Earth & Space
A Family-Style Science Program

Michelle Copher and Karen Loutzenhiser

Published by HooDoo Publishing
United States of America
© 2023 Layers of Learning

ISBN 978-1-7360624-8-7

Copies of worksheets or activities may be made for a particular family or classroom. All other rights reserved. Printed in the United States of America.

(Grilled Cheese BTN Font) © Fontdiner - www.fontdiner.com

If you wish to reproduce or print excerpts of this publication, please contact us at contact@layers-of-learning.com for permission. Thank you for respecting copyright laws.

Available at Layers-of-Learning.com

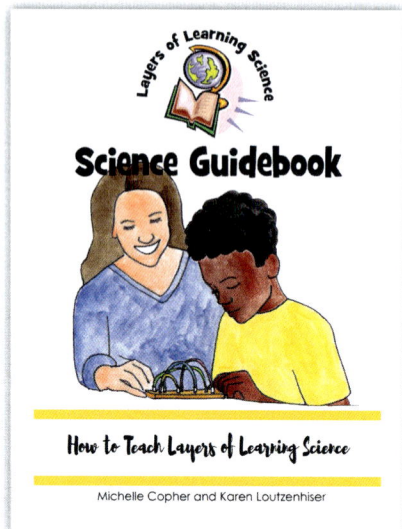

Science Guidebook: How To Teach Layers of Learning Science

Learn the philosophy behind Layers of Learning Science, how to plan a unit, how to schedule your learning, and how to assess and grade.

This is a valuable and inexpensive PDF guide to using the curriculum effectively.

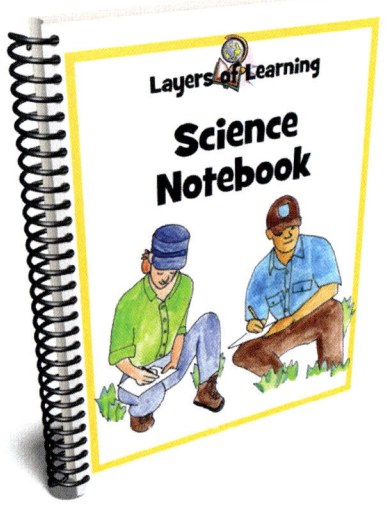

Science Notebook

The Science Notebook is modeled after the notebooks that real scientists keep. Students record data and sketches from experiments and observations. They also add foldables, take notes, and record their learning. The science courses include instructions on filling in the Science Notebook.

Printable Packs

If you purchased this book directly from Layers of Learning, your Printable Packs were included on your receipt. If you purchased it elsewhere you can retrieve your free Printable Packs with the coupon code: FREEPACK.

Scan the QR code to visit the Earth & Space Resources page.

How To Use This Course

Earth & Space is a family-style program, which means your whole family, from ages six to eighteen and beyond, can use the program together. The activities are meant to be a family affair, with individual expectations being tailored to the ages and abilities of each child. We also encourage you to share completed individual work, like reports, posters, and projects.

Like all of Layers of Learning, *Earth & Space* is a pick-and-choose curriculum; you don't need to complete everything in the book. Instead, browse through and choose the library books, Explorations, and sidebars that appeal to you and are appropriate for your kids. Generally, you will choose one or two Explorations to do together each week.

Scheduling

Each unit within this book is designed to last about a month and then be repeated in subsequent years, but the exact schedule and timing are completely up to you. If your kids are engaged and enthusiastic about a topic, feel free to carry on for a little while longer.

In *Earth & Space*, each Exploration is one complete lesson plan. The exact length of each one varies and depends on your needs, the ages of the students, and how absorbed in a lesson you get. However, you can generally plan on one to two hours per lesson. Science should be a weekly part of your educational plan.

Sidebars

You will find sidebars throughout *Earth & Space*. The sidebars are little snippets of information you can read aloud while children work, things you can touch on during a Morning Meeting, or springboards for lessons you create on your own. Do as many or as few as you like.

Printable Packs

This curriculum includes printables. For printing convenience and to keep your costs down, the printables are found in digital Printable Packs that you can retrieve from the Layers of Learning catalog. Find the product page for this book and scroll down to the link to download the Printable Pack. If you purchased this book directly from Layers of Learning, you will see a link to download the printables on your receipt. Otherwise, use the coupon code FREEPACK at checkout to get the Printable Packs for free.

Resources

Every unit comes with its own YouTube playlist of videos to use as enrichment or as video lectures to supplement lessons. The videos can be played during a lesson. Frequently, Explorations include instructions to watch a video. The videos are curated in these playlists.

On the Layers of Learning website, you can also find links to websites and resources that are especially useful when teaching each unit. The web links are located under "Resources" on the main menu.

At Layers of Learning, we believe learning is about exploring and we invite you to joyfully explore with us. In the words of Robert Louis Stevenson, "The world is so full of a number of things, I'm sure we should all be as happy as kings."

Table of Contents

How Science Works   6
- Tools of the Scientist   8
- History of Science   15
- Scientific Method   23

Planet Earth   34
- Structure of the Earth   37
- Age & Formation of Earth   45
- Oceans   52

Plate Tectonics   64
- Moving Plates   66
- Volcanoes   73
- Earthquakes   80
- Mountain Building   84

Rocks   94
- Minerals   98
- Igneous   103
- Sedimentary   108
- Metamorphic   112
- Weathering & Erosion   116

Fossils   124
- How Fossils Form   126
- The Fossil Record   133
- Dinosaurs   142

Seasons & Climate   152
- Seasons   155
- Atmosphere   162
- Climate   169

Weather   182
- Recording & Forecasting   185
- Precipitation   197
- Storms   200
- Special Effects   204

Universe   212
- Outer Space   215
- Stars   222
- Star Clusters & Galaxies   229

Solar System   240
- Planets   243
- Comets, Asteroids, Meteors   253
- Humans in Space   258

Glossary   268

People   272

Earth & Space

Unit Overview

Key Concepts:
- Scientists use tools and record their observations, experiments, and conclusions so they can be repeatable.
- There are four basic branches of science: biology, chemistry, physics, and earth & space.
- Scientists use the Scientific Method to make conclusions.

Vocabulary:
- Science
- Qualitative observations
- Quantitative observations
- Earth & Space
- Biology
- Chemistry
- Physics
- Scientific Method
- Hypothesis
- Law
- Theory
- Control group
- Experimental group
- Independent variable
- Dependent variable
- Double blind

Science Skills:
- SI Units
- Measurement Conversions
- Scientific Notation
- Significant Figures

HOW SCIENCE WORKS

Science is the study of the natural world, from the reason things fall when they are dropped to how ants work together in a group. People have been curious about animals, plants, clouds, water, and all sorts of things about the universe since ancient times. But science is more than just casual curiosity. It is the methodical observation and testing of physical things in the universe.

Over time, scientists have developed sets of standards to practice so that their observations and experiments aren't incomplete or tainted by human prejudice. This is called the scientific method. Scientists also use careful standard measurements using the SI system (International System of Units). The SI system uses meters, grams, degrees Kelvin, and seconds, to name a few. Scientists all over the world from every culture use the same measurements so there is no confusion when they share their work.

Step 1: Library List

Choose books from your library that go with this topic. Here's a list of some favorites and also a list of search terms so you can utilize what your library offers. Read the books with your kids and/or assign them some to read independently. It is from these books your kids will learn most of the facts they need from this unit.

Search for: what is science, history of science, scientific revolution, modern science history, famous scientists, scientific method, SI units, measuring

How Science Works

- 😊 😊 😊 *Encyclopedia of Science* from DK. Read "How Scientists Work" on pages 14-15.

- 😊 😊 😊 *The Usborne Science Encyclopedia*. Peruse some of the reference pages at the end for a quick rundown on scientific measurements, important scientists, pages 404-417.

- 😊 😊 😊 *The Kingfisher Science Encyclopedia*. Skim through the Ready Reference section at the back to familiarize yourself with measurements, conversions, famous scientists, and inventions and discoveries, pages 466-473.

- 😊 *Mad Margaret Experiments With the Scientific Method* by Eric Mark Braun. When Margaret's friend, Jasper, can't stop sneezing, Margaret uses the scientific method to find out why.

- 😊 😊 *What is the Scientific Method?* by Baby Professor. Clearly describes the systematic way scientific experiments are carried out so errors are reduced.

- 😊 😊 *How to Think Like A Scientist* by Stephen P. Kramer. How can you find the answers to your questions about the world? How can you know if you are right?

- 😊 😊 *A Child's Introduction to Natural History* by Heather Alexander. An excellent overview of the fields of science and some of the scientists who have made breakthroughs.

- 😊 😊 *Zoey and Sassafras: Dragons and Marshmallows* by Asia Citro. A sick baby dragon appears in Zoey's backyard looking for help. Zoey has to use scientific observations to discover what's wrong and help the dragon before it's too late. First chapter book in a series for young readers.

- 😊 😊 *Investigating the Scientific Method* with Max Axiom, Super Scientist by Donal B. Lemke. In graphic novel format, Max Axiom must figure out the best materials to use to build a levee to protect his city from flood waters. He uses the scientific method to do it.

- 😊 *Lives of the Scientists* by Kathleen Krull. Mini-biographies of twenty important scientists.

- 😊 *Archimedes and the Door of Science* by Jeanne Benedick. Introduces the reader to the life and work of Archimedes, one of the earliest scientists. Look for other titles in this series as well.

- 😊 😊 *Science Year By Year* by DK. A visual feast and timeline of science showing the greatest discoveries and inventions throughout history.

Family School Levels

The colored smilies in this unit help you choose the correct levels of books and activities for your child.

😊 = Ages 6-9
😊 = Ages 10-13
😊 = Ages 14-18

On the Web

For videos, web pages, games, and more to add to this unit, visit the Earth & Space Resources at Layers-of-Learning.com.

You will find a link to video playlists, web links, and more.

Bookworms

If you're looking for a family read-aloud, we'd like to suggest this one.

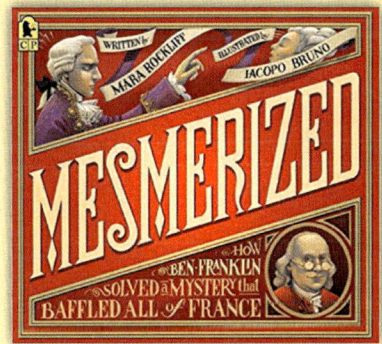

Mesmerized, by Mara Rockliff, is a picture book you can read with your kids in one sitting.

Learn how Dr. Mesmer had everyone in Paris agog with his ability to heal through his invisible force. Everyone in Paris was mesmerized, until Ben Franklin came to town and used the scientific method to prove Dr. Mesmer wasn't what he seemed.

Earth & Space

Memorization Station

Memorize the definition of science.

Science: the study of nature and the way things in nature behave

Additional Layer

Rounding numbers is an important skill in science. Often, measurements like temperature or mass need to be rounded. Take several measurements and then practice rounding them to two decimal points.

Additional Layer

Science Notebooks aren't just for school. Real scientists use them every day to take notes, record observations, and keep track of data. This herpetologist is taking notes while in the field as he studies bog turtles. What kind of science would you be most interested in studying?

○ ○ *The Story of Science: Aristotle Leads the Way* by Joy Hakim. This is the first of a series of three books on the history of science.

○ *Galileo and the Scientific Revolution* by Laura Fermi and Gilberto Bernardini. At just over 100 pages, this is a great introduction to Galileo and his importance to science.

○ *The Story of Western Science* by Susan Wise Bauer. Explains the most crucial advances in science since ancient times in chronological order with guides to the original writings of scientists. Interested students can use this as a springboard for reading the original scientists in their own words.

○ *Exploring the Scientific Method: Cases and Questions* by Steven Gimbel. The reader chooses a branch of science, such as chemistry or astronomy, then reads about an actual scientist's work in that field to see what science looks like beyond the classroom. Also explains basic thought methods including deductive vs. inductive reasoning.

○ *International System of Units (SI): How the World Measures Almost Everything, and the People Who Made It Possible* by Edmund Isakov. A 300-page book about the history of the SI system and how and why it is used.

○ *The Demon-Haunted World* by Carl Sagan. Talks about how myths we once used to explain the world can now be explained by science. The universe is governed by predictable, stable rules. We can learn to think past pseudoscience.

Step 2: Explore

Choose a few hands-on explorations from this section to work on as a family. They should be appealing activities that will create mental hooks so your kids remember the information in the unit. Save the rest of the explorations for the next time you do this unit in four years when your kids are older. You can also read the sidebars together and explore some little rabbit trails.

This unit includes printables. See the introduction for instructions on retrieving your Printable Pack.

Tools of the Scientist

○ ○ ○ **EXPLORATION: Science Notebook**

For this activity, you will need:

- Science Notebook - You will need a Science Notebook

How Science Works

for each student for each year. You can purchase them from Layers-of-learning.com or use spiral bound notebooks or composition books.
- A handful of interesting rocks or other natural objects
- Colored pencils

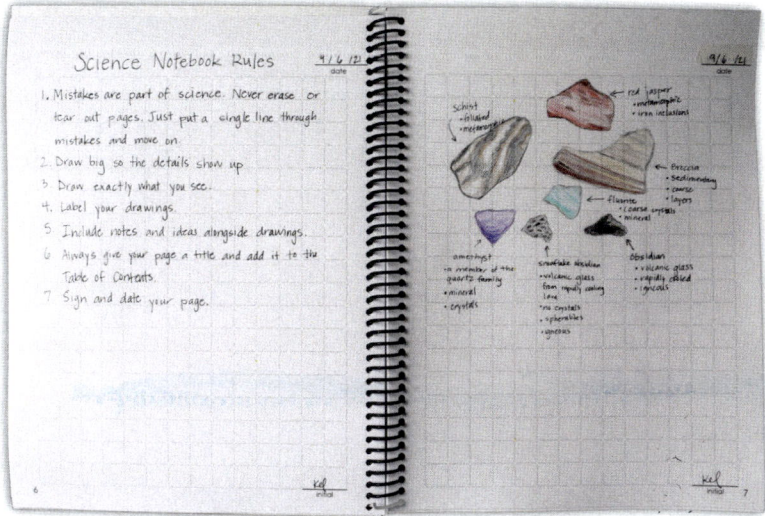

Science is the study of nature and the way things behave in nature. Scientists, throughout time, have been observing and experimenting on the things they see in the natural world to learn more about them. Scientists keep notebooks with sketches, notes, and observations. This year you will be learning about Earth and space and keeping track of everything you learn in your own personal Science Notebook.

1. Write your name and the date inside the front cover of your Science Notebook.

2. Find the Table of Contents at the front of your Science Notebook. If you are making your own notebook, write "Table of Contents" at the top of the first page. Then skip three pages before you begin numbering the pages.

3. At the top of the first page, write "Science Notebook Rules" and add that title to your "Table of Contents" page. Write the page number before your entry.

   If you are making your own Science Notebook, you will need to number each page in the bottom corner. You can start by just numbering a few pages and then adding more as you proceed through the notebook.

4. On the Science Notebook Rules page, write these rules:
   - Mistakes are part of science. Never erase or tear out pages. Just put a single line through mistakes and move on.

Fabulous Fact

The first recorded brain surgeries were done in ancient Egypt.

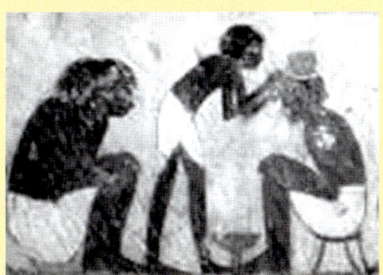

The Greeks also used Egyptian medicine and improved on it. Somehow, knowledge of these types of surgeries was lost and not revived again until 1884 when Englishman Rickman Godlee performed the first modern removal of a tumor from a patient's brain.

Additional Layer

Étienne Léopold Trouvelot lived in the middle of the 1800s when photography was still pretty new. He thought better, more beautiful renderings of nature could be done by hand and produced hundreds of skilled drawings of astronomical objects.

Here is his drawing of Jupiter.

Consider how nature inspires art. How else do you think art and nature are connected?

Try your own drawings of things you find in nature.

Earth & Space

Fabulous Fact

This is a logo that includes the seven base SI units.

- cd = candela, a measure of luminosity
- kg = kilogram, a measure of mass
- m = meter, a measure of distance
- s = second, a measure of time
- A = ampere, a measure of electric current
- K = kelvin, a measure of temperature
- mol = mole, a measure of substance

Memorization Station

Qualitative observations: data that is focused on characteristics or qualities

Quantitative observations: data that can quantified, or expressed using numbers and values (They must be measured as accurately as possible.)

Example of a qualitative observation:

"The finches have broad beaks."

Example of a quantitative observation:

"The ball fell 20 meters."

- Draw big so the details show up.
- Draw exactly what you see.
- Label your drawings.
- Include notes and ideas alongside drawings.
- Always give your page a title and add it to the Table of Contents.
- Sign and date your page.

5. On the "Science Notebook Rules" page, sketch a rock (or another natural object) in as much detail as you can. Make the sketch fill up at least a quarter of the page. Color the sketch realistically. Write labels and notes. For example, you could tell where the rock was collected and when. You could also label any inclusions, like pyrite or quartz, that you already know about.

EXPLORATION: Qualitative and Quantitative

For this activity, you will need:

- "Qualitative and Quantitative" printable from the Printable Pack
- An item to observe
- Tape measure, scale, thermometer, or other measuring tools
- Drawing and coloring utensils

Scientists use both **qualitative observations** and **quantitative observations**. Qualitative observations focus on qualities and characteristics, often observed using the five senses - sight, smell, taste, touch, and hearing. They do not use numbers or measurements. For example, you could observe that there are clouds in the sky today.

Quantitative observations can be quantified. You use numbers or measurements for them, and so, you must be as accurate as possible. For example, you may note that the temperature outside is 26 degrees Celsius today.

1. Begin by choosing something you can observe. It might be a dog, an orange, a glass of water, or a potted plant. On the "Qualitative and Quantitative" printable, write the definitions of each kind of observation in the top two boxes and then draw a simple picture of the item you are observing.

2. Next, record observations of each kind. If you are observing a dog, write some qualitative observations in green. For example, it has black fur, it has blue eyes, or its tail is wagging. While observing the same dog, write some quantitative observations in blue. The dog weighs 32 pounds. It has four paws. It is 40 centimeters tall.

How Science Works

3. Finally, think like a scientist and reflect on your observations in the last box. Both kinds of observations are valuable, but quantitative observations are more precise and exact. It's important to be aware of both kinds of observations when you experiment. Add your page to the Science section of your Layers of Learning Notebook.

😊 🙂 **EXPLORATION: Scientific Measurements**

For this activity, you will need:

- Meter stick
- Scientific balance or scale that measures to .01 grams
- Graduated cylinder that holds at least 100 ml and/or a set of beakers
- Lab thermometer, digital or glass (Celsius, not Fahrenheit)
- Stopwatch
- Calculator

Scientists all over the world measure in the exact same ways. They use a system called the International System of Units (abbreviated SI units from the French *Système International*). Below is a chart of the basic SI units.

1. Head a new page in your Science Notebook "Scientific Measurements" and add it to your Table of Contents. Copy this chart into your Science Notebook.

Quantity	Unit	Symbol
time	seconds	s
length	meters	m
mass	grams	g
temperature	Kelvin	K
volume	liter*	L

*Technically the liter is not an SI unit, but it is commonly used by scientists alongside SI units and is the measurement on the side of your graduated cylinder or beaker. The SI way of measuring volume is in cubic centimeters (abbreviated as cm^3 or cc).

There are other base units that we will learn about as we progress through science. Things like moles, for measuring amounts of substances, and candelas, for measuring the amount of light.

Besides the base units, there are derived units, units that are a combination of two or more base units. For example, a Newton is a unit of force that is defined as kilograms times meters all divided by seconds squared

Additional Layer

Basic measuring tools you will use over and over in science include:

- Metric ruler or meter stick
- Celsius thermometer
- Balance - an electronic scale that measures to the hundredths place
- Stopwatch
- Graduated cylinders
- Beakers

Spend some time using these tools and learning to measure accurately with them.

When you measure with an electronic balance, don't forget to hit the "tare" button after you set your weighing dish or container on the balance. This zeros out the balance so your measurement is accurate.

When you measure liquid, set the container on a surface, look at the liquid at eye level, and wait for the liquid to still.

On the Web

There are lots of online lessons and quizzes to help you master measurements, unit conversions, scientific notation, and significant figures. You'll find some on the Earth & Space Resources page at Layers of Learning online.

Earth & Space

Expedition
Go out into a natural setting with your Science Notebook a few times throughout this unit. Set a timer and just spend the time observing something in nature closely and taking detailed notes. You can draw pictures and diagrams or write observations of what you see, hear, touch, taste, or smell.

Deep Thoughts
Can science answer all of mankind's questions?

Explain why you think it can or can't. Give examples.

Additional Layer
Countries and kings have used standard sets of measurements for thousands of years so that trade and taxes could be conducted fairly.

Find out more about how standardized measurements are used for things other than science.

Fabulous Fact
The prefixes chart, to the left, is incomplete. It includes the most commonly used prefixes, but there are actually more. The largest prefix in the SI system is a yotta, which is 10^{24}. The smallest prefix is the yocto, which is 10^{-24}.

You can look up more prefixes online and add them to your chart if you like.

($Kg \cdot m \cdot s^{-2}$). We will cover these one by one as they come up; for now, it's just important to know the most basic units and that there will be more to follow.

Most of these measurements are probably familiar to you, with the exception perhaps of Kelvin for measuring temperature. The Kelvin system uses absolute zero, the coldest possible temperature in the universe, as its base. 0° K is the coldest possible temperature at which all atoms and parts of atoms stop moving. Kelvin uses the same space between each degree as the Celsius scale, so it is easy to convert between them by just adding 273.15 degrees to your Celsius measurements.

2. Measure 5-8 temperatures of various things around your house with your scientific thermometer, which will be in Celsius. Write down each measurement on a chart like the one here.

3. Convert each of your Celsius temperatures to Kelvin and add them to the chart as well. Remember, just add 273.15 to your Celsius measurements to get Kelvin.

stuff	°C	°K
jello in my fridge	4	277.15
inside my mouth	35	
tap water	18	
air in my house	25	
boiling water	100	

Scientists use Celsius all the time and so will we in Layers of Learning, but sometimes scientists use Kelvin too, so it's good to know how Celsius and Kelvin are related. Did you figure out why we add 273.15 degrees when converting from Celsius to Kelvin?

4. Each of the base units can have prefixes added to them. Here is a list of the most common prefixes. Copy this chart into your Science Notebook as well.

Prefix	Conversion	Symbol
milli-	x 1000	m
centi-	x 100	c
deci-	x 10	d
deca-	x 0.1	da
hecto-	x 0.01	h
kilo-	x 0.001	k

You can put "milli" onto meters to make millimeters. Or

How Science Works

you can add kilo onto grams to make kilograms. Any of these prefixes can be added on to any of the base units.

5. Take one measurement with each of the base units (time, length, mass, temperature, and volume) using your meter stick, balance scale, beakers, and so on. In your Science Notebook, draw a picture of each thing you measured and write down the measurement next to it. Then, write down a prefix combined with each base unit and convert the number into the form you chose.

To add a prefix, move the decimal to the left or the right by multiplying by a power of ten. Conversions are easy to do if you remember to set the problem up correctly.

Start by writing down your measurement with the units Always write the units! Below, the units are meters (m).

$$1.8 \text{ m}$$

Draw a multiplication symbol with a long fraction line after it. I'm converting meters (m) into centimeters (cm).

$$1.8 \text{ m} \times \frac{\text{cm}}{\text{m}}$$

On top of the line, near the right end, you will write the units you are converting to. Beneath the line at the far right end, you will write the units you started with.

Then, you write the conversion number in the correct place. I know that there are 100 cm for every 1 m. So I will write 100 next to the cm and 1 next to the m.

$$1.8 \text{ m} \times \frac{100 \text{ cm}}{1 \text{ m}}$$

Now, I can do the calculation in my head or with a calculator. I multiply by everything on top of the line. I divide by everything below the line, because a fraction is a division problem.

$$1.8 \cancel{\text{m}} \times \frac{100 \text{ cm}}{1 \cancel{\text{m}}} = 180 \text{ cm}$$

Notice how I crossed out the m and the m? The units

Fabulous Fact

Many scientists study certain things for a purpose, like to cure cancer or put a man on the moon. Others study nature just because it's fascinating.

You don't have to have a science degree to be fascinated by the world, observe nature, and do some testing of your own.

Additional Layer

Whenever you are doing science, make sure you are using SI units. In this curriculum, SI units will always be used for science. We won't also give you the English standard measurements to help you out. We want you immersed.

SI is the universal language of science and it's important for kids to understand it fluently.

This unit introduces basic SI units. More units of measure will be added as they become relevant. For example, moles will be introduced when students study chemistry.

Practice using various types of measurements in your everyday life.

Earth & Space

Fabulous Fact

A negative power, like 10^{-3}, means that the 10 is actually being divided.

So 7.345×10^{-3} is the same as:

$$\frac{7.345}{10^3}$$

Or we could write:

$7.543 \div 10 \div 10 \div 10$

These all equal .007345.

Because these are powers of ten, that means we can just move the decimal over three spaces to the left.

Negative powers will move that number of decimal places to the left while positive powers will move that number of places to the right.

Teaching Tip

If you need more help on metric conversions, scientific notation, or significant figures, you'll find several great videos in this unit's YouTube playlist.

Fabulous Fact

Whenever you solve math problems in science, you use only significant figures in your answers. Solve the problems just as you normally would, but once you get the answers, take a moment and check the significant figures and make sure that you are only listing the correct number of significant figures in your final answer. Scientists call them "sig figs."

are multiplied and divided as well as the numbers being multiplied and divided, so the only unit left in the answer is the cm because m ÷ m = 1. Just like 5 ÷ 5 = 1.

As conversion problems get more complicated, it will be very important to do these steps exactly, so practice them the right way now.

☺ ● EXPLORATION: Scientific Notation

For this activity, you will need:

- Paper and pencil

Scientific notation (standard form to you, British folks) is a way to write very large or very small numbers. Instead of writing 1,000,000,000,000,000,000, I can write 1×10^{18}. Or instead of writing .0000000000001, I can write 1×10^{-12}.

1. Examine both sets of numbers above very carefully and see if you can figure out where the 18 and the -12 came from.

    How can you write 700 in scientific notation? **(7×10^2)**

    The "$\times 10^2$" means we multiply the seven by ten two times. Is 7 x 10 x 10 equal to 700?

2. Write down some scientific notation conversions for someone else and have them solve yours while you solve theirs.

☺ ● EXPLORATION: Significant Figures

For this activity, you will need:

- "Significant Figures" from the Printable Pack
- "Significant Figures Answers" from the Printable Pack
- Paper and pencil
- Calculator

Significant figures are digits that carry meaning in terms of measurements, like when measuring temperature or length. Significant figures include:

- Non-zero digits.
- Zeros between two or more significant digits. The 0 in 208 is significant, but the 0 in 074 is not, neither is the 0 in 390.
- Zeros following a non-zero after a decimal are significant. The two 0s furthest to the right in 0.00200 are significant, but the others aren't. The non-significant zeros are place holders only.

Significant figures do not apply to exact numbers, like when

How Science Works

you are counting the number of cars in a parking lot or the number of apples in your grocery cart. They only apply to measurements like speed or temperature.

If you are doing calculations with significant figures, your final answer should show the least precise measurement.

For example: 2.4 x 3.13 = 7.512 but 2.4 only has two significant figures, so your answer should only have two significant figures. 2.4 x 3.13 = 7.5 Round extra digits.

1. Complete the "Significant Figures" worksheet from the Printable Pack. Use a calculator if you'd like. Then, check your answers using the answer sheet.

History of Science

🙂 🙂 🙂 **EXPLORATION: History of Science Cascading Book**

For this activity, you will need:

- "History of Science" from the Printable Pack
- Colored paper
- Glue
- Scissors
- Ruler
- Stapler

Make a layered book that shows the eras of scientific knowledge and illustrate it.

1. Cut apart the squares on the "History of Science" printable.

2. Fold your colored paper in half the long way, hot dog-style. Glue your paper squares to the colored paper.

3. Trim each paper to the length you need in order to make a cascading book. The first sheet, with the cover, should be about 7.5 cm long. Add another 2.5 cm in length to each subsequent page.

Deep Thoughts

Since the scientific revolution, western science has rejected non-scientific sources of knowledge.

For example, in Australia, natives described certain birds they call "'firehawks" that would carry burning sticks to intentionally spread fires. Modern scientists dismissed these stories out of hand. But it turns out it's true. The birds feed on animals fleeing fires, so they purposely start new fires from old ones.

Natives in Africa had been using the bark of the Olon tree to kill malaria mosquitoes for centuries, but only recently have scientists begun examining this native knowledge. They found that not only does the bark kill mosquitoes that carry malaria but also the parasite that causes the disease.

Natives of the Pacific Northwest coast in North America have purposely cultivated clam gardens with perfect habitats so they could harvest more clams. Their ecological understanding was dismissed until very recently because it wasn't based on the scientific method.

The scientific method is valuable, but is it the only way to gain knowledge?

Where else does knowledge come from?

Earth & Space

Famous Folks

Aryabhata was an Indian mathematician and astronomer who invented the first trigonometric functions, like sine and cosine, when he was in his early twenties. He also invented the quadratic equation and calculated pi to five decimal places.

It was from his writings that medieval European mathematicians learned their trigonometry and algebra. His writings are still in existence today.

Writer's Workshop

Choose a scientist to learn about. Do some research about the scientist's life, education, and work. Write a true story about him or her.

The True Stories unit from *Writer's Workshop* can help you learn to write true stories.

Share your story with your family or another audience.

4. Learn what science was like in each of the ages on the printable by reading the descriptions together. Write what you learned on each page of the book. Add illustrations if you like.

5. Staple all the pages together at the top. Keep it as a mini-book or paste the book into your Science Notebook. If you put it in your Science Notebook, be sure to add a title and add it to your Table of Contents.

☺☺☺ EXPLORATION: Be A Natural Philosopher

For this activity, you will need:

- Science Notebook
- Pencil or pen
- Colored pencils (optional)

Ancient and medieval scientists referred to themselves as "natural philosophers." They observed natural phenomenon, like the way things moved or the patterns in the stars. They thought about the universal laws governing nature. They used mathematics to describe the motion of the stars or to measure the circumference of the earth. They observed lots of things, but they rarely did experiments.

1. Spend time sitting quietly observing nature outdoors. You could watch ants, clouds, birds, someone swinging on a swing set, or anything else that interests you.

2. Write and sketch your observations in your Science Notebook.

3. Think about the laws of nature that govern what you are observing. Why do ants all travel one after the other in a straight line? Why do clouds stay afloat even though they are made of heavy water? Why do the stars move across the sky as the night progresses? Write down why you think the things you observe are happening.

☺☺☺ EXPLORATION: Astrology Observation of the Stars

For this activity, you will need:

- "My Sign Is ___" printable from the Printable Pack
- Colored paper
- Glue
- Scissors
- A guidebook, website, or app to help you find constellations in the night sky

Astrologers were people who foretold events based on the stars and planets. Sometimes they would help a king decide when the best moment to go to battle against his enemies would be based on the night sky. They also

How Science Works

kept track of time using the movement of the sun, moon, and stars. They kept careful observations and records and wrote star charts. They became very good at predicting mathematically when an eclipse would happen or when Orion would line up with Venus. Because of their careful observations, they laid the foundations for later scientific studies of the night sky.

Astrologers thought that the stars that were highest in the sky when a person was born were important and could predict what kind of person the baby would turn out to be. They divided the sky into 12 equal sections, 30 degrees each. A different constellation was within each section. Today, we still know of the 12 constellations of the zodiac and most people know their "sign," the constellation that was high in the sky when they were born.

1. Learn a little bit about your sign and the constellation that goes with it.
2. Learn to find your constellation in the night sky. This will be easiest to do in the months surrounding your birthday. If you were born in the summer, you won't be able to see your constellation in the middle of winter and vice versa.
3. Observe the movement of the zodiac constellations

Famous Folks

Kidinnu was a Babylonian astronomer who studied and defined the movements of the sun and moon and calculated the solar and lunar years, time periods we still use today.

Scientists and thinkers who followed him referred to his work and quoted him often. There is a crater of the moon named after him.

Writer's Workshop

People are naturally curious. We spend a lot of time and energy learning about things that don't do anything for us in a practical way. We read about people we will never meet, places we will never go, and random facts we will never need.

Social media sites like Instagram and Pinterest capitalize on curiosity by providing you with an endless scrolling screen that leads you from one random thing to the next.

Humans are especially good at learning, and a big part of that is all the practice we get learning useless stuff by poking our noses in wherever.

Start a list of random things you are curious about.

Earth & Space

Famous Folks

Max Planck is a great example of how science works to refine knowledge so we get ever closer to the truth.

Planck was a theoretical physicist who found problems with Newton's long-accepted laws of motion. Planck's greater understanding led to quantum theory and the harnessing of the atom.

Fabulous Fact

There are hundreds of jobs within the broad category "scientist":

- Doctor
- Environmental Scientist
- Meteorologist
- Farmer
- Conservationist
- Plant Pathologist
- Park Ranger
- Waste Treatment Operator
- Astronomer
- Chemist
- Food Scientist
- Structural Engineer
- Nuclear Plant Operator
- Science Teacher

over a period of two weeks or so. Can you see the constellations moving across the sky each night and progressing further each day? Notice how the constellations are all rotating across the same plane near the equator, in the same path the sun moves in.

4. Cut out the "My Sign Is ___" label. Write in your sign in the blank space. Glue the label onto a slightly larger piece of colored paper so there is a frame around the label. Cut the colored paper to size. Glue the top edge of your framed label to a page in your Science Notebook to create a flap. Under the flap, write some information about your observations and research about your constellation or the other zodiac constellations.

On the same printable page, there are some additional printables you can use as labels or flaps to add to pages in your Science Notebook.

5. Put the title in the table of contents in your Science Notebook. Initial and date your page.

😊 😊 **EXPLORATION: Alchemy and the Philosophers' Stone Craft**

For this activity, you will need:

- Small rock, washed clean
- Paint in various colors like blue, gold, silver, pink, etc.
- Glitter
- Glue

Alchemists used chemicals to try to turn cheap metals, like lead, into silver or gold. They searched for the universal solvent that could dissolve everything and the elixir of life that could cure any disease. The alchemists never found what they were looking for, but, in the process of trying, they invented distillation methods and apparatus, vessels

How Science Works

that would withstand great heat, and flame-producing lamps. They also discovered hydrochloric acid, antimony, arsenic, phosphorus, and zinc. They invented dyes, inks, metal ore extraction techniques, medicines, glass-making methods, and more. They learned that metals could color glass blue, red, purple, and many other colors. They may have been wrong about a lot of things, but they also discovered some pretty neat things in the process.

Alchemists believed there were four elements: earth, air, water, and fire. Different combinations of these elements made up everything on Earth and in the universe. They thought if you could manipulate these elements at will, then you could heal any disease, create any substance, and live forever. The key to manipulating the elements was a philosophers' stone, a magical object that was the ultimate goal of all alchemists.

1. Make your own philosophers' stone. Paint your clean rock with any colors you like, completely covering it. Spread on glue and then sprinkle on glitter.

2. Research a famous alchemist together to learn more about his or her life. Here are some to choose from: Mary the Jewess, John Dee, Nicholas Flamel, Kanada of India, Zhang Guo the Elder, Johann Faust, Tycho Brahe, Roger Bacon.

☺ ☺ ☺ **EXPLORATION: Scientists of the Scientific Revolution**
For this activity, you will need:

- "Scientific Revolution" from the Printable Pack
- Colored paper
- Scissors
- Glue
- Colored pencils, pens, or crayons

Beginning in the 1500s, science underwent a revolution. People stopped seeing the world through a mystical lens and started to systematically and logically discover why things in nature behave the way they do.

1. Cut apart and color the famous scientist cards and the scientific method card from the "Scientific Revolution" printable.

2. Glue the cards onto pieces of colored paper that are slightly larger than the cards so the colored paper makes a border.

3. Look up each scientist to find out what made him famous. Take a few notes about him on the back of his card. Discuss why you think his ideas might be

Famous Folks

Nicolas Flamel was a real life alchemist who lived in medieval Paris and strove to create the philosopher's stone, a means to eternal life.

He is a favorite with authors who have cast him in books including *Harry Potter and the Philosopher's Stone*, *The Hunchback of Notre Dame*, and *The Alchemist: The Secrets of the Immortal Nicholas Flamel* series.

Earth & Space

Deep Thoughts

The invention of the printing press had a lot to do with the scientific revolution because, for the first time in history, ideas could be preserved and transported around the world easily.

Discuss how the invention of the printing press compares to the invention of the internet. Do you think the internet is having and will have an enormous affect on world history?

Fabulous Fact

The four branches of science are artificial divisions between the sciences. In reality, there is a lot of overlap. A biologist usually has to have a good background in chemistry to understand what is going on with living systems, for example.

An astrophysicist uses chemistry, astronomy, and physics to study what stars are made of.

A soil scientist has to understand not only rocks and erosion, but microbes and worms and the roots of plants.

considered revolutionary. What was revolutionary about the scientific method? What were the colleges and societies that gathered scientists to discuss ideas?

4. Glue the Scientific Revolution card onto a piece of colored paper large enough to create a pocket on another piece of paper in your Science Notebook. Put all of your cards in the pocket.

☻EXPLORATION: Four Branches of Science Flap Book

For this activity, you will need:

- "Four Branches of Science" from the Printable Pack
- Square piece of paper, about 12.5 cm x 12.5 cm
- Pencil or pen
- Glue

There are four main branches of science that were established during the scientific revolution. They are biology, chemistry, physics, and earth & space science. Within

How Science Works

these branches are many specific disciplines. For example, an entomologist is a biologist who specializes in studying insects. Also, there is a lot of overlap between these main branches. A paleontologist who studies fossils needs to be part geologist and part biologist. It is useful to understand the four main branches and some of the specialties within them.

1. Use the "Four Branches of Science" printable as an anchor chart to help identify the four branches and some of the specific fields within them.

2. Fold your square piece of paper in half one way, then open it and fold it in half the other way. Where the fold creases meet is the center of your paper.

3. Fold each corner of the square into the center so all the corners just touch.

4. On each folded piece, write one of the branches of science. Inside the flap for each branch, write some of the specific fields that exist within that branch. For example, ecology is a sub-branch within biology.

5. Glue the entire flap book onto another sheet of paper, then add it to the Science section of your Layers of Learning Notebook along with the anchor chart.

😊 😊 😊 **EXPLORATION: Top Ten Inventions Timeline**

For this activity, you will need:

- "Modern Inventions That Changed Everything" timeline from the Printable Pack
- Colored pencils, pens, or crayons

New things are invented all the time, but only a few inventions have had major impacts on humanity.

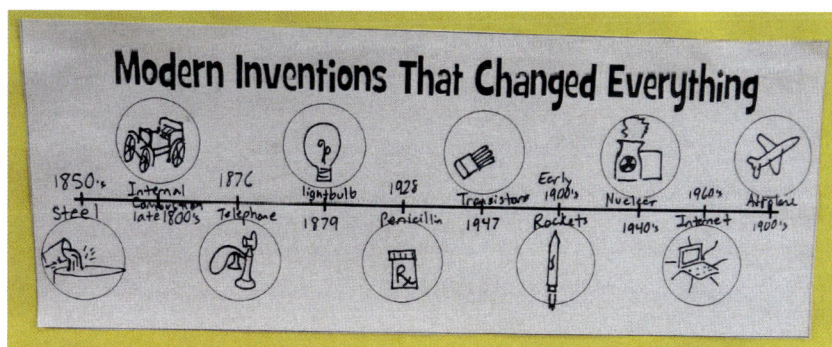

1. Together, brainstorm a list of the most important inventions you can think of. Then, narrow your list down to the top nine most important, in your opinion.

2. Find out when each of your top nine was invented

Memorization Station

Memorize the four branches of science.

Earth & Space: study of Earth and the universe

Biology: study of life

Chemistry: study of materials and how they combine

Physics: study of motion, forces, and energy on a large and atomic scale

Additional Layer

Rationalism is a philosophical view that reason can be used to find truth. Sometimes people go so far as to say that all truth can found by reason.

Empiricism is another philosophy that says we learn truth through our senses, by observing, smelling, feeling, and experiencing.

Historically, rationalism and empiricism were opposites, but modern science unites them. Scientists observe, touch, taste, and feel, but then they use their rational minds to make connections that take us further than either observation or reason could alone.

Read more about the philosophies of rationalism and empiricism.

Additional Layer

Leonardo da Vinci, Thomas Edison, Nikola Tesla, Benjamin Franklin, and Thales of Miletus were all brilliant inventors. Look up quotes by them or about them and see if you can discover why they were so smart.

Earth & Space

Memorization Station

Memorize the steps of the scientific method.

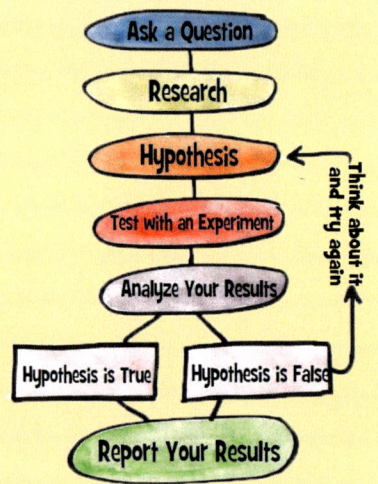

You can find this anchor chart in the Printable Pack.

On the Web

Since at least 1975, some scientists, such as Thomas Kuhn and Lee Smolin, have argued that there is no such thing as the scientific method.

They say that scientists think creatively and find solutions rather then following steps or methodologies.

In their view, science is messy and sometimes unpredictable.

Look up Lee Smolin's article "There is No Scientific Method" and see if you agree or not.

Writer's Workshop

George Bernard Shaw said, "Science never solves a problem without creating ten more." Write about what you think he meant.

and place them on the timeline. There is space on the timeline to add illustrations. Add this to the Science section of your Layers of Learning Notebook.

😊 😊 😊 **EXPLORATION: Biography of a Modern Scientist**

For this activity, you will need:

- "Scientist Report Notes" from the Printable Pack
- Library books and/or internet resources
- Project supplies (varies)

1. Choose a scientist who lived in the modern era, anytime after 1800. Research your scientist.

   Some possible scientists include:

   - Marie Curie
   - Edwin Hubble
   - Charles Darwin
   - George Washington Carver
   - Albert Einstein
   - Jane Goodall
   - Thomas Edison
   - Tim Berners-Lee

2. Research your scientist using books, videos, or articles. Use the "Scientist Report Notes" to organize your information and take notes on during your research.

3. Make a project about your scientist. Possible project ideas:

   - Recreate his or her experiment
   - Create a video slide show with images and your own voiceover
   - Create a poster with images and captions
   - Dress in a costume and give a speech as though you are the scientist telling about your own life.
   - Create a mobile with parts that hang from a hanger or hoop and give details about your scientist.

4. Present your project to an audience and teach them all about your scientist and what he or she is known for.

How Science Works

Scientific Method

The **scientific method** is a series of steps scientists use to answer questions about the natural world. They begin by making observations and identifying a question or problem. Next, they research to learn all they can and then make a **hypothesis**, or prediction about the outcome of an experiment they will conduct. Next, they design and conduct an experiment. They analyze the results and then draw a conclusion. Along the way, they document everything. The scientific method is the process scientists use over and over again to learn about the natural world.

😊😊😊 EXPLORATION: Scientific Method Wheel

For this activity, you will need:

- "The Scientific Method" wheel from the Printable Pack
- Scissors
- Brass brad (split pin)

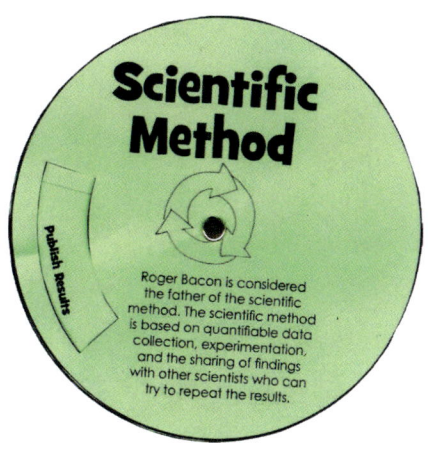

Modern scientists make careful measurements, observe closely, set up experiments so the results are accurate, and publish their methods and results so other scientists can confirm or reject their findings. This careful investigation of the natural world is called the scientific method.

There are steps to the scientific method:

- Observe & question
- Research
- Hypothesize (make a prediction)
- Experiment
- Analyze
- Conclude

However, the steps aren't always followed exactly and sometimes they are out of order or skipped. Albert Einstein, for example, never did any experiments. He just thought deeply, did the math, and came to conclusions, which other scientists after him have confirmed through experimentation.

1. Cut out each of the large circles from "The Scientific Method" printable. Cut out the window.
2. Fasten the two circles together with a brass brad in the center with the circle containing the window on top.

Memorization Station

Scientific method: A method of research in which a problem is identified, relevant data are gathered, a hypothesis is formulated from these data, and the hypothesis is empirically tested

Hypothesis: Prediction of what will happen in an experiment

Teaching Tip

The circular shape of the scientific method craft is intentional as it highlights how scientists don't just experiment once. They try again and again and then pass it along to others to try. If they make mistakes, then scientists rethink and redesign experiments and start all over.

Famous Folks

Roger Bacon is considered the father of the scientific method. He described a repeating cycle of observation, hypothesis, and experimentation as well as the need for others to confirm the results.

Earth & Space

Deep Thoughts

Make sure your hypotheses are falsifiable, in other words it must be possible to prove it wrong.

Just because something can't be proven wrong doesn't mean it isn't true, but it does mean it's not scientific - at least not with the tools we have at the moment.

Check out these hypotheses and decide if they are falsifiable or not.

a. Bigfoot exists.
b. If red and blue are mixed, they make purple.
c. Aliens abducted my cousin.
d. All red apples are sweet.
e. Cheating on a test is wrong.

Only b and d are falsifiable. It is possible that someone could mix red and blue and not get purple. If they did, then this hypothesis would be proved wrong.

It is also possible that someone could eat a red apple that is not sweet. If they did, then this hypothesis would be proved wrong.

It is not possible to absolutely prove that Bigfoot does not exist. You can't prove a negative. Neither is it possible to prove your cousin was not abducted by aliens. All you can find is an absence of evidence. And, as for cheating, that is an ethical statement and can not be proved.

Discuss falsifiability. How does this limit science and how does this strengthen science?

How does this strengthen other ways of knowing?

3. Read through all of the steps on the circle as you discuss the scientific method. Can you think of a simple experiment you could describe to show an example of what each of these steps would look like?

4. Add the craft to your Science Notebook. Make sure to add the title to the table of contents and date and initial your page.

😊 😊 **EXPLORATION: Hypotheses, Theories, and Laws**

For this activity, you will need:

- "Hypothesis Sentence" from the Printable Pack
- Scissors
- Paper and pencils for recording data
- A sheet of white art paper for each child
- Colored markers, paint pens, or watercolor paints

A hypothesis is a prediction of what will happen during an experiment. It is based on observations and research, not

How Science Works

wild guesses. Because I've observed this with other items, I may hypothesize: *If I drop this book, it will fall to the ground.*

A **law** is a description of what happens in a particular situation. Often laws can be described by fairly simple mathematical equations. *When a book is dropped, it falls to the ground* (Newton's Law of Gravitation).

A **theory** explains why something happens in nature. Theories are based on repeated and rigorous experimentation and evidence by many scientists over time. *A dropped book falls to the ground because the mass of the earth curves space so that the book falls toward the center of the mass of the earth* (Theory of Relativity).

Laws and theories are pretty reliable, but they aren't absolute. Future evidence, new questions asked, or better methods and tools for gathering data can overturn or refine a law or theory.

Science is based on the idea that we come closer and closer to the truth rather than doing our best to make sure we are right. Science is constantly refining itself and questioning.

1. Follow the directions on the "Hypothesis Sentence" printable. Prepare this ahead of time so the kids don't see the words.
2. Let the kids work through the process without help. You may need to prompt them about smart ways to collect or organize data, but hold off until they are completely stymied.
3. Once they believe they have the answer, discuss how the process they went through was similar to scientists getting one little piece of the puzzle at a time. Finally, they arrive at a theory, but even then they can't be absolutely sure because perhaps they never saw all the pieces.
4. Make anchor charts about scientific hypotheses, theories, and laws for each of the kids to put in the Science sections of their Layers of Learning Notebooks (see the example in this Exploration.). Use your creativity and markers or paints.
5. Reveal the actual sentence the kids were trying to discover.

Answer: Around the rose bushes, we stacked rocks while wearing pleated, pink tutus and singing show tunes from *The Sound of Music*.

Memorization Station

Law: a description of what happens in a natural process, often expressed with mathematics

Theory: explains the mechanism of a natural process

Make sure to point out to your kids that the scientific definitions for theory and law are not the same as the common definitions.

Fabulous Fact

Science uses mostly inductive reasoning, which begins with an observation and then attempts to find out why it is so.

Sometimes scientists use deductive reasoning, which begins with a general hypothesis and then searches for evidence to confirm the hypothesis or evidence that proves the hypothesis wrong.

Additional Layer

Every time you find an answer to a scientific question, you get more questions.

If you discover that red and blue combine to make purple, then what questions occur to you?

Practice asking lots and lots of questions and looking for the whys behind the facts.

That's real science.

Earth & Space

Memorization Station

Control group: a group in which all variable factors are kept constant

Experimental group: a group in which one variable is changed to test its effects

Independent variable: the variable that is changed in a scientific experiment

Dependent variable: the variable being tested, it will change depending on the independent variable

It can be helpful to think of them in relation to cause and effect. The independent variable is what you change, and the dependent variable is what happens because of the change in the experimental group you're testing.

Additional Layer

Accuracy is important in science measurements.

Set up an exercise where there are several things to measure - the length of a pencil, the amount of water in a container, the temperature of the inside of the fridge, the time it takes a ball to fall 2 meters, etc.

Have each of your children measure as accurately as possible. Compare the measurements you got.

Human error will mean that there are slight differences even when people are measuring the same thing.

Often scientists will take several measurements of the same thing and then average the measurements together to get the closest possible.

☺☺☺ EXPERIMENT: Scientific Controls Plant Growth

For this activity you need:

- Video about experiment variables from this unit's YouTube playlist
- Bean seeds
- Potting soil
- Disposable cups or small planting pots
- Water
- Ruler
- Permanent marker
- "Experiment" sheet or template from the Printable Pack

Within an experiment, there's often a **control group** and an **experimental group**. In the control group, you keep everything the same. Then you can compare the outcome of that to a second group, the experimental group. Within the experimental group, you will just change one thing - the **independent variable**. An independent variable is a variable that is not affected by any other variable. You can think of it as the cause in the experiment. The independent variable will cause a change in the **dependent variable**. The dependent variable is the variable you are testing for. You can think of it as the effect.

Not all experiments require a control, but they are useful. Use a control whenever you need to have a base to compare your experimental group to.

1. Watch some videos about the variables in experiments and learn the difference between independent variables, dependent variables, and controls.

2. Fill two plant pots or disposable cups with potting soil so you leave about 2 cm from the top of the soil to the rim of the container.

3. Poke ten holes in the soil to the first knuckle of your

How Science Works

pointer finger in each container of soil. Drop one bean seed in each hole. Cover the beans with soil.

4. Decide which container will be your control and which container will be your experiment. Label the containers with a permanent marker. You can also put a piece of masking tape on each container and mark the masking tape.

5. In this experiment, we will test the effect of water on bean plant growth. The water is your independent variable. The bean plant growth is your dependent variable. To test the effect of water on sprouting bean seeds, you will water your experimental beans with a set amount of water each day, 2 milliliters, and not water the control at all.

   You will need to make sure everything else, besides water, is the same. They need the same amount of light and heat, for example. These are your controls.

   Use the "Experiment" sheet to write your Experiment, Purpose, Materials, Hypothesis, and Procedure down. Plan a procedure carefully and write down the steps.

6. Observe your experiment every day as you water the experimental beans only, and take notes on development. Take measurements, like number of seeds sprouted or the height of the sprouts daily. Record your measurements.

7. At the end of a set time, count your bean sprouts in each experiment and their condition (height, color, number of leaves per sprout, etc.). Compare your control to your experiment and write down your results and conclusions. Young kids can use the colorful "Experiment" printable. Older kids can type up their own using the template from the Printable Pack as a guide.

8. Add your write-up to the Science section of your Layers of Learning Notebook.

😊 😊 😊 **EXPERIMENT: Scientific Method Cookies**

For this activity, you will need:

- Science Notebook
- Science "Experiment" sheet or template (for high schoolers) from the Printable Pack
- Favorite brownie or cookie recipe (that's a biscuit if you're not from North America)
- Ingredients and supplies to make your recipe, enough for at least two batches
- Artificial sweetener

Writer's Workshop

Write a paragraph explaining the difference between a control group and an experimental group.

In a second paragraph, give an example of a science experiment and identify the control group and the experimental group in the example you gave.

Famous Folks

Shen Kuo was a Chinese scientist and mathematician who discovered the compass and its use in navigation. He also studied climate change.

Deep Thoughts

To the alchemists, science and experimentation went hand in hand with religion and magic.

They believed the physical world was a reflection of the spiritual world and combined religion, magic, and science.

How does their way of seeing the world differ from yours? Are there any similarities?

Earth & Space

Memorization Station

Double blind: When neither the scientist nor his test subjects know which sample is which

It is as though both the scientists and his subjects are blindfolded. Double blind studies are the most accurate when dealing with human test subjects.

Fabulous Fact

There are different levels of validity in scientific studies.

The best science involves experiments with controlled variables in a double blind study and lots of trials or subjects, so the scientists and subjects do not know who is receiving the independent variable and who is not.

The next best experiments involve controlled variables in a closed system with lots of trials or subjects, but without a double blind. This means the scientist's prejudices could get in the way.

The third best science is when there are no controlled experiments, just observation and data gathering.

The worst science involves computer models without any actual experiment. Computer models are only as good as the data entered into them. They really shouldn't be considered valid science at all, only a tool for scientist to use to explore possibilities.

- Writing utensils, including a marker
- Two labeled paper plates (Plate A and Plate B)
- Taste testers and a cookie server

Scientists do good, high quality science when they change only one variable and keep everything else in the experiment the same. In this experiment, you will be changing nothing but the sweetener. Everything else must be carefully measured so it is precise.

The second part of being a good scientist is controlling for bias. You will be doing a **double blind** test to ensure that no one, not the cookie server and not your testers, know which sweetener is in which cookie. That way nothing in the scientist's attitude or voice can give away information to the testers.

1. Design an experiment using the scientific method to determine how artificial sweetener compares to white cane sugar in a recipe. You should compare both taste and texture. How can you conduct the experiment so the results are scientific? Make sure that part of your design involves an uninformed server giving the cookies to the taste testers so there is no bias. Keep careful notes in your Science Notebook of the process and the results.

2. Do your results suggest new ways you could take the experiment further?

3. If you'd like, you can also write up your experiment using the "Experiment" template or type it yourself using the template for older kids as a guide. Make sure someone else could repeat your experiment exactly, using only your write-up as a guide. Add it to the Science section of your Layers of Learning Notebook.

How Science Works

😊 😊 EXPERIMENT: Scientific Method Marble Art

For this activity, you will need:

- Science Notebook
- Various colors of poster paint
- Box or pan with high sides
- Paper
- Marbles
- Scissors (if you need to trim the paper to fit your container)

1. Predict what will happen when colors are mixed together. What color will result from mixing blue and yellow? Red and brown? Orange and purple? Write up your methods and findings in your Science Notebook.

2. Use a box or pan with high sides. Place a piece of paper in the bottom, cut to fit.

3. Put dollops of paint in various places around the paper.

4. Put marbles in the container and tip the container to roll them around and through the paint, over and over.

5. Were your predictions correct? Were your results reliable? Once your paint is dry, glue your picture into your Science Notebook. Write a bit about your results. Make sure to initial your page and add it to your Table of Contents.

😊 😊 EXPLORATION: Recipe For Rigorous Science

For this activity, you will need:

- Video about rigorous science or the reproducibility or repeatability crisis in science
- "Recipe for Rigorous Science" from the Printable Pack
- Scissors
- Glue stick
- Science Notebook

Not all science is equally convincing, which is part of the reason why people disagree about scientific results even when a credentialed scientist presents them. To be highly convincing, scientific results have to be rigorous and have:

Additional Layer

Often scientists conduct a series of multiple experiments to learn more and more. Frederick Griffith was curious about how certain bacteria affected mice. He injected two different bacterial strains into two groups of mice. The one which was infected with the first strain developed pneumonia and died while the mice with the second strain injected stayed alive.

In the second stage, Griffith heated the first strain to kill it before injecting it into mice, and the mice stayed alive. Then, he mixed the heat-killed first strain with some of the live second-strain bacteria. This mixture was injected into mice and they died.

Fabulous Fact

There are two main types of scientists: experimental and applied.

Experimental scientists work on theory and experiments to discover new truths or refine old hypotheses.

Applied scientists make new inventions, methods, or products for commercial purposes.

Earth & Space

Deep Thoughts

In the 1960s, the sugar industry paid three Harvard scientists $50,000 to say that heart disease was most likely caused by saturated fat. After their report was published, diets concentrating on low fat gained the endorsement of many health authorities. To replace the flavor that fat once provided, sugar was added to many foods. Why do you think the sugar industry would want that information to be published?

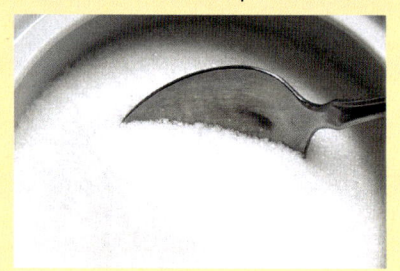

Fabulous Fact

During the Siege of Leningrad that lasted almost 900 days during World War II, there were Soviet scientists who defended the world's largest seed bank in Leningrad. The Nazis had the area surrounded and wanted to starve the people out. Nine scientists starved during the siege even though they were surrounded by seeds, crops, and fruit that they were protecting. They refused to destroy the future of Russia and would not eat them.

- Clear, testable hypothesis - The hypothesis must test one thing and be possible to prove wrong. No hypothesis can absolutely be proved right; we can only say that in this particular experiment it worked out. But even one negative result (if the experiment was performed carefully) will prove a hypothesis wrong.
- Careful design - The experiment must have controls in place to test only one thing or variable at a time and with systemic random sampling, so the scientist can't pick and choose which data or test subjects to use.
- Repeatability - An experiment or process has to be possible to repeat over and over and obtain the same results to be considered reliable. Some science, by its very nature, isn't repeatable. For example, we can't go back and simulate the extinction event that killed the dinosaurs. Any single event that happened in the past fails to be repeatable. Also, if an experiment is repeated and fails to achieve the same results, then the science is called into question.
- Impartiality - Scientists are humans and all humans are biased. Good scientists control for their biases through careful experimental design and careful measurement. They are aware that they are biased and try to minimize the effect of their bias. They carefully report their results so they state accurately what the research actually showed, not an extrapolation or exaggeration of what the research showed. They don't cherry pick the results that back up their hypothesis while throwing out the data that doesn't. Good scientists are more concerned with discovering the truth than being right.
- Accurate and direct measurements - Results that can be measured with tools like rulers, balances, speedometers, and graduated cylinders are always superior to results that are qualitative or subjective. If your measurement devices aren't accurate or reliable, then the rest of your science is called into question. If you can only measure something in a secondary way, like extrapolating the atmosphere of Earth 10,000 years ago from some tiny frozen air bubbles in a glacier, it will never be as accurate or as reliable as a direct measurement would be.

Science that meets all of these requirements is rigorous. Science that meets none or only one of these requirements is imprecise. In between, there are varying degrees of confidence in the results. No science is ever 100% correct or true, without a doubt. The very nature of science is that it can always be proved wrong or incomplete in the future, no matter how rigorous. Throughout Layers of Learning

How Science Works

Science, we will see again and again how scientists have been proved wrong. We will also see that it is when old, established ideas are proved wrong that science advances.

1. Watch a video about rigorous science or the reproducibility crisis in science.

2. Read the card on the "Recipe For Rigorous Science" printable.

3. Read each of the brief summaries of real-life flawed scientific studies. Put a check mark in the box or boxes that indicate which parts of rigorous science were left out of the recipe. Discuss your ideas with a mentor or another student. Why did you check the boxes you checked?

4. Put the "Recipe For Rigorous Science" in you Layers of Learning Notebook behind the Science divider.

😊 😊 😊 EXPEDITION: Tour a Lab 😊

For this activity, you will need:

- A lab or research facility to visit in your area
- Preparation so you can ask intelligent questions

Plan a tour of a science lab or a research facility and arrange to talk with an experimental or applied scientist. Look for universities, commercial labs, government-funded organizations, zoos, hospital labs, or astronomical observatories in your area. Call ahead to see if you can arrange a tour. Make sure they know you are interested in the methods scientists use to ensure experiments have reliable results. Prepare your children so they each have at least one intelligent question to ask the tour guide about experiments, the scientific method, or research they have participated in.

Step 3: Show What You Know

During this unit, choose one of the assignments below to show what you have learned during the unit. Add this work to your Layers of Learning Notebook. You can also use this assignment to show your supervising teacher or your charter school as a sample of what you've been working on in your homeschool, if needed.

There are more ideas for writing assignments in the "Writer's Workshop" sidebars.

Writer's Workshop

Albert Einstein received a letter from a little girl once, in which she complained that she could not be a scientist because she was a girl. He responded, "I do not mind that you are a girl, but the main thing is that you yourself do not mind. There is no reason for it."

Write a letter to the little girl explaining to her some of the reasons girls can and should be scientists if they choose to.

Famous Folks

Marie Maynard Daly experimented with the effects of cholesterol, sugars, and other nutrients on the heart. She discovered how high cholesterol foods clog arteries. She was also the first African American woman to earn a Ph.D. in chemistry.

Earth & Space

Unit Trivia Questions

1. Name the four main branches of science.

   Earth & Space Science, Biology, Chemistry, Physics

2. True or false - A hypothesis is a wild guess about how an experiment will turn out.

   False - a hypothesis should be an educated prediction based on observation and research.

3. Each time you walk into the garage, you smell gasoline. This is most closely associated with which step in the scientific method?

   Making an observation

4. After formulating a hypothesis, the next step in the scientific method is to _____.

   Conduct an experiment

5. Does the experimental group or the control group contain the independent variable?

   The experimental group

6. Which of these explains why or how something happens in the natural world: Law, hypothesis, theory?

   Theory

7. True or false - To be certain about their measurements, good scientists only measure once.

   False - good scientists measure carefully, but they also often repeat their measurements and then take the average of all of them.

Coloring or Narration Page

For this activity, you will need:

- "How Science Works" printable from the Printable Pack
- Writing or drawing utensils

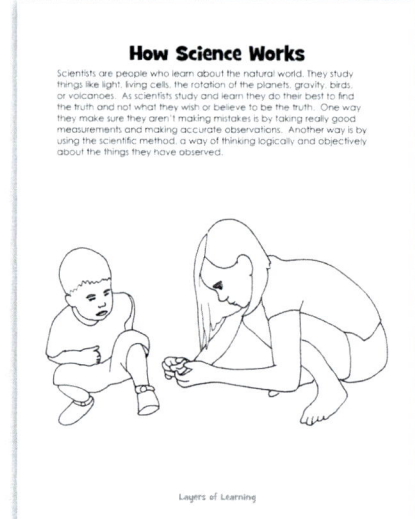

1. Depending on the age and ability of the child, choose either the "How Science Works" coloring sheet or the "How Science Works" narration page from the Printable Pack.

2. Younger kids can color the coloring sheet as you review some of the things you learned about during this unit. You might talk about observations, the history of science, or the scientific method. You may even make a list of the four branches of science - earth and space, biology, chemistry, and physics. On the bottom of the coloring page, kids can write a sentence about what they learned. Very young children can explain their ideas orally while a parent writes for them.

3. Older kids can write about some of the concepts you learned on the narration page and color the picture as well.

4. Add this to the Science section of your Layers of Learning Notebook.

Science Experiment Write-Up

For this activity, you will need:

- The "Experiment" write-up or "Experiment Report Template" from the Printable Pack

1. Choose one of the experiments you completed during this unit and create a careful and complete experiment write-up for it. Make sure you have included every specific detail of each step so your experiment could be repeated by anyone who wanted to try it.

2. Do a careful revision and edit of your write-up, taking it through the writing process, before you turn it in for grading.

How Science Works

😊😊😊 Three Things Page
For this activity, you will need:

- Paper
- Writing and coloring utensils

1. Divide a sheet of paper into three sections. In each of the sections, write and illustrate the three most important things you learned during this unit.

2. Present your three things out loud to an audience. Give the audience an opportunity to ask you questions about what you learned.

😊😊😊 Big Book of Knowledge
For this activity, you will need:

- "Big Book of Knowledge: How Science Works" printable from the Printable Pack, printed on card stock
- Writing or drawing utensils
- Big Book of Knowledge

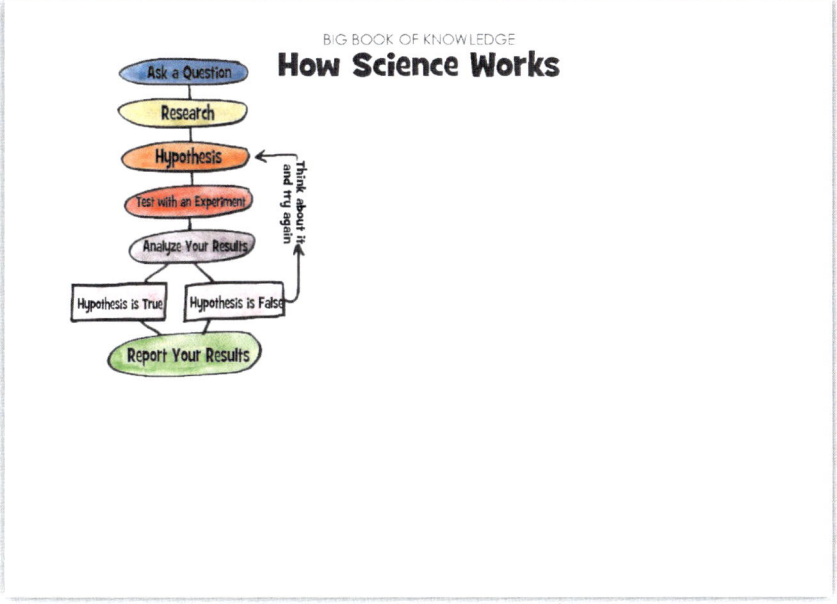

1. Color, draw on, or write on the Big Book of Knowledge page. Record concepts, definitions, and facts you learned during this unit. It's a record of the things you learned and hope to remember. Add the page to your Big Book of Knowledge.

2. Use your Big Book of Knowledge regularly to help you review, quiz, or create games that will help you commit the things you've learned to memory.

Big Book of Knowledge

The Big Book of Knowledge is a book for you, the mentor, to use as a constant review of all of the things you're learning about. You can use it to quiz your kids or prepare tests or review games. Whenever you learn something in Layers of Learning that you want your kids to remember, add it to your Big Book of Knowledge.

Assemble your Big Book of Knowledge in a binder or with binder rings. Divide it into sections for each subject.

In the Printable Pack for this unit you will find a "Big Book of Knowledge" sheet. You can add this sheet to others you collect or create yourself as you progress through the Layers of Learning curriculum. Customize the Big Book of Knowledge to your family by adding facts and topics that you enjoyed exploring as you were learning.

Visit Layers of Learning online to find more information on how to assemble and use your own Big Book of Knowledge.

You will also find cover and section pages to print along with creative games to play with your Big Book of Knowledge to keep school, even the tests, fun!

Earth & Space

Unit Overview

Key Concepts:
- The earth is made up of layers, including the crust, mantle, outer core, and inner core.
- Earth has a magnetic field caused by convection cells in the mantle.
- Earth has had three atmospheres: methane, carbon dioxide and water vapor, and an oxygen-rich atmosphere.
- Oceans have five zones: sunlight, twilight, midnight, abyss, and trenches.
- Ocean currents are caused by differences in salinity and temperature.
- Oceans regulate global temperatures.

Vocabulary:
- Crust
- Mantle
- Outer core
- Inner core
- Continental crust
- Oceanic crust
- MYA
- BYA
- Saltwater
- Freshwater
- Brackish water
- Salinity
- Current
- Specific heat
- Water Cycle

Theories, Laws, & Hypotheses:
- Dynamo theory
- Uniformitarianism theory
- Whole mantle convection hypothesis
- Plume convection hypothesis
- Great Oxygenation Event
- Late Heavy Bombardment hypothesis
- Giant impact hypothesis

PLANET EARTH

Earth is the third planet from the sun and is the only planet known to support life. Its distance from the sun and atmosphere make it a perfect environment for us to live. It also has oxygen and water, two very important things we need to live. The structure of Earth allows it to create magnetic fields which protect us from the sun and objects in space, produce new rock (including minerals and gases that we use on a regular basis), act as a vast recycling plant of air, water, rock, soil, and everything else. This recycling feature means it can repair and heal itself. Besides that, understanding the structure of the earth helps us understand and partially predict earthquakes and volcanoes.

Deep down under the crust are all the materials we need to not just survive, but to thrive, and they are there in such incredible abundance. It is a changing, dynamic, regenerating place, so unlike the deadness and cold hostility of the moon. It is largely because of what goes on beneath the surface that Earth is called a living planet.

Step 1: Library List

Choose books from your library that go with this topic. Here's a list of some favorites and also a list of search terms so you can utilize what your library offers. Read the books with your kids and/or assign them some to read independently. It is from these books your kids will learn most of the facts they need from this unit.

Search for: Earth, structure of the earth, layers of the earth, oceans, water cycle

😊 😊 😊 *Encyclopedia of Science* from DK. Read ""Earth" and "Structure of the Earth" on pages 209-213 and "Seas and Oceans," "Waves, Tides, and Currents," and "Shoreline" on pages 234-237.

😊 😊 😊 *The Usborne Science Encyclopedia*. Read "The Earth & Moon" on pages 166-167.

Planet Earth

✓ 😊😊😊 *The Kingfisher Science Encyclopedia*. Read "Earth and the Solar System" and "Earth's Rotation" on pages 2-3. Read "Earth's Structure," "Earth's Atmosphere," "The Oceans," and "The Ocean Floor" on pages 8-15.

💧 😊😊😊 *My Tourist Guide To The Center of the Earth* by Lizzie Munsie. This book takes you all of the way from the atmosphere to the center of the earth with some really neat stops along the way.

😊 *Magic School Bus Inside the Earth* by Joanna Cole. A quirky teacher takes her students on a field trip inside the earth. Along the way, they learn about each layer before being spewed back out through a volcano. Also look for *The Magic School Bus on the Ocean Floor*, *The Magic School Bus Wet All Over*, and *The Magic School Bus at the Waterworks*.

💧 😊 *Follow the Water from Brook to Ocean* by Arthur Dorros. A book about how water shapes the planet as it flows across the land and to the sea to introduce the water cycle.

💧 😊 *Water* by Melissa Stewart. This is an easy reader from National Geographic all about the water cycle.

😊 *Down Comes the Rain* by Dr. Franklyn M. Branley. A picture book about the water cycle with lots of details.

💧 😊 *Water Cycle* by Monica Hughes. A picture book that explains the role of water on the earth and then shows the water cycle.

😊 *Planet Earth/Inside Out* by Gail Gibbons. Talks about the formation of the earth 4.5 billion years ago. Discusses the features of Earth, from its bulging equator to the inner core.

😊 *Earth! My First 4.54 Billion Years* by Stacy McAnulty. Told in first person by Earth herself, this is full of facts from where Earth is in the solar system to how old she is to what's been going on with her since she was formed.

💧 😊😊 *Earth: The Water Planet* by E.C. Hill. A short chapter book about how Earth is unique because of its water.

💧 😊😊 *Solving the Puzzle Under the Sea: Maria Tharp Maps the Ocean Floor* by Robert Burleigh. A picture book about the first person to map the sea floor and the obstacles she faced.

😊😊 *Ocean: the Definitive Visual Guide* by Robert Dinwiddie. This is a DK visual book that is full of photos, illustrations, and text about the physical characteristics of

Family School Levels

The colored smilies in this unit help you choose the correct levels of books and activities for your child.
😊 = Ages 6-9
😊 = Ages 10-13
😊 = Ages 14-18

On the Web

For videos, web pages, games, and more to add to this unit, visit the Earth & Space Resources at Layers-of-Learning.com.

You will find a link to video playlists, web links, and more.

Bookworms

If you're looking for a family read-aloud, we'd like to suggest this one.

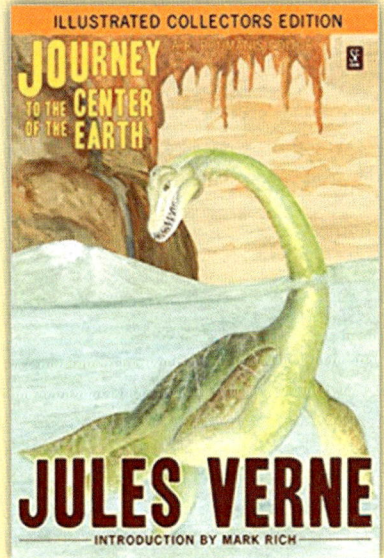

Journey to the Center of the Earth by Jules Verne is an imaginary journey to deep under the earth's surface. It was written before we knew what was down there. If you have young children, look for an abridged version.

Earth & Space

Deep Thoughts

Ask and answer some "what if" questions about the structure of the earth.

What if Earth had cooled clear through like the moon?

What if Earth didn't have a magnetic field?

What if Earth spun at a faster or slower rate than it does?

Think of some "what if" questions of your own.

Fabulous Fact

Silicates are minerals that are composed of silicon and oxygen. 90% of the rocks in the earth's crust are based on silicates. Minerals like topaz, hornblende, talc, biotite, quartz, emerald, and dozens of others begin with a silicon and oxygen base. For example, the mineral zircon has a formula of $ZrSiO_4$.

The other 10% of the earth's crust is made of things like iron, gold, silver, platinum, rare earth elements, carbon, copper, arsenic, and their compounds.

Memorization Station

Memorize the layers of the earth. For younger kids, use the layers on the "Structure of the Earth" diagram.

High schoolers can memorize the more detailed "Earth's Layers" diagram.

Try drawing a chalk diagram of Earth's layers outside on some pavement. Move around the chalk diagram as you recite the layers. The movement and recitation will solidify the information.

---

the water, sea floor, and oceans.

🙂🙂*Super Earth Encyclopedia* by DK. Includes vibrant visual information on the formation and structure of Earth and also weather, formations, oceans, and other topics that will be covered in Layers of Learning Earth & Space.

🙂🙂*The New Ocean Book* by Frank Sherwin. This is part of the "Wonders of Creation" series and is Christian-based. It discusses the composition of water in oceans, tides, currents, coral reefs, ocean life, and the Genesis flood in relation to oceans today.

🙂*The Tide: The Science and Stories Behind the Greatest Force on Earth* by Hugh Aldersey-Williams. Tells the story of how people have explained the tides scientifically and visits some the most interesting tidal phenomenon on Earth.

🙂*Mapping the Deep* by Robert Kunzig. A tour of the oceans from the seafloor to submerged islands to the collapse of the cod fisheries. This book is an easy read for the advanced topics of what we know and don't know about the oceans.

🙂*The Story of Earth* by Robert M. Hazen. Details the history of the earth from the gathering of stardust and the emergence of continents to the formation of the atmosphere and the beginnings of life. Contains evolutionary biology.

🙂*The Wonder of Water* by Michael Denton. This book is profoundly awe-inspiring. Water, something we all take for granted, is amazing. Without its abundance on Earth, we could not exist. The author is a biologist and this book is focused on the many chemical and physical properties of water that make life possible. This book is a page-turner.

🙂*The Biblical Case For An Old Earth* by David Snoke. Especially for Christians. Snoke is a physicist and devout Christian who accepts the timeline scientists give for the age of the earth.

🙂*Earth: The Definitive Visual Guide* by Douglas Palmer, et. al. (DK). A beautiful book packed with vibrant photos and detailed text about all sorts of aspects of the earth - the formation of Earth, its structure mountains, volcanoes, rivers, and more. This book will be a valuable resource for the entire Layers of Learning Earth & Space course.

🙂*AP/College Environmental Science* by KhanAcademy.org. For a more traditional high school experience, you can add a Khan Academy course. During this unit, study "Earth Systems and Resources." You will learn about plate tectonics, soil, air, water, seasons, and climate.

Planet Earth

Step 2: Explore

Choose a few hands-on explorations from this section to work on as a family. They should be appealing activities that will create mental hooks so your kids remember the information in the unit. Save the rest of the explorations for the next time you do this unit in four years when your kids are older. You can also read the sidebars together and explore some little rabbit trails.

This unit includes printables. See the introduction for instructions on retrieving your Printable Pack.

Structure of the Earth

💧 😊 😊 😊 **EXPLORATION: Earth's Layers**
For this activity, you will need:

- Video or book about the structure of the earth from this unit's Library List or YouTube playlist
- Colorful play dough
- "Structure of the Earth" from the Printable Pack (a simple diagram for younger kids up to about 11 or 12 years old)
- "Earth's Layers" from the Printable Pack (a more detailed diagram for older kids)
- "Structure of the Earth Answers" and "Earth's Layers Answers" from the Printable Pack
- Colored pencils, crayons, or pens

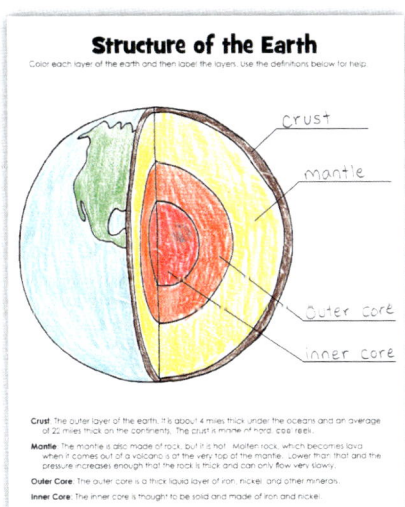
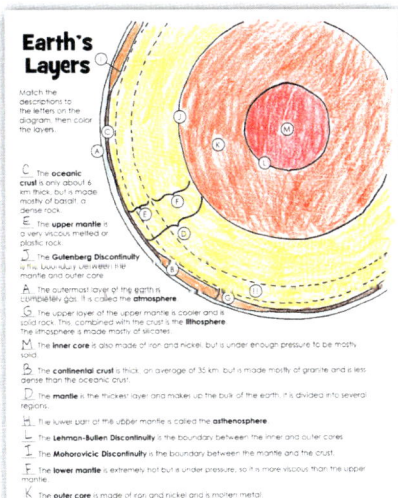

Earth is not just a solid ball of rock with random big basins where water gathers. Earth is complex and layered. The outside of the earth is called the **crust**. It's the part we see, stand on, dig holes in, and live on. Beneath the crust are layers of really hot molten rock, called the **mantle**. Below that is the **outer core**. At the very center is a solid **inner core**

Famous Folks

In 1936, a Danish geophysicist and mathematician named Inge Lehmann discovered the solid inner core and the molten outer core of the earth.

She carefully and mathematically analyzed the data from earthquakes and realized that the entire inner parts of the earth could not be one single molten mass.

Fabulous Fact

Between the layers of the earth are boundaries called "discontinuities." These are places where the seismic velocities actually change. There is something really there, not just a boundary line on paper.

The Mohorovicic Discontinuity, or Moho, is thought to be a place where the composition changes from feldspar rocks above to non-feldspar rocks below. So, besides differences in temperature and viscosity, there are differences in chemical composition between the various layers of the earth too.

37

Earth & Space

Additional Layer

We have told you that the inner core of the earth is a solid, but the truth is that we only know that it *acts* like a solid, deflecting the seismic waves as it does. As we speak, scientists are hard at work trying to figure out what the core really is. Go read all about it.

Memorization Station

Crust: the thin outermost layer that wraps around the earth

Mantle: the layer of the earth between the crust and the core that is made of silicate rock

Outer core: a fluid layer of the earth composed mostly of iron and nickel

Inner core: the solid material in the center of the earth that is at an extremely high temperature and pressure

Additional Layer

The interiors of the other rocky planets in the solar system are probably very similar to Earth's layers. We know they have volcanoes, for example. This is the inside of Venus. Look up information on other planets' cores.

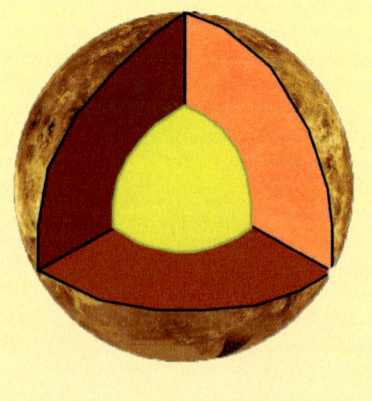

made of metal.

There are several ways of thinking about the layers of the earth. You can think of it in terms of physical properties, like liquid or solid; in terms of chemical properties and what each layer is made of; or in terms of mathematical physics of waves passing through the earth. The printable for older kids includes aspects of all three properties of Earth while the printable for younger kids just includes the chemical properties.

1. Watch a video or read a book about the structure of the earth.

2. Make your own model of the layers of the earth using colorful play dough. Start by making a ball that represents the inner core, then add a layer for the outer core, another for the mantle, and finally, a thin layer for the crust. You can even add oceanic as well as continental crust if you'd like to.

3. Color the printable of your choice, using the "Answers" sheets as a guide.

😊😊😊 EXPERIMENT: Layers of the Earth in a Jar 🔵

For this activity, you will need:

- Clear jar
- Vanilla pudding (2-3 boxes, depending on the size of your jar)
- Food coloring
- Graham cracker crumbs
- "Layers of the Earth Labels" from the Printable Pack

Memorize the layers of the earth by making a layers of the earth jar and practicing sticking labels to each layer in the proper places. You can also learn the names of the boundaries where each of these layers meets.

1. Make a batch of vanilla pudding and divide it into three bowls. Use food coloring to dye one of the bowls red,

Planet Earth

one orange, and leave one the creamy color of vanilla pudding.

2. Add a cream layer to the bottom of the jar, followed by a layer of orange, and then a thick layer of red. Smash the cookies into crumbs and place them across the top, creating a layer that represents the earth's crust. Adhere the labels to each layer - inner core, outer core, mantle, and crust.

3. Now, label the boundaries between the layers. The Mohorovičić discontinuity, often called the Moho, is the boundary between the crust and the mantle. The Gutenberg Discontinuity is the lowermost part of the core that sits at the boundary between the mantle and the outer core. The Lehman-Bullen Discontinuity is where the inner core and outer core meet. Practice grabbing a label and matching it with each layer and boundary in the jar until you have them all memorized.

😊 😊 😊 EXPERIMENT: P-Waves and the Inner Earth

For this activity, you will need:

- String
- Scissors
- Tape
- Science Notebook

Scientists compare the time a particular earthquake's waves are recorded by a seismometer to the time the earthquake actually took place. That tells them how fast the waves passed through the earth. Sound waves pass through different materials at different speeds. This helps us know what the materials inside of the earth are made of. When sound waves change speed they also change direction. Seismometers can also be used to find these directional changes, helping us learn the density and thickness of the inner layers of the earth. Furthermore, something in the center of the earth deflects or blocks

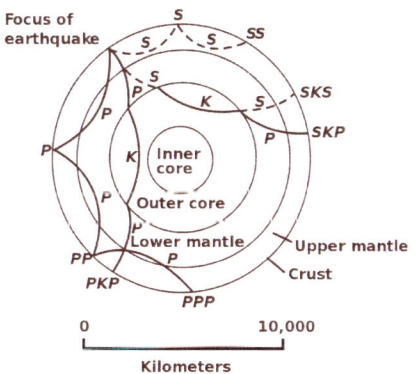

Additional Layer

Since the earth's outer core is not rigidly connected to the mantle, some scientists think that the core may be rotating at a different rate from the rest of the planet.

They use the seismology readings and magnetic field to study the possibility.

Research more on this area of exploration in earth science.

Famous Folks

Francis Birch was an American geophysicist who built on the work of Lehmann to discover the chemical composition of the layers of the earth. It was he who determined that the mantle was made of silicates and the core was most likely iron.

Teaching Tip

Show your kids a hard boiled egg to help them visualize the earth's layers. The core is like the yolk, the mantle is like the white, and the thin shell is like the crust of the earth.

Earth & Space

Fabulous Fact

The word "earth" is a Germanic word that means "ground." It became the English name of our planet about 1,000 years ago or so.

Earth is capitalized when it is used as the name of the planet and is not preceded by "the." So we write: We live on Earth. The earth is our home.

Additional Layer

Felsic lava, which forms continental granite rock, occurs when continental rock is melted into the mafic lava already under the earth, increasing its silica levels. The other rocky planets in our solar system have crusts made of basalt, like Earth's oceans. Without our continental rock, the whole earth would be ocean.

So, how did the continental rock form in the first place if new continental rock always starts out with old continental rock?

Do some research and see if you can find out the latest hypotheses on how the continents got their start.

---

sound waves from passing through that point, so we know something very solid and dense is in the center.

1. Cut a piece of string about 2 feet long. Tape one end of the string to a table or countertop. You might need someone to hold the string and tape in place.

2. Stretch the string taut and flick it with your finger to create noise.

3. Wrap the loose end (the end not taped to the table) around your pointer finger and insert your finger into your ear. Flick the string again. The sound is much louder now. The first time, the sound was passing through air to your ear. The second time, it was passing through the solid string to your ear. Waves passing through different materials have different effects that can be detected.

4. Head a new page in your Science Notebook "P-Waves" and add it to your table of contents. Draw a labeled diagram of your experiment, then draw a diagram of how p-waves pass through the earth.

😊 😊 EXPERIMENT: Wobbly Earth

For this activity, you will need:

- Two eggs
- Saucepan with water
- Stove

The earth wobbles a bit on its axis. This wobbling occurs because the inside of the earth is not a solid but is at least partially a viscous liquid.

1. Boil one egg in a saucepan of water on the stove until it is cooked. Leave the other egg raw.

2. Spin the two eggs. Compare the movement of the raw egg to the boiled egg. The raw egg wobbles more and slows down much more quickly than the boiled egg, which has a solid center.

Because the inner part of the earth is liquid enough

Planet Earth

to flow, it can spin at a different rate and exert forces contrary to the overriding force of the earth's orbit, throwing the whole thing off just a little.

3. Head a new page in your Science Notebook "Wobbly Earth" and add it to your table of contents. Draw a labeled diagram of the experiment you did. Add a sentence or two about how the liquid center of the earth makes it wobble in its revolutions.

☺ ☺ **EXPERIMENT: Bulging Equator**

For this activity, you will need:

- Paper cut into strips (approximately 55 cm by 4 cm)
- Scissors
- Tape or glue
- Pencil

The earth is almost a sphere, but not quite. It bulges at the equator because it is spinning.

1. Make a paper sphere with two long strips of paper taped at right angles to one another. Curve the long arms up and tape them together to make a sphere shape.
2. Poke a sharpened pencil through the center of one of the axes. Spin the pencil between your hands and watch the shape of the spinning sphere.
3. Head a new page in your Science Notebook "Bulging Equator" and add it to your table of contents. Draw a labeled diagram of the experiment you did. In a sentence or two, explain how your experiment relates to the way Earth's equator bulges just a little.

Fabulous Fact

This is what our magnetic field would look like if we could see it.

The magnetic field is essential in protecting the earth from solar radiation.

In what appears to be complete randomness, the direction of the magnetic field can reverse, flopping the North and South Poles.

Evidence for reversed magnetic poles can be found in sea floor basalt where metallic minerals line up north to south. None of these flops have occurred during human history, but you never know, maybe this will be our lucky year.

Go find out what would happen if the magnetic field did reverse. How would it affect animals, plants, and humans?

Fabulous Fact

The Dynamo Theory says that Earth's magnetic field is caused by the flowing magma inside of the earth, which causes electrons to flow and creates a magnetic field.

This is a scientific theory and not a scientific law because it explains *how* the magnetic field is formed.

Earth & Space

Memorization Station

Continental crust: the relatively thick part of the earth's crust that forms landmasses

Oceanic crust: the relatively thin part of the earth's crust which is found under the oceans

Together, these two types make up what we call the crust of the earth.

Additional Layer

People create models and experiments for things we can't possibly observe first-hand, like the inner workings of Earth.

This works fairly well because the principles of physics are constant. This idea, that the physical laws of the universe are unchanging, is called uniformitarianism.

Palouse Falls in Washington State was formed during a cataclysmic flood from the end of the ice age. Photo by David Lee, CC by SA 2.0 Wikimedia.

Some geologists also say that the rate of change is constant and slow, but this idea is recently being revised to accept that the slow rate of change on Earth is sometimes punctuated by a rapid catastrophic event like the Missoula Flood in North America.

EXPERIMENT: Earth's Magnetic Field

For this activity, you will need:

- Iron filings
- Bar magnet
- Video about Earth's magnetic field from the YouTube playlist for this unit

We know Earth has a magnetic field, because compasses always point north, but why? Where does the magnetic field come from, and how is it maintained? The current theory is that because the insides of the earth are so hot, they flow. This movement causes moving electrons, and moving electrons can create a magnetic field. This theory is called the dynamo theory.

1. Get some iron filings and a magnet to see what a magnetic field looks like. Just scatter the iron filings over a small area and then place the magnet in the middle. The iron filings will line up along the lines of the magnetic field.

2. Head a new page in your Science Notebook" Earth's Magnetic Field" and add it to your table of contents. Draw a detailed diagram of the magnetic field you observed with the iron filings and magnet. Don't forget to label your diagram and add your observations.

3. Watch a video about the Earth's magnetic field. As you watch, take notes in your lab notebook. You can pause the video from time to time so you have enough time to write and draw diagrams.

EXPERIMENT: Why is the Earth Hot Inside?

For this activity, you will need:

- Glass bottle with a narrow neck
- Circle of heavy paper that fits over the mouth of the bottle
- Freezer

Why is the earth hot inside? Well, the earth started out hot because the material used to make it was molten in the beginning. Secondly, inside of the earth there are many chemical reactions involving radioactive decay, which gives off heat. Finally, there is a lot of friction because of the moving rocks and lava and bits of metal inside of the earth slide past one another as the earth spins.

We can demonstrate how friction produces heat.

1. Put an empty glass bottle in a freezer for 20 minutes.
2. Take the bottle out of the freezer and place the paper

Planet Earth

circle over the top of the bottle.

3. Rub your hands together vigorously until you can feel the heat from the friction. Place your warm hands around the cold bottle. Watch as the circle of heavy paper lifts and falls back down over and over as the heat from your hands warms the air inside the bottle.

4. Head a new page in your Science Notebook "Why Is the Earth Hot Inside?" and add it to your table of contents. Draw a labeled diagram of the experiment you did.

5. Add a list of reasons the inside of the Earth is hot:
   - It started with molten materials.
   - Chemical reactions continue to give off heat.
   - Friction among the rocks inside the earth produces heat.

😊 😊 😊 EXPLORATION: Two Types of Crust

For this activity, you will need:

- Red, orange, yellow, blue, and green felt
- Scissors
- Glue
- Card stock
- Books or websites about the earth's crust
- Video about the earth's crust from the YouTube playlist for this unit

The earth's crust is made up of two different types of material. One is **continental crust**, which is made of felsic rock which forms all sorts of igneous rocks and then transforms into sedimentary or metamorphic rock. The other is **oceanic crust**, which is made of mafic rock which forms into either basalt or gabbro. Continental crust is much thicker and older than oceanic crust. Oceanic crust is much denser than continental crust. Because oceanic crust is thinner and denser than continental crust, it sinks lower into the molten layers of Earth below it and forms the deep basins that are the oceans.

1. Do some research on the earth's crust. Head a new page in your Science Notebook "Earth's Crust" and add it to your table of contents. Take some notes about what you learn. Also, make a table of facts in your Science Notebook comparing the oceanic and continental crust. It should look like this:

Crust	Thickness	Density	Composition	Rock Types
Oceanic				
Continental				

Additional Layer

We can make good estimates of Earth's age by finding the oldest rocks possible and dating them using radiometric dating techniques. So far, the oldest rock ever found is from the Jack Hills in western Australia.

The areas of Earth with the oldest rocks are in Australia, southern Africa, and on the Canadian Shield.

The Kaapvaal Craton in southern Africa is a big hunk of crust from around 3 billion years ago. It is the source of the rich gold deposits and diamonds of South Africa.

Find out more about the oldest rocks on Earth.

Writer's Workshop

There are two hypotheses about convection in the mantle.

In "whole mantle convection," the entire mantle is flowing the way the hot oil flows when heated in a pan.

In "plume convection," heat is carried up from the core in plumes and then much smaller convection cells near the surface occur.

No one knows which hypothesis is right or if either is correct.

Read up on both hypotheses, draw diagrams of each, then make lists of the evidence for each. Are there questions each hypothesis fails to answer? Which hypothesis do you like better?

Earth & Space

Additional Layer

Without the atmosphere, liquid water would not exist on the surface of Earth. Air presses down and it provides pressure. Without that pressure, the water would evaporate more quickly than it could be produced.

This is a plastic bottle that was sealed on top of a mountain. When it was brought down the mountain to sea level, the weight of the air crushed it.

That is one of the reasons it is believed that the atmosphere formed pretty early, because we know there were oceans pretty early in Earth's history.

Writer's Workshop

Imagine how different our planet would be if its crust had mostly land with just a small amount of oceanic crust on the surface of the planet. Write a descriptive paragraph about what you think it would be like and how you think it would affect our planet.

Memorization Station

MYA: million years ago

BYA: billion years ago

This dating system is used for geologic time and paleontology. It is always an approximation and dates backward from "today."

2. Make a model of the oceanic and continental crusts with felt. Begin by reviewing the internal layers of the earth as you create an inner core, an outer core, and magma using red, orange, and yellow felt circles.

3. To differentiate between the oceanic and continental crust, you will add thin areas of blue oceanic crust, and thicker areas of green continental crust that rises up above the oceanic crust. The continental crust should be thick, with lots of mountains and rough ground. The oceanic crust should be thinner, reside beneath the continents, and have fewer mountains. Once your earth model is complete, glue it to a sheet of card stock.

4. Add labels and a caption to your model and add it to the Science section of your Layers of Learning Notebook.

😊 🔵 EXPERIMENT: Earth's Mantle

WARNING: This experiment uses hot oil. Adult supervision is needed.

For this activity, you will need:

- Glitter
- Cooking oil
- Saucepan
- Stove

The center of the earth heats the liquid mantle above it much like a stove heats a pot of water. The heat rises toward the surface and then falls again as it cools. This creates a current called a convection current. The convection cells in the mantle refine and separate the minerals in the earth's core into felsic and mafic rock compositions, making the oceanic and continental crusts.

1. To watch a convection current, add a spoonful of glitter to a saucepan. Pour cooking oil into a saucepan until it is about 3/4 full.

2. Put the saucepan on medium heat and watch. As the oil heats, the pieces of glitter are carried to the top of the oil and then they flow back down toward the bottom.

Planet Earth

3. Head a new page in your Science Notebook "Earth's Mantle" and add it to your table of contents. Watch a video about the earth's mantle. As you watch, take notes. Pause the video on a diagram of what scientists think the convection currents in the mantle look like. Copy the diagram into your Science Notebook.

😊 😊 **EXPERIMENT: Scale Model of Earth Challenge**

For this activity, you will need:

- Play dough or clay in three colors: red, orange, yellow
- Fine sand
- Ruler
- Calculator
- Fishing line or waxed string
- "Scale Model of Earth Challenge" printable from the Printable Pack

The challenge is to build a scale model of the layers of the earth using play dough or clay. A scale model is an exact replica of the real thing, but in a different size. Your scale model of the earth will be much smaller than the real earth, but each layer needs to be proportionally the same as the real thing.

1. Using the "Scale Model of Earth Challenge" printable, scale down the model of the earth and determine (in centimeters) how thick to make each of the layers.

   Hint: Since measurements are in km on the printable, you can easily convert into centimeters for your model.

2. Use the three colors of play dough to construct a scale model of earth, then roll the ball in a thin layer of sand to simulate the crust.

3. Slice your model in half with the fishing line to see the layers.

Age & Formation of Earth

> **WARNING: This section assumes an Old Earth model. If you don't agree with this model, you can teach your kids your own beliefs or explain that we don't know but that some scientists believe in this.**

😊 😊 😊 **EXPLORATION: Geologic Time Scale**

For this activity, you will need:

- Roll of freezer paper or other long roll of paper
- Metric ruler or meter stick

Bookworms

The Pebble in My Pocket by Meredith Hooper is a picture book story of a tiny rock from 480 million years ago.

Fabulous Fact

The geologic timeline does not contain biological events of life, only geologic ones of rocks, continents, and mountains because this unit is focused on geology.

You might want to point out that though life in the form of microorganisms appeared very early, it wasn't until the beginning of the Cambrian period that larger, more complex life forms appeared. This is related to the time when there was enough oxygen to support animals.

This is a trilobite fossil from the Cambrian Period.

You will learn more about fossils and ancient life in the *Earth & Space: Fossils* unit.

Earth & Space

Bookworms

The Story of the Earth in 25 Rocks by Donald R. Protero answers the question "but how do we know?"

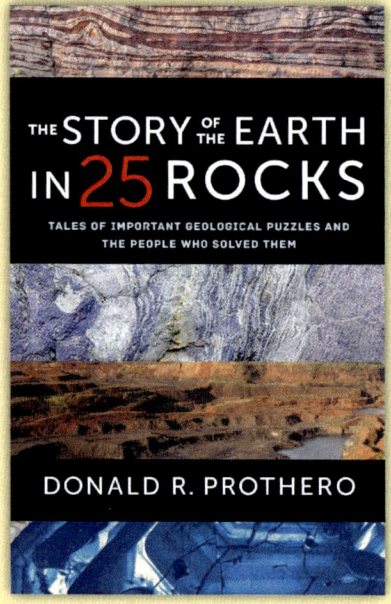

How do we know how old the earth is or when the oceans first appeared or when the first life took root? The record is in the rocks.

For age 14 and up.

Deep Thoughts

The moon is not geologically active and does not have water or an atmosphere to cause erosion. The moon is preserved, like a time capsule, from the earliest ages of its formation. It was formed just after Earth and contains old lava fields, crater impacts, and a shared chemical composition with Earth.

If we study the moon, we can find out more about early Earth.

But consider: why didn't the moon end up with water and active volcanoes and an atmosphere like Earth did?

- Permanent markers
- "Geologic Time Scale" printable from the Printable Pack
- Crayons, colored pencils, or colored markers
- Scissors
- Glue stick or school glue

Scientists estimate the age of the earth at about 4.5 billion years. When they are speaking of such vast time spans, they use the acronyms **MYA** or **BYA** to describe them. To visualize this vast amount of time, use a long roll of paper.

1. Cut your roll of paper 4.5 meters long. This represents the whole history of the earth. One meter represents one billion years.

2. Choose one end of the paper that represents the beginning of the earth and the other end that represents today. Mark your paper with important dates starting with "today" and going backward. Use this chart as a guide to help you place your marks.

cm from "Today"	Era	Important Features
0.2	Pleistocene	Continents in present position
2.3	Neogene	Himalayas and Zagros Mountains formed
6.6	Paleogene	Alps and Rocky Mountains formed

Planet Earth

14.5	Cretaceous	Andes Mountains formed, current continents take shape
20.1	Jurassic	Pangaea breaks up
25.2	Triassic	Pangaea formed
29.9	Permian	Appalachian and MacDonald Mountains formed
35.9	Carboniferous	Ural Mountains formed
41.9	Devonian	High sea levels covered North America
44.4	Silurian	Mountains of Wales, Scotland, and Scandinavia formed
48.5	Ordovician	Gondwana supercontinent formed
54.1	Cambrian	Pannotia supercontinent first formed
250	Proterozoic	Bacteria began to produce oxygen, forming the atmosphere
400	Archean	First life appears in the oceans, earliest continents emerge
450	Hadean	Earth is formed from debris rotating around the sun. Temperatures are extremely hot. Moon is formed due to a collision with another planet. First oceans form toward the end of this time.

3. Color and cut apart the super continents and other important dates from the "Geologic Time Scale" printable. Paste them on the timeline in the correct places. The cm from "today" are shown on each date.

4. There will be lots of white space left on your timeline. Let the kids illustrate it any way they like. They can add volcanoes, meteor showers, dinosaurs, and so on.

🙂🙂🙂 **EXPLORATION: Evolving Atmosphere Craft**
For this activity, you will need:

- Three identical foam balls - about 4 cm in diameter
- Three paper plates
- Paints and paintbrushes

Over time, Earth's atmosphere has changed drastically. Evidence of this can be found in layers of sedimentary rocks. Because of the composition of the rocks, scientists can tell they developed in an atmosphere that contained little oxygen because of how quickly the atmospheric oxygen combined with iron and other minerals.

1. Cut holes in the centers of your paper plates, just large

Fabulous Fact

There is a hypothesis that a big uptick in impacts from space debris occurred about 3.8 BYA in an event known as the Late Heavy Bombardment. This is based on the observed age of the craters of the moon and other rocky planets. However, it's possible that earlier craters were obscured by more recent ones.

Fabulous Fact

After the moon was formed, both it and Earth continued to be hit by vast quantities of space debris. Both bodies would have been cratered and pitted. The moon still shows these marks while the earth, because of erosion and plate tectonics, does not.

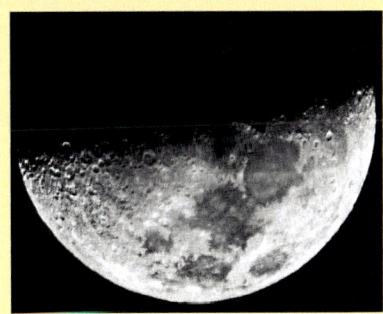

By about halfway through the history of the moon and the earth, around 2.4 BYA, the majority of space debris in the solar system would have either already collided with something or be in a regular orbit around the sun, and so the rate of collisions dropped.

Earth & Space

Additional Layer

The Great Oxygenation Event, where the atmosphere became saturated with oxygen, was necessary for the forms of life we see on this planet today. However, the microbes that lived on Earth prior to the GOE would have been largely wiped out when oxygen became a factor. It would have been toxic to them.

The GOE is thought to be the first major extinction event on the planet.

Besides being responsible for multicellular life, an oxygen-rich atmosphere also makes possible more than 2,500 different minerals. These minerals contain oxygen, obtained from the air and water.

This is an astonishing theory because it suggests that life shaped the planet at least as much as the planet shaped life.

Below is a type of rock called banded iron. It is a sedimentary rock, laid down in layers. Oxygen-rich layers alternate with oxygen-poor layers. Rocks like this are part of the evidence for an emerging oxygen-rich atmosphere and ocean.

Read up more on the Great Oxygenation Event and the emerging ideas surrounding it.

enough for your foam balls to fit inside.

2. Paint the first ball to look like the early earth with lots of red molten surfaces, many craters, and dark rock.

3. Paint the first paper plate disc to look like the earliest atmosphere. The sky should be orange-yellow because of all the methane, with a larger than normal moon. The moon is moving away from the earth, so, in earliest Earth, it would have looked about twice as big.

4. Paint the second foam ball to look like the earth during Earth's second atmosphere. There are vast shallow seas of a greenish tinge and many volcanoes on large rocky continents that are spewing clouds of water vapor and gases into the atmosphere. There are still many craters on the surface. Photosynthetic microorganisms are producing oxygen, but it's all getting snapped up by iron and other elements that combine with oxygen.

5. Paint the second paper plate disc like the second atmosphere of Earth, with skies that are still orange-yellow, but now, there are clouds raining down water and lighting storms. Tons of meteors, comets, and asteroids are slamming into the earth, so you might show some streaking through the sky. The moon is still large.

6. Paint the third foam ball to look like the earth at the beginning of earth's third atmosphere. The oceans have turned blue, reflecting the sky, and the continents and islands are covered with green plants, obscuring the craters. There are still some volcanoes.

7. Paint the third paper plate disc to look like the earth's third atmosphere. The sky is now blue because the amount of methane in the atmosphere has greatly reduced. There are fluffy, white clouds everywhere and

Planet Earth

the moon has receded somewhat. The iron and other oxygen-loving elements have been largely used up, so oxygen from photosynthesis in the ocean and on land is starting to build up. This is known as the Great Oxygenation Event and will soon make it possible for animals to live.

8. Insert each of your foam Earth balls into the paper plate disc it belongs with. You can hang these from your ceiling if you'd like.

🙂 🙂 🙂 **EXPERIMENT: Forming Clouds From Volcanoes**
For this activity, you will need:

- Water
- Pan to heat water
- Stove
- Glass jar with a lid
- Ice
- Colored paper, paints, markers, scissors, glue, and poster board

Water was part of the dust and rocks that formed the giant solar cloud scientists theorize coalesced to make Earth and the other planets. Even more water would have had to come to Earth in the early days when comets and meteors were bombarding the new planet. Once Earth cooled enough for liquid water to exist on the surface, clouds would have formed and rained and rained. Volcanoes spewed out more water from the rocks under the surface, and then, more clouds formed and more rain fell. There was so much water that vast oceans formed. The water you drink and wash with has been on Earth since the beginning.

1. Use paper, paint, or markers to decorate the sides of

Fabulous Fact

There are competing hypotheses about where the water on Earth came from.

One side says the water came from comets bombarding the earth.

The other side says the water came from the earth itself, rising out the rocks and spewing out of the volcanoes.

Either way, the first water on the hot, molten earth would all have been water vapor. As the earth cooled to below 100° C, it began to rain and rain and rain for centuries.

Fabulous Fact

When the two planets that preceded Earth collided, Earth became large enough to have a magnetic field that could protect our atmosphere from the sun. The axis of the earth also became tilted to give us seasons. Finally, an extremely large moon began causing the tides and, therefore, the possibility of sea life on the earth.

All three of these parameters of Earth are essential to life. Without that collision at the precise speed and angle, we would not be here.

Earth & Space

Fabulous Fact

All of the oxygen in the atmosphere of the Earth was formed by living things in the oceans.

This is a NASA photo of the Bay of Biscay off the coast of France. The swirling clouds of white in the water are blooms of oxygen producing phytoplankton.

Today 70% of all the oxygen in the atmosphere is still produced by living things in the ocean.

Deep Thoughts

If the Earth were just a little bit bigger, gravity would be too great for a proper atmosphere. If it were just a tiny bit smaller, Earth wouldn't have enough of a magnetic field to keep the harmful radiation of the sun from stripping away our atmosphere.

The size, position, and composition of Earth and its moon have to be exactly the way they are for life to exist here. Earth is sometimes called the Goldilocks planet. It has to be just right.

Brainstorm some things that are just right, allowing life to thrive on Earth.

your jar to make it look like a volcano. Create some background decorations of more volcanoes, oceans, rain clouds, and rocks on a poster. Set it behind your jar to show the whole scene in early Earth.

2. Heat water until it is steaming. Pour hot water into a jar until the jar is 1/3 full. Then, place a lid on the jar. Observe the steam rising from the water into the air inside the jar. Water from inside the earth is released by volcanoes into the air this way.

3. Put some ice cubes on top of the jar's lid and observe and discuss what happens.

🙂 🙂 🙂 EXPLORATION: Formation of the Moon

For this activity, you will need:

- 18" round balloons (be careful not to get oval)
- Plaster of Paris bandage strips or paper maché (1 cup water and 1 cup flour)
- Rubber gloves
- Scissors
- Glue
- Paints in gray, red, yellow, and white, plus brushes

The giant-impact hypothesis proposes that Earth hit another large body, something around the size of Mars, right near the beginning of its life. When the two bodies collided, the energy would have melted any rocks that had hardened. Then, debris would have splashed up and coalesced into the moon. Exactly how this might have happened is not yet understood. We do know that the direction of Earth's spin matches the moon's orbit. We can also tell that the rocks on the moon's surface were once molten. The rocks on Earth and the moon have similarities not found elsewhere in the solar system. Plus, there is evidence of other collisions in the solar system producing debris discs. This is a picture of the process that might have happened:

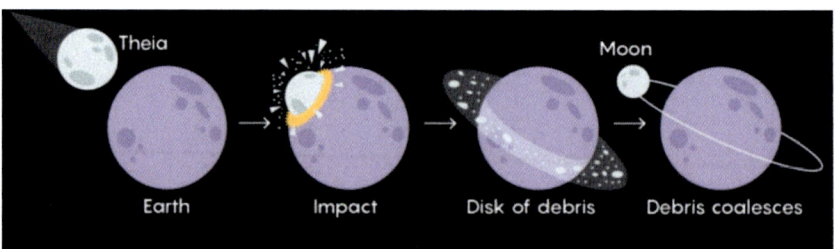

Image by Citronade, CC by SA 4.0 Wikimedia

We're going to make a model showing the moment of impact.

1. Blow up two round balloons so that one is a little smaller than the other. These represent the two bodies that collided with each other.

50

Planet Earth

2. Cut the plaster of Paris strips into 15 cm lengths. Wearing gloves, wet the strips one at a time and apply them to the surfaces of the balloons until they are both covered.

3. Let the balloons dry. Cut one side off of the smaller balloon, then snip up the sides a bit so you can fold the edge flat and glue the smaller ball to the larger ball.

4. Once the glue has dried, cover both balls with another layer of plaster of Paris strips.

5. Once this has dried, paint your planet collision in gray for any solid rock and red, yellow, and white for molten rocks. The area around the collision site will be white hot.

6. Cut tissue paper into squares, crumple it up, and glue it to the collision area. White is the hottest and should be in the middle with red, yellow, and orange "splashing" up around it.

😊 😐 😊 **EXPEDITION: Visit a Rock Formation Near You**

For this activity, you will need:

- Internet
- Camera
- Glue stick
- Science Notebook

Take a trip to see interesting rock formations near you.

1. Search online for "rock formations near me" or "geologic map of ____," filling in the state, province, or country where you live. Have

Writer's Workshop

Would you ever take a trip to the moon in a rocket if you had the chance? Write about your answer and include at least three reasons why.

Additional Layer

Learn a bit more about the moon. Find out how many people have traveled to the moon, how much it cost NASA to send people there, and who owns the moon today.

Fabulous Fact

On the east coast of Greenland, the water is significantly warmer than the water on the west coast of Iceland.

When the two waters mix, the cold water dives deep beneath the warm water, dropping 3,505 meters. This underwater waterfall is called the Denmark Strait Cataract.

Earth & Space

Fabulous Fact

There are currents deep under the ocean as well as on the surface. These deep currents are driven by changes in density. Parts of the ocean are more salty and colder than other parts and this means the water is more dense in some places than in others. These differences mean the water flows in streams, like giant rivers. These streams circle the whole globe, mixing the oceans.

These global streams in the oceans are called thermohaline circulation or the "ocean conveyor belt."

Memorization Station

Saltwater: contains high concentrations of dissolved salts and minerals

Freshwater: water that is not salty, like the water within lakes, streams, and rivers

Brackish water: water that has more salt than freshwater, but less than saltwater, usually occurs where fresh ground water mixes with water from the ocean

---

each person in the family find one to three facts about the rock formation and share them with each other before you go to see it. Pay special attention to how old the rock formation is and place it on the timeline from the Geologic Time Scale Exploration.

2. Take lots of photos when you are there. If you are allowed, take a few samples of the rock as well.

3. When you get back home, print your favorite photo and glue it into your Science Notebook. Write down your observations along with the date and a title. Don't forget to put the title in your table of contents.

Oceans

😊 😊 😊 EXPLORATION: Ocean Zones

For this activity, you will need:

- "Ocean Zones" from the Printable Pack
- Card stock
- Markers and/or crayons
- Hole punch
- Yarn or string
- Internet or books about ocean zones

Different depths of the ocean receive different amounts of light and support different types of life. The ocean zones are named according to how much light they get. The top layer is the sunlight zone, then the twilight zone, the midnight zone, the abyss, and finally, the trenches.

1. Print "Ocean Zones" onto card stock. Cut the pieces apart.

2. Research each zone. Draw pictures of the types of things that live in each zone and write facts about what each zone is like. Use the front and the back of each of your card stock rectangles.

3. Punch five holes across the bottom of the "Ocean Zones" rectangle. Then punch a hole in the top center of each remaining card stock rectangle.

52

Planet Earth

4. Tie a string through each hole of the zone cards. The shortest string should be on the "Sunlight Zone" and the longest on "The Trenches" so that the rectangles are at increasing depths.

5. Tie each zone to a hole at the bottom of the "Ocean Zones" rectangle to make a mobile.

😊 😊 😊 **EXPLORATION: Salty, Brackish, and Fresh Water** 💧

For this activity, you will need:

- Three containers for holding water
- Graduated cylinder
- Table salt
- Stirring spoon
- Balance for measuring weight
- Distilled water

The oceans are made of **saltwater** because all of the salt dissolved in the water on earth collects there. Most water on land is **freshwater**; it has a very low salt content. **Brackish water** can be found where salt and fresh water mix, like an estuary where a river pours into the sea.

1. Measure out 250 milliliters of water into each of the three containers.

2. Measure 8.75 grams of salt with a balance and stir it into the first container. Label this container "saltwater."

3. Measure 5 grams of salt with a balance and stir it into the second container. Label this container "brackish water."

4. Measure .05 grams of salt with a balance and stir it into the final container of water. Label it "freshwater."

Famous Folks

Walter Munk was a prolific American oceanographer, or ocean scientist, who pioneered the study of surface waves, tides, sound waves under water, sea level rise, global ocean temperatures, and climate change.

He also was the one to coin the term "ocean gyres" and predict their locations.

During Wold War II, he predicted the surf conditions for the Allied landing in North Africa as well as during D-Day in France. During the war, he was responsible for determining the currents, tides, and diffusion potential for the nuclear bomb testing at Bikini Atoll.

Learn more about the profound changes in ocean understanding that Munk introduced.

Deep Thoughts

Some people believe that faith and science are incompatible.

Do believe this is true? Can you believe in God and also believe in the radiometric dating of rocks?

Do you struggle with conflicts in your belief system? How do you resolve these conflicts?

Earth & Space

Additional Layer

There is an ongoing international research project, begun in 2000, that deployed thousands of floats that bob about 1,000 feet beneath the surface of the oceans. They measure speed, density, salinity, temperature, pressure, and other aspects of the ocean.

The floats are called the Argo Project, and the four satellites that monitor the floats are called Jason.

Go read up on the Argo Project and the kinds of information that scientists are gathering.

Additional Layer

The Argo Project, like many scientific objects, tools, and endeavors is named after ancient mythology.

Jason is a hero from ancient Greek myths. He led a team of adventurers called the Argonauts who sailed on a ship called the Argo. The Argonauts went on a sea voyage quest to find a magical golden fleece.

You can learn more about the ancient Greeks and their mythology in the *Ancient History: Ancient Greece* unit.

5. Take a tiny taste of the plain distilled water. It should taste very flat and unappealing. Then, dip a finger into each of the three containers of water and taste each of them.

6. Discuss the difference between saltwater, brackish water, and freshwater and where each can be found in nature. Point out that even freshwater has some salt dissolved in it.

7. Head a new page in your Science Notebook "Saltwater, Brackish Water, and Freshwater" and add it to your table of contents. Draw a labeled diagram of your experiment. Write down your observations.

😊 😊 😊 EXPERIMENT: Salinity

WARNING: This experiment includes hot water. Use caution.

For this activity, you will need:

- Table salt
- 2 liters of water set out so it becomes room temperature
- Plastic shoe box-size container
- Graduated cylinder
- Freezer
- Several containers for water
- Saucepan and stove
- Balance
- Food coloring - red and blue

Salinity is the saltiness of water. All natural water on Earth has at least some salts dissolved in it. Much of the salt dissolved in water is sodium chloride, table salt, but water also contains many other salts, like magnesium sulfate, potassium nitrate, and sodium bicarbonate.

Saltwater in the oceans varies in salinity from place to place on the globe, but it averages about 35 grams of salt per kilogram of water. The salts in the oceans move and mix as the currents carry water around the globe. The currents are driven mostly by differing temperatures of ocean waters, but also depend on salinity. Water in less salty places moves towards more salty areas, contributing to currents.

1. Weigh out 35 grams of table salt using a balance. Add the salt to 1 liter of room temperature water. This is approximately how salty water within the ocean is. Dip your finger in and taste it.

2. Measure out 50 ml of saltwater and put it in a freezer to cool it for 15 minutes. At the same time, measure out 50 ml of saltwater and warm it in a saucepan on the stove until it begins to steam.

3. Add another 1 liter of water to the plastic box. This

Planet Earth

makes it deep enough for the next part.

4. While you are waiting, head a new page in your Science Notebook "Salinity" and add it to your table of contents. Draw a labeled diagram of what you have done so far.

   Make a hypothesis about which waters, the hot or the cold, will rise or sink when poured into room temperature water. Write your hypothesis in your Science Notebook.

5. Add 2-3 drops of blue food coloring to the cold saltwater. Add 2-3 drops red food coloring to the hot saltwater. Stir each solution.

6. Gently pour the cold saltwater into one end of the box full of room temperature water. Then gently pour hot seawater into the other end of the box.

7. Draw a diagram of what happened in your Science Notebook. Write your observations and conclusions.

Additional Layer

For a simple way to think about surface-level currents, fill a baking dish with water and place two rocks in it that stick out of the surface. Put a different color of food coloring in each of the four corners.

First, place an ice cube right in the center and watch what happens. This is simulating the various temperatures and how they interact in the sea.

Next, use a straw to blow air across the surface of the water in a variety of directions. As you blow into the straw, you are simulating the wind. Watch what happens to the food coloring.

Discuss how what happened in your baking dish relates to what happens in the oceans every day.

😊 😊 😊 EXPERIMENT: Currents

For this activity, you will need:

- Two identical small clear jars
- Salt
- Water
- Blue and red food coloring
- Stiff piece of paper, like an index card

A **current** is a steady flow of a fluid. Ocean currents are the flow of water around the globe. There are currents deep in the oceans and currents on the surface. Deep currents are caused by differences in salinity and temperature of ocean waters. Surface currents are caused by prevailing winds.

Memorization Station

Salinity: the amount of salt in water

Current: a steady flow of fluid

Fabulous Fact

The Agulhas Current, which flows south along Africa's western coast, takes warm saltwater from the Indian Ocean and dumps it in the south Atlantic, a sea which is cold and less salty. This is one example of how the ocean currents are driven by temperature and salinity.

Learn more about African geography in the *People & Planet: Africa* unit.

Earth & Space

Fabulous Fact

Water is the most important factor that makes Earth a changing, living planet.

Water does these jobs:

- Absorbs, stores, and releases heat energy
- Transmits sunlight
- Expands and becomes less dense when it freezes
- Exists in liquid form at the same temperatures that are best for life
- Dissolves many things, allowing water to transport minerals and nutrients
- Flows and erodes rock
- Lowers the melting point of rocks
- Makes molten rock less viscous, meaning the planet changes more quickly, renewing itself because of water
- Evaporates at low enough temperatures to form clouds and be transported around the globe

Bookworms

Ocean Speaks by Jess Keating is a picture book biography of Maria Tharp, the woman who mapped the ocean floors. For ages 5 to 8.

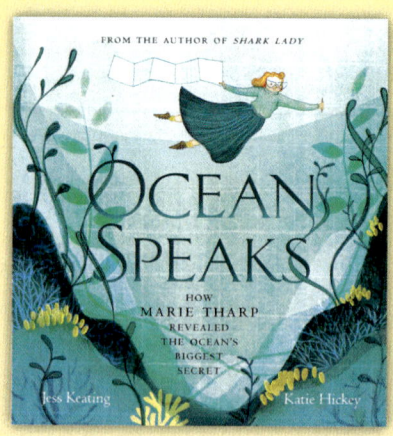

The tides and the shapes of the shorelines around the world also affect currents.

1. Fill a small jar with water. Add two or three drops of blue food coloring. Stir in salt until no more will dissolve.

2. Fill a second small jar with water. Add two to three drops of red food coloring.

3. Place an index card over the opening of the salty jar. Invert it and line it up with the freshwater jar. Remove the card so the water from the two jars can mingle. Observe.

4. Head a new page in your Science Notebook "Currents" and add it to your table of contents. Draw a labeled diagram of your experiment and write down your observations.

5. Repeat this experiment with hot and cold water instead of salty and fresh.

😊 😊 😊 **EXPLORATION: Map of Surface Ocean Currents**

For this activity, you will need:

- "Ocean Currents" from the Printable Pack
- Colored pencils
- World map

Planet Earth

Oceans and ocean currents drastically change the weather and climate of the whole planet. Cities that are far inland, like Chicago or Moscow, experience very cold winters and very hot summers. There is no ocean nearby to mitigate the effect of the sun. Cities at high latitudes, like London or Juneau, have much milder weather because of warm ocean currents.

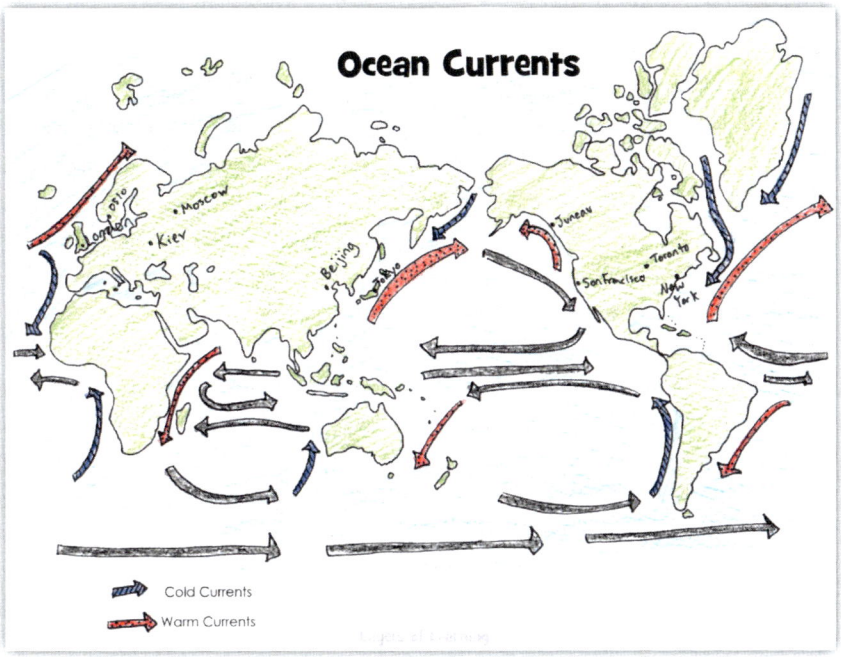

1. Color the "Ocean Currents" map from the Printable Pack. Start by coloring the oceans light blue and the land green.

2. Then, color the ocean currents, warm ocean currents in red and cold in blue. The remaining ocean currents aren't especially cold or warm and can be colored in black.

3. Use a world map to compare coastal cities affected by a warm current with cities at a similar latitude that are inland. Also, compare cities near cold currents with those near warm currents. Mark these cities on your map: London, Oslo, Moscow, Kiev, Juneau, San Francisco, Toronto, New York. What difference does the ocean make to the climate?

😊 😊 EXPLORATION: Ocean Floor Challenge
For this activity, you will need:

- All-purpose flour
- Water
- Salt
- Cooking oil
- Bowl
- Spoon for stirring
- Medium box with lid
- Small straw or wooden

Expedition
Go visit a body of water near you. It could be a lake, river, pond, stream, sea, or ocean. Bring a blanket to spread out and some books to read about this unit. Read and talk about the concepts of this unit while you are there so your family can connect the lessons with the real world.

Famous Folks
Maria Tharp was the first person to map the ocean floor during World War II.

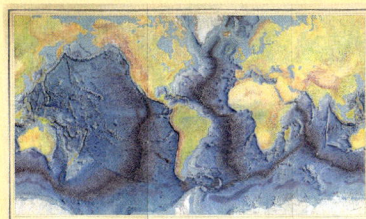

This is an artist's rendering of the ocean floor features that Tharp found.

Before Tharp, people had a general idea that the ocean floor was a flat, muddy plain. Her work revealed mountain chains, deep chasms, cliffs, hills, and, most importantly, a single, long, deep rift valley running the length of the Atlantic Ocean.

We shall see why this discovery was so important in the next unit on *Plate Tectonics*.

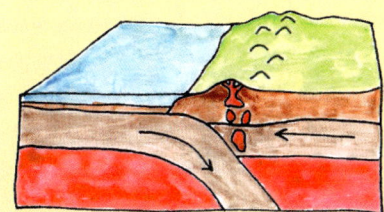

Earth & Space

Fabulous Fact
Less than 5% of the oceans have been explored. Even the ocean floor and all its nuances are only known in a very general way. In fact, we have better maps of Mars than we do of our ocean floors.

Additional Layer
The oceans, like the rest of Earth, are in a state of constant change. We know that ocean waters flow and that the flow alters from year to year. We know that salinity is uneven and this alters over time. We know that sea levels rise and fall. What we don't know is how much of these changes are natural and how much may be affected by mankind. What kind of effect do you think humans can have on big systems like the oceans?

Teaching Tip
Get your kids' attention by holding out a glass of water and asking them how old they think the water is. After they've guessed, explain that all of the water on earth is at least as old as the earth itself, we're talking billions of years. It's just been recycled lots and lots of times.

Memorization Station
Specific heat: the energy required to raise 1 gram, 1 degree

Water cycle: the continuous recycling of the earth's water that causes it to circulate within the earth and the atmosphere

- skewers
- Graph paper
- Metric ruler

The ocean floor isn't flat. It has mountain ranges, valleys, cliffs, rolling hills, canyons, and volcanoes, just like the continents do.

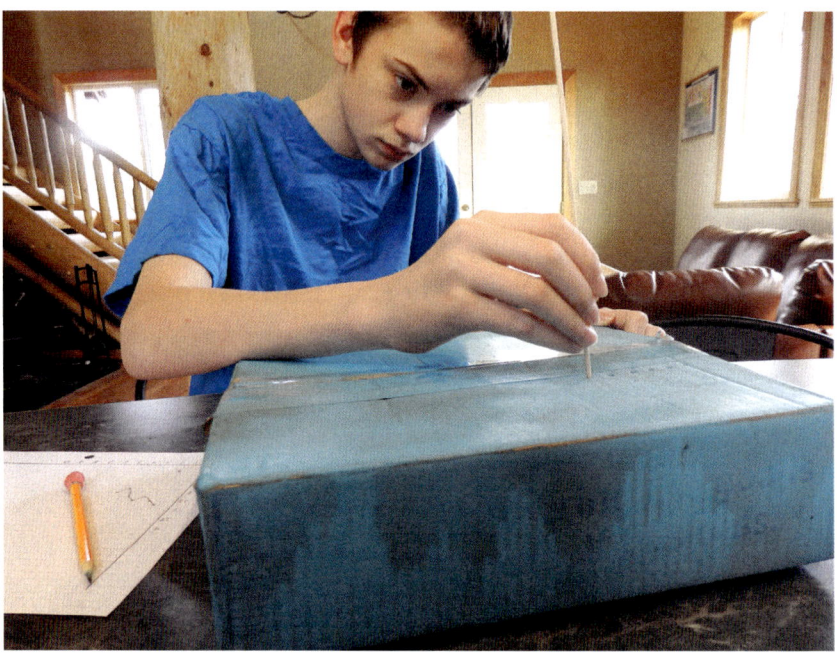

1. Mix up some salt dough by stirring together 1/2 cup of warm tap water, 1/4 cup salt, 4 tablespoons cooking oil, and 2 cups all-purpose flour. You will need one batch for each child.

2. In the bottom of your box, design a section of ocean floor with valleys, mountains and other variations using your salt dough. Put the lid on the box.

3. Swap boxes with another person. Challenge each child to discover a profile shape of the ocean floor inside the box without taking the lid off. Give them skewers or coffee straws, a ruler, and some graph paper to draw the profile on.

   HINT: Poke a series of small holes in the box lid in a straight line right down the center. Poke a skewer down in the first hole, marking when it hits the "bottom." Draw the profile of the ocean floor on graph paper. When you are finished, take the lid off and see how close you got to the "real" ocean floor inside the box.

☺ ☺ **EXPERIMENT: Oceans Regulate the Temperature**

WARNING: This experiment includes boiling water. Be careful!

Planet Earth

For this activity, you will need:

- "Experiment" sheet from the Printable Pack or "Experiment Report Template" for 12 and up.
- Water at room temperature
- Beaker or graduated cylinder for measuring
- Pot
- Scientific thermometer
- Stove or hot plate or Bunsen burner
- Watch or timer
- Graph paper

Specific heat is the amount of energy required to raise 1 gram of something 1 degree Celsius. Water has a high specific heat, so it takes a lot of energy to raise the temperature of water. This also means that once water has absorbed heat, it holds on to it longer and releases it gradually. This aspect of water, combined with the vast sizes of our oceans, helps to regulate the temperature of the entire planet.

As water evaporates into the air, this warm, moist air is transported around the globe and toward the poles. At the same time, the cold polar water circulates toward the equator, regulating and evening out the climate of the planet as a whole. Without the oceans, temperatures in different parts of the world would be much more extreme, both hotter and colder.

1. Use the "Experiment" report forms to record your experiment. Before you begin, write a hypothesis about how long you think it will take to heat water to boiling compared with how long it will take to cool water back to room temperature.
2. Measure 250 ml of water into a pot.
3. Measure and record the temperature of your water.
4. Put the pot on the stove over high heat. Measure the temperature every thirty seconds, keeping a record of the measurements as you go.
5. Once the water is boiling, note the time and remove it from the heat.
6. Continue to make and record temperature measurements every 30 seconds until the temperature returns to the previous level.
7. Pick a variable of the experiment to change: starting temperature of the water, level of heat on the stove, amount of water in the pot, and so on. Run the experiment again, keeping careful measurements. You

Deep Thoughts

Scientists who study Earth are sometimes paid by a company, organization, or government agency with an interest in finding a certain type of answer.

For example, a study analyzing the Environmental Protection Agency's greenhouse gas regulations was conducted by scientists who were paid by the EPA. In another case, a scientist testing contamination of groundwater where fracking was being done was paid by an energy company.

Can scientists be trusted in these cases? How do you think conflicts of interest should be handled?

Bookworms

Water Cycles by DK is about everything water.

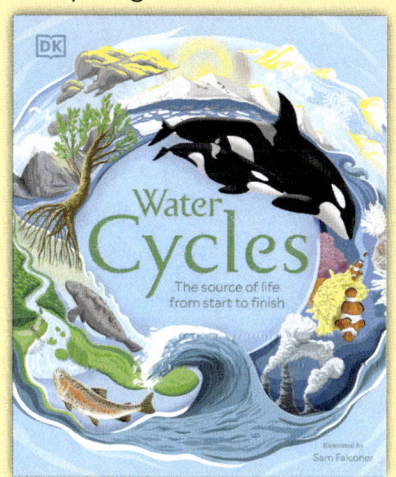

It includes how water moves from the sea to the air to the rivers and back to the sea. You will also find the formation of early oceans, how life depends on water, the physical properties of water, and how humans use water. For all ages.

Earth & Space

Famous Folks

Sir John Murray is the father of oceanography. He began his studies of the ocean while serving as the ship's surgeon on a whaler called the Jan Mayen.

Later, he served as a naturalist on the famous 1872 Challenger Expedition, a four-year voyage of discovery sponsored by the Royal Society of London.

On that expedition he laid tho foundations for oceanography. He and other scientists discovered 4,000 species, mapped ocean currents, took samples of the ocean floor, determined the surface density of the seas, and sounded the depths.

The voyage gave its name to the deepest part of the ocean, Challenger Deep, a discovery made on the voyage.

Find out more about John Murray and the Challenger Expedition.

can run it a third time with new variables if you'd like.

8. Plot the data from each experiment on a graph. What do you notice about how water absorbs and releases heat? How do you think this affects the globe with the oceans absorbing and releasing heat?

😊 😊 😊 EXPLORATION: Water Cycle

For this activity, you will need:

- Large clear glass bowl or jar
- Smaller dish
- Plastic wrap
- Large rubber band
- Small rock
- Poster board - white
- Markers or crayons
- "The Water Cycle" from the Printable Pack
- Glue stick
- Science Notebook
- Colored pencils or crayons

The water you drank today has been on earth since the formation of the planet. Water gets a regular cleaning and recycling through something called the **water cycle**. Water collects in the oceans, then it evaporates into the air where it becomes water vapor and forms clouds. Finally, it rains down on the planet. Rain washes the sky and cleans the surfaces of earth. Then, the rainwater filters down through the soil and the rocks, which cleans out the dirt and bacteria. Water reemerges and collects in streams, rivers, and lakes. And the cycle starts all over again.

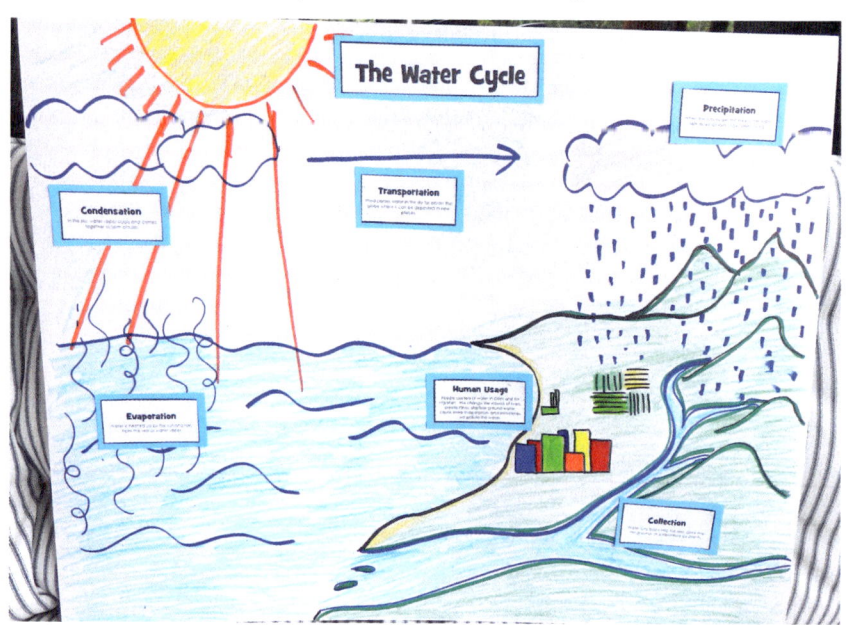

1. Pour about 5 cm of water into the bottom of your large glass bowl or jar. Set a smaller dish inside the center of the large jar.

2. Cover the jar with plastic wrap, held in place with a

Planet Earth

rubber band. Put a small rock in the center of the plastic wrap to make a dip where the water can collect and run off.

The moisture in the jar will evaporate and collect on the walls and plastic wrap at the top of the jar. The water will then drip back down into the smaller dish like rain.

3. Experiment with different conditions like cool temperatures, direct sunlight, or dappled sunlight. How do the sun and temperature affect the water cycle?

4. Make a poster with a diagram of the water cycle. Use word strips from "The Water Cycle" printable. Add your own illustrations. Take turns using the poster to describe the water cycle.

5. Draw and label a diagram of the water cycle in your Science Notebook. Give it a title and put it in your table of contents.

Step 3: Show What You Know

During this unit, choose one of the assignments below to show what you have learned during the unit. Add this work to your Layers of Learning Notebook. You can also use this assignment to show your supervising teacher or your charter school as a sample of what you've been working on in your homeschool, if needed.

There are more ideas for writing assignments in the "Writer's Workshop" sidebars.

🙂 🙂 Coloring or Narration Page 💧

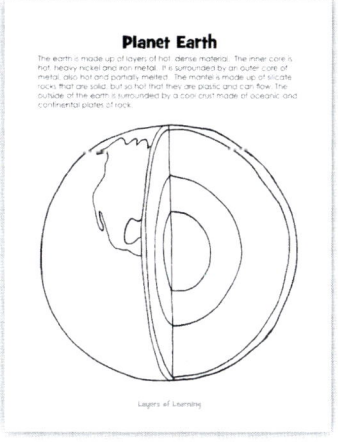

For this activity, you will need:

- "Planet Earth" from the Printable Pack
- Writing or drawing utensils

1. Depending on the age and ability of the child, choose either the "Planet Earth" coloring sheet or the "Planet Earth" narration page from the Printable Pack.

2. Younger kids can color the coloring sheet as you review some of the things you learned about during this unit. On the bottom of the coloring page, kids can write a sentence about what they learned. Very young children can explain their ideas orally while a parent writes for them.

Writer's Workshop

Write a shape poem about water and how important it is to you and to life!

Draw a droplet of water and then have the words of your poem travel around the shape of the droplet. You can turn the page as you write to make it easier.

Decorate and color your page after you've written your poem.

Additional Layer

Play sink or float. Fill two bowls with water and then add salt to one until no more salt will dissolve in it. Now, gather some items from your home.

- A pencil eraser
- A die
- A marshmallow
- A crayon
- A piece of candy, like Starburst
- A grape

One by one, place each item into each of the bowls and determine whether or not the item sinks or floats. You may want to record your predictions and observations in your Science Notebook. Once you're finished, write about what you observed and why you think you got the results you did. What causes items to sink or float?

Hint: Relative density is what causes things to sink or float. The saltwater is more dense than the freshwater, so some things will float in it even though they won't float in freshwater.

Earth & Space

Unit Trivia Questions

1. Name the four main layers of the earth.

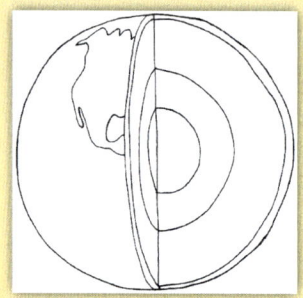

   Inner core, outer core, mantle, crust

2. Which is thinner and denser, continental crust or oceanic crust?

   Oceanic crust

3. The magnetic field is caused by
   a) Rays from the sun
   b) The spinning of the earth
   c) Convection cells in the mantle

4. True or false - Earth is about 4.5 million years old.

   False. Earth is 4.5 billion years old

5. Name the top zone of the ocean.

   Sunlight zone

6. What causes ocean currents?

   Differences in temperature and salinity.

7. True or false - Scientists have determined that the Great Oxygenation Event definitely happened, so it is a scientific theory.

   False. The Great Oxygenation event is a hypothesis; there isn't enough proof yet to call it a theory.

---

3. Older kids can write about some of the concepts you learned on the narration page and color the picture as well.
4. Add this to the Science section of your Layers of Learning Notebook.

😊 😊 😊 Science Experiment Write-Up

For this activity, you will need:

- The "Experiment" write-up or "Experiment Report Template" from the Printable Pack

1. Choose one of the experiments you completed during this unit and create a careful and complete experiment write-up for it. Make sure you have included every specific detail of each step so your experiment could be repeated by anyone who wanted to try it.
2. Do a careful revision and edit of your write-up, taking it through the writing process, before you turn it in for grading.

😊 😊 😊 Layers of the Earth & Oceans Sorting Quiz

For this activity, you will need:

- "Layers of the Earth & Oceans Sorting Quiz" printables from the Printable Pack, including the answer key

1. Have your kids sort the words from the word bank on the printable quiz. They will have to identify which words are describing layers of the earth and which are describing layers of the oceans. Then, they will write them in descending order to see if they can recall the order of each of the layers.

😊 😊 😊 Writer's Workshop

For this activity, you will need:

- A computer or a piece of paper and a writing utensil

Choose from one of the ideas below or write about something else you learned during this unit. Each of these prompts corresponds with one of the units from the Layers of Learning Writer's Workshop curriculum, so you may choose to coordinate the assignment with the monthly unit you are learning about in Writer's Workshop.

- **Sentences, Paragraphs, & Narrations:** Look up an underwater photograph of an ocean and write a detailed, complete sentence about it.
- **Descriptions & Instructions:** Create similes about

Planet Earth

each of the layers of the earth, describing each one figuratively. (The crust is like...)
- **Fanciful Stories**: Write a short story about an ocean animal who goes on an adventure through the ocean zones.
- **Poetry:** Compose a quatrain (4-line poem) about ocean currents that rhymes. Draw an ocean scene in the background.
- **True Stories:** Write about an experience you've had at the ocean.
- **Reports and Essays:** Compare and contrast freshwater versus saltwater or the crust versus the mantle.
- **Letters:** Create a post card that shows the water cycle and give it to someone along with a water bottle as a gift.
- **Persuasive Writing:** Would you rather explore the land or explore the ocean? Write about it and why.

😊 😊 😊 Big Book of Knowledge

For this activity, you will need:

- "Big Book of Knowledge: Planet Earth" printable from the Printable Pack, printed on card stock
- Writing or drawing utensils
- Big Book of Knowledge

1. Color, draw on, or write on the Big Book of Knowledge page. Record concepts, definitions, and facts you learned during this unit. It's a record of the things you learned and hope to remember. Add the page to your Big Book of Knowledge.

2. Use your Big Book of Knowledge regularly to help you review, quiz, or create games that will help you commit the things you've learned to memory.

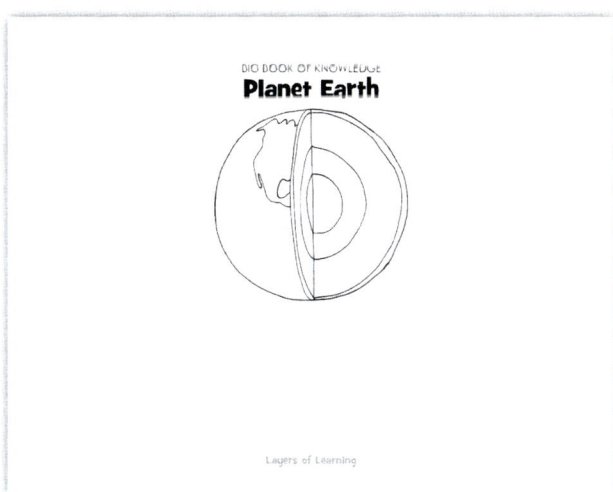

Big Book of Knowledge

The Big Book of Knowledge is a book for you, the mentor, to use as a constant review of all of the things you're learning about. You can use it to quiz your kids or prepare tests or review games. Whenever you learn something in Layers of Learning that you want your kids to remember, add it to your Big Book of Knowledge.

Assemble your Big Book of Knowledge in a binder or with binder rings. Divide it into sections for each subject.

In the Printable Pack for this unit you will find a "Big Book of Knowledge" sheet. You can add this sheet to others you collect or create yourself as you progress through the Layers of Learning curriculum. Customize the Big Book of Knowledge to your family by adding facts and topics that you enjoyed exploring as you were learning.

Visit Layers of Learning online to find more information on how to assemble and use your own Big Book of Knowledge.

You will also find cover and section pages to print along with creative games to play with your Big Book of Knowledge to keep school, even the tests, fun!

Earth & Space

Unit Overview

Key Concepts:
- The crust is broken into large plates and these plates move.
- Volcanoes, earthquakes, and mountain building are caused by the movement of the plates.

Vocabulary:
- Plate
- Convergent boundary
- Divergent boundary
- Transform boundary
- Pangaea
- Supercontinent
- Unifying theory
- Volcano
- Magma
- Lava
- Explosive eruption
- Effusive eruption
- Pyroclastic flow
- Earthquake
- Focus
- Epicenter
- Seismometer
- Seismic waves
- P waves
- S waves
- Volcanic mountains
- Fold mountains
- Block mountains
- Folding
- Faulting
- Volcanic activity
- Igneous intrusion
- Metamorphism

Important Scientists:
- Alfred Wegener

Theories, Laws, & Hypotheses:
- Plate tectonic theory
- Fold mountain theory
- Hot spot hypothesis
- Elastic rebound theory

PLATE TECTONICS

In the 1960s, geologists established tectonic theory. It describes that the earth's surface is broken into large plates and that these plates are moving, or drifting, over the surface. They grind against one another, push each other out of the way, slide past each other, and, over time, change the face of the earth. In fact, the continents are drifting so much that at one time there was a super continent called Pangaea. Even before that, they surmise that there were many other continents and super continents that had formed, broken up, and reformed.

Today, we can observe that the Atlantic Ocean gets a little bit bigger each year while the Pacific Ocean gets just a tad smaller. We can also see how the coastlines of Africa and South America look like they could fit together.

Tectonic activity makes volcanoes erupt, earthquakes shake, and mountains form. Most of the tectonic activity is so slow that the face of the earth changes imperceptibly over the lifespan of a human. Once in awhile though, we can watch as a volcano forms a mountain in a matter of weeks or an earthquake rips a rift in the earth inside a minute.

Step 1: Library List

Choose books from your library that go with this topic. Here's a list of some favorites and also a list of search terms so you can utilize what your library offers. Read the books with your kids and/or assign them some to read independently. It is from these books your kids will learn most of the facts they need from this unit.

Plate Tectonics

Search for: plate tectonics, volcanoes, earthquakes, mountains, Pangaea, Alfred Wegener

🙂 🙂 🙂 *Encyclopedia of Science* from DK. Read "Moving Continents," "Volcanoes," "Mountain Building," and "Earthquakes" on pages 214-220.

🙂 🙂 🙂 *The Usborne Science Encyclopedia*. Read "Earth's Structure" on pages 180-183.

🙂 🙂 🙂 *The Kingfisher Science Encyclopedia*. Read "Continental Drift," "Volcanoes," "Earthquakes," and "Building Mountains" on pages 16-23.

🙂 🙂 🙂 *Continental Drift: the Evolution of Our World from the Origins of Life to the Far Future* by Martin Ince. Beautiful illustrations. Explores the way moving continents affect life on Earth. Contains theory of evolution material.

🙂 🙂 🙂 *Volcano: Eruption and Healing of Mt. St. Helens* by Patricia Lauber. Fairly dense text that introduces children to many scientific terms. This is a case study of a real volcano.

🙂 🙂 🙂 *Ring of Fire* by Leonard Hort. Great read-aloud to explore volcanoes, earthquakes, and plates.

🙂 *How Mountains Are Made* by Kathleen Weidner Zoehfeld. Some kids hike up a tall mountain and find a seashell. How did it get there?

🙂 *Eruption! The Story of Volcanoes* by Anita Ganeri. Volcano basics for little ones.

🙂 *Volcanoes* by Dr. Franklyn M. Branley. Just right for young children. Packed with facts and pictures. Look for *Earthquakes* by Dr. Franklyn M. Branley too.

🙂 🙂 *Volcanoes* by Seymour Simon. Thorough information with gorgeous photos from a favorite science author. Also look for *Mountains* by the same author.

🙂 🙂 *Why do Tectonic Plates Crash and Slip?* by Baby Professor. A great early book for kids about tectonic theory.

🙂 🙂 *Plate Tectonics: The Engine Inside the Earth* by Judith Hubbard. College-level concepts in kid-level language. Read it with your kids. It also comes with experiments to try.

🙂 *The Incredible Plate Tectonics Comic* by Kanani K.M. Lee. In graphic form, this is an easy read for middle grades kids.

🙂 🙂 *When the Earth Shakes: Earthquakes, Volcanoes, and Tsunamis* by Simon Winchester. The first time the author felt

Family School Levels

The colored smilies in this unit help you choose the correct levels of books and activities for your child.
🙂 = Ages 6-9
🙂 = Ages 10-13
🙂 = Ages 14-18

On the Web

For videos, web pages, games, and more to add to this unit, visit the Earth & Space Resources at Layers-of-Learning.com.

You will find a link to video playlists, web links, and more.

Bookworms

If you're looking for a family read-aloud, we'd like to suggest this one.

The Big Wave by Pearl S. Buck is about two friends, one lives on the mountainside and one by the sea. When a tsunami wave washes the seaside village away along with Jiya's entire family, the young boy must work through the grief.

Earth & Space

Memorization Station

Plate: a large piece of Earth's crust that reacts and moves as a unit

Teaching Tip

You can learn lots more about volcanoes, earthquakes, and other natural disasters in *Layers of Learning People & Planet: Asia*.

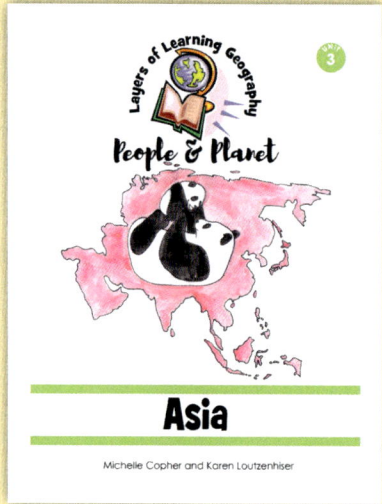

Famous Folks

Maurice Ewing was an American oceanographer who mapped the sea floor, discovering the mid-ocean ridges, during World War II. His work was instrumental to the theory of plate tectonics.

Maurice Ewing performed most of his research from aboard a navy research vessel called the Atlantis. Since the 1940s, there have been a series of vessels with the same name, all performing oceanic research.

an earthquake was during a trip to New Zealand. Starting with that story, the author explains what is happening when the earth shakes.

☺ *The Tectonic Plates Are Moving!* by Roy Livermore. A popular level book about all the advances in plate tectonic theory since the 1960s. Excellent text.

☺ *The Origin of Continents and Oceans* by Alfred Wegener. This is the original book about the theory of plate tectonics by the geologist that invented it. Just read chapter 8.

☺ *Cosmology and Astronomy* from KhanAcademy.org. For a high school lecture experience, you can add a Khan Academy course. During this unit, study "Earth Geological and Climatic History: Plate Tectonics."

Step 2: Explore

Choose a few hands-on explorations from this section to work on as a family. They should be appealing activities that will create mental hooks so your kids remember the information in the unit. Save the rest of the explorations for the next time you do this unit in four years when your kids are older. You can also read the sidebars together and explore some little rabbit trails.

This unit includes printables. See the introduction for instructions on retrieving your Printable Pack.

Moving Plates

The crust of the earth is broken up into big sections called **plates**. The plates are moving with the forces created by the molten mantle under the crust.

☺☺ **EXPLORATION: Tectonic Cookie Continents**

For this activity, you will need:

- Book or video about tectonic plates from the Library List or YouTube playlist for this unit
- Sugar cookie dough
- Baking sheet
- Oven
- Frosting in green, blue, brown
- Science Notebook

The crust of the earth is cold and hard, a brittle crust over a plastic molten planet. Brittle things break. Under the crust is hot molten rock which allows for the slow movement of the crust plates over the surface.

Plate Tectonics

1. Read a book or watch a video about tectonic plates.
2. Mix together a batch of sugar cookie dough.
3. Give each child a portion of the dough to shape into a continent.
4. Bake the cookies for 12 minutes or until they are crisp. Let them cool for ten minutes.
5. While the cookies are cooling, head the next page in your Science Notebook "Tectonic Plates" and add the title to your table of contents. Draw a picture of plates and write a few facts that you learned from the video.

6. Break the continent cookie into smaller pieces. Frost the continent with different colors of frosting. Put a little pressure on the sides of your continent with your fingers. Watch as it moves along the plate edges.
7. Have each child take a turn describing how tectonic plates work on their continent.

😊 😊 😊 **EXPLORATION: Plate Boundaries**

For this activity, you will need:

- Book or video about plate boundaries from the Library List or YouTube playlist
- "Plate Boundaries" printable from the Printable Pack. (Choose between the two versions, one with diagrams to color and one left blank for you to illustrate.)
- Crayons, colored pencils, or pens

There are three main types of boundaries between plates. They are convergent, divergent, and transform.

Famous Folks

The geophysicist who finally put the whole theory of plate tectonics together was Canadian John Tuzo Wilson.

Photo by Stephen Morris, CC license, Wikimedia

He first described and named transform faults like the San Andreas and hot spots like the one under Hawaii.

The whole concept of seabed expansion and contraction (the moving sea floor) is called the Wilson Cycle after him.

Teaching Tip

You can learn more about how we make maps of the earth in *Layers of Learning People & Planet: Maps and Globes.*

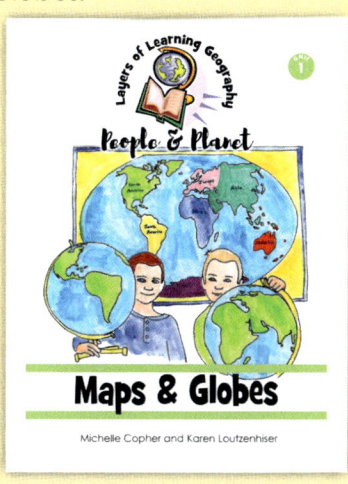

Earth & Space

Famous Folks

Hugo Benioff and Kiyoo Wadati were seismologists who charted deep earthquakes along plate margins in the Pacific Ocean, noticing that the epicenters follow a slanted trajectory, getting deeper as you move further inland. These slanted subduction zones are called Wadati-Benioff zones.

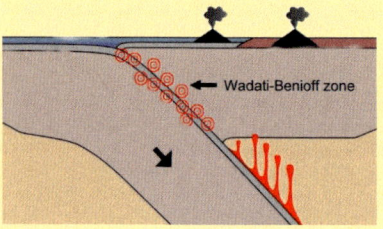

CC by SA 3.0 Wikimedia

Additional Layer

Do you live in an earthquake zone? A volcano zone? A tsunami zone? Prepare a family emergency plan for disasters.

Memorization Station

Convergent boundary: place where plates are moving toward one another and colliding

Divergent boundary: place where plates are moving apart from one another

Transform boundary: place where plates are sliding past one another longitudinally

Pangaea: a supercontinent that formed about 335 million years ago and has since broken apart due to plate tectonics

Supercontinent: when all of Earth's land masses assemble into one big continent

Convergent boundaries are moving toward one another. Asia and India have moved toward each other to create the Himalayas Mountains. If an oceanic plate and a continental plate converge, the denser oceanic plate will slide under the continental plate.

Divergent boundaries are moving away from each other. The mid-Atlantic Ridge in the middle of the Atlantic Ocean is being formed by divergent plates.

Transform boundaries are sliding past one another horizontally. The San Andreas Fault in California is an example of a transform fault.

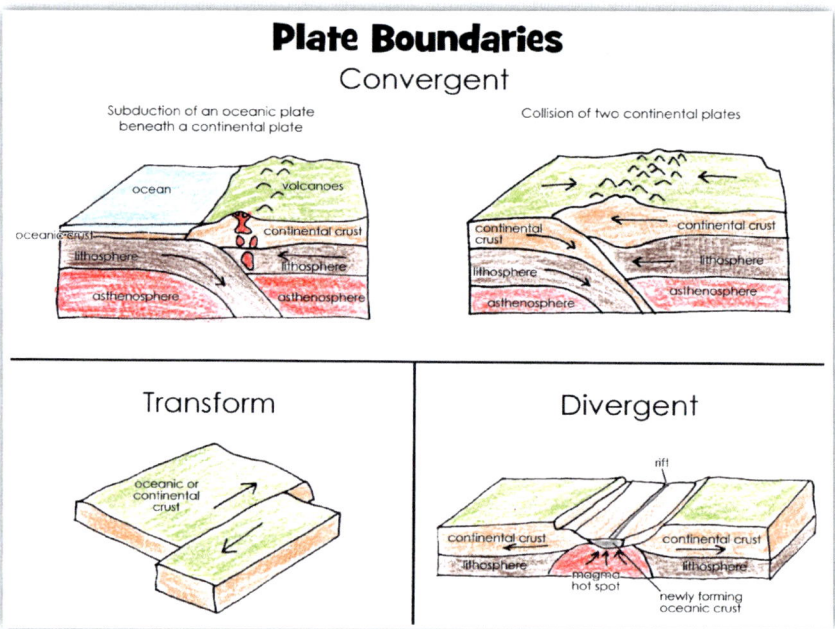

1. Read a book or watch a video about plate boundaries.
2. Color and label the "Plate Boundaries" sheet.
3. As you complete the sheet, look up any words or concepts that you don't understand.
4. Put the Plate Boundaries sheet into the Science section of your Layers of Learning Notebook.

😊😊😊 EXPLORATION: Tectonic Plates Puzzle

For this activity, you will need:

- "Earth's Tectonic Plates" printable from the Printable Pack, printed onto card stock
- Crayons, colored pencils, or markers
- Scissors
- Student atlas for kids ages 12 and up
- Envelope
- Glue stick
- Science Notebook

Plate Tectonics

1. Color the "Earth's Tectonic Plates" map so that each plate is a different color.

2. 😊 😊 Older kids should use a student atlas to research the direction some of the plates are moving and add arrows to the map in the appropriate places.

3. Cut the map apart on the heavy lines. These lines are the boundaries between the plates.

4. Practice putting the map together like a puzzle.

5. Glue an envelope to a page labeled "Tectonic Plates" in your Science Notebook and keep the puzzle pieces inside.

😊 😊 EXPLORATION: Pangaea
For this activity, you will need:

- Three sheets of card stock
- Scissors
- Dinner plate
- White school glue
- Paints and paintbrushes
- String or yarn
- Paper hole punch
- A map of today's Earth

Pangaea became a **supercontinent** about 335 mya and lasted for around 165 million years. A supercontinent happens when all, or nearly all, of the earth's continents merge together into one land mass. Pangaea is the most recent of the supercontinents.

1. Trace a dinner plate onto three sheets of card stock. Cut out each circle.

Additional Layer
The earth has fourteen plates, but a crack in the African plate is making a new plate at the East African Rift.

Learn more about the East African Rift and make a model of it out of clay.

Explain the model and what it shows to other students.

Famous Folks
Ted Irving of Canada was the first scientist to provide hard evidence for the theory of continental drift. He studied paleomagnetism, the history of the earth's magnetic field and the way it had flipped over long eons of time. The successive bands of flipped magnetic sections on the ocean floor gave evidence that the sea floor was spreading.

Additional Layer
Newly formed ocean plates have quite a bit of iron in them. Iron, as you know, responds to magnetic forces. The earth is one big magnet. So when new material spews out of the ocean vents and cools into new rock, the iron in the rock aligns with the magnetic poles of the earth.

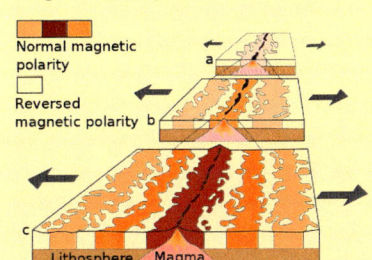

Learn more about paleomagnetism.

Earth & Space

Additional Layer

You can create your own Pangaea flip book using the "Continental Drift" printable from the Printable Pack. Color the pages and then compile the booklet, stapling it at the edge.

As you flip through it, you can watch the progression of the continents moving from one supercontinent to the seven continents we have today.

Famous Folks

Alfred Wegener proposed tectonic theory in 1912, but he was resisted fiercely by the scientific community. It wasn't until the 1960s that scientists finally accepted plate tectonic theory.

Wegener was also an explorer who pioneered polar research. He died while on an expedition in Greenland in 1930.

Wegener is on the left in this picture. His companion is Rasmus Villumsen, an Inuit who helped Wegener in his research.

2. Use a current map of the world as a reference to paint a freehand map on the first circle with green continents and blue oceans.

3. On the second plate, paint a freehand version of the continents sort of squished together, but still recognizable as continents we know today.

4. On the third plate, paint a supercontinent that you envision as Pangaea. Make the continents fit together into one landmass.

5. Once the paint dries, label each plate: "Earth Today," "Separating Continents," and "Pangaea."

6. Fold each plate in half from the North Pole to the South Pole. Then, glue the plates together to make a mobile. Hang it by a string from your ceiling.

😊 🙂 EXPLORATION: Wegener and the Evidence

For this activity, you will need:

- "Alfred Wegener" from the Printable Pack
- "Unifying Theory of Geology" from the Printable Pack
- Scissors
- Glue stick
- Colored pencils or crayons
- Books, videos, or websites about Alfred Wegener.
- Science Notebook

Alfred Wegener was a German scientist who was the first to hypothesize that the continents are slowly drifting along the surface of the earth. He had three evidences for his theory:

- The shorelines of Europe and Africa fit together with the

Plate Tectonics

shorelines of the Americas and rock formations span continents as well.
- Fossil types across widely separated continents like Africa and South America matched.
- Fossils of tropical plants and animals have been found in polar climates.

Wegener's hypothesis was tested and examined by scientists from 1915, when it was proposed, until the 1960s, when it was accepted as a scientific theory. Plate tectonics is the **unifying theory** of geology because it explains the reasons behind all of the geological processes on Earth, from the rock cycle and why earthquakes happen to how mountains are formed and beyond.

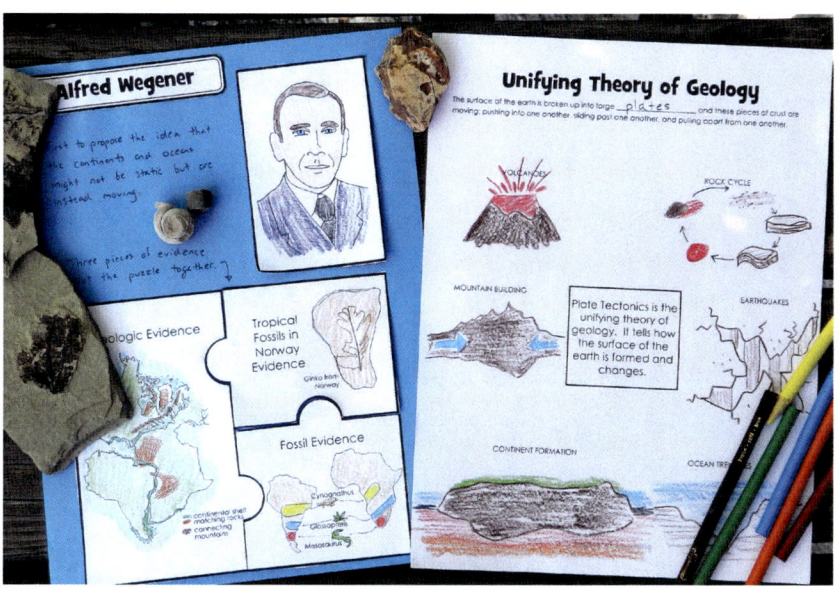

1. Read a book or watch a video about Alfred Wegener.
2. Color the "Alfred Wegener" printable. Cut apart the pieces on the heavy lines. Glue the pieces to a page in your Science Notebook with the title at the top. Add the title to your table of contents. The puzzle pieces should be glued down along one edge only to create flaps.
3. Write a brief description of each kind of evidence for continental drift under the puzzle pieces.
4. Illustrate the "Unifying Theory of Geology" printable with the different kids of phenomenon that plate tectonics explains. In the blank, fill in the word "plate."
5. Glue this sheet into your Science Notebook as well. Write "Unifying Theory of Geology" on your table of contents.
6. Discuss how Alfred Wegener's theory of plate tectonics is a unifying theory in geology.

Fabulous Fact

In the early 1900s, there was a vehement debate between "drifters" who thought the plates of Earth were moving and "fixists" who thought the continents were static. Alfred Wegener started the debate and cited the similar rock structure of the Newfoundland and Scotland highlands and the Caledonian and Appalachian Ranges as evidence that they had once been joined. But Wegener could not provide a mechanism by which continental rock could plow through oceanic rock, and so he wasn't taken seriously by most scientists.

Intriguingly, there is still not a definite mechanism known by which this happens, but the evidence that it does happen has mounted until the theory of plate tectonics is generally accepted by scientists.

Memorization Station

Unifying theory: an overall idea that explains how everything else within a scientific discipline works

The unifying theory of geology is plate tectonics.

If plate tectonics were to be proven wrong, it would destroy all the other knowledge about geologic processes that we have. Our concept of volcanoes, earthquakes, and mountain formation would be completely altered. Unifying theories are very important to their disciplines.

Earth & Space

Fabulous Fact

There are two main types of eruptions: effusive and explosive.

Effusive eruptions occur when magma wells out of the ground somewhat slowly and flows across the surface. Mauna Loa in Hawaii has effusive eruptions.

Explosive eruptions are sudden and violent, with huge plumes of ash and lava spewing high into the air and mud flows racing down the sides of the mountain. Eyjafjallajökull in Iceland had an explosive eruption in 2010.

EXPLORATION: Ocean Ridges

For this activity, you will need:

- Book or video about ocean ridges
- "Ocean Ridges" and "Ocean Ridges Answers" from the Printable Pack
- Colored pencils or crayons
- Scissors
- Glue stick
- Science Notebook

Ocean ridges are mountain chains that run the length of the oceans, right down the middle. They are spots where the ocean crust is cracked in two and spreading apart, allowing for lots of volcanic activity and mountain building along the crack. The Mid-Atlantic Ridge is the reason that the Atlantic Ocean is growing a little bigger each year.

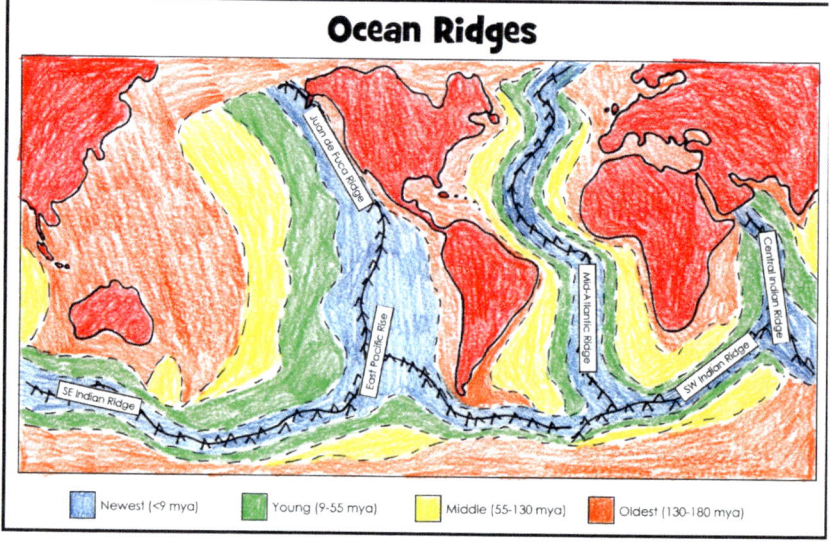

1. Read a book or watch a video about ocean ridges.
2. Choose five colors. On the "Ocean Ridges" printable, color the boxes in the key four different colors.
3. Use your fifth color to color the continents on the map. Name each of the continents out loud. Continental crust, in general, is much older than oceanic crust.
4. Color the rest of the map according to the colors you chose for the key. Where is the oldest rock in the oceans? Where is the youngest rock?
5. Cut out the little tags at the bottom of the map. The thick lines with mountains running across them are the ocean ridges. They are in the areas with the youngest rock. Glue the tags to the map in the correct places. Use the "Ocean Ridges Answers" as a guide.
6. Cut out the map on the heavy line. Glue it into your Science Notebook.

Plate Tectonics

Volcanoes

Volcanoes are ruptures, or breaks, in the earth's crust where hot **magma**, gases, and ash can escape from the interior of the earth to the surface. Volcanoes are part of the plate tectonic system of moving, broken up pieces of crust. Most volcanoes can be found on the boundaries of plates.

😊 😊 **EXPERIMENT: Baking Soda and Vinegar Volcano**

For this activity, you will need:

- Book or video about volcanoes
- A bottle or flask
- Salt dough (1½ cups salt, 1½ cups warm water, ¾ cup cooking oil, 6 cups flour)
- Paints and paintbrushes
- Warm water
- Vinegar
- Baking soda (sodium bicarbonate)
- Dish soap
- Red food coloring
- A large pan or tray to stand your volcano within

When hot magma under the earth builds up pressure, it erupts out of the earth and flows out as **lava**, ash, and gas.

1. Read a book or watch a video about volcanoes.
2. Mix up the salt dough.
3. Set your bottle or flask in the center of a large pan or tray (to catch the mess!) and use the clay to build a volcano shape around the bottle.
4. You can paint the volcano right away unless you want to keep it. In that case, let it dry for a few days first. You can also add action figures, toy animals, or other scenery to the area if you'd like.

Memorization Station

In your Science Notebook, draw illustrations to show the meanings of each of these words:

Volcano: a place where the earth's crust is ruptured and lava, gas, and ash escape from inside the earth to the surface

Magma: hot molten rock found under the surface of the crust

Lava: hot molten rock on the surface of the crust

Additional Layer

Not all volcanoes have the typical lava flowing down the sides of the mountains as we picture when we think of a volcano. Learn more about the various types of eruptions and lava flows you can see in volcanoes. Here are a few you can learn about:

Explosive eruption: a violent volcanic eruption where gas, ash, and magma are forcibly ejected from a fissure

Effusive eruption: lava steadily and slowly flows from a fissure

Pyroclastic flow: a fast moving "river" of hot ash and rock that flows out of a volcano and along the ground

Earth & Space

Writer's Workshop

Choose one of these topics to do a five-minute quick write about:

- If you could visit any one volcano, past or present, to watch erupt, which one would you want to see?
- Would you want to see a volcano erupt in person?
- What is the difference between magma and lava?
- If there were a new chain of islands made from eruptions like Hawaii was, would you want to be the first citizens to live there?
- If a volcanic lava flow were headed toward your house, what ten items would you grab before you evacuated?

Writer's Workshop

Obviously, volcanoes can be very dangerous and destructive, but do they do anything good?

Find out and write about the good points of a volcano from the point of view of the volcano.

What benefits do we get from volcanoes and geothermal energy? Are there any rocks, minerals, or other resources we use that are volcanic? Do volcanoes help people in any other ways? What would a volcano think of humans?

5. When you are ready to explode your volcano, put warm water into your bottle (you might need a funnel) until it is about ½ full.
6. Add several drops of red food coloring and a squirt of dish soap. Then, add 3 spoonfuls of baking soda.
7. Pour in ¼ cup of vinegar to set off the explosion.
8. You can set your volcano off as many times as you like by adding more baking soda and vinegar.

😊 😊 😊 EXPLORATION: Model Volcano

For this activity, you will need:

- Book or video about volcanoes
- Colored play dough or homemade salt dough, one batch per child (½ cup warm tap water, ¼ cup salt, 4 tablespoons cooking oil, 2 cups flour)
- Food coloring (optional)
- "Parts of a Volcano" from the Printable Pack
- Glue stick
- Scissors
- Science Notebook

From the outside, a volcano usually just looks like a normal mountain, but inside, it is more complex. There are tunnels and chambers full of hot magma, cracks forced through the rocks by the pressure, and places where hot steam is building.

1. Read a book or watch a video about volcanoes.

Plate Tectonics

2. Make a model of a volcano out of play dough or salt dough in cross section so you can see the insides. If you are using salt dough, color the dough red, brown, light brown, and any other colors you think you might want.

   Use the "Parts of Volcano" printable as a guide as you build your volcano.

3. Cut out the "Parts of a Volcano" printable on the solid outline. Glue it into your Science Notebook. Add the title to your table of contents.

4. Practice until you can name all the parts from memory.

☺ ☺ ☺ **EXPLORATION: Escape the Volcano Game**

For this activity, you will need:

- Book or video about volcanoes
- Large cardboard box
- Spray paint, green or brown
- Small glass or plastic jar, like a baby food jar
- Paper bowl
- Scissors
- Tiny plastic or paper cups
- Salt dough (1½ cups salt, 1½ cups warm water, ¾ cup cooking oil, 6 cups flour)
- Paint and paintbrushes
- Branches from trees, rocks, action figures, toy dinosaurs (optional)
- Vinegar
- Baking Soda

Use this game to review facts after you have done some reading or watched videos about volcanoes. As you read and watch, have your kids take notes so that they can come up with questions to ask each other during the game.

1. Cut a box down so it has short sides. Spray paint the box in a background color (green or brown).

2. Build a volcano around the small jar right on the box. Use an upside-down paper bowl with the bottom cut out to add more volume to your volcano so you can get away with less dough.

3. Press tiny plastic or paper cups into the dough to make "spaces" on the game board. These will be the spots your pieces rest on as you play the game. Each player will have his or her own path down the mountain, so make as many paths as you have players. If you have more than four players, you'll want to play on teams or build a second volcano.

4. Paint the volcano any way you like; no need to wait for the dough to dry. We painted each of our paths down the mountain in a different color for each player and added a couple of painted on spaces to the flat area

Additional Layer

There are 16 volcanoes around the world that are classified as "Decade Volcanoes" because they are especially dangerous to human beings. These volcanoes are all pretty active and are located near large population centers.

They are called "decade volcanoes" because they were identified during the UN's International Decade for Natural Disaster Reduction in the 1990s.

Learn more about these volcanoes and where they are located. What makes them especially dangerous?

Mount Rainier in Washington is a decade volcano.

Fabulous Fact

Volcanoes can be plateaus or just vents in the earth.

Lakagigar Fissure in Iceland is a crack in the earth that vented steam, gas, and lava for eight months in 1783-84. It killed most of the livestock and a quarter of the people in Iceland.

Photo by Anne Schöpa, CC by SA 3.0 Wikimedia

Earth & Space

Fabulous Fact

The people of Indonesia throw offerings of flowers, money, and livestock into Mount Bromo once a year during the Yadnya Kasada Ceremony to appease the volcano and commemorate the first offering: a human sacrifice by ancient monarchs.

Photo by CEphoto, Uwe Aranas

Bookworms

The Magic School Bus Blows Its Top: A Book About Volcanoes by Joanna Cole is an excellent picture book for teaching kids the science behind volcanoes. Ms. Frizzle and her class discover an underwater volcano that is creating a new island.

of the box. Each of our players had five steps to travel from the top to safety.

5. Let the paint dry, then add trees, rocks, moss, action figures, dinosaurs, or anything that makes it fun for your kids.

6. The little cups then become the game pieces. You can draw faces on the cups and label them with the players' names.

7. Pour about a half cup of vinegar into the container in the center of the volcano and add a teaspoon of baking soda to each player's cup.

To Play: Everyone starts at the top, in the space nearest the rim of the volcano. The first person asks the player on their left a question about volcanoes from the reading or video. A correct answer moves down the volcano toward safety. A wrong answer moves toward the volcano. Move around the table asking questions. If someone gets a question wrong and they are standing on the rim of the volcano, then they dump the contents of their cup into the volcano, and the volcano explodes. If this happens, refill your volcano with vinegar. Play until everyone is either to safety or has made the volcano explode.

😊 😊 😊 **EXPERIMENT: Mud Pots Pudding**

For this activity, you will need:

- Sugar
- Water
- Cocoa powder
- Corn starch

Plate Tectonics

- Salt
- Vanilla extract
- Milk
- Butter
- Stove
- Whisk
- Saucepan and glass bowl or a double boiler
- Video about mud pots

Mud pots are boiling puddles or pools of mud. Mud pots are indirectly heated by magma, which heats groundwater. The groundwater boils and steams underground, heating the earth above it. Surface water collected in puddles and pools is then heated by the groundwater. It's a lot like a double boiler in your kitchen.

1. Stir together in a glass mixing bowl (or if you own a double boiler, use that):

    2/3 cup sugar
    1/4 cup cocoa powder
    1/2 cup corn starch
    1/4 teaspoon salt

2. Gradually stir in 2 ¼ cups milk, whisking as you go.
3. Set a pot, half-filled with water, on the stove. The stove is like the magma under the surface. The water is like the groundwater that is heated by the magma.
4. Set your bowl full of "mud" on top of the pot of water. Turn the heat on high. Keep cooking and stirring until the "mud" on top is thickened, about 15 minutes.
5. While the pudding is cooking, head a new page in your Science Notebook "Mud Pots" and add it to your table of contents.
6. Draw and label a picture of your experiment.
7. Watch a video about mud pots and other geothermal

Additional Layer

Read more about one of these famous volcanic eruptions in history:

- Thera c. 1500 BC
- Mt. Vesuvius AD 79
- Mount Tambora 1815
- Mauna Loa 1843-now
- Krakatoa 1883
- Mount Pelee 1902
- Paracutin 1943
- Mt. St. Helens 1980
- Nevado del Ruiz 1985
- Mount Pinatubo 1991

Famous Folks

Katia and Maurice Krafft were French volcanologists who filmed and photographed volcanoes all around the world.

Tragically, they died in a pyroclastic flow on Mount Unzen in Japan in June 1991.

Earth & Space

Fabulous Fact

Not everyone buys into the mantle plume/hot spot hypothesis. Some volcanologists think that volcanoes in the middle of tectonic plates can be explained as places of stretching or thinning in the plate. In this hypothesis, the mantle isn't any hotter in these places; it's just closer to the surface.

Fabulous Fact

You can tell whether a chain of islands has formed above a hot spot or along a plate boundary because if it has formed above a hot spot, the islands will all be different ages, with the youngest directly above the hot spot and the islands getting older the further you go from the hot spot. If the islands are all about the same age, then they have formed along a plate boundary.

landscape features. As you watch, take notes in your Science Notebook.

8. Discuss how the hot pudding is like a mud pot.

9. Stir in 2 tablespoons of butter and 1 teaspoon of vanilla extract. Spoon into individual dishes and cool in the refrigerator for two hours or more. Then you can eat it.

😊😊😊 EXPERIMENT: Geyser Model

WARNING: Kids should stand back to prevent scalds from the hot water. Wear eye protection and heat protection for your hands.

For this activity you need:

- Tempered glass jar (canning jar or chemistry flask)
- Drinking straw
- Play dough or clay
- Stove
- Water
- Book or video about geysers from the Library List or YouTube playlist for this unit

Sometimes the magma and heat from the interior of the earth is very close to the surface. Underground streams feed water into hot underground pools. If the path of the water to the surface is constricted through a narrow opening, then the heating water builds up pressure until the water erupts out as a geyser.

1. Fill the bottle or flask three quarters full with warm water. If you use a canning jar, punch a hole in the lid big enough to fit your straw through and then put the lid on the jar.

2. Insert a straw, and stop up the edges around the straw at the neck of the bottle with clay or play dough. Make sure the straw is near the bottom of the bottle, but *not directly touching* the bottom.

3. Heat on a stove top until the water in the bottle is hot enough to spurt out.

4. Finish by reading a book or watching a video about geysers.

Plate Tectonics

☻ **EXPLORATION: Plot Real Volcanoes on a World Map**
For this exploration you will need:

- "Volcanoes of the World" and "List of Volcanoes of the World" from the Printable Pack
- Internet
- Colored pencils

Most volcanoes are found at either convergent or divergent plate boundaries, but some are found in the middle of a plate. These are less understood. Many scientists think that directly underneath the volcano is a hot plume in the mantle, a place where the mantle is rising toward the surface. The hypothesis is that this movement decreases pressure and makes it easier for the rock to melt. There are about fifty different hot spots on Earth, mostly under the oceans. Hawaii, the Society Islands, and Yellowstone National Park are all sitting above hot spots.

1. Color the key for your "Volcanoes of the World" map. Have a different color for each type of volcano: divergent plate boundary, convergent plate boundary, or hot spot.
2. Plot the locations of the volcanoes from the "List of Volcanoes of the World" onto the "Volcanoes of the World" map.
3. Look up information about the volcanoes to determine which type of volcano each is. Be able to explain why the conditions at the volcano's location make it so eruptable.
4. Put the Volcanoes of the World Map into your Layers of Learning Notebook in the Science section.

☻ ☻ ☻ **EXPLORATION: Types of Volcanic Eruptions**
For this activity, you will need:

- Freezer paper or a long roll of paper
- Paints and paintbrushes
- Books or websites about volcanoes

There are six types of eruptions. Here they are from the least violent to the most violent: Hawaiian, Strombolian, Vulcanian, Surtseyan, Pelean, Plinian.

1. Research each type of volcanic eruption, taking a few notes about each.
2. On a long sheet of freezer paper, paint six volcanoes in a row. Paint what each type of eruption looks like.
3. After the paint dries, label each type of eruption.

Additional Layer

This is a painting by Pompeo Batoni called *Vulcan*.

It depicts the Roman God, Vulcan. Vulcan was the god of fire, and he gave his name to volcanoes. He was known as Hephaestus to the Greeks. Learn more about him. Then learn about other volcano and fire gods and goddesses from world mythology.

Additional Layer

Old Faithful is a famous geyser in Yellowstone National Park in the United States. Learn more about it.

Earth & Space

Writer's Workshop
Earthquakes are usually caused by movement of the earth's crust along faults, but they can also be caused by volcanoes, landslides, nuclear tests, or asteroid impacts. Write about an earthquake that takes place in the middle of the Siberian Craton, far from a fault. What might have caused it?

Memorization Station
Earthquake: shaking of the earth caused by moving plates

Focus: the spot in the crust at the center of the earthquake, also called a hypocenter

Epicenter: the spot on the surface directly above the focus of an earthquake

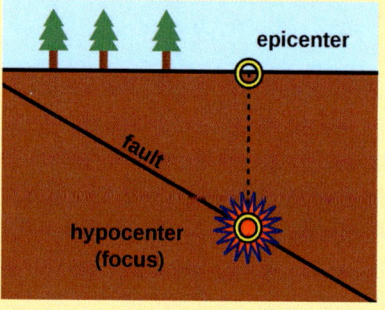

Additional Layer
Research the Moment Magnitude Scale and how it is used to measure the size and severity of earthquakes.

"Earthquake Scales" from the Printable Pack can be used to create pages in your Science Notebook.

Cut apart the table so each "magnitude" is in its own section. Make an illustration to go with each section.

4. Display your volcano chart on your wall until this unit is over.

Earthquakes

Earthquakes are a shaking of the earth caused by moving plates. The plates try to slide past one another, but they are stopped by friction. The energy builds up until they give way, resulting in shaking. The spot in the earth's crust at the center of the earthquake is called the **focus,** or hypocenter. The spot on the surface just above the focus is called the **epicenter**.

🙂🙂🙂 EXPERIMENT: Strike-Slip Fault Simulator
For this activity, you will need:

- A brick or heavy rock
- Large heavy-duty rubber band
- Piece of wood larger than the brick or rock
- Book or video about earthquakes
- Science Notebook

Why does the earth seem to stay nice and still for long periods of time and then suddenly shake violently without warning? Why does it settle back into a quiet period afterward, as though nothing had ever happened?

A strike-slip fault is made up of two massive chunks of rock sliding horizontally past one another.

1. Wrap a heavy-duty rubber band or two around a brick. Set the brick on the piece of plywood.
2. Slowly stretch the rubber band until the brick gives way and slides.

   The brick doesn't move until the force becomes great enough to overcome inertia. This is true in the crust of the earth too. The blocks of rock will sit still with pressure building and building until suddenly . . . slip . . . you have an earthquake. Then, the pressure is relieved, and it starts to build again.

Plate Tectonics

3. Read a book or watch a video about earthquakes.

4. Head a page in your Science Notebook "Earthquakes" and draw a picture of your experiment. Add the title to your table of contents. In your own words, explain how pressure builds up in the earth, gives way, and causes an earthquake.

😊 😊 😊 EXPERIMENT: Seismometer

For this activity, you will need:

- Cardboard box
- Plastic or paper cup
- String
- Pen
- Tape
- Paper
- Scissors
- Small weights, like pebbles or coins
- Science Notebook

A **seismometer** measures the shaking of the earth. Basically, it works by a hanging, heavy weight suspended over a moving sheet of paper with a pen attached to the weight. The pen just touches the paper and creates a straight line when the weight remains still. But if the weight begins to move due to shaking in the earth, then the pen will draw a squiggly line - the more squiggly, the more the earth is shaking.

1. Cut the flaps off the cardboard box so one side is completely open.

2. Cut two long slits in the bottom of the opposite sides of the box. This is where you will thread paper through one side of the box and out the other.

3. Poke two holes adjacent to one another on a short side of the box.

4. Punch two holes into the rim of your cup. Punch a hole in the center bottom of your cup.

Memorization Station

Seismometer: an instrument that detects and records earthquakes

Additional Layer

The Chinese were the first people we know of who set up earthquake detectors. Find out more about ancient Chinese earthquake detectors.

Famous Folks

Charles Richter was a Caltech professor and researcher who created a scale and seismograph to measure earthquakes with the help of his colleague, Beno Gutenberg.

Earth & Space

Additional Layer

It takes an enormous amount of force to shift the rocks that make up the crust of the earth. The force doesn't happen all at once, but it builds over time until suddenly . . . snap . . . the plates shift and you get an earthquake. This theory, that energy is stored in the rocks as they deform and stretch and then is suddenly released all at once, is called Elastic Rebound Theory.

You can simulate this process by wrapping a watermelon with more and more rubber bands until it explodes.

Additional Layer

The 2011 Tohoku Earthquake was one of the most destructive in recorded history. It wasn't the shaking that did the damage though; it was the tsunami.

Find out what happened in that earthquake.

5. Insert a pen through the hole in the bottom of the cup, so the tip is facing down. Fill the cup with something heavy like pebbles or coins.

6. Thread the string through the cup rim and then through the holes you made in the box. Tape the strings in place so that the pen is just touching the paper below.

7. Make a long strip of paper by cutting one sheet in thirds, hot dog-style, and then taping the three pieces together, end to end.

8. Place the paper through the slots in the box and under the hanging cup and slowly pull it through while someone shakes the table.

9. Head a new page in your Science Notebook "Seismometer." Sketch and label a picture of your experiment. Write down how a seismometer works.

🙂 🙂 EXPERIMENT: Seismic Waves in Sand

For this activity, you will need:

- Two toilet paper tubes
- Paper towels
- Rice
- Clay or play dough
- Rubber bands

Seismic waves are waves of energy that travel through the earth. They are usually caused by earthquakes and volcanoes. They do not move the same through all materials. When waves pass through sand, they move very

Plate Tectonics

slowly and are distributed away from the center.

1. Head a page in your Science Notebook "Seismic Waves" and add it to your table of contents. Write down the definition of "seismic waves."
2. Place a paper towel across one opening of each toilet paper tube and secure with a rubber band.
3. Fill one tube with rice and one with clay or play dough. Cover the other end of each toilet paper tube with another paper towel secured with a rubber band.
4. Press down on the contents of each tube with your fingers, putting pressure on the paper towel. What happens? The clay should bust through the paper towel, but the rice doesn't. Like sand, rice is made up of tiny individual particles that do not simply move forward when pressed on by a force. They move sideways and even backward as well as forward.
5. Draw a picture of your experiment and write down your observations.

☺ ☺ ☺ **EXPERIMENT: Shake Table Earthquake Simulator**
For this activity, you will need:

- Plastic lid from a coffee can or similar container
- Marbles
- Stiff flat platform, like a piece of wood or a cutting board
- Blocks or cups to build "buildings" with

There are two different kinds of seismic waves created by earthquakes. **P waves**, or primary waves, travel through

Additional Layer

Rocks near the surface of the earth are cold and brittle, meaning they can crack and break, but the rock miles deep is hot and plastic. When forces are placed on them they ought to just deform, like play dough. Quite frequently though, it turns out they do suddenly release large amounts of energy all at once.

There are four different hypotheses out there right now about how these deep earthquakes occur.

- Solid state phase transitions
- Dehydration embrittlement
- Transformational faulting
- Shear instability

Look up information about each of these ideas. Divide a page in your Science Notebook into four quadrants and draw a picture or write facts about each hypothesis in the quadrants.

Memorization Station

Seismic waves: waves of energy that travel through the earth

P waves: or primary waves, travel through the ground like a water wave

S waves: or secondary waves, shake the ground up and down, perpendicular to the direction the P wave is moving

Earth & Space

Additional Layer

You probably don't think of Oregon and Washington as earthquake zones, but the two states are sitting right along the Cascadia fault line. This is a deep fault line in a subduction zone just off the coast. When it goes, the results will be a massive tsunami.

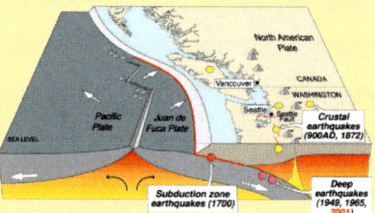

Learn more about the Cascadia fault.

Fabulous Fact

This image shows the theory of continental collisions forming major mountain ranges like the Alps and Himalayas.

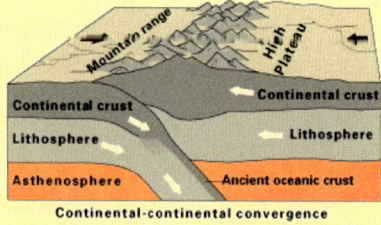

This image shows mountain building due to subduction of an oceanic plate beneath a continental plate, as is happening to form the Andes Mountains.

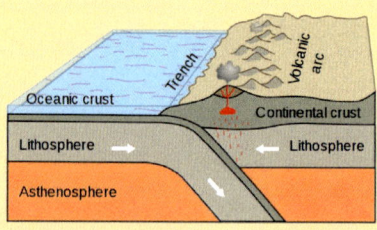

the ground like a water wave. They travel quickly and are the first to be picked up by seismometers. **S waves**, or secondary waves, shake the ground up and down, perpendicular to the direction the main wave is moving. S waves are slower but do more damage than P waves.

1. Set your lid down on a stable surface and fill it with 10-20 marbles. Set your platform on top so it is more or less centered.

2. Now, you can build various structures, buildings and bridges, and test which stands up to shaking better. Shaking back and forth with small rapid movements simulates P waves. Moving up and down vertically or side to side in small rapid movements demonstrates S waves.

3. Head a new page in your Science Notebook "Earthquake Simulator" and add it to your table of contents. Draw a labeled diagram of your experiment. Include all of your observations.

Mountain Building

We learned in the volcanoes section about how volcanoes can form mountains, but that isn't the only way mountains are formed. There are three ways mountains are formed, and the mountains are named after the ways they are formed: **volcanic mountains**, **fold mountains**, and **block mountains**. We'll take a look at fold mountains as well as block mountains in this section and also learn a few more principles of mountain building.

Plate Tectonics

😊 😊 EXPLORATION: Fold Mountains

For this activity, you will need:

- Play dough in three or more colors
- Rolling pin or round jar

The Himalayas, Alps, Andes, and Rockies are fold mountains. The tallest mountain ranges in the world are all fold mountains.

Fold mountains are formed when two plates collide. The forces involved are slow but immense. In fold mountain theory, an oceanic plate submerges beneath a continental plate. The continental plate crumples into deep folds, making mountains. It turns out that the folding up is matched by the folding down. High mountains also have deep roots, protruding deep into the mantle.

1. Start by rolling several colors of play dough into thin sheets with a rolling pin. Stack them on top of one another. Don't press them together or you won't be able to separate your colors out later. This represents layers of rock forming, either on the sea floor or from volcanic activity.

2. Next, gently fold and arrange the slabs into rolling hills. Those are the first two steps in the formation of fold mountains.

3. The final step is erosion. Erosion keeps the mountains from being nicely rounded and makes jagged peaks, deep valleys, and other formations.

4. Draw a picture of the fold mountains you made in your Science Notebook. Write down the three steps to creating fold mountains. Title your page "Fold Mountains" and put it in your table of contents.

Additional Layer

Find out which is the tallest mountain peak on each continent. Make a scale model of each of these tallest peaks. Label them with their names, the continent they are from, and how high they are.

Which mountains do you think are oldest? Can you find out?

Mt. Denali, North America's Tallest Peak

Memorization Station

Sketch and define these terms in your Science Notebook.

Volcanic mountains: occur along the margins of plates where oceanic crust is pushed underneath continental crust, causing melting of crust material

Fold mountains: occur where two plates collide, pushing the continental material up

Block mountains: caused by faults in the crust where blocks of rock move past each other

Earth & Space

Additional Layer

Sometimes rifts, places where continental crust is being dragged apart, can create mountains with low, broad valleys between them. These mountains are lower than mountains caused by collisions.

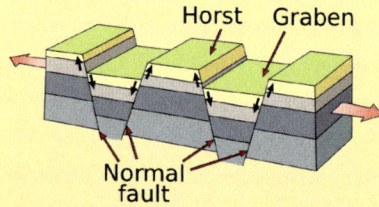

The high places are called horsts and the low valleys are called grabens. The Upper Rhine Valley in Europe is a graben between the Black Forest horst and the Vosges Mountain horst.

Deep Thoughts

The Scandinavian Mountains in Norway and Sweden are an exception to how mountains typically form. There is currently a lot of debate about exactly how they did form.

The problem is that they are located along a passive continental margin, a place where no relative movement is taking place at all. In such a spot, no mountains ought to exist if mountains are formed by crustal movements.

Research the Scandinavian Mountains and then have a discussion about some possibilities of how they could have formed. Let all the wild and crazy ideas come out along with the sensible ones. In science, it's important to listen to all ideas before you reject them.

☺ ☻ EXPLORATION: Types of Folds

For this activity, you will need:

- Video about geologic folding
- Paper and pen or pencil
- Scissors
- Glue stick
- "Some Types of Folds" from the Printable Pack
- Science Notebook

Folds are a deformation in rock that happens when rocks bend instead of breaking under stress. Folds can be small in scale or they can be as large as mountains. Folds can be classified into many different types based on their size, shape, dip (syncline or anticline), and the tilt of the axis.

Anticline: A fold where the newest material is on the outside of the fold. Often this fold will be turned downward like a frown, but it could be turned on its side or even on its head.

Syncline: A fold with the newest material in the center of the fold. It too can be turned sideways or upside down.

Recumbent: A fold where the axis has been tilted so that the layers are horizontal.

Angular: The fold has square or sharp corners.

Chevron: The fold repeats itself in tight folds. These folds can be rounded or angular.

1. Watch a video about geologic folding.
2. Cut out the title, pictures, and tags from the "Some Types of Folds" printable.
3. Match photos with labels. Glue them in your Science Notebook.

Plate Tectonics

Answers: A: Anticline; B: Recumbent; C: Angular; D: Syncline; E: Chevron

There are many more types of folds than the five in this exploration. All of the folds in this Exploration are two-dimensional, but folds can be three-dimensional as well.

😊 😊 😊 EXPLORATION: Block Mountains Model
For this activity, you will need:

- Salt dough (½ cup warm water, ¼ cup salt, 4 tablespoons cooking oil, 4 drops red, 2 drops yellow, and 2 drops green food coloring, 2 cups flour)
- Plaster of Paris

The Sierra Nevada Mountains in California and Nevada are block mountains. They were formed from pockets of granite that hardened deep underground. An oceanic plate began to submerge beneath the North American continental plate, creating lots of volcanic activity, most of which took place deep inside the crust. The volcanic activity created a batholith, a massive intrusion of granite inside the crust. This batholith began to tilt with the continued force of the oceanic plate crushing against the continental plate. As it tilted, the corner thrust upward, forming mountain peaks. Glaciers, rivers, and water eroded the rock, forming canyons and carving the peaks. The Sierra Nevada Mountains are still uplifting from the Pacific Plate's continual pushing against California. Frequent earthquakes in the Sierra Nevadas are evidence of this.

1. Make a model of a fault block mountain. Pat the dough out into a slab that is fairly thick but flattened.

2. Now, mold out a hollow space, almost as deep as your dough. This is the space that molten lava will fill in your crust to form a batholith. Pour the mixed up plaster of Paris into the hollow space.

Famous Folks
Charles Lyell, a British geologist, was the first scientist to explain clearly that the earth is undergoing constant changes.

The plates move, volcanoes build land, mountains are built up and then eroded, and so on.

Deep Thoughts
Most mountains are part of ranges, but sometimes lone mountains form. Would a lone mountain be more likely to be volcanic or fold?

Explain your reasoning.

Fabulous Fact
Tsunamis are giant waves, or surges of ocean water, that happen after an underwater earthquake. They are deadly, killing everyone who gets caught in them.

Earth & Space

Memorization Station

Memorize this short poem about mountains by Beth Wren.

Take me to the mountains

For that's where I belong.

Just birds and trees

And wind and leaves

And silence is my song.

Memorization Station

There are five major processes that can lead to mountains being built up. As you go through the explorations in this unit, can you identify any of these processes?

Folding: layers of rock are bent or curved in a permanent deformation.

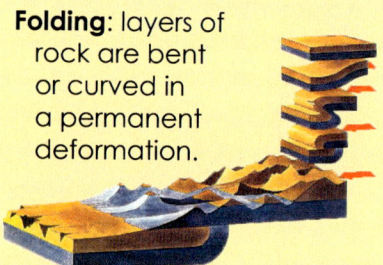

Faulting: the crust fractures and mass displacement of rock layers occurs

Volcanic activity: a rupture in the earth's crust allows hot material from the magma chamber to rise and spill out onto the surface

Igneous intrusion: magma pushes upward beneath the surface, cooling and solidifying underground

Metamorphism: heat and pressure deep in the crust deform rocks and pushes them into ridges and folds

Learn about each of these and memorize the definitions.

3. Allow it to harden for a couple of hours.

4. Now, turn the slab of "crust" over and push on one side of the formation. What happens to the batholith portion of the crust?

😊 😊 😊 EXPLORATION: Dome Mountain Cream Puffs

For this activity, you will need:

- Cream puff pastry (recipe below)
- 2 pkg (6.8 oz) instant pudding mix
- Mixing bowl and whisk
- Refrigerator
- Saucepan
- Electric mixer
- Baking sheet
- Parchment paper
- Oven
- Pastry bag with wide tip or a large, clean, plastic syringe
- Science Notebook

The Adirondack Mountains are dome mountains. They formed when hot magma welled up beneath the surface of the earth, lifting the overlying rock. The magma never broke the surface, but instead, hardened under the surface into granite. The result is rounded tops and gentle foothills.

To demonstrate how this happens, we'll make cream puffs.

1. Mix together 2 packages vanilla instant pudding mix, 2 cups heavy cream, and 1 cup milk. Cover and refrigerate to set.

2. Preheat oven to 425° F (220° C).

3. In a large pot, bring 1 cup water and ½ cup butter to a rolling boil. Remove from heat. Stir in 1 cup flour and ¼ teaspoon of salt until the mixture forms a ball. Transfer the dough to a large mixing bowl. Let the dough cool for ten minutes.

4. Using an electric mixer, beat in 4 eggs, one at a time,

Plate Tectonics

mixing well after each. Beat in 2 tablespoons of sugar and 1 teaspoon of vanilla. Drop by tablespoonfuls onto an ungreased baking sheet that is lined with parchment paper.

5. Bake for 20 to 25 minutes in the preheated oven, until golden brown. Centers should be dry.

6. When the shells are cool, poke a small hole in the side, gently flatten the shell with your hand, and use a pastry bag to pipe the pudding into the shells.

    Adding the pudding mix will make the pastry puff up, just as magma being injected into overlying ground can make the ground puff up.

7. Watch a video about mountains while you eat your dome mountain cream puffs.

8. Title a page in your Science Notebook "Types of Mountains" and draw a picture of your dome mountain cream puffs. Explain how dome mountains are formed. On the same page, you can also draw fault-block mountains, volcanic mountains, and fold mountains if you have learned about them in your reading.

😊 🙂 EXPLORATION: Delamination

For this activity, you will need:

- Paper and pen or pencil
- Science Notebook

Sometimes in places where continental plates collide, the lower, dense lithosphere can become separated from the upper lithosphere and replaced by less dense asthenosphere (the next layer down in the earth). This is called delamination. This causes the now lighter crust to be uplifted and creates a new mountain chain. This is how the Sierra Nevada Mountains in California were and are being created.

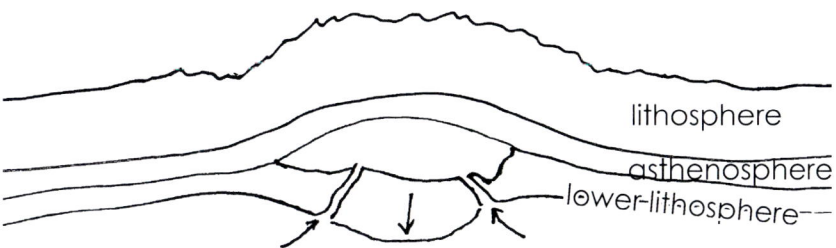

1. Copy this diagram into your Science Notebook and label it to show the delamination process.

Fabulous Fact

Scientists use the word "orogenesis" to mean mountain building. It comes from Greek and means "creation of mountains."

All of the greenish blue patches on this map show places of current orogenesis on earth, or places where mountains are currently being built.

Additional Layer

Mountains go through a cycle called the orogenic cycle, which has three stages.

1. Accumulation of sediments and deposits, creating a thick area of continental crust
2. Crustal movements, causing folds and igneous intrusions
3. Upheaval of deformed crust, creating mountain ranges

Learn more about the orogenic cycle and add it to your Science Notebook.

Famous Folks

Delamination is a theory that was introduced by Peter Bird of UCLA in 1978. Most, but not all, geologists have accepted it as a mechanism for mountain uplift.

Earth & Space

Bookworms

My Side of the Mountain, by Jean Craighead George, is the story of a young boy who runs away to the Catskill Mountains to live off the land. He befriends animals and learns to fish, gather berries, and take care of himself in the mountains.

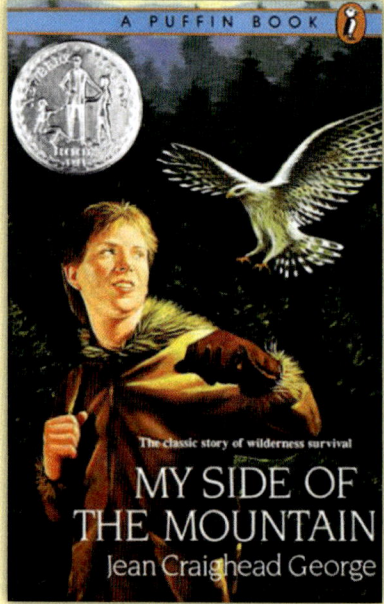

Fabulous Facts

- Mountains make up about one-fifth of the world's landscape.
- About one-tenth of the world's people live in mountainous areas.
- Earth isn't the only planet with mountains. Olympus Mons on Mars is far larger than any of Earth's mountains.

Writer's Workshop

Many of the planets under the sea are uncharted and have never been visited by humans. Write about whether or not you would want to explore some of them.

2. Other substances that are formed in layers go through delamination, causing bubbles in their surface. Plastics, the surface of RVs and boats, plywood, and laminate flooring can all experience delamination.

   See if you can find examples of these types of delamination around your home or neighborhood, and compare this to what happens under the earth.

3. Discuss what has to happen for the delamination process to begin. Write about delamination in your Science Notebook. Give your page a title - "Delamination." Add it to your table of contents.

😊 😊 😊 **EXPLORATION: Design a Model Mountain**

For this activity, you will need:

- Modeling clay and modeling tools
- Paints
- Internet

Many mountain ranges in the world are being actively formed right now.

1. Go online and research one of these mountain ranges to find out how they are being built:

   - The Zagros Mountains of Iran
   - Cascade Mountains of North America
   - Himalayas Mountains of Asia
   - Mediterranean Ridge

2. Using modeling clay, design a model of the mountains, with a cut-away section that shows what is happening under the surface of the earth to form the mountains.

😊 😊 😊 **EXPEDITION: Mountain Trip**

For this activity, you will need:

- Internet
- Science Notebook

1. Look up information on mountains near you. How were

Plate Tectonics

the mountains formed? Are there any impressive rock formations to check out? How old are the mountains?

2. Drive into mountains near you. Look for exposed outcroppings of rock and see which formations you can identify. Can you see layers in the rock? Are the layers tilted or folded?

3. Make sketches in your Science Notebook while you are there. Include notes about the way the mountains formed.

Step 3: Show What You Know

During this unit, choose one of the assignments below to show what you have learned during the unit. Add this work to your Layers of Learning Notebook. You can also use this assignment to show your supervising teacher or your charter school as a sample of what you've been working on in your homeschool, if needed.

There are more ideas for writing assignments in the "Writer's Workshop" sidebars.

😊 🙂 Coloring or Narration Page

For this activity, you will need:

- "Plate Tectonics" from the Printable Pack
- Writing or drawing utensils

1. Depending on the age and ability of the child, choose either the "Plate Tectonics" coloring sheet or the "Plate Tectonics" narration page from the Printable Pack.

Deep Thoughts

Normally, folded mountain ranges are formed with at least one continental plate as the backdrop, but the New Guinea Highlands are an exception.

They are formed between two oceanic plates. Yet, the New Guinea Highlands are, themselves, made of continental crust, folded, metamorphosed, and intruded with magma multiple times. They are like a floating random piece of crust in the middle of vast ocean plates.

Think about this phenomenon and possibilities for scientific discovery based on the New Guinea Highlands. Have a discussion about the kinds of studies or experiments that you think could be done in this unique part of Earth.

Writer's Workshop

Choose an animal that makes its home in the mountains and learn all about it. Write a simple animal report. If you need help, *Writer's Workshop: Reports & Essays* has instructions. Here are some animals that may interest you: mountain goat, chinchilla, lynx, big horn sheep, Himalayan tahr, vicuna, ibex, snow leopard, Andean condor, alpine marmot, or chamois.

Earth & Space

Unit Trivia

1. What is the name for the big sections of crust on the earth?

    Plates

2. What are the three main types of boundaries between plates called?

    Convergent, divergent, and transform.

3. Fill in the blanks - The spot in the earth's crust at the center of the earthquake is called the _____, or hypocenter. The spot on the surface just above that is called the _____.

    focus, epicenter

4. These are seismic waves that travel through the ground like a water wave.

    P waves

5. Which type of evidence was NOT used to support the continental drift hypothesis?

    a) Evidence from landforms

    b) Evidence from fossils

    c) Evidence from human remains

    d) Evidence from climate zones

6. True or False - Volcanoes only exist on land.

    False - There are lots of volcanoes under the oceans. Some of them even erupt to the point that they create new islands.

7. Most volcanoes are concentrated around the "Ring of Fire," which forms a circle through which ocean?

    The Pacific Ocean

2. Younger kids can color the coloring sheet as you review some of the things you learned about during this unit. On the bottom of the coloring page, kids can write a sentence about what they learned. Very young children can explain their ideas orally while a parent writes for them.

3. Older kids can write about some of the concepts you learned on the narration page and color the picture as well.

4. Add this to the Science section of your Layers of Learning Notebook.

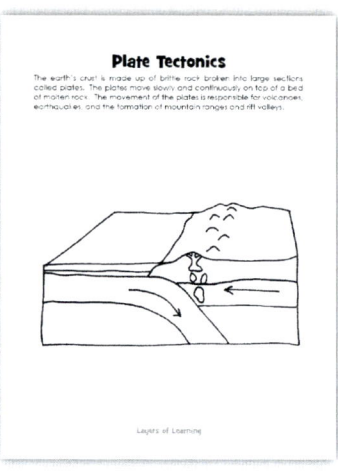

😊 😊 😊 Science Experiment Write-Up

For this activity, you will need:

- The "Experiment" write-up or "Experiment Report Template" from the Printable Pack

1. Choose one of the experiments you completed during this unit and create a careful and complete experiment write-up for it. Make sure you have included every specific detail of each step so your experiment could be repeated by anyone who wanted to try it.

2. Do a careful revision and edit of your write-up, taking it through the writing process, before you turn it in for grading.

😊 😊 😊 Parts of a Volcano Quiz

For this activity, you will need:

- "Parts of a Volcano Quiz" from the Printable Pack

1. Take the quiz to see how much everyone learns and remembers about the parts of a volcano.

Answers: 1 - Inactive volcano, 2 - Fumarole, 3 - Secondary volcanic pipe, 4 - Volcanic pipe, 5 - Crater, 6 - Ash cloud, 7 - Volcanic bomb, 8 - Volcanic cone, 9 - Ash bed, 10 - Solid lava flow, 11 - Lava flow, 12 - Magmatic chamber

Plate Tectonics

😊 😊 😊 **Plate Tectonics Short Answer Questions**
For this activity, you will need:

- Paper and writing utensils

1. Answer these short answer questions to show what you've learned throughout this unit.

    - Describe tectonic plates and some of the effects they have on our earth.
    - Explain some of the reasons scientists believe our continents used to be a supercontinent called Pangaea.
    - Explain the three main ways mountains are built.

😊 😊 😊 **Big Book of Knowledge**
For this activity, you will need:

- "Big Book of Knowledge: Plate Tectonics" printable from the Printable Pack, printed on card stock
- Writing or drawing utensils
- Big Book of Knowledge

1. Color, draw on, or write on the Big Book of Knowledge page. Record concepts, definitions, and facts you learned during this unit. It's a record of the things you learned and hope to remember. Add the page to your Big Book of Knowledge.

2. Use your Big Book of Knowledge regularly to help you review, quiz, or create games that will help you commit the things you've learned to memory.

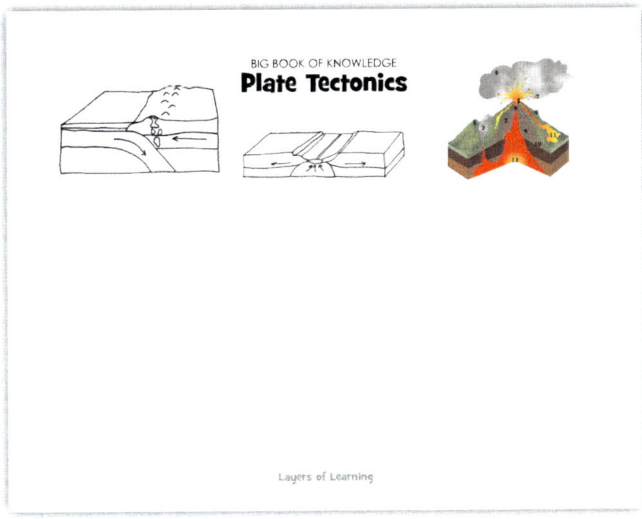

Big Book of Knowledge

The Big Book of Knowledge is a book for you, the mentor, to use as a constant review of all of the things you're learning about. You can use it to quiz your kids or prepare tests or review games. Whenever you learn something in Layers of Learning that you want your kids to remember, add it to your Big Book of Knowledge.

Assemble your Big Book of Knowledge in a binder or with binder rings. Divide it into sections for each subject.

In the Printable Pack for this unit you will find a "Big Book of Knowledge" sheet. You can add this sheet to others you collect or create yourself as you progress through the Layers of Learning curriculum. Customize the Big Book of Knowledge to your family by adding facts and topics that you enjoyed exploring as you were learning.

Visit Layers of Learning online to find more information on how to assemble and use your own Big Book of Knowledge.

You will also find cover and section pages to print along with creative games to play with your Big Book of Knowledge to keep school, even the tests, fun!

Earth & Space

Unit Overview

Key Concepts:
- Minerals are the building blocks that make up rocks.
- There are three types of rock: igneous, sedimentary, and metamorphic.
- Rocks go through a cycle from formation to erosion to new forms of rock and then, finally, back to being melted under the surface.
- Rocks are eroded by wind and water.
- Soil is a complex system of eroded rock, organic matter, water, air, and small creatures.

Vocabulary:
- Minerals
- Crystals
- Igneous
- Sedimentary
- Metamorphic
- Mafic
- Felsic
- Magma
- Lava
- Sediment
- Foliation
- Regional metamorphism
- Contact metamorphism
- Weathering
- Erosion
- Deposition
- Soil horizon
- Soil profile

Theories, Laws, & Hypotheses:
- Law of superposition

ROCKS

There are three types of rocks: igneous, sedimentary, and metamorphic. Igneous rocks are formed when magma from under the earth cools and hardens.

This is Craters of the Moon National Monument, Idaho, USA. The whole area is a huge basalt plain of igneous rock.

After the rock forms, it can be exposed to weathering, pressure, and other forces. Weathering from ice, wind, rain, and temperature changes can break rock apart into smaller pieces. If those little pieces get pressed together over time, they can form sedimentary rocks, made up of the sediments, or tiny pieces of other rocks.

On the left are some sandstone rock faces at Arches National Park, Utah, USA. On the right is a sedimentary geode.

Rocks

If rock is subjected to high temperatures and pressure under the surface, the rock can be transformed into new types of rock. These are known as metamorphic. Metamorphe means "change of form" in Greek.

This is a metamorphic rock called gneiss. It forms from granite. Often "granite" counter tops are actually made of gneiss.

Step 1: Library List

Choose books from your library that go with this topic. Here's a list of some favorites and also a list of search terms so you can utilize what your library offers. Read the books with your kids and/or assign them some to read independently. It is from these books your kids will learn most of the facts they need from this unit.

Search for: geology, rocks, igneous, sedimentary, metamorphic, weathering, soil

🙂 🙂 🙂 *Encyclopedia of Science* from DK. Read "Rocks and Minerals," "Igneous Rocks," "Sedimentary Rocks," and "Metamorphic Rocks" on pages 221-224. Also see "Ice and Glaciers," "Weathering and Erosion," and "Soils" on pages 228-232.

🙂 🙂 🙂 *Kingfisher Science Encyclopedia*. Read "Building Rocks," "Ores and Gems," "Igneous Rock," "Metamorphic Rock," Sedimentary Rock," and "Erosion and Weathering" on pages 24-33.

🙂 🙂 🙂 *The Usborne Science Encyclopedia*. Read "Earth's Resources" on page 198.

🙂 🙂 🙂 *Rocks and Minerals* by Lindsay A. Caputo. A good read-aloud overview of rocks, the rock cycle, and minerals.

🙂 *Let's Go Rock Collecting* by Roma Gans. This book teaches how rocks are formed: igneous, sedimentary, and metamorphic. Also tells how rocks are used every day.

Family School Levels

The colored smilies in this unit help you choose the correct levels of books and activities for your child.

🙂 = Ages 6-9
🙂 = Ages 10-13
🙂 = Ages 14-18

On the Web

For videos, web pages, games, and more to add to this unit, visit the Earth & Space Resources at Layers-of-Learning.com.

You will find a link to video playlists, web links, and more.

Bookworms

If you're looking for a family read-aloud, we'd like to suggest this one.

Jake and the Quake by Cary I. Sneider takes place in the weeks leading up to and during the San Francisco earthquake of 1989. Jake finds a weird rock near the Golden Gate Bridge and, with help from some other middle schoolers, figures out what it means.

Earth & Space

Writer's Workshop

Find ten or more images of mountain peaks online; print them or collect them in a digital form.

Invent a classification system for the mountain peaks. How will you group them, arrange them, and name them?

Write down your mountain peak classification system so that someone can arrange your mountain peak images into the groups you decided on.

For help with this kind of writing, check out the *Writer's Workshop: Descriptions & Instructions* unit.

Bookworms

Where She Fell by Kaitlyn Ward is about a teenage girl named Eliza who falls into a sinkhole and disappears into an underground cavern system where she finds a colony of other people who have also become lost in the caverns.

Eliza's geology interests might help her survive, but her anxieties could cancel all of that out.

My Book of Rocks & Minerals by Devin Dennie. Explains how rocks are formed and the different types of rocks and also gives tips on how to collect rocks.

Rocks: Hard, Soft, Smooth, and Rough by Natalie Myra Rosinsky. A science book that reads like a storybook. This is illustrated and simple for your youngest kids.

The Pebble in My Pocket by Meredith Hooper. Illustrated picture book about the rock cycle and how the pebble in your pocket might be millions of years old.

A Chip Off the Old Block by Jody Jensen Shaffer. A picture book about a little rock chip who is related to pretty famous rocks like Uncle Gibraltar, Aunt Etna, and Grandma Half-Dome.

Grand Canyon by Jason Chin. A father and daughter hike through the Grand Canyon discovering the story the layers of rock tell about the geological history of the area.

Dirt: The Scoop On Soil by Natalie Myra Rosinsky. A simple, illustrated book about soil and what it is made of.

The Magic School Bus: Inside the Earth by Joanna Cole. A classic your kids will love.

Geology Lab For Kids: 52 Projects to Explore Rocks, Gems, Geodes, Crystals, Fossils, and Other Wonders of the Earth's Surface by Garret Romaine. Get this if your kids are real rock hounds and want to do more and more!

Rocks & Minerals by Seymour Simon. One of our favorite science writers. This book has full-color photos on every page along with facts about how to identify rocks.

Cracking Up: A Story About Erosion by Jacqui Bailey. How a cliff becomes a beach, with lots of illustrations.

I Wonder Why Stalactites Hang Down and Other Questions About Caves by Jackie Gaff. Fun Q&A book.

Rocks, Minerals, & Gems by Miranda Smith and Sean Callery. This book explains how rocks are formed and then has descriptions of many individual rocks. It can act as an identifying guide.

Rocks and Minerals: A Gem of a Book by Simon Basher and Dan Green. Brings geology to life.

Science Comics: Rocks and Minerals: Geology from Caverns to the Cosmos by Andy Hirsch. A famous rock hunter and a crazy-for-crystals kid go on a journey.

Outdoor School: Rock, Fossil, and Shell Hunting by

Rocks

Jennifer Swanson. Includes information, activities, and space to journal your own adventures.

🙂 🙂 *The Geology Book* by John D. Morris. Presents a young earth theory viewpoint. From the Wonders of Creation series.

🙂 *What's That Rock or Mineral?* by DK. A field guide that teaches you to look for the properties of rocks in order to identify them in the field. This guide is only for North America.

🙂 *The Practical Geologist* by Dougal Dixon. Easy to read and accessible but more thorough than an introductory university course.

🙂 *Geology: A Self-Teaching Guide* by Barbara W. Murck. A full course for high school geology.

Step 2: Explore

Choose a few hands-on explorations from this section to work on as a family. They should be appealing activities that will create mental hooks so your kids remember the information in the unit. Save the rest of the explorations for the next time you do this unit in four years when your kids are older. You can also read the sidebars together and explore some little rabbit trails.

This unit includes printables. See the introduction for instructions on retrieving your Printable Pack.

🙂 🙂 🙂 EXPEDITION: Rock Collecting

For this activity, you will need:

- Book or video about rocks from the Library List or playlist
- Rock identification guide for your part of the world
- Internet or an expert on rocks in your area
- Science Notebook
- Masking tape or dot stickers
- Permanent marker
- Container to put your rocks in
- Shoe box, egg carton, glass jar or another way to display your rocks

This activity is best to do at the beginning of this unit, after you have read a book or watched a video about the basics of rocks. You will use your rocks in future Explorations in this unit.

1. Read a book or watch a video about rocks to get some basic information before you begin collecting.

Fabulous Fact

Rock collecting isn't legal everywhere. If you are on land that does not belong to you, make sure it is okay for you to collect rocks from that location.

Rock collection is prohibited in all U.S. National Parks, for example, but you can freely collect rocks on Forest Service land.

Teaching Tip

It's much easier to identify rocks from a pre-selected batch of samples from a science supplier than it is to identify rocks that you find in nature.

When you fail to identify some of the rocks that your kids find, point out that having all the answers isn't necessarily the point. How much can you notice and learn about the rock, even if you don't know its official name?

Earth & Space

Famous Folks

James Hutton was the first geologist ever.

He was also the first plutonist, or scientist who believed rocks formed from magma. He believed that geological processes were usually slow and continuously happening through time.

Writer's Workshop

Which would you rather visit: a cave deep underground or a canyon carved by a river?

Explain your choice and reasoning in a paragraph.

Teaching Tip

Set up a rocks and minerals exploration station and let your kids explore rock samples, notice the crystals, and examine the details of rocks all on their own.

2. You can find rocks in your backyard, but you'll want to go a little further afield to find different types of rocks. The internet can be a good resource. There also may be rock hound clubs in your area or a geology professor who could point you to some good spots. Get out and find some rocks! Try to find some igneous, some sedimentary, and some metamorphic examples.

3. When you select a rock to keep, tear off a piece of masking tape, use a permanent marker to label the tape with a letter, starting with "A." Put the label on your rock. Then, in your Science Notebook, write an "A" and make notes about where you found the rock and the date. Sketch the site or the rock. Leave space so you can add more notes later when you identify the rock.

4. Keep your labeled rocks in a box or bag to take home.

5. At home, clean your rocks, being careful to keep track of which label goes with which rock. Let the rocks dry, relabel them with their letters, then sort them into a display using a box, egg carton, or glass jar.

6. Use a rock identification book to identify the rocks to the best of your ability.

Minerals

😊 😊 EXPLORATION: Minerals Make Rocks

For this activity, you will need:

- Book or websites about minerals

Rocks

- Chocolate chips
- Mini marshmallows
- Peanuts
- Walnuts
- Raisins
- Coconut
- Cookie chunks
- Butterscotch chips
- Cupcake papers
- Microwave oven

Minerals are the building blocks that make up rocks. Minerals are made from specific elements and can form regular **crystals**. For example, quartz is a mineral with the chemical composition SiO_2. It is made of a silicon atom combined with two oxygen atoms. If quartz has enough space to grow, it will form a tetrahedron-shaped crystal.

Feldspar is another mineral. If quartz and feldspar mix together to form rocks under the surface of the earth, then you get granite, an igneous rock.

Here is a list of some other minerals that combine in different ways to get unique rocks.

quartz	gypsum	copper
feldspar	calcite	mica
pyrite	apatite	diamond

1. Put the chocolate chips and other ingredients in individual bowls on a table. Label each of the ingredients with a tag, each representing a real mineral.

2. Look up information in books or online about each of the minerals so kids can see pictures of the real minerals and get an idea of what they are and how they look.

3. Let each child choose which ingredients to include in a "rock" by adding those ingredients to a cupcake paper.

4. Put the cups in the microwave for one minute to melt the chocolate and marshmallows. Give the candy a little stir to combine everything. Then, let it cool.

Memorization Station

Minerals: made of specific elements and often forming regular crystals, minerals are the building blocks of rocks

Crystals: a homogeneous substance that has a regular geometric shape

Writer's Workshop

Gems are minerals that are highly valued because of their beauty and rarity. They are harder and clearer than other minerals and often form deeper underground so they are more difficult to find and retrieve.

Look up different types of gemstones. Choose one to research. Draw a picture of your gem in the center of a piece of paper then write facts about it around the picture. Share your findings with a group in an oral report, using your picture as a visual guide.

Bookworms

Geology Activity Book by Jenny Jacoby is a great solution for kids who get really into this unit and want to go further.

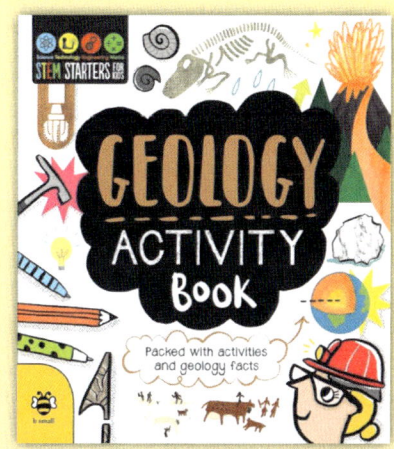

Earth & Space

Bookworms

The Atlas Obscura Explorer's Guide for the World's Most Adventurous Kid by Dylan Thuras is a world tour of amazing places to visit including crystal caves in Mexico, Blood Falls in Antarctica, and ice caves in Argentina.

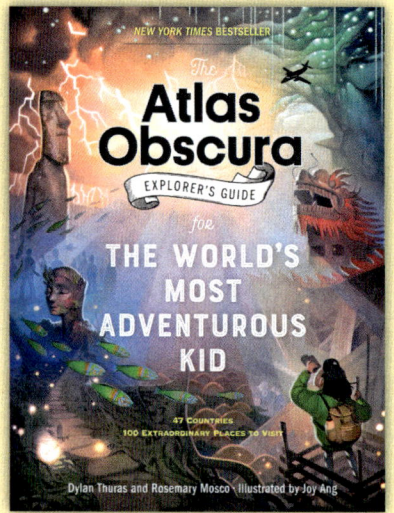

Bookworms

The Map That Changed the World by Simon Winchester is a well-written biography of the father of geology for ages 14 and up.

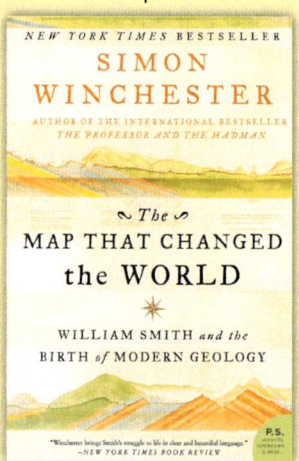

William Smith began his career as a poor canal digger. But his life's work was a map of the rocks.

Each "rock" formed is different because it began with different minerals and amounts of minerals.

😊 😊 😊 EXPERIMENT: Identifying Minerals

For this activity, you will need:

- Mineral sample kit with nine or more minerals
- Sticky dot labels
- Permanent marker
- "Mohs Mineral Hardness Scale" printables (2 pages)
- "Identification of Common Minerals" flowchart from the Printable Pack
- Unglazed white tile
- Steel nail
- White vinegar
- Magnet (if one of your samples is magnetite)
- Science Notebook

Minerals are classified by how hard they are. A harder mineral can scratch a softer one. This means you can try scratching one mineral with another to determine which is harder.

1. Label each of your mineral samples with letters A through I using the sticky dots and a permanent marker.

2. Use the "Mohs Mineral Hardness Scale" printable and try to put your minerals in order from softest to hardest by scratching them against one another.

3. Next, check for luster. Does your sample look metallic? Is it shiny or glassy? Does it look waxy or dull? Record your observations in your Science Notebook.

4. Check whether each sample can be scratched by your fingernail or not. Then check if each sample can be scratched by a nail or not. Record your observations.

100

Rocks

5. The way a mineral breaks is distinctive too. If your mineral breaks into even flat sheets, it has good cleavage. If it splits irregularly or shatters, then it has poor cleavage. Minerals can break into regular shapes like cubes as well. Record whether your mineral samples have good or poor cleavage or other distinctive breaking trends.

6. Minerals leave distinctive colored streaks on unglazed white tile. You can do streak tests to further narrow down what type of minerals you have.

    Scrape each of your samples across a piece of tile to determine its streak color. Record the streak color.

7. Apply a drop or two of vinegar to each of your samples to see if a chemical reaction occurs (bubbling or fizzing). Record your observations.

8. If you have magnetite in your sample collection, have the kids test the rocks to see if any are magnetic.

9. Use the "Identification of Common Minerals" flowchart to identify your minerals.

😊 😊 EXPERIMENT: Growing Crystals

WARNING: This experiment uses boiling water. Be careful!

For this activity, you will need:

- Chenille stems
- Borax (laundry aisle)
- Pencils
- Clear jars or cups
- Food coloring (any color)
- 250 ml or larger beaker
- String
- Scissors
- Water
- Magnifying glass
- Samples of minerals
- Science Notebook

Many minerals have a definite crystal structure. Calcite often forms into 12-sided elongated crystals. Salt forms into

Additional Layer

The United States Geological Survey (USGS) studies and maps all of the natural resources within the U.S., not just rocks and minerals. Learn more about what they do. Or, if you're not from the U.S., learn about agencies in your country that map and track natural resources.

Famous Folks

Florence Bascom was a member of the USGS (United States Geological Survey) and a college professor who taught geology.

She developed better methods for identifying rocks.

Additional Layer

Make rock candy by boiling 4 cups of sugar in 2 cups water on the stove, stirring continuously. Dip string into the sugar water repeatedly then lay it out to dry for a week as crystals form.

Earth & Space

Deep Thoughts

Geologists didn't always know where rocks came from. As late as the 1700s, some scientists believed that all rocks crystallized from ocean water. Eventually, the Neptunists, or people who believed that all rocks came from water, were replaced by geologists who witnessed volcanic activity. Plutonists (scientists who believed rocks formed from within the earth) went on an expedition to Iceland around the 1730s and watched lava flow from fissures in the earth. They saw rocks form from magma and dispelled the theories of the Neptunists.

In this photo by Anne Burgess you can see rocks the Neptunists relied on for their ideas. Sea creatures called ammonites were found fossilized in this rock, which was so hard it was thought to be basalt. It turns out this rock is mudstone.

Discuss the nature of science as a process of discovery. It's okay not to know everything. It's okay to be still learning. And it's okay to be wrong sometimes while we get closer to truth.

Add an entry to your Science Notebook about Neptunists and Plutonists. Divide a box into two halves. Write "Neptunists" on one half and draw a picture of how they believed rocks formed. Write "Plutonists" on the other half and draw a picture of rocks forming from magma

cube shapes. Mica forms into flat sheets of hexagonal crystals.

1. Look at some samples of minerals with a magnifying glass. Can you see crystal structures? Some minerals have microscopic crystal structures that you probably can't see. Others don't form crystals at all. You can sort your minerals into two groups: those with a visible crystal structure, and those without. Draw what you see in your Science Notebook.

2. Bend a chenille stem into a shape you like: a snowflake, a star, a circle, and so on. Tie it to a piece of string and the other end to a pencil.

3. Combine 250 ml of boiling water with borax, one spoonful at a time, until your solution is saturated (until no more borax will dissolve in the water when you stir).

4. Add 2-3 drops of food coloring to the borax water and stir.

5. Pour the borax water into a jar. Place your chenille stem into the jar with the pencil laid across the top of the jar so that the chenille stem is suspended above the bottom of the jar, completely in the liquid.

6. Let the solution sit overnight. Remove your crystals from the jar and examine them with a magnifying glass. Draw a sketch of what you see in your Science Notebook.

🙂🙂🙂 EXPERIMENT: Make a Geode

WARNING: This experiment uses boiling water. Be careful!

For this activity, you will need:

- Egg shell halves, cleaned of egg
- School glue
- Paintbrush
- Borax
- Water, boiling
- 50 ml or larger graduated cylinder
- 100 ml or larger beaker
- Food coloring (optional)
- Small dish
- Magnifying glass

A geode is a hollow rock which has mineral crystals growing inside it. You may want to look up some image of geodes to see what they look like. In this experiment, you will simulate how crystals grow inside a hollow rock.

1. Paint the inside of the clean egg shell halves with glue. Sprinkle borax directly onto the wet glue so it coats the inside of the egg shell. Let it dry for an hour.

2. Measure out 60 ml of boiling water into a beaker. Add

Rocks

borax to the boiling water, one spoonful at a time until the solution is saturated (you can get no more borax to dissolve). Add food coloring, if desired. Let the solution cool for 30 minutes.

3. Set your egg shell half into a small dish, just larger than your egg shell. Pour the saturated borax solution over the egg shell until it is completely submerged.

4. Let the egg shell sit for several days. Check each day to see how well your crystals are growing. Once they are to your satisfaction, remove the egg shell from the solution and set it out to dry. Examine your crystals with a magnifying glass and talk about how crystals form.

Igneous

😊 😊 😊 EXPLORATION: The Rock Cycle

For this activity, you will need:

- "The Rock Cycle" and "The Rock Cycle Answers" from the Printable Pack (choose between simple and advanced)
- One example each of an igneous rock, sedimentary rock, and metamorphic rock
- Science Notebook, including 5-step cycle printable

The rock cycle describes how each of the three types of rocks - **igneous**, **sedimentary**, and **metamorphic** - are related to each other.

When rocks are pushed deep under the surface of the earth, they may melt into magma. If magma is pushed near or above the surface, then it will cool into igneous rock. Igneous rock exposed to the surface with temperature changes, wind, and water may break down into smaller

Memorization Station

Memorize the three types of rock and their definitions.

Igneous: rocks that solidify from magma

Sedimentary: rocks that form from sediment deposited by water or wind

Metamorphic: rocks that are transformed by heat or pressure (or both) deep in the crust

Writer's Workshop

Write a children's story from the point of view of a rock going through the rock cycle.

Include illustrations and read it to a younger child.

Fabulous Fact

The word "igneous" comes from the Latin for fire.

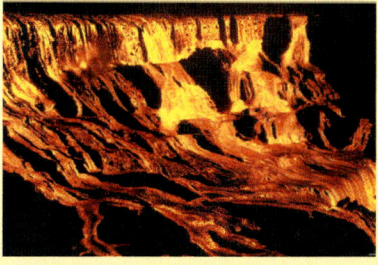

When this lava from Kilauea, Hawaii cools, it will become brand new rock.

Earth & Space

pieces of sediment.

If those sediments are compressed, they may form sedimentary rocks. Then, if either igneous or sedimentary rocks are subjected to pressure and heat under the surface of the earth, they may transform into metamorphic rock.

Additional Layer

Your kids may enjoy making a crayon rock cycle on a large sheet of butcher paper.

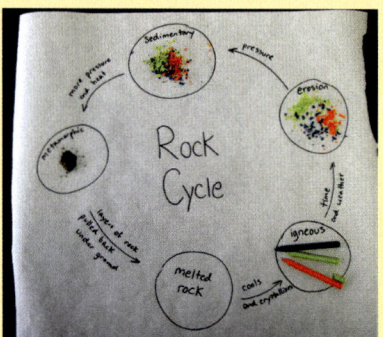

Use crayons to show the different stages of the rock cycle. Solid crayons represent igneous rock, then grate them to show erosion, gently press them together to show sedimentary and then heat and squeeze them to show metamorphic.

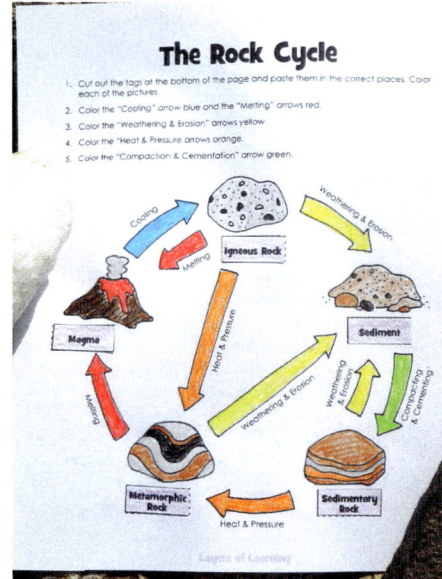

1. Fill out one of "The Rock Cycle" printables, either the simple cycle or the more advanced version.

2. Examine your three rock samples. Notice as many details about them as possible. Can you identify which is igneous, which is sedimentary, and which is metamorphic?

3. Place the three samples on the correct places on top of "The Rock Cycle" printable. Talk through the process of how rocks can move through the rock cycle. How does the rock cycle relate to plate tectonics?

4. If you purchased the Science Notebook, there are "cycle" printables included. Find a 5-step cycle printable. Use it to draw and label the rock cycle in your Science Notebook.

Memorization Station

Mafic: rocks that are dense and dark in color

Felsic: rocks that are lighter in color and less dense

Fabulous Fact

Most of the ocean floor is made of mafic rock: basalt and gabbro. Most of the continental crust is made of felsic rock, especially granite.

Oceanic crust is denser than continental crust and that is why oceanic plates sink beneath continental crust at the edges, making earthquake and volcano zones on the earth.

😊 😊 EXPLORATION: Mafic & Felsic

For this activity, you will need:

- "Formation of Mafic and Felsic Rock" from the Printable Pack
- Colored pencils

Mafic rocks are high in magnesium, iron, calcium, and sodium. The word "mafic" is made up the first two letters of magnesium and from the Latin spelling of iron (ferric). Mafic

Rocks

rocks are dense and dark in color. These rocks are formed from magma that is recently melted in places where the crust is spreading, mostly on the ocean floor. Basalt and gabbro are two common mafic rocks.

Felsic rocks are made of lighter elements like silicon, oxygen, aluminum, and potassium. The word "felsic" is made up of letters from feldspar and silica, the most common minerals in these rocks. They are lighter in color and less dense. The most common felsic rock is granite.

Some rocks are partially mafic and partially felsic. They are called intermediate rocks.

Deep inside the earth, the rock is melted and flowing, and gravity is still at work. Even deeper inside the earth, the hot rock is under so much pressure that it seems solid, but it does flow slowly - just centimeters per year. It flows in convection cycles, with deep materials being brought near the surface where the pressure is relieved enough that the rock can become truly liquid. The lighter materials, silicas and feldspars, float to the top near the upper mantle. The heavier materials, like iron and magnesium, sink back toward the center of the earth. That is why Earth's core is iron, all the heavy stuff has been sinking for a long time.

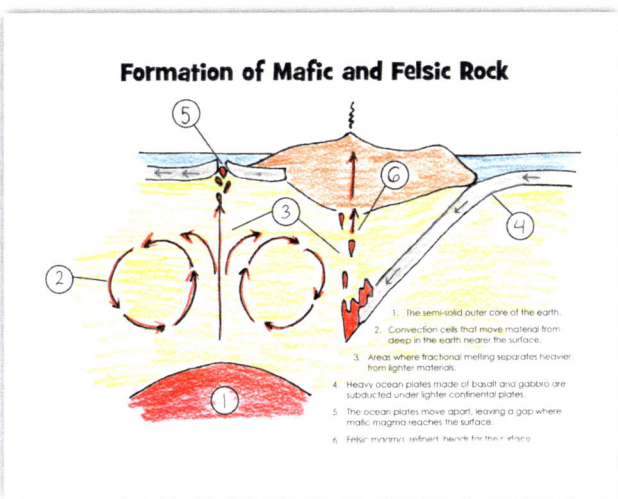

1. Read the information above out loud and color the "Formation of Mafic and Felsic Rock" sheet, placing the correct numbers into the circles using the descriptions. The answers are above.

2. Add this page to the Science section of your Layers of Learning Notebook.

😊 😊 **EXPLORATION: How Igneous Rocks Form**
For this activity, you will need:

- Book or video about igneous rocks

Additional Layer

There are four families of igneous rock:

- Periodite
- Basalt-Gabbro
- Andesite-Diorite
- Granite-Ryolite

Find examples from each of these families, either actual rocks or images of rocks, and make a display explaining the characteristics of each family.

Additional Layer

As magma cools, it goes through a process called fractional crystallization.

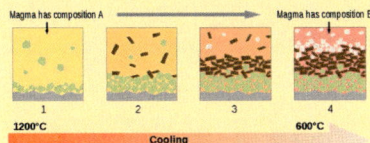

Minerals crystallize out at different temperatures and pressures. The exact conditions, including pressure, temperature, and the presence of water will lead to different types of rock being formed, even if you started with the exact same magma.

Older students can research more about the specific ways that rocks form from magma.

Fabulous Fact

Basalt is an extrusive rock, while gabbro is intrusive. The difference in these rocks is based on where they formed, not what minerals they are made of. They have the same chemical composition.

Earth & Space

Fabulous Fact

Today, all igneous rock is produced through tectonic forces when old plate material is dragged under the surface, melted, and then reformed into new rock.

When the baby earth was first cooling enough to form a crust though, there couldn't have been tectonic forces creating continental or oceanic crust. There were no plates.

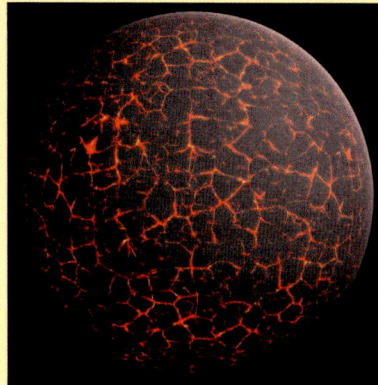

How did two distinct types of crust form, one perfect to act as basins for an ocean and the other perfect to act as higher ground for plants and animals to colonize?

No one knows.

A NASA scientist, Dr. Tim Johnson, has a hypothesis. He believes that a multistage process of magma solidifying, melting, refining, and then solidifying again and again eventually created the right chemical composition for the continental crust.

Memorization Station

Magma: hot molten rock found under the surface of the crust

Lava: hot molten rock on the surface of the crust

- "How Igneous Rocks Form" from the Printable Pack
- Colored pencils or markers

When magma cools, it forms igneous rocks. Magma can cool above the surface, extrusive rock, or beneath the surface of the earth, intrusive rock.

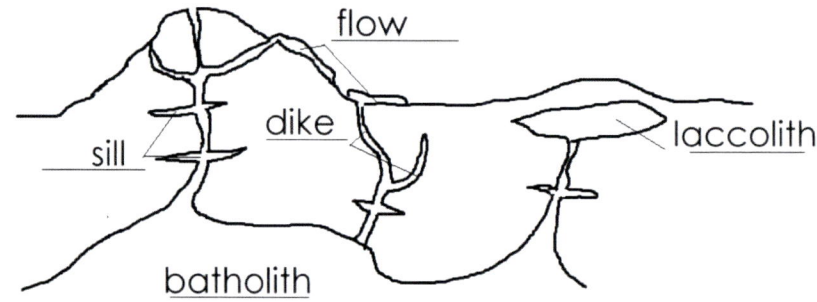

1. Read a book or watch a video about igneous rocks.
2. Read the paragraph from the "How Igneous Rocks Form" printable. Label the diagram, then color it.
3. Put the sheet in the Science section of your Layers of Learning Notebook.

🙂 **EXPLORATION: Make Your Own "Magma"**

For this activity, you will need:

- Liquid starch
- White school glue
- Bowl & spoon for mixing
- Food coloring
- Science Notebook

Scientists use the term **magma** for molten rock that is underground. **Lava** is molten rock that breaks through the earth's surface. Magma is very viscous; it doesn't flow easily. After it breaks the surface, there is a lot less pressure, so lava can sometimes flow more quickly.

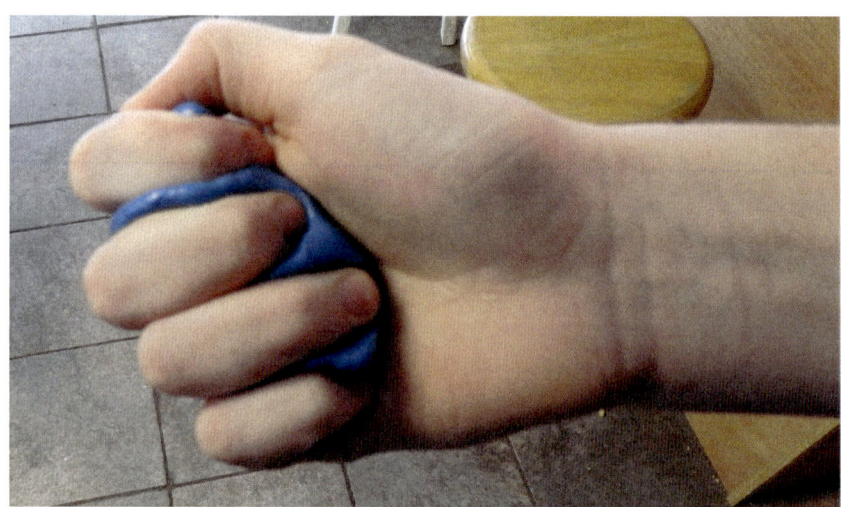

Rocks

1. Add 125 ml glue and 60 ml liquid starch to a bowl.
2. Add red food coloring, a little at a time, until it is a shade you like. Stir the mixture with a spoon. You will have to switch to kneading with your hands as it thickens.
3. The putty you made, like magma, is very viscous. If you hold it in your hand it doesn't flow much, but if you squeeze it in your fist, it will squish out between your fingers.
4. Write down what you did and draw a picture in your Science Notebook. Record your observations and thoughts on the viscosity of magma, how it flows, and the differences between lava and magma.

🙂🙂🙂 **EXPERIMENT: Textures of Igneous Rocks**

WARNING: This experiment uses boiling water. Be careful.

For this activity, you will need:

- Sugar
- Water
- Saucepan
- Stove or hot plate
- Two small bowls and a small plate
- Fridge and freezer
- Science Notebook

Igneous rocks have different textures depending on the conditions as they were cooling. If lava cools slowly, crystals have time to form. When crystals are big enough to be visible to the naked eye, we say the rock has a phaneritic texture. If lava cools a bit faster, fewer crystals have time to form. They are only visible with magnification; we call that an aphanitic texture. If lava cools very rapidly, then there are no crystals at all; you get glass.

1. Combine 60 ml of water with 215 g of sugar in a saucepan. Bring it to a hard boil. Remove from heat.

Fabulous Fact

Mafic lava is runnier than felsic lava. Trapped air can make its way out of mafic lava more easily than out of felsic lava. If you've ever tried to boil a thick tomato sauce on the stove top, you've seen how explosive a thick felsic lava can be. Mafic lava flows are usually quieter.

Fabulous Fact

Pahoehoe and a'a are two varieties of lava flows.

Pahoehoe results in smooth, hardened basaltic rock because the lava is less viscous and hotter than a'a.

A'a results in rough basalt surfaces.

Pahoehoe and a'a are Hawaiian words.

In this picture you can see a smooth, pillowy pahoehoe flow over the top of a rough a'a flow.

You might enjoy watching YouTube videos of these lava flows so you can see them form.

Earth & Space

Additional Layer

When rock is laid in layers, the oldest rocks will always be the bottom layer.

This is the law of superposition, first defined by William Smith, an English geologist. Smith produced the first ever geological map showing the underlying rock beneath all of Britain.

This photo of a rock formation in Norway shows layers of rock, one laid down on top of the other. The oldest rocks must be on the bottom.

Write the law of superposition and its definition in your Science Notebook.

Make a model of superposition with scissors, glue, and construction paper.

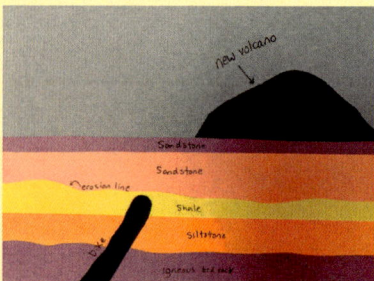

Number the rock in the order it must have formed. What about the igneous dike?

2. Pour hot sugar water onto the plate to make a thin layer. Place this in the fridge.

3. Pour the remaining sugar water in roughly equal amounts into the two bowls. Place one bowl in the freezer and leave the other one on the counter.

4. Let it sit six hours to overnight.

5. Compare the textures in the three dishes. Which cooled fastest and which cooled slowest? How can you tell? Write about the results of your experiment in your Science Notebook.

Sedimentary

🙂🙂🙂 **EXPERIMENT: Settling Sediments**

For this activity, you will need:

- Clear 2-liter bottle or quart size jar with lid
- Funnel
- Sand and rocks from outside with lots of tiny rocks and sand or clay (not just organic matter)
- Water
- Science Notebook

When **sediment** settles to the bottom of a lake or the ocean, it settles in layers.

1. Put the sand and rocks in the bottle or jar with a funnel. You want the sand and rocks to fill about a quarter of the bottle. Fill the bottle with water about 3/4 full.

Rocks

2. Next, predict what you think will happen if you shake it up and then let it sit. Write down your hypothesis In your Science Notebook. Give the page a title, add it to your table of contents, and then write down the procedure and materials.

3. Give the bottle a good shake to get the contents thoroughly mixed.

4. Let your sediment settle for a full 24 hours without disturbing the bottle. Record the results and as many observations as you can come up with.

🙂 🙂 🙂 **EXPERIMENT: Make a Sedimentary Rock**

For this activity, you will need:

- Sand
- Clay (from outside, not the kind you do art with)
- Small pebbles
- Epsom salts
- Disposable cups
- Warm tap water
- Craft sticks
- Science Notebook

Sedimentary rocks are made up of small pieces of sand, silt, clay, and marine shells. The sediment primarily comes from weathering of igneous rocks. Rivers carry the sediment down to lakes or to the ocean where it settles down to the bottom along with shells of marine animals. The weight of the water and layers of sediment press down on the deposits. Water is squeezed between and through the spaces between the grains, leaving behind crystalline material which cements the grains together. Calcite,

Memorization Station

Sediment: solid material that is moved and deposited in a new location

Sediment can be made of minerals, rocks, plants, and animals. It can be tiny, like sand, or giant, like a boulder.

Deep Thoughts

There is a growing movement to move away from coal as a source of energy. Burning coal causes carbon dioxide and other waste to be released into the atmosphere. On the other hand, coal is inexpensive, many people rely on it for jobs, and using coal has become cleaner than it once was. So, there is a public controversy. Public controversies become political, with one side trying to force the other side to their way of thinking.

Scientific controversies are different. Scientists definitely want to win arguments, but they rely on data, experimentation, and formal debates in research journals and meetings. As evidence persuades more scientists to one side, the other arguments fade away.

But science can't tell us what is ethical or right to do.

Compare the difference between public and scientific controversies.

Earth & Space

quartz, and silica are all common cements in sedimentary rocks.

Mostly, this process is slow and continuous, building up little bit by little bit over the years. But sometimes, a big flood event can carry and deposit large amounts of sediment very quickly.

1. Mix sand, clay, and pebbles in any proportions you like. Experiment with this, making some mixtures only sand, some clay and pebbles, and so on. Put the mixtures into disposable cups so the cups are about a quarter full.

2. Record your experiment in your Science Notebook. Don't forget to give your page a title and add it to the table of contents.

3. Label your cups with letters like "A" and "B." Write down the labels and what they mean in your Science Notebook.

4. Dissolve Epsom salts into warm tap water until no more will dissolve. Then pour the salt water into each half of the cups until the water is just at the level of the sand and pebbles. Pour plain water into the remainder of the cups.

5. Let the cups dry in a warm place for a week or until the water is evaporated.

6. Carefully remove the "rocks" from the cups and let them dry for another day. Keep track of the labels of your cups. Test the rocks to see if they are firm or not. What did you discover?

☺ ☺ ☺ EXPERIMENT: Dissolving Limestone

For this activity, you will need:

- Limestone rock (find one outside, buy one from a craft supplier, or use chalk, which is a kind of limestone)
- Vinegar
- Clear jar or beaker
- Science Notebook

Limestone is a type of sedimentary rock made from fragments of marine organisms, like coral and mollusks.

1. Put your limestone in a clear jar or beaker.

2. In your Science Notebook, record your hypothesis of what you think will happen when vinegar, an acid, is added to the limestone.

3. Pour vinegar over the limestone until it is covered with

Additional Layer

Coal is a sedimentary rock made mostly of materials that were once living. Plants in a wetland die, sink down to the bottom of the swamp, decompose, and then are covered by more rotting vegetation, over and over. The vegetation is compacted under layers of mud and sand sediment, pushed deeper and deeper. Lignite coal is brownish black and often has fossils of plants remaining in it. Bituminous coal results from lignite coal being buried even deeper with more pressure. Bituminous coal is darker, shiny, and has very few fossils. Anthracite coal, a metamorphic form of coal, is even deeper, glassy, and very hard, with no fossils remaining.

This is a miner holding a piece of bituminous coal. Photo by Peabody Energy, CC by SA 3.0

Purchase two or more types of coal to compare the samples. Use the Mohs hardness test and a magnifying glass to inspect the samples closely.

Deep Thoughts

Fossils are found in sedimentary rock, rarely in metamorphic rock, and never in igneous rock.

Why do you think that is?

Rocks

liquid. Observe and record the results.

Limestone reacts and dissolves in acids. All rainwater is slightly acidic (not nearly as acidic as vinegar, though) so limestone deposits often form caves and karst landscapes. The Rock of Gibraltar and the White Cliffs of Dover are both limestone formations. So are the Mammoth Caves in Kentucky. Water seeps through the soil, dissolving rock, then depositing it again to make the formations you find in caves.

😊 😊 😊 EXPERIMENT: Classifying Sedimentary Rocks

For this activity, you will need:

- "Classification of Sedimentary Rocks" from the Printable Pack (and provided answer key)
- Scissors
- Glue stick
- Rocks you have collected or a purchased rock set
- Paper to make tags for your rocks

There are two main types of sedimentary rock: clastic and chemical. Clastic rocks are made of bits of other rocks that have been eroded down and then re-cemented together under pressure. Chemical rocks are made of once-living things, like plants or seashells.

1. Cut the tags from the bottom of the "Classification of Sedimentary Rocks" worksheet. Paste the tags in the correct places on the worksheet, using the key below as a guide.

2. Now, sort through your rock collection. Do you have any sedimentary rocks in your collection? Use the flow chart to determine which types of sedimentary rocks you have and sort them by type.

Expedition

Devils Tower National Monument is in Wyoming, USA. In an area formed of sandstone from the bed of an ancient sea, a tower of harder, erosion-resistant sandstone rises.

Take a virtual expedition at the National Park website.

Additional Layer

If you have a microscope, put some rocks under it. Under a microscope you can see the individual grains and many more of the colors that are in minerals and rocks.

Additional Layer

Physical weathering involves the effects of water and wind. Chemical weathering involves chemical reactions that break up rock.

Carbon dioxide dissolved in rainwater can cause rocks to weaken, making them more susceptible to physical weathering.

Design an experiment with rock samples, carbonated water, and the MOH's hardness test to see how chemical weathering affects different types of rocks.

Are all types of rocks equally affected?

Earth & Space

Additional Layer

Gneiss (pronounced "nice") has coarse grained pieces that are visible to the naked eye. The minerals making up gneiss can vary widely and have nothing to do with classification as gneiss.

Photo taken in Montana USA by James St. John, CC by SA 2.0

Gneiss is a foliated rock with bands of minerals forming layers. The layers are often wavy or bent and folded.

Make a model of gneiss with several layers of colored play dough. Cut your play dough model in half to see your gneiss layers.

Additional Layer

You could do an entire unit just on caves! Learn more about caves, how they are formed, cave formations, mineral resources within them, and wildlife that lives them.

You can also learn more about cave paintings within *Layers of Learning Art Beginnings: Prehistoric Art*.

😊 😊 😊 EXPEDITION: Visit a Cave

For this activity, you will need:

- Books or videos about caves
- Information about a cave near you
- A day for a field trip

1. Read a book or watch a video about caves.
2. Find a cave within driving distance. Make arrangements to visit the cave. Make sure you look for the things you learned about caves. Can you see water dripping? Are there any animals or signs of animals? Are there cave formations like stalactites and stalagmites? If you will have a guide in the cave, come prepared with a question or two to ask the guide.

Metamorphic

😊 😊 😊 EXPLORATION: Metamorphic Candy Bar Model

For this activity, you will need:

- Candy bar with layers, like a Snickers with layers of peanuts, chocolate and nougat
- Cutting board or other flat object
- Knife
- Plastic wrap
- Science Notebook

Metamorphic rocks change from igneous or sedimentary to a whole new type of rock when they are subjected to heat

Rocks

and pressure under the surface of the earth.

1. Cut a candy bar in half so you can see all the layers. In your Science Notebook, draw a detailed diagram of the candy bar with all of the different layers labeled.

2. Wrap the candy bar loosely with plastic wrap and squish it under a cutting board, pressing down hard to get it as flat as possible.

3. Peel the plastic off and draw a new diagram of the candy bar. Can you still see layers?

    The candy bar is made of the same ingredients as before, but the way it looks and feels is different. It is denser and more compact. This is what happens with metamorphic rocks as well.

😊 😊 😊 EXPERIMENT: Foliation & Regional Metamorphism

For this activity, you will need:

- Play dough or salt dough (1/2 cup warm water, 1/4 cup salt, 4 tablespoons cooking oil, 2 cups flour, food dye)
- Glitter
- Cutting board
- Science Notebook

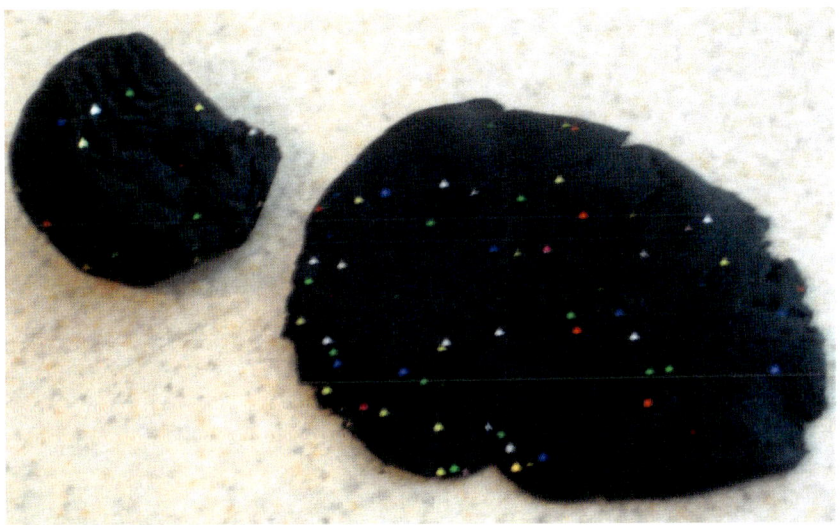

Foliation means minerals in a rock are oriented parallel to one another. Igneous rocks will usually have haphazard minerals facing all directions while metamorphic rocks often have strong foliation, with all the minerals pointed in the same direction.

Regional metamorphism is caused by pressure. Two plates from the earth's crust push against one another, building up enormous pressure and compressing and bending the rock, forming metamorphic rock. Metamorphic rocks of this type

Fabulous Fact

This is quartzite, a metamorphic rock that formed from quartz sandstone.

Photo by zarmel, CC by SA 3.0

When you see folds like this, the rock is almost certainly metamorphic.

Memorization Station

Foliation: the parallel arrangement of mineral grains that give rocks a striped appearance

Regional metamorphism: occurs when rocks are heated by nearby magma

For example, metamorphic rock is formed when tectonic plates collide and the pressure compresses and bends the rock.

Contact metamorphism: occurs deep in the earth where pressure builds up and are able to create a chemical change in rocks

For example, when rock is exposed to intense heat from magma under the surface of the earth, it creates metamorphic rock

Earth & Space

Fabulous Fact

Slate is a foliated metamorphic rock that forms from shale. It is made of very fine grains and breaks easily along flat planes called cleavage lines.

Photo by Si Griffiths, CC by SA 3.0

This slate is on a beach in Cornwall, Great Britain. You can easily see the cleavage lines.

Additional Layer

To help you remember that metamorphic rocks are formed with either contact or regional metamorphism, complete the "How Are Metamorphic Rocks Formed?" printable from the Printable Pack.

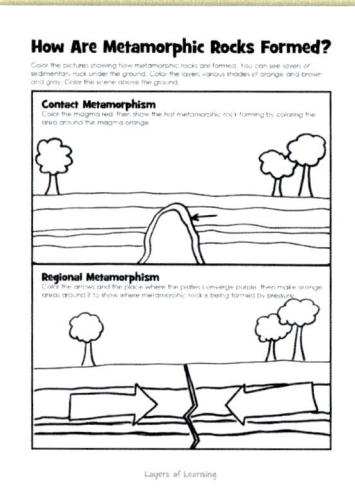

will have strong foliation; you can see the layers and often those layers are bent and folded.

1. Knead a spoonful of glitter into a batch of play dough so the glitter is spread all through. Rocks that have formed without great pressure will have this type of foliation, with the minerals pointing all directions.

2. Next flatten the play dough by squishing it under a cutting board with your hands pressed down on top. Observe the glitter in the dough. After pressing it hard, the glitter pieces all orient in the same direction, they have parallel foliation.

3. Label a page in your Science Notebook "Foliation" and add it to your table of contents. Draw a picture of what you did. Label the picture and describe what happens to the minerals under pressure. Write a definition of regional metamorphism in your Science Notebook.

😊 😊 😊 EXPLORATION: Contact Metamorphism

WARNING: This experiment uses boiling water. Be careful.

For this activity, you will need:

- Medium glass bowl
- Narrow glass jar or beaker
- 3 eggs
- Kettle or pan with a lid
- Water
- Stove or a hot plate

Contact metamorphism is caused by intense heat, usually from magma. An intrusion of magma forces its way up

Rocks

through the layers of rock. All of the existing rock around this intrusion will be heated. If the rocks melt, they become magma, but if they just get hot enough to become partially plastic and then cool and reform, they become metamorphic rock. The heat causes chemical changes and recrystallization of the rock's minerals.

1. Separate egg whites and yolks. Break an egg in half and tip the yolk from one half of the shell to the other over a medium glass bowl. The white will fall into the bowl. You can put your yolks in another bowl. The egg white represents existing rock deep underground.

2. Heat water to boiling in a kettle or a covered pot.

3. Place the narrow jar or beaker in the center of the bowl with the egg whites. Pour boiling hot water into the beaker. The boiling water represents an intrusion of magma.

4. Observe the egg whites closely. Did the color, structure, or any other factor of the egg whites change when heated by contact with the boiling water? This is similar to the way that heat from magma underground forms metamorphic rock.

😊 😊 😊 **EXPERIMENT: Rock Identification Lab**

For this activity, you will need:

- Rocks you have collected or a rock sample kit
- Magnifying glass
- Butcher paper
- Colored markers
- Vinegar

Before you begin this experiment, read about igneous, sedimentary, and metamorphic rocks and how they form.

Fabulous Fact

Because metamorphic rocks are more rare, they also tend to be more valuable. They are used as building materials and ingredients in cosmetics, paint, and lubricants.

shale *slate*

phyllite *schist*

gneiss

Fabulous Fact

The pressure of layers of rock on top of one another is not enough to cause metamorphism. It requires the pressures exerted during mountain building where plates are converging.

Fabulous Fact

This is a metaconglomerate, a conglomerate rock made of pebbles cemented together which has undergone metamorphism.

Photo by Zimbras, CC by SA 2.5

The cement between the pebbles becomes as strong as the pebbles.

Earth & Space

Fabulous Fact

Not all metamorphic rock is foliated. Marble is a metamorphic rock that is not foliated.

This is an ancient sculpture from about AD 200. The statue has survived all these years because it is made of hard, metamorphic marble.

Additional Layer

Some metamorphic rock will continue to change as more and more heat and pressure is applied. For example, shale becomes slate and then phyllite, and then schist, and eventually gneiss when it is exposed to greater and greater amounts of heat and pressure.

Get samples of these types of rock and compare their foliation and grains.

1. Cover a table with butcher paper to protect the surface, then spread out a bunch of rocks that you have collected or purchased.

2. Use magnifying glasses to observe the rocks closely. Find crystals within the rocks, notice the cleavage (how the rocks break), and any other distinctive characteristics.

3. Sort your rocks into families: igneous, sedimentary, and metamorphic, based on your reading.

4. Draw two large circles on the butcher paper with your markers. Label one "mafic" and the other "felsic." Sort your igneous rocks into these two groups. Mafic rocks are igneous rocks rich in magnesium and iron and tend to be darkly colored. Felsic rocks are igneous rocks that are rich in feldspar and quartz and tend to be lightly colored. Mostly light rocks with dark inclusions are considered felsic.

5. Draw some of the rocks in your Science Notebook. Write down some of the characteristics of each rock. If you know the type of rock, then label it with its name.

Weathering & Erosion

With water, wind, and time, rocks break apart in a process called **weathering**. The broken apart material is carried away by water, wind and gravity in a process called **erosion**. Finally, the material is dropped in a new location, where it settles, in a process called **deposition**. These processes are how mountains are worn away into hills, deep canyons are cut through rock, and valleys are scoured out of highlands.

😊 😀 EXPERIMENT: Wind and Water Erosion

For this activity, you will need:

- Sand
- Drinking straw
- Baking sheet or tray
- Disposable cup
- Pencil
- Water

Wind and water can both erode rock. Some types of rock are softer and easier to erode than others, but all rock can be broken down by the weather over time.

1. Make a mound of damp sand in the middle of the baking sheet or tray.

2. Go outside. Blow through a straw at the sand. The "wind" you blow across the sand breaks it down and changes the shape of the hill.

Rocks

3. Poke several holes in the bottom of a disposable cup with a pencil. Fill the cup with water and hold it over the sand hill to make it "rain" on the sand. The water washes away the sand wherever it hits.

😊 😊 😊 **EXPERIMENT: Freezing & Thawing Erosion**
For this activity, you will need:

- Electronic balance
- Chalk
- Freezer
- Clear plastic cups
- Paper plates
- Permanent marker
- Science Notebook
- Book or video about erosion from the Library List or YouTube playlist

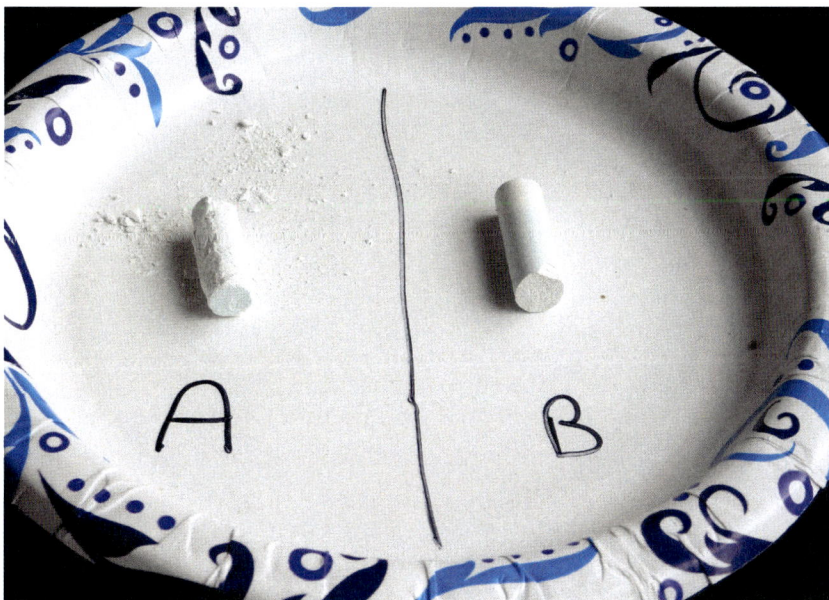

Rocks can absorb water. When they absorb the water and then freeze, the expanding water can break them down

Additional Layer
You can also play with a hose in a sand box to show how a stream of water can easily erode land.

Memorization Station
Weathering: the breaking down of rocks and minerals

Erosion: the movement of sediment from one location to another by means of ice, wind, or water

Deposition: when sediment is dropped or deposited in a new location

Additional Layer
Paint rocks and leave them for others to find. You can simply leave them for people to find around your area just to brighten their day, or you can join an online rock hunting group that posts hashtags and information about where the rocks have traveled.

Earth & Space

Famous Folks

Dr. Rattan Lal won the 2020 World Food Prize for his work in researching and promoting no-till farming, mulching, cover crops, and returning carbon to degraded soils.

Dr. Lal was born into a Pakistani refugee family in a poverty stricken village in India. To escape poverty, the government offered a small scholarship to study at university for students who could remain in the top 5% of their class. He graduated with honors.

He went on to teach soil science at Ohio State University in Columbus, Ohio, USA.

Deep Thoughts

Erosion is a natural process, but human activities have increased soil erosion by approximately ten times the natural rate. In some places, it is closer to forty times the natural rate or even higher.

The end result of advanced soil erosion is desertification; the soil can no longer support plants and the land becomes barren. It also results in damage to waterways.

Discuss the value of healthy soil and how you think its loss could be prevented.

---

into sediments. Chalk is a soft type of limestone rock.

1. Draw a line down the middle of a paper plate. Label one half A and the other half B.

2. Break a piece of chalk in half and drop one half into water, then pull it out after ten seconds. Place the wet chalk on the A side of the plate and the dry chalk on the B side of the plate. Put the plate in the freezer. Set a timer for 30 minutes.

3. While you are waiting, write a "Freezing & Thawing Erosion" header on a page in your Science Notebook and add it to your table of contents. Draw a labeled diagram of your experiment and write down your hypothesis.

4. Read a book or watch a video about erosion.

5. Compare the soaked and dry chalk. Has the freezing of the water helped the chalk to break apart? Which chalk pieces ended up softer? Record your results.

EXPEDITION: Erosion, Weathering, or Deposition

For this activity, you will need:

- "Erosion, Weathering, or Deposition" game from the Printable Pack (3 pages)
- Scissors
- Fly swatters (optional)
- Rock candy (optional) or a sheet of paper to keep score

1. Cut apart the weathering, erosion, and deposition definition cards and place them on a table where everyone can see them and easily reach them. Cut apart the situation cards and place them upside down in a stack.

2. A mentor or players, in turn, will draw a card off the top of the stack and read it. The players will slap the definition they think the card is describing (using fly swatters to do the slapping is fun). The first person to slap the correct definition should get two points. Everyone else who slapped the correct definition should get one point.

3. Keep track of points with a tally on a piece of paper or by giving out pieces of rock candy for each point scored. Play until the cards are all gone.

EXPEDITION: Soil Horizons & Profiles

For this activity, you will need:

Rocks

- "Soil Horizons" from the Printable Pack
- Garden spade
- Area of soil outside where you can dig a big hole
- Science Notebook
- Meter stick
- Colored pencils
- "Soil Profile" cards from the Printable Pack, printed on card stock
- 1" wide double sided carpet tape
- Scissors

If you've ever seen a deep hole or a cut along a roadside, you've noticed that the soil has layers, or horizons. Every area of soil has its own pattern of **soil horizons** and this is called the **soil profile**.

1. Use the "Soil Horizons" printable to learn about the basic horizons. Follow the directions on the worksheet. The answers are down the sheet in this order: **O, A, B, C, D**
2. Print out the "Soil Profile" cards onto card stock. Cut out each card.
3. Go outside to a location where you can dig a deep hole. Alternatively, you can go to a spot where soil horizons are already exposed, like a roadside cut. Dig a hole deep enough to expose the soil horizons. Draw a sketch of what the soil horizons look like in your Science Notebook. Color the soil horizon sketch with colored pencils. Label the layers you can see: O, A, B, C
4. Collect a bit of soil from the A, B, and C layers. Measure from the surface to the deepest point on each layer. Mark these measurements in your sketch in your Science Notebook.
5. Attach a short strip of double-sided carpet tape to a

Memorization Station

Soil horizon: the layers of the soil that are revealed as you dig down from the surface

Soil profile: the pattern of soil horizons in a particular location

Additional Layer

There are two types of rock weathering: physical and chemical.

Physical weathering involves the effects of water and wind.

Chemical weathering involves chemical reactions that break up rocks. Carbon dioxide dissolved in rainwater can cause rocks to weaken, making them more susceptible to physical weathering.

Design an experiment with rock samples, carbonated water, and the Mohs hardness test to see how chemical weathering affects different types of rock.

Fabulous Facts

Erosion causes minerals to be dissolved and carried away in water which is then later taken up into plants and animals. Without erosion and the ability of water to carry minerals, life could not exist. Life needs minerals to function.

Earth & Space

Famous Folks

Vasily Dokuchaev, a Russian scientist, was the first to consider soil as distinct from bedrock and see it as a living natural body worthy of study on its own.

Here is Dokuchaev pictured with a big block of chernozem, a black colored rich soil found in Russia and elsewhere.

He believed soil was affected and formed by much more than the rock it was eroded from. He considered the parent rock, the climate, the plant life, the topography, and the amount of time the soil had to form.

These were revolutionary ideas and formed the basis of modern soil science.

Writer's Workshop

Soil is valuable. So much so that there has been a problem with black market sales of especially fertile soils in the Ukraine, Russia, China, and elsewhere.

Create an INTERPOL wanted poster for an international soil smuggler.

"Soil Profile" card in the long rectangle section. Peel back the tape to expose the sticky to the level of the first layer of soil. Sprinkle some soil from the A layer onto the sticky tape, pressing it firmly. Tap off the excess soil.

6. Peel the tape back further to expose sticky to the bottom of the B layer. Sprinkle some B soil, pressing it firmly. Tap off the excess soil.

7. Peel back the rest of the tape. Sprinkle C soil onto the tape, and press it in firmly. Tap off the excess soil. Glue the cards into your Science Notebook. You can repeat this experiment in other areas to get different soil profiles.

😊 😊 😊 EXPERIMENT: Soil Is a Filter

For this activity, you will need:

- Kitchen funnel
- Clear jar
- Soil from outside
- Powdered drink mix in a dark color

Soil acts as a filter to clean contaminants out of water. This also means that contaminants can be trapped in soil and make their way into the plants people and animals eat. Soil filtering is beneficial, but nonetheless, we need to be careful about what we send into the soil in the first place.

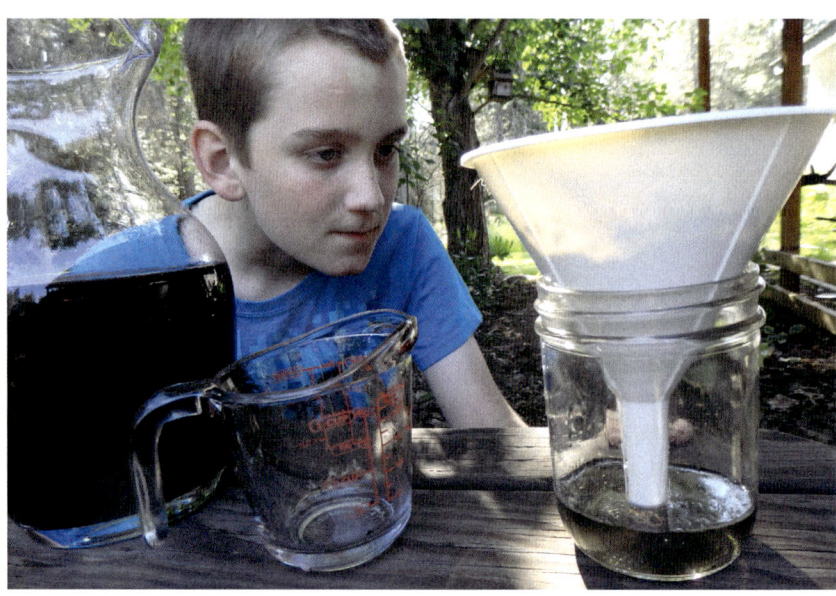

1. Mix powdered drink mix into 1.5 liters of water.
2. Fill the kitchen funnel half full of soil. Place the kitchen funnel into the jar.
3. Pour 120 ml of drink mix into the funnel and allow it to filter down into the jar.
4. Observe the color of the water in the jar and compare it

Rocks

to the original color of the water.

5. Repeat the experiment again with different types of soil or plain sand. You can also try filtering the same water, you collected again to see if repeated filtering removes more pollutants.

😊 😊 😊 **EXPERIMENT: Soil Glue**

For this activity, you will need:

- Two clods of soil, one from an undisturbed spot and one from a garden bed or somewhere soil has been disturbed recently
- Two large clear jars filled with water
- Screen mesh
- Rubber band or metal ring if using a canning jar
- Science Notebook

Soil that is undisturbed contains fungi that produce something called glomalin. Glomalin is like glue that holds the soil particles together.

1. Shape your screen mesh, one for each jar, into a basket that dips down into the water and is secured at the top of the jar with either a metal ring or a rubber band.

2. Set one clod of soil in each mesh basket. Observe the results. Does the undisturbed soil hold together better than the disturbed soil? What does glomalin do to help prevent soil erosion? How do you think glomalin might help plant roots?

3. Draw a labeled sketch of your experiment in your Science Notebook. Record your results.

Famous Folks

Vera Baltz was a Russian soil scientist, born in Saint Petersburg in 1866. She specialized in soil structure, engineering, and road building.

In 1930, she was arrested by the Soviet government who thought she was an anti-government agitator. She spent three years in a Siberian forced labor camp then was released and lived with her niece.

She died of starvation at the age of 76 after giving up her rationed food portions for her young relatives who had none.

Famous Folk

The Mohs Hardness Scale was named after German geologist, Friedrich Mohs.

Earth & Space

Unit Trivia Questions

1. Name the three families of rocks.

   Igneous, Sedimentary, Metamorphic

2. Which type of rock is made from magma?

   a) Igneous

   b) Sedimentary

   c) Metamorphic

3. Explain how rocks are made from minerals.

   Minerals are the building blocks of rocks that combine to make all the rocks on the earth.

4. What causes erosion?

   Weathering from wind and water

5. The hardness of rocks is one way to identify them. This is done with the _____ Mineral Hardness Test.

   Mohs

6. When rocks are deformed and changed from the heat of nearby magma, it is called:

   a) Contact metamorphism

   b) Regional metamorphism

   c) Igneous rock

7. Name the basic steps of the rock cycle in order.

   Magma, igneous rock, sediment, sedimentary rock, metamorphic rock, melting

8. Which of these things is present in soil:

   a) Sediment from rocks

   b) Living things

   c) Air

   d) Water

   e) All of the above

Step 3: Show What You Know

During this unit, choose one of the assignments below to show what you have learned during the unit. Add this work to your Layers of Learning Notebook. You can also use this assignment to show your supervising teacher or your charter school as a sample of what you've been working on in your homeschool, if needed.

There are more ideas for writing assignments in the "Writer's Workshop" sidebars.

🙂 🙂 Coloring or Narration Page

For this activity, you will need:

- "Rocks" from the Printable Pack
- Writing or drawing utensils

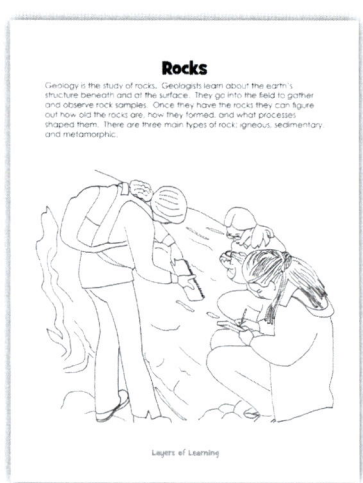

1. Depending on the age and ability of the child, choose either the "Rocks" coloring sheet or the "Rocks" narration page from the Printable Pack.

2. Younger kids can color the coloring sheet as you review some of the things you learned about during this unit. On the bottom of the coloring page, kids can write a sentence about what they learned. Very young children can explain their ideas orally while a parent writes for them.

3. Older kids can write about some of the concepts you learned on the narration page and color the picture as well.

4. Add this to the Science section of your Layers of Learning Notebook.

🙂 🙂 🙂 Science Experiment Write-Up

For this activity, you will need:

- The "Experiment" write-up or "Experiment Report Template" from the Printable Pack

1. Choose one of the experiments you completed during this unit and create a careful and complete experiment write-up for it. Make sure you have included every specific detail of each step so your experiment could be repeated by anyone who wanted to try it.

Rocks

2. Do a careful revision and edit of your write-up, taking it through the writing process, before you turn it in for grading.

😊 😊 😊 Game or Quiz

For this activity, you will need:

- Index cards
- Mineral or rock samples

1. Have everyone gather together and write down your own trivia questions about what you read about, watched, and explored during this unit. Each trivia question should be written on a card with the question and answer.

2. Play a trivia game with the cards. You can also hold up rock or mineral samples and ask questions about what you see. Make special rules if you are playing with multiple ages.

😊 😊 😊 Big Book of Knowledge

For this activity, you will need:

- "Big Book of Knowledge: Rocks" printable from the Printable Pack, printed on card stock
- Writing or drawing utensils
- Big Book of Knowledge

1. Color, draw on, or write on the Big Book of Knowledge page. Record concepts, definitions, and facts you learned during this unit. It's a record of the things you learned and hope to remember. Add the page to your Big Book of Knowledge.

2. Use your Big Book of Knowledge regularly to help you review, quiz, or create games that will help you commit the things you've learned to memory.

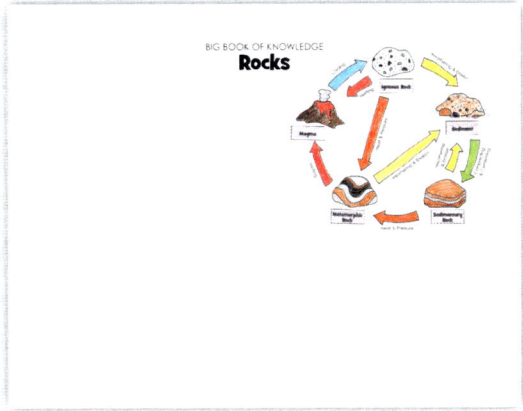

Big Book of Knowledge

The Big Book of Knowledge is a book for you, the mentor, to use as a constant review of all of the things you're learning about. You can use it to quiz your kids or prepare tests or review games. Whenever you learn something in Layers of Learning that you want your kids to remember, add it to your Big Book of Knowledge.

Assemble your Big Book of Knowledge in a binder or with binder rings. Divide it into sections for each subject.

In the Printable Pack for this unit you will find a "Big Book of Knowledge" sheet. You can add this sheet to others you collect or create yourself as you progress through the Layers of Learning curriculum. Customize the Big Book of Knowledge to your family by adding facts and topics that you enjoyed exploring as you were learning.

Visit Layers of Learning online to find more information on how to assemble and use your own Big Book of Knowledge.

You will also find cover and section pages to print along with creative games to play with your Big Book of Knowledge to keep school, even the tests, fun!

Earth & Space

Unit Overview

Key Concepts:
- Fossils are preserved remains that can provide us with clues about things that lived long ago.
- There are several kinds of fossils including permineralization, casts, carbon films, amber, and trace fossils.
- The fossil record is comprised of the clues we can learn about the history of our earth by examining its rock layers, fossils, and more.
- Dinosaurs are just one type of prehistoric animal. We have learned a lot about them by examining their fossil remains.

Vocabulary:
- Fossil
- Paleontology
- Extinct
- Permineralization
- Fossil cast
- Carbon film
- Amber
- Trace fossils
- Strata
- Index fossils
- Paleontologist
- Dinosaur
- Herbivore
- Carnivore
- Omnivore

Theories, Laws, & Hypotheses:
- Extinction Theory
- Law of Superposition
- Alvarez Hypothesis
- Deccan Traps Hypothesis

FOSSILS

Fossils are preserved remains or traces of something that was once living. Footprints, egg shells, leaf imprints, bones, and wood can all become fossils. Enormous trees, gargantuan dinosaurs, tiny insects, and microscopic bacteria can all be found in the fossil record.

The fossil record is comprised of all of the fossils ever found. It is a record of life on Earth, from the earliest to the most recent. The record is mainly preserved in rocks. Fossils can become mineralized into rocks or rocks can bear the traces or imprints of living things. Most fossils are found in sedimentary rocks but, sometimes, they can be seen in metamorphic rocks too.

Paleontologists study fossils and the fossil record to learn about past life on Earth. A paleontologist is part earth scientist and part biologist. Paleontologists try to reconstruct what living things looked like and how they behaved in the past. This is a rapidly growing and changing field as new discoveries challenge what we thought we knew.

Dinosaurs are a large group of vertebrate (backbone) animals that paleontologists study. They are often drawn to look like reptiles, but their legs are attached straight down from the body instead of splayed out sideways like modern reptiles. Today, most paleontologists believe that modern birds are related to dinosaurs because of the way birds' legs are attached to their bodies. Also, birds and dinosaurs both have scales and they both lay eggs. There are some other compelling similarities between bird and dinosaur skeletons too, like large eye sockets and thin, hollow bones. Some newer illustrations of dinosaurs include feathers, though whether certain species had feathers or not is still debatable.

This is an artist's idea of what Deinonychus may have looked like based on the latest research. Old illustrations of dinosaurs never showed feathers and always depicted dinosaurs in drab colors. Image by Fred Wierum, CC by SA 4.0

Fossils

Step 1: Library List

Choose books from your library that go with this topic. Here's a list of some favorites and also a list of search terms so you can utilize what your library offers. Read the books with your kids and/or assign them some to read independently. It is from these books your kids will learn most of the facts they need from this unit.

Search for: fossils, dinosaurs, paleontology

WARNING: All of these books assume evolution and a long timeline of life on earth, unless otherwise stated.

🙂 🙂 🙂 *Encyclopedia of Science* from DK. Read "Fossils" and "Record in the Rocks" on pages 225-227.

🙂 🙂 🙂 *Kingfisher Science Encyclopedia*. Read "Fossils & Geologic Time" on pages 4-5.

🙂 🙂 🙂 *The Usborne Science Encyclopedia*. Read "Life on Earth" on pages 186-187.

🙂 *Fossils Tell of Long Ago* by Aliki. Explains how fossils are records of life, from leaf prints to bones that turned to stone.

🙂 *Digging Up Dinosaurs* by Aliki. Describes the work of paleontologists and how dinosaur bones get from the ground to a museum.

🙂 *Dinosaur Lady: The Daring Discoveries of Mary Anning, the First Paleontologist.* A biography of paleontologist Mary Anning that includes lots of facts about dinosaurs along with the story of her life.

🙂 🙂 *The Dinosaur Book* by DK. Full of full-color illustrations and facts, this is a highly browsable book. Includes life before dinosaurs as well as the emergence of mammals.

🙂 🙂 *Science Comics: Dinosaurs: Fossils and Feathers* by MK Reed. Real science told in graphic format. Perfect for visual learners. Includes the history of paleontology and how dinosaurs become fossils.

🙂 *Dinosaur Mummies: Beyond Bare-Bone Fossils* by Kelly Milner Halls. Recently, paleontologists discovered preserved soft tissues of dinosaurs. This book tells about it.

🙂 *Fossil Hunter: How Mary Anning Changed the Science of Prehistoric Life* by Cheryl Blackford. This is a biography about a pioneer fossil hunter and scientist.

🙂 🙂 *Dinosaurs: The Grand Tour* by Keiron Pim. Lots of illustrations, size comparison charts, fast facts, and plenty of info on dozens of dinosaur species and families. This is a

Family School Levels

The colored smilies in this unit help you choose the correct levels of books and activities for your child.
🙂 = Ages 6-9
🙂 = Ages 10-13
🙂 = Ages 14-18

On the Web

For videos, web pages, games, and more to add to this unit, visit the Earth & Space Resources at Layers-of-Learning.com.

You will find a link to video playlists, web links, and more.

Bookworms

If you're looking for a family read-aloud, we'd like to suggest this one.

The Bone Wars by Katherine Lasky is about a young man, Thad, who gets caught up in the frantic search for fossils in the American West.

It's based on real, hair-raising, events from history.

125

Earth & Space

Teaching Tip
When you study fossils, you will inevitably be presented with Old Earth theories. Whether you believe in an old or young Earth, you can still teach your family about the theories some scientists believe so they can have a good understanding of how scientists are always looking to explain the things we presently see by theorizing about past events. Use those sources and explorations as a starting place for a discussion about your beliefs.

Memorization Station
Fossil: a remnant or trace of a deceased ancient organism

Paleontology: the study of fossilized animals and plants from the past

Extinct: when a species dies out completely and there are no more left on Earth

book to browse through more than read cover to cover.

😊😊 *The Fossil Book* by Gary Parker. Told from a creationist point of view, this book explains how fossils are created and what they reveal about life on Earth. Includes young earth dates for fossils and explores the differences between evolutionist and creationist views.

😊😊 *Dinosaur Bones And What They Tell Us* by Rob Colson. Starts with things that lived before the dinosaurs and moves through the timeline in chronological order. It includes sea creatures and mammals as well as dinosaurs. Excellent illustrations.

😊 *Weird Dinosaurs: The Strange New Fossils Challenging Everything We Thought We Knew* by John Pickrell. Contains some of the latest findings in paleontology and how our perception of what dinosaurs were has changed so drastically. Well-written and entertaining.

😊 *Remarkable Creatures* by Tracy Chevalier. A historical novel about the life of Mary Anning, a pioneering paleontologist. Really highlights the struggles of being a woman scholar in the 1800s as well as shines a light on the beginnings of this science.

😊 *Sea Dragons: Predators of the Prehistoric Oceans* by Richard Ellis. All about the sea creatures that existed at the same time dinosaurs were walking the earth.

Step 2: Explore
Choose a few hands-on explorations from this section to work on as a family. They should be appealing activities that will create mental hooks so your kids remember the information in the unit. Save the rest of the explorations for the next time you do this unit in four years when your kids are older. You can also read the sidebars together and explore some little rabbit trails.

This unit includes printables. See the introduction for instructions on retrieving your Printable Pack.

How Fossils Form

The study of **fossils** is called **paleontology**. Paleontologists study **extinct**, no longer living, animals and plants. It is a relatively new branch of science which began in the late 1700s. Paleontology is a vibrant area of research today with tons of new information coming to light and old hypotheses being refined constantly.

Fossils

😊 😊 😊 **EXPLORATION: How Fossils Form**

For this activity, you will need:

- Video about how fossils form from this unit's YouTube playlist
- Science Notebook
- Crayons, markers, or colored pencils

Most of the animals that die never become fossils. It takes very special conditions to allow a fossil to form. Generally, if an animal dies and then is quickly buried by sand or mud that is carried by water, it has the potential to become a fossil.

1. Watch a video about the formation of fossils. While you are watching, take notes in your Science Notebook.

2. Draw a picture of the conditions needed for a fossil to form. Nearby, add some things that would likely happen to prevent the fossil from forming if the animal isn't quickly buried.

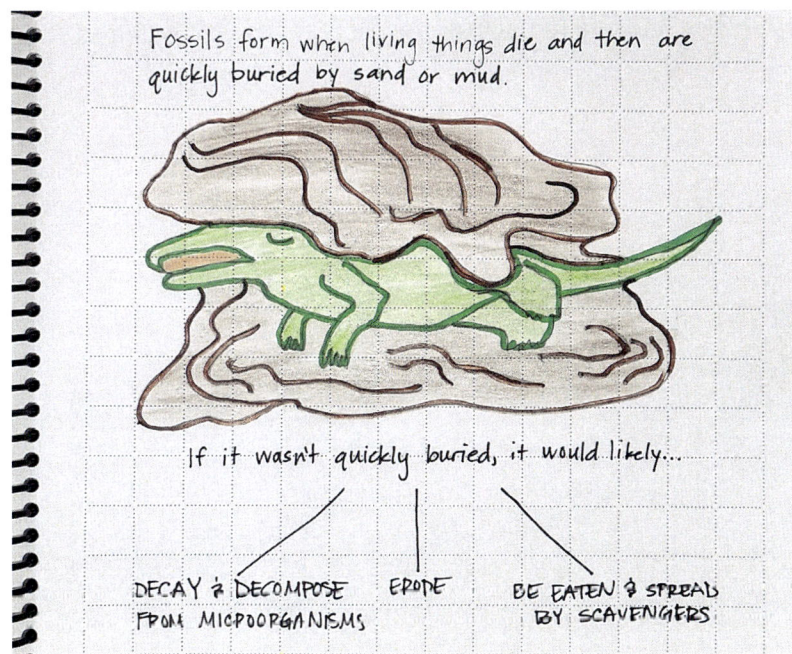

😊 😊 😊 **EXPLORATION: Fossilization Game**

For this activity, you will need:

- Video about how fossils form from this unit's YouTube playlist
- "Fossilization Game" from the Printable Pack
- Colored pencils or crayons
- Small objects to use as a place markers
- Die
- Science Notebook

Famous Folks

A young girl named Mary Anning collected fossils on the shore near her home to sell in her family's shop.

When she grew up, her interest in fossils remained. She became a respected expert on fossils and discovered many species.

Fabulous Fact

Early mammal fossils are rarer than dinosaur fossils because early mammals were small and didn't live on flood plains. Flood plains are the best possible place for an animal to be if it is to become a fossil because it could be buried quickly by flood waters and mud.

Image by FunkMonk (Michael B. H.), CC by SA 3.0.

This is a Morganucodon, the earliest known mammal. First discovered in Wales, it appeared in the late Triassic and was just 10 cm long.

Earth & Space

Famous Folks

Georges Cuvier was a French naturalist. He spent most of his career comparing living animals with fossilized ones.

He is known as the father of paleontology.

Bookworms

Finding Esme by Suzanne Crowley is about a twelve-year-old girl who finds dinosaur bones on her family's Texas farm.

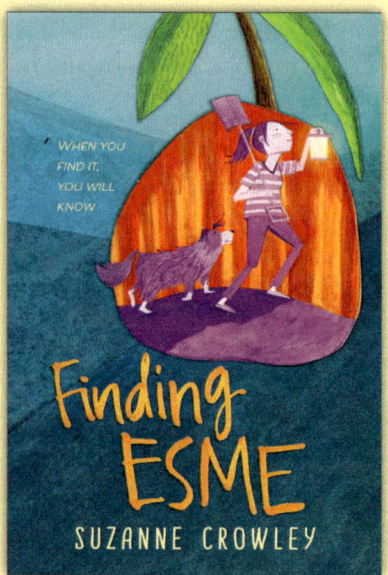

It's an adventure and mystery with a little dose of magic thrown in.

For ages 8 to 12.

Most plants and animals decompose and no trace is left behind after they die. Sometimes though, if conditions are just right, a fossil can form. First, it is more likely for something with hard body parts like bones or a shell to become fossilized than something with only soft body parts. Second, the animal or plant must be covered by sediment quickly and completely. If they are not, then scavengers, insects, and bacteria will break the body down. Third, the sediment the living thing is buried in must be wet so water can carry minerals in to replace the bone or shell. Finally, the sediment must become compressed under further layers and become rock.

Most fossils are of sea creatures with hard shells. The next most common are plants, which fall into still ponds or swamps. The least common fossils are of land animals. Land animals are much less likely to die and fall into a watery place and be covered quickly with mud or sand.

Because it is so hard to become a fossil and then be discovered, there are likely thousands and thousands of species that we have never found evidence of at all.

1. Watch a video about how fossils form. While you are watching, color the game board any way you like.

2. Each player should have a small piece to act as his or her marker. Place the markers on the START space.

3. Take turns rolling a die. Move your marker the number of spaces shown on the die. Follow the directions on the spaces. The first one to the end becomes a fossil and wins!

4. Add a passage in your Science Notebook about the conditions required for fossilization to occur.

Fossils

😊 😊 😊 **EXPLORATION: Making Fossils**

WARNING: Be careful not to get burned on the hot water!

For this activity, you will need:

- Kitchen sponge (the cheap cellulose kind is perfect)
- Scissors
- Epsom salts
- Tap water
- Pot and stove for boiling the water
- Spoon
- Shallow dish

To become a fossil, many organisms go through a process called **permineralization**. Minerals dissolved in water are carried into all the spaces in organic tissue, like inside of the cells. The minerals crystallize and create a perfect cast of the organism, right down to the cellular level. Most dinosaur bones are permineralized as are petrified wood and many sea creatures.

1. Cut your sponge into a bone shape, just for fun.

2. Make a saturated solution of Epsom salts and water. Heat 2 cups of water to boiling in a saucepan. Add a little bit of Epsom salts at a time, stirring as you go, until no more salt will dissolve in.

3. Set your bone shaped sponge in a shallow dish. Pour salt water over the sponge. Let the water evaporate from the sponge for several days until it is dry.

The salt, a mineral, moves in and fills the spaces in the sponge, turning it into a "rock." This is what happens to

Fabulous Fact

The extinct dodo bird

People used to believe animals and plants could not go extinct. George Cuvier proposed that extinction was possible in a 1796 lecture. He then spent the rest of his career trying to convince everyone else.

It wasn't until Charles Darwin that people began to accept that extinction could occur, and not until 1982 did people accept that mass extinction events were real.

Extinction Theory is now generally accepted.

Fabulous Fact

Paleontologists find fossils from more recent geological periods more often and in greater numbers. Older samples are less likely to be preserved as the rock cycle eats up old rock.

Memorization Station

Memorize these types of fossils:

Permineralization: dissolved minerals in water replace the bone with rock

Fossil cast: a complete impression of soft tissues is left on the rock

Earth & Space

Famous Folks

Charles Doolittle Walcott studied the Burgess Shale fossils in British Columbia, Canada beginning in 1909. These fossils are 508 million years old and showed the soft body carbon film imprints of thousands of species.

Walcott visited the formation and collected specimens with his family for 15 years.

This is Walcott, his daughter Helen, and his son, Sidney, searching the shale for fossils.

The significance of his find and how these fossils told a story about how life developed on Earth was not understood until the 1960s. Paleontologists are still finding new species in the Burgess Shale every year.

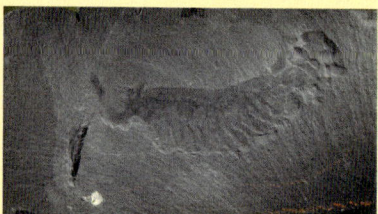

This is a fossil of an Opabinia from the Burgess Shale. It is weird, nothing at all like animals we see today.

Writer's Workshop

Look up animals discovered in the Burgess Shale. Pick one.

Imagine you discovered a living one and you decided to keep it as a pet. Write a story about taking it to a pet show.

---

animal bones when permineralization takes place. The soft tissues, like the skin, muscles, and organs, all decompose before permineralization can take place, but the bone takes longer to decompose, so it is preserved as rock.

😊😊😊 EXPLORATION: Fossil Cast

For this activity, you will need:

- Modeling clay
- Plaster of Paris
- Water
- Disposable cup and spoon - two for each cast
- Hard plastic toy dinosaur or animal

Rarely, a fossil includes an entire impression of an animal, even including the skin texture or the presence of feathers and other tiny details. This happens when an animal is covered quickly and the fossilization process happens quickly, before the skin and other softer parts can decompose. A **fossil cast** is made of the entire animal.

1. Press the clay down into the bottom of a disposable cup or bowl. You may need to soften it a bit by kneading a little extra water into the clay.

2. Press a toy dinosaur or animal into the deep into the clay so it makes a good impression, then pull it back out. If you don't have a toy dinosaur, you can also make "footprints" with the eraser end of a pencil.

3. Mix a little Plaster of Paris in a disposable cup with a disposable spoon. We used 2 tablespoons of plaster and 1 tablespoon of water for each of our casts. Spoon the Plaster of Paris into the footprint and let it dry for at least an hour.

4. Remove the plaster from the mold to see your preserved

Fossils

animal cast. You can cut the disposable container down the side to release the cast if you need to.

> **WARNING: Throw Plaster of Paris and all of the mess into the garbage afterward. Do NOT rinse it down the sink!**

😊 😊 😊 EXPLORATION: Carbon Film Fossils

For this activity, you will need:

- Brown or black paint
- Paintbrushes
- Fresh leaves, several species
- Paper
- Clean flat rocks, a little bigger than your leaves

All living things are based on carbon. Under some circumstances, animals and plants without skeletons, shells, or woody trunks decompose while being compressed between layers of sediment. They will leave nothing behind but a carbon silhouette of the original organism. This is called a **carbon film**.

The animals of the famous Burgess Shale Formation left this type of fossil. Most plant fossils are also carbon film fossils.

1. Paint one side of a leaf with brown or black paint.
2. Place the painted leaf on the flat surface of a rock.
3. Place a piece of paper over the painted leaf and press down carefully on the entire surface. Then remove the paper and the leaf. Let the paint dry.
4. Repeat with different species of leaf. After the paint dries, can you identify the species from the imprint? What details do you see that help you know which is which? Are there any details that are missing in your imprint?

Bookworms

Boy, Were We Wrong About Dinosaurs! by Kathleen V. Kudlinski is a picture book about what ancient people, early modern people, and modern people have gotten wrong about dinosaurs.

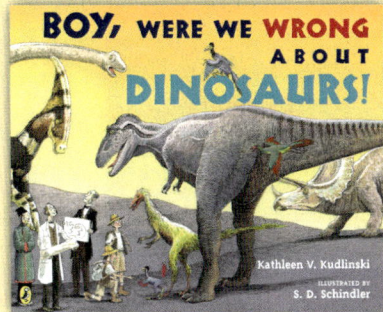

It explains how those misconceptions have been corrected. This is an excellent book for highlighting how real science takes many wrong turns along the way to truth.

Fabulous Fact

Not all fossils are old. Younger fossils and partially mineralized fossils are called "sub-fossils" by paleontologists.

Memorization Station

Memorize these types of fossils:

Carbon film: the organism is compressed between layers of sedimentary rock, leaving only an outline or impression

Amber: a small organism is trapped in sap, which fossilizes into rock

Trace fossils: a fossil of a footprint, trail, burrow, or other trace of an animal rather than of the animal itself

Earth & Space

Fabulous Fact

The dating of fossils is not perfect. The best we can do is give a range of when a creature probably lived. This is because most fossils and the rock they are in cannot be directly dated using radiometric dating. We use nearby rock layers and relative dating to make an estimate.

Only igneous rock can be dated with radiometric dating methods. Radiometric dating depends on the moment of rock formation. Since sedimentary rock, the rock that fossils are found in, is always formed of other, older rock, you can't tell when the sedimentary rock was formed based on the chemicals within the rock.

The exception is when an animal or plant is buried in layers of ash from a volcano.

We also know that an animal can be missing from the fossil record when it is actually still alive.

Maybe you will be the one to find a more reliable and accurate method of dating fossils.

On the Web

Search online for a dinosaur dig kit. There are dozens of choices to give your kids a fun, interactive afternoon activity.

EXPLORATION: Amber Fossils

For this activity, you will need:

- Plastic toy insect or dinosaur
- Small cup or dish
- Yellow, lemon gelatin
- Refrigerator
- Internet

Insects are sometimes found fossilized in **amber**. Amber is hardened tree sap. Long ago, the insect got caught in sap, the sap encased the insect, and then it hardened. The insect is now a fossil.

1. Mix up gelatin according to the directions on the package. Pour gelatin into a small plastic cup until it is nearly full. Place a clean plastic bug toy into the gelatin. Put it in the refrigerator for 6 hours or overnight.

2. Remove the gelatin from the cup. Talk about how sometimes an insect or very small creature could be trapped in sap from a tree. The sap hardens over time to amber, which is like a rock.

3. The insect in gelatin represents a preserved amber fossil. Look up some examples of insects preserved in amber online.

EXPLORATION: Trace Fossil Sugar Cookies

For this activity, you will need:

- Sugar cookie dough
- Toy dinosaurs (cleaned with soap and water and dried)
- Milk chocolate chips or candy bars, melted

Fossils can be parts of an animal, a plant, a microorganism, or they can be **trace fossils**. Trace fossils are not part of

Fossils

living things, but evidence of behavior from a living thing like animal poop, a footprint, or a burrow.

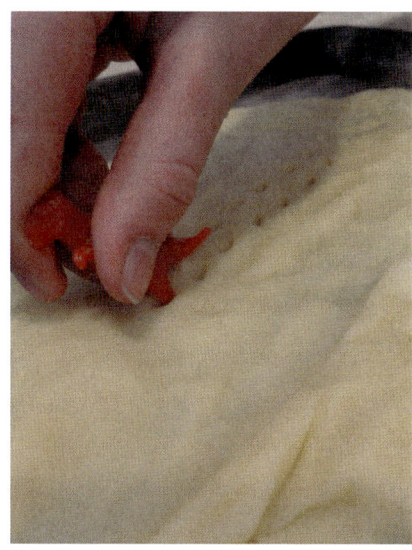 

1. Roll sugar cookie dough out flat. Then shape it with clean hands to look like a mud flat or a sandy river bank.

2. Press the clean toy dinosaur footprints deeply into the sugar cookie dough "land." Make it look like your dinosaur is ambling along slowly or running. You could have two dinosaurs interacting and make a story if you like.

3. Bake the sugar cookie dough according to the recipe directions. Let it cool completely. This is like the sun drying out a stretch of riverbank and making the footprints harden.

4. Melt chocolate in a microwave or double boiler. Pour melted chocolate over the area where the footprints are located. Let the chocolate cool and harden. This is like a new layer of mud being carried by a spring flood to quickly cover the tracks.

5. Uncover your dinosaur tracks under the mud to discover the trace fossils.

6. Take turns explaining the definition of a trace fossil and how it is different than other fossils.

The Fossil Record

😊😊😊 **EXPLORATION: Fossil Record**
For this activity, you will need:
- "The Fossil Record" from the Printable Pack plus all the pages of animal and plant cards that follow (8 pgs. total)

Memorization Station

Memorize the periods of geologic time in order from the present to the formation of the earth:

Cenozoic	Quaternary
	Neogene
	Paleogene
Mesozoic	Cretaceous
	Jurassic
	Triassic
Paleozoic	Permian
	Carboniferous
	Devonian
	Silurian
	Ordovician
	Cambrian
	Precambrian

The periods in the geologic time scale are for the convenience of people as we talk about the long ago past of the earth.

Note that the Precambrian Period is likely around ten times as long as the rest of the periods put together. The first bacteria appeared fairly early in the Precambrian and the first multi-celled life appeared toward the end of this period.

At the end of the Permian Period, Pangaea had formed and the first dinosaur species had emerged. The dinosaurs died out at the end of the Cretaceous Period, so the Mesozoic was the age of dinosaurs.

Earth & Space

Bookworms

Time by Roger Reid is a mystery set in Alabama during a dinosaur dig.

A fun, action-packed read. For kids ages 10 and up.

Expedition

You can easily see rock strata in places like the Grand Canyon.

Go visit a location near you where rock strata has been exposed. The oldest rocks are on the bottom. Can you spot the layers of rock?

Memorization Station

Strata: layers of rock

- Colored pencils
- Scissors
- Glue

Paleontologists and earth scientists use the geologic time scale to relate rocks and the evidence of life that they reveal. Most scientists estimate the age of the earth at about 4.5 billion years. The fossil record, a history of life as documented by fossils we've found, shows that the first life appeared about 2 billion years ago, halfway through Earth's existence.

Scientists divide the time periods of Earth's history into supereons, eons, periods, epochs, and ages. In this exploration, we will focus on periods because those time divisions are used most often when talking about dinosaurs.

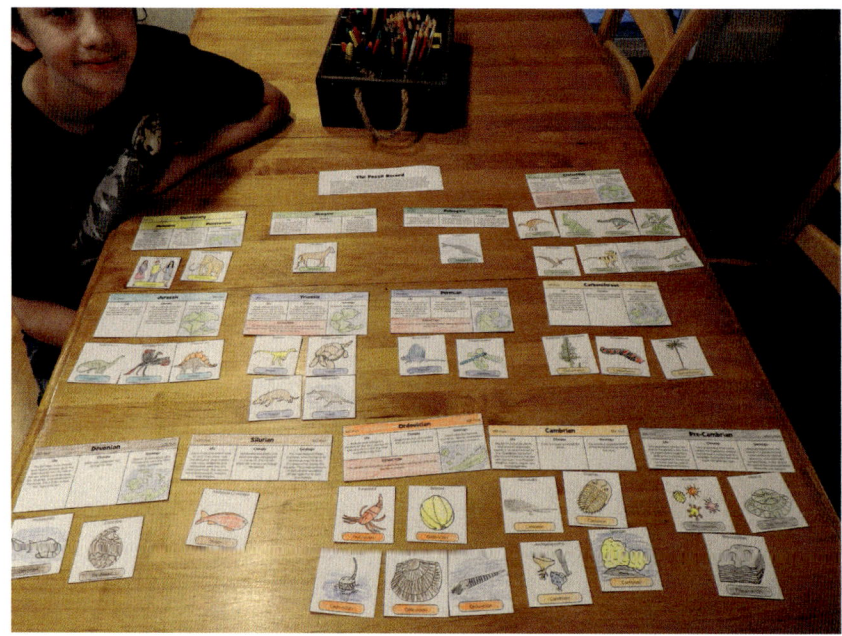

1. Cut apart "The Fossil Record" strips.
2. Color each period - Quaternary, Neogene, Paleogene, and so on - with a different color.
3. Then cut apart the plant and animal cards. Color the plants and animals. Color the period on each animal or plant card to match the colors on your period cards.
4. Arrange the cards from most recent to the most distant. Read the descriptions of each period as you go. Match the animals and plants to their periods.
5. There are some blank cards so you can look up more living things from the fossil record to include in your history of life on Earth.

Fossils

🙂 🙂 **EXPLORATION: Law of Superposition Paper Collage**

For this activity, you will need:

- Video about superposition (We like "Law of Superposition" from Bozeman Science.)
- Scissors
- Construction paper in several colors
- Glue stick
- Markers

Layers of rock are called **strata**. You can see strata of rock in a canyon where a river has eroded deeply into the ground. When rock strata are formed, they are laid down horizontally and left where water or wind or flowing lava deposited them. The oldest rock is the bottom layer and the newest rock is the top layer. This is the **law of superposition**.

If you find two fossils, each in different layers of rock, the fossil in the lower layer will be older than the fossil in the upper layer. Understanding this allows you to date the fossils relative to each other. You can't tell, by this method, exactly how old a fossil is, just that is younger or older than another fossil.

1. Watch a video about the law of superposition.
1. Choose a piece of colored construction paper to be your background.
2. Cut or tear strips of paper in other colors to make layers of rock on the background. Glue each strip to the background. Label each layer with different types of rock. Make sure to include some layers of sedimentary rock, as this is the type of rock that fossils are mostly found in.

On the Web

If you haven't learned about half-life in chemistry, you may want to watch a video from YouTube about this topic to get caught up on the fly so you understand radiometric dating better.

Just search for "half-life" and watch a video by Mr. Anderson or Khan Academy.

Fabulous Fact

Radiometric dating is not perfect. It depends on

- The sample not being contaminated or altered since the formation of the rock.
- A large enough sample to test accurately.
- Multiple samples taken through a particular rock zone so that natural variations in concentration of radioactive material can be averaged out.

Accuracy can be improved if more than one radioactive element in a sample can be tested to check the samples against one another.

In addition, radiometric dating has several methods of calculation and no one knows which is the most accurate. Often, multiple methods are used and compared when testing a sample. At best, scientists can get a date within 2-3 million years in a sample that is 2 billion or more years old. Perhaps in the future even better methods will be found.

Earth & Space

Fabulous Fact

Paleontologists who discover the fossils of new species get to name the species. In the late 19th century, many of them were racing to discover new species in the fossil record.

Famous Folks

In 1907, Bertram Boltwood was the first to suggest that rocks and the earth itself could be dated using the brand new understanding of radioactive decay.

He also proved that the product of the breakdown of Uranium-238 was lead, an essential piece necessary to dating very old rock.

Writer's Workshop

Choose a dinosaur that interests you, research it, and then write a report about it. Include these things:

- Where and when the fossils were first found.
- How the dinosaur is classified and what its name means.
- What researchers believe the habitat and life of this dinosaur was like.

Share your report out loud when you're finished.

3. In each sedimentary layer, draw fossil animals or plants. Remember that fossils are usually found in sedimentary rock. Limestone will include sea creatures. Sandstone could include dinosaurs. Coal will include lots of plants.

4. Show off your collage and explain which of your fossils are older or younger than others according to the law of superposition.

☺ ☻ EXPLORATION: Radiometric Dating

For this activity, you will need:

- Box with a lid
- Package of M&Ms candy
- Book or video about radiometric dating from the Library List or YouTube playlist for this unit
- Science Notebook

All matter is made of elements, the ingredients of the universe. All elements are made of a single type of atom. Lead is made of lead atoms, carbon is made of carbon atoms, uranium is made of uranium atoms, and so on.

Each atom can have variations, or isotopes. All uranium atoms have 92 protons; that's what makes it uranium. Uranium is radioactive and breaks down over time at a steady, predictable rate. When it does, the uranium atom is split in two and you get lead. Lead is stable and does not break down.

Zircon is a common mineral in igneous rock in the earth's crust. When zircon forms, it contains uranium, but it rejects lead. As the uranium breaks down over time, lead is left behind in the zircon. So, if you compare how much uranium

Fossils

is in a zircon crystal in a rock with how much lead there is, you can fairly accurately tell how long it has been since the rock formed.

This method only works on igneous rock, in which it is usually not possible for fossils to exist. Geologists examine nearby rock layers for extra clues though. For example, if you have a sedimentary layer of rock just above or just beneath an igneous layer of rock, you can tell if a fossil is older or younger than the igneous rock layer. It helps narrow down the age of the fossil.

1. Place all the M&Ms candies in a box with the printed "m" side up. The "m" side represents a radioactive element like uranium-235, which turns into lead-207. When a rock first forms, the zircon crystals in the rock contain only uranium and no lead.

2. Put the lid on the box and give it a good shake. Uranium-235 has a half-life of 700 million years, so it takes 700 million years for half of the uranium to turn to lead. Shaking the box once represents 700 million years going by. When you open the box, about half of the M&Ms will be facing up with the "m" showing and half will be facing down. The ones that are facing down have decayed into lead. Remove the "lead" from the box because lead is stable and is not subject to the passage of time; it will stay lead forever.

3. Shake the box again. Another 700 million years have passed. Open the box and remove all the face down M&Ms that have turned to "lead."

4. Repeat the process several times, keeping track of how often you shake the box. Count the number of face up "m" pieces and the number of face down pieces.

5. Compare how much uranium you have left to how much lead you have. How many times did you shake the box? How many years have gone by? Does the amount of uranium remaining correlate to the number of years that have passed?

6. Read a book or watch a video about radiometric dating and then discuss how your M&M experiment relates to radiometric dating. Write about it in your Science Notebook.

😊 😊 😊 **EXPLORATION: Index Fossils**

For this activity, you will need:

- "Index Fossils" from the Printable Pack (2 pgs.)
- Scissors

Additional Layer

Edward Cope and Othniel Marsh went head to head in a rush to find the best fossils in the American West. They both tried bribery, sabotage, theft, vandalism, and defamation to destroy one another.

Learn more about the Bone Wars.

Writer's Workshop

Read a book about fossils.

Draw a picture of your favorite part of the book. Write the information about your favorite part in your own words.

Compare what you remembered and wrote to what the book originally told. How much did you remember? Did you explain the ideas well in your own words?

Fabulous Fact

Paleontologists have to be good geologists and good biologists. They have to understand rocks and life.

Paleontology has become such a fruitful field that people now specialize in one area of fossils such as paleobotany (fossil plants) or paleoecology (ancient ecosystems).

Earth & Space

Additional Layer

Why did the dinosaurs go extinct? There are two main competing hypotheses:

The Alvarez Hypothesis contends that a major asteroid hit earth, causing earthquakes, debris, and a darkening of the sky across the globe for at least a year. Evidence has been found that debris from an asteroid was spread across various parts of the globe in a thin layer called the K-Pg (Cretaceous-Paleogene) boundary and an impact site in Mexico has been found.

Luis and Walter Alvarez, a father-son team, first proposed that a massive asteroid may have killed the dinosaurs.

The other major theory is the Deccan Traps Volcanoes, a massive super volcano that erupted at about the time the dinosaurs were dying out. The volcano was big enough to have impacted global climates.

Since the early 1990s, the Alvarez hypothesis has been gaining ground, but the Deccan Traps are thought to have been a contributing factor. Learn more.

- Glue stick
- Colored pencils
- Extra piece of colored, blank paper

Certain types of fossils are so common all over the world that they can be used to help date other fossils. These common fossils are called **index fossils**. Index fossils have to be widespread, distinctive from other fossils, exist for only a limited period of time, and be found in relatively large numbers. Most index fossils are sea creatures because the species could easily spread widely throughout the oceans. However, because life in the sea tends to be very vulnerable to changes in climate, these species usually only lasted for relatively short periods of time.

Trilobites are a great index fossil. They lived in all parts of the ocean from the Cambrian through the Permian time periods. They had hard shells which they molted like modern arthropods, leaving easily fossilized body parts all

Fossils

over the sea bed. Today, trilobite fossils are found on every continent where ancient sea beds have become part of continental crust. If you find a species of trilobites in a layer of rock in western Australia and the same trilobite species in a layer of rock in British Columbia, Canada, then you know that both layers of rock formed at around the same time during the period during which the trilobite species was living. You also know that any other fossils in either of those rock layers are about the same age as the trilobites.

1. Color the rock types in the key on the "Index Fossils" printable. Talk about each type of rock and whether it is sedimentary, metamorphic, or igneous. Only sedimentary rocks have fossils (with a few exceptions). Also, even though conglomerate is a sedimentary rock, it doesn't normally contain fossils. Shale, limestone, mudstone, and sandstone are all sedimentary and great places to find fossils.

2. Color the layers of rock in the columns on the first page of the "Index Fossils" printable so they match your key. Cut them apart on the solid lines. Given what you know of the relative ages of the fossils in these rock layers, put the layers in order, gluing the columns together so they make one long column.

3. On the second page of the "Index Fossils" printable, some of the layers of rock have already been added. Color these to match your key. Color in the rest of the rock layers any way you like, according to the key.

4. The columns on this page will be assembled into two columns, as though each column had been found in different parts of the world. Cut apart the columns and cut out the fossils.

5. Design the columns and index fossils in a way that makes sense. Younger fossils should be above older fossils. Fossils should not be in igneous, metamorphic, or conglomerate rock layers. You can use all or just some of the fossils.

6. If you have two fossils of the same type, what does that tell you about those rock layers? What if you found another creature in the same layer as one of your index fossils? What would that tell you about the new creature?

7. Trim your key down. Glue the key and the three columns of rocks with fossils to a second piece of paper.

8. Add this to the Science section of your Layers of Learning Notebook.

Memorization Station

Index fossils: fossils that are useful for dating and correlating the strata in which it is found

Bookworms

The Lie Tree by Frances Hardinge is a Costa Book of the Year award winner.

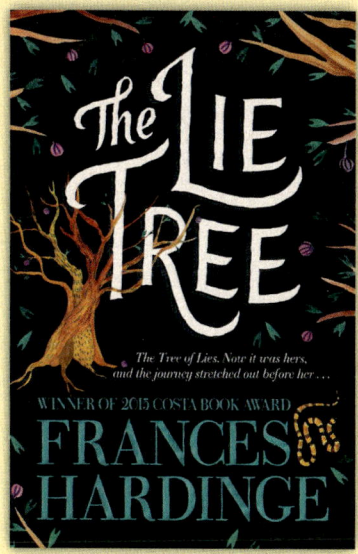

Faith is the daughter of a minister, naturalist, and fossil hunter from Victorian England. Her father dies in mysterious circumstances. Before he dies, Faith helps him hide a secret. Can she use the secret to find out what happened to her father?

Faith's curiosity and hunger are at odds with society's expectations, but she can't help being interested in her father's fossils. 14 and up.

Earth & Space

Additional Layer

Paleoart is art depicting ancient ecosystems, animals, and plants. It's important mainly because it communicates scientific ideas to the general public, gets people interested, and helps provide funding for research.

This painting is by Charles R. Knight and was done in 1987.

Paleoart can include paintings, sculptures, films, books, and more.

Find a how-to-draw of a dinosaur and make your own paleoart with a background.

Additional Layer

Plesiosaur, megalodon, and basilosaurus are all ancient extinct sea creatures.

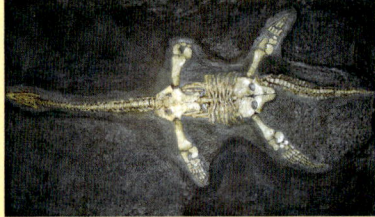

Learn more about these ancient sea creatures.

Deep Thoughts

There is no Nobel Prize for paleontology or many other scientific areas. Do you think there should be? Why or why not?

😊 😊 😊 EXPLORATION: The Cambrian Explosion

For this activity, you will need:

- "Cambrian Explosion Timeline" from the Printable Pack (2 pgs.)
- Scissors
- Colored pencils or crayons
- Small cardboard box, just big enough for the strips of the timeline to fit through
- Paints, paintbrushes, and a water cup

About halfway through Earth's history, bacteria and other microorganisms showed up in the fossil record. Then suddenly, the fossils of many different animals quickly appeared in a wide variety of body styles. Spinal chords and hard shells and eyes suddenly existed where none had been before. This sudden appearance of a wide variety of animals is known as the Cambrian Explosion. It's an explosion of life.

Scientists are still actively investigating why and how the Cambrian Explosion happened. There are some hypotheses. Some scientists hypothesize that oxygen levels in the atmosphere finally reached levels that animals needed to survive. Others think that perhaps enough ozone had finally formed to protect Earth from the deadly UV radiation levels that existed without it. It's also possible that volcanoes released calcium, needed for shells and bones, into the oceans. Maybe there was a major extinction event just before the Cambrian Explosion that left room for new species to develop. Some say there wasn't an explosion at all; it's just that we don't have all the facts yet because the fossil record is incomplete.

Fossils

1. Cut the strips of the "Cambrian Explosion Timeline" on the solid lines.
2. Color each of the strips. Glue the pieces together, end to end, in order.
3. Paint a small box any way you want so it represents the explosion of life or the fossil record. Cut slits in each side of the front of the box.
4. Thread your "Cambrian Explosion Timeline" through the slits, from the back to the front, and then back. Glue the two ends of the "Cambrian Explosion Timeline" together to make a loop.
5. Read the story of the Cambrian Explosion as you draw your timeline loop through the box.

☺ ☺ ☺ **EXPEDITION: Tour a Fossil Dig**

For this activity, you will need:

- Internet to find nearby fossil dig
- Science Notebook

Find out if there is an active fossil dig or petrified forest near you that is open to the public.

This is the Mammoth Site & Museum in South Dakota. It is an active dig that you can watch as the scientists work.

1. Take a trip to see a fossil dig, armed with at least one good question. Try to get your question answered either by reading displays or asking a guide.
2. Write about what you saw in your Science Notebook

On the Web

Many states, provinces, and countries have official fossils. Usually, these are fossils that have been found in the region. Search online to find out what yours is.

Print a picture of it and paste it into your Science Notebook with a few facts about the fossil.

This is the Idaho state fossil, the Hagerman Horse.

Additional Layer

Dinosaurs are just one category of ancient animals. We also have fossils of ancient mammals, amphibians, insects, shellfish, fish, and more. Learn more.

Famous Folks

Joan Wiffen was a self-taught paleontologist who wanted to prove that dinosaurs once lived in New Zealand, her home. She achieved her goal in spades.

This is artist, Joel Field's, concept of what Joan's first find, a Theropod, may have looked like.

Earth & Space

Additional Layer

Paleontologists separate dinosaurs into two big groups: avian and non-avian. Since today it is believed that modern birds descended from dinosaurs, avian dinosaurs are modern birds.

This kingfisher is an avian dinosaur.

All other dinosaurs, including almost all of the ancient extinct species, are non-avian.

This Styracosaurus is a non-avian dinosaur.

This unit deals with non-avian dinosaurs, but you can learn more about both types.

Deep Thoughts

Fossil smuggling is when a fossil specimen is illegally sold and transported, usually out of the country of origin to a private collector or museum.

What do you think are the problems with fossil smuggling and how would you stop it?

and record a few things you learned while at the dig site.

😊 😃 EXPEDITION: Real Life Paleontologist

For this activity, you will need:

- Two 30cm long pieces of 1x2 wood
- Two 45cm long pieces of 1x2 wood
- Brad nails and hammer
- 1/4 inch metal screen
- Screws
- Screw driver
- Bucket
- Large garden shovel

Build a fossil screen to sift for fossils in a stream like a real **paleontologist** in the wild. This is a wet, dirty expedition, so be prepared!

1. Make a rectangular frame with the 30 cm and 45 cm pieces of wood. Nail the wood together at the corners. Then screw the screen across the top.

2. Research a site to sift for fossils in a stream. The stream must have public access and be in an area of sedimentary rock. It's also good if you know fossils have been found in the area before.

3. Use a bucket and shovel to get dirt and rocks from the bottom of the stream. Dump it into the screen and frame. Shake the screen to remove the smaller debris. Search for fossils as you go. Remember that fossils can be of plants, shells, foot prints or fragments of bone. It is unlikely that you will find a complete intact bone fossil.

Dinosaurs

There are lots of prehistoric animals in the fossil record; **dinosaurs** are just one kind. Dinosaur fossils have been

Fossils

found all over the world. Paleontologists carefully excavate the fossilized remains and then study them to learn clues about what dinosaurs were like and what may have caused their extinction.

😊 🟢 EXPLORATION: Dino Dig

For this activity, you will need:

- Toy dinosaurs, chicken bones, and/or shells
- Clay
- Plaster of Paris
- Disposable cup and spoon for mixing plaster
- Tools for digging, like a toothbrush, metal picks (like the ones for getting nuts out of a shell), and so on

Fossils are hard, mineralized rock, usually found in layers of softer rock. The softer rock is chipped carefully away to reveal the hard fossils.

1. Prepare the dino dig ahead of time for younger kids or have older kids prepare the dig for younger ones.
2. Start by pressing toy dinosaurs, chicken bones, or shells deep into soft clay. Remove the object and then pour in prepared Plaster of Paris (use the directions on the package) into the cavities left by the objects. Let the plaster harden.
3. Bury the plaster objects in a thick layer of clay. Let the clay dry for several days or a week. You can also bury it in a sandbox or sandy area if you have one.
4. Give children toothbrushes, small metal picks, and other tools to dig the harder plaster "fossils" out of the softer brittle clay.

Writer's Workshop

Paleontologists often name dinosaurs with Latin names that tell about the dinosaur's characteristics.

For example, tyrannos means tyrant. Saurus means lizard. And rex means king.

So tyrannosaurus rex means tyrant lizard king.

In the Printable Pack, you will find a "Name A Dinosaur" sheet with Latin roots you can combine to make up a new dinosaur.

Draw a picture of your dinosaur in the box and then fill in the blanks in the story.

Memorization Station

Paleontologist: a scientist who specializes in the study of fossils and prehistoric life forms

Dinosaur: extinct, warm-blooded reptiles that lay eggs, have hind limbs extending directly beneath the body, have a simple hinge ankle joint, have a hole between the eye socket and nostril, and live most of life on land

Earth & Space

Writer's Workshop

Write a 6-line rhyming dinosaur poem.

Use an AABBCC rhyme scheme so the first two lines rhyme, the third and fourth lines rhyme with each other, and the last two lines rhyme.

Make lists of words that rhyme with:

- Roar
- Stomp
- Tail

Use the words you came up with as the basis of your poem.

Famous Folks

The Shaximiao Formation is a site of rich dinosaur fossils in central China. It was discovered by paleontologist Dong Zhiming in 1980.

Dong successfully campaigned to get an expensive public works project halted in communist China to preserve the site.

The site is a rare Middle Jurassic bed and contains dozens of examples of stegosaurs and other dinosaurs not found elsewhere.

Dong discovered more than 40 species of dinosaurs. One dinosaur, the *Sinraptor dongi*, is named after him.

This is the Sinoraptor dongi in the Anhui Geological Museum, Hefei.

EXPLORATION: What Is A Dinosaur?

For this activity, you will need:

- "What Is A Dinosaur?" from the Printable Pack, plus the answer key
- Colored pencils or crayons

There were many different kinds of animals that lived in prehistoric times and can be found in the fossil record, but only some of those are actually dinosaurs. To be a dinosaur, you have to have these characteristics:

- Warm-blooded
- Egg laying
- Hind limbs beneath the body, instead of legs splayed to the sides
- Simple hinge ankle joint
- A hole between the eye socket and nostril
- Live most of their life on land

1. On the "What Is A Dinosaur?" printable, draw a line from the center circle to each animal that is a dinosaur. Hint: look for how the legs are attached first!

2. Check the answer key to see if you are right.

3. Color all the animals as desired. If you like, you can look up each animal to find out more about it.

4. Add your finished page to the Science section of your Layers of Learning Notebook.

EXPLORATION: Dinosaur Groups Target Practice

For this activity, you will need:

- "Dinosaur Groups" from the Printable Pack as well as the two pages of dinosaur cards that follow
- Crayons or colored pencils
- White card stock
- Scissors
- Six similarly-sized boxes or buckets
- Masking tape or packaging tape
- A bean bag, small ball, or wadded ball of paper for each child

There are six major groups of dinosaurs.

- **Ankylosaurians** - These are the armored dinosaurs like Ankylosaurus and Edmontonia. Their backs were covered with bony armor plates. They walked on four legs and lived from the early Jurassic until the end of the Cretaceous. Their fossils have been found on every continent.
- **Stegosaurians** - These are dinosaurs with tail spikes

144

Fossils

and spikes or plates running along their backs. They walked on four legs, with the hind legs longer than the front legs so their tails were elevated and could be used as weapons. Their heads were very small for their body size. They had hoof-like toes on all four limbs. This group includes the Stegosaurus, Huayangosaurus, Craterosaurus, and others.

- **Ceratopsians** - They were herbivorous dinosaurs with beaks. Members of this species walked on four legs and had horns on their faces and frills around their heads. Their skulls were large and heavy and thick. Triceratops, Polyonax, and Leptoceratops are three examples of this group.
- **Ornithopods** - These dinosaurs ran about on two legs and dropped to four legs to amble along or graze on grasses. They had three toes, no armor, and a horny beak. Some of them had duck-bills. They ranged in size from one meter long to fifteen meters long. Some examples of this group include Parasaurolophus, Edmontosaurus, and Iguanodon.
- **Theropods** - These dinosaurs had hollow bones, three toes on their feet, always walked on their hind legs and most of them had tiny forelegs. Most of them were carnivorous but a few were omnivores or even herbivores. Examples of this type of dinosaur include Tyrannosaurus Rex, Gigantosaurus, and Velociraptor. These ranged in size from as small as a crow to as much as eighteen meters long. Many, or perhaps all, of this group had feathers on at least part of their bodies.
- **Sauropodomorphs** - This group includes the largest animals ever to live on land like Brontosaurus, Apatosaurus, and Diplodocus. They lived on every continent, had long necks, walked on all four legs, and ate plants. The smallest adult dinosaurs in this group were 6 meters long and the largest, Argentinosaurus, was nearly 40 meters long.

1. Print the "Dinosaur Groups" and dinosaur cards onto white card stock.
2. Color the dinosaurs any way you like. Cut apart the cards on the solid lines.
3. Put your six boxes or buckets at one end of an open space. Tape the six dinosaur group cards, one to each box or bucket. Gather the dinosaur cards into a pile in random order.
4. Read the description of each group of dinosaur from this Exploration. Read the name and facts from the first dinosaur card and show the picture of the dinosaur.

Additional Layer
Print a world map from the internet. Choose ten dinosaurs to research. Mark on the world map where the dinosaur bones were found.

On the Web
Find a "how-to-draw a dinosaur" tutorial online. Practice until you are satisfied with your dinosaur. Draw and paint or color your dinosaur.

Then, on the internet, find a background scene you can print to put your dinosaur in. It could be a realistic Cretaceous background or it could be Mars, a city, or whatever you like.

Cut your dinosaur out carefully and glue it into the background scene.

Bookworms
Time Flies by Eris Rohmann is a Caldecott Honor book. It is filled with magical pictures (and no words) of a dinosaur museum that comes to life after a bird gets trapped inside.

Earth & Space

Bookworms

My Daniel by Pam Conrad. This book was first published in 1989 and is no longer in print. If you can find a copy, you will not forget the young girl who witnessed the dinosaur rush of the 1800s tear apart her beloved older brother and destroy their dream of saving the family farm. Well-written and emotionally captivating.

Ages 8 and up.

Additional Layer

This is a megalodon tooth.

There are many myths surrounding these creatures.

5. Standing back a little ways, have each child toss a beanbag into the dinosaur group bucket she or he thinks the dinosaur on the card belongs in.

6. Check the key, just below, to see the correct answer. Everyone who tossed their ball into the correct bucket gets a point. Continue until you have finished all the dinosaur cards.

Answers:
- **Ankylosaurians: Edmontonia, Ankylosaurus, Antarctopelta**
- **Stegosaurians: Craterosaurus, Stegosaurus, Huayangosaurus**
- **Ceratopsians: Triceratops, Titanoceratops, Leptoceratops**
- **Ornithopods: Edmontosaurus, Parasaurolophus, Iguanodon**
- **Theropods: Anchiornis, Tyrannosaurus Rex, Velociraptor**
- **Sauropodomorphs: Diplodocus, Apatosaurus, Brontosaurus**

🙂 🙂 🙂 **EXPLORATION: Teeth**

For this activity, you will need:

- Book or video about dinosaurs' diets
- Internet
- Paper
- Drawing utensils

Fossils can lend insights about the behaviors of animals that lived long ago. For example, some dinosaurs were **herbivores**, some were **carnivores**, and some were **omnivores**. We can tell what kinds of food they ate by examining their fossilized teeth. Herbivores had wide, flat teeth with ridges. They mashed and ground tough vegetation with their teeth. Carnivores had sharp, serrated teeth that could slice and tear flesh. Omnivores primarily had both of these kinds of teeth. Some, like ornithomimus,

Fossils

didn't have any teeth at all, but instead, used their beaks like scissors. Because we can look at the shapes of their teeth, we know the kinds of food they ate even though we've never actually watched a dinosaur eat anything.

1. Read a book or watch a video about dinosaurs' diets.
2. Divide a sheet of paper into three columns and write one of each of these titles above each column - herbivore, carnivore, omnivore.
3. Go online and find examples of each of these to add to that column. Also, do some research about the teeth of each kind.
4. What kind of teeth would reveal that a dinosaur was an herbivore? A carnivore? An omnivore? Even though we can't see the dinosaurs actively eating, we can learn about their diets and the kinds of things they would have eaten by examining their fossil remains. Draw examples of each kind of teeth that would be common within each column.
5. Add your page to the Science section of your Layers of Learning Notebook.

☺ ☺ ☺ EXPLORATION: How Big?
For this activity, you will need:

- Book or video about dinosaurs
- Sidewalk chalk (and a large concrete area for drawing)
- Tape measure

Fabulous Fact

In 1996, a shocking discovery was made in northeastern China in the Yixian Formation. It was a clear impression of a feathered dinosaur now called the *Sinosauropteryx* which means "Chinese reptilian wing."

Photo by Sam / Olai Ose / Skjaervoy from Zhangjiagang, China, CC by SA 2.0

It was discovered by Li Yumin, a farmer and amateur fossil hunter who sold his specimens to collectors and museums.

Before 1996, some paleontologists had hypothesized that modern birds were descended from dinosaurs, but there was no definite proof. The primitive feather structures on this specimen gave the first direct evidence that birds and dinosaurs had similarities beyond hollow bones and the way their hips were joined.

Memorization Station

Herbivore: an animal that feeds on plants

Carnivore: an animal that feeds on flesh, or other animals

Omnivore: an animal that eats both plants and flesh, or other animals

Earth & Space

Writer's Workshop

Make a list of the equipment you would need to explore a remote location if you were looking for fossils.

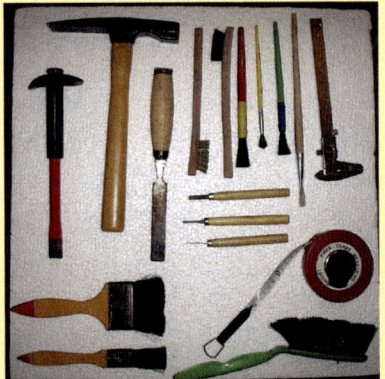

You will need tools for digging, but also camping equipment, food, and first aid supplies.

Additional Layer

We have a general idea of the geography of the world during the age of the dinosaurs. We can see where ancient oceans used to be, we can calculate the movement of the plates backward in time, and we can tell where land animals lived versus sea animals.

Original paleogeographic map of the Cretaceous Period (90 Ma) by Ron Blakey, CC by SA 3.0.

Learn about paleogeography, the study of ancient locations, formations, and continents.

Dinosaurs were many different shapes and sizes. During this exploration, we'll compare the sizes of several kinds of dinosaurs.

Can you imagine what it would be like to encounter one of the enormous species in person? Compare the height of a Brontosaurus to a giraffe, the world's tallest land mammal, and calculate the difference. During this Exploration, we'll take a look at some of the sizes of various species of dinosaurs.

Tyrannosaurus Rex footprint by Chris Kirkman, shared under CC 2.0 license

1. Read a book or watch a video about dinosaurs.

2. Go outside with sidewalk chalk and measure out the lengths of several kinds of dinosaurs so you can see how big they really were. Use the tape measure to show the length, then mark it off with chalk. Below, you will find some approximate measurements for various species.

   - Tyrannosaurus Rex   12 meters (40 feet)
   - Stegosaurus   9 meters (30 feet)
   - Diplodocus   24 meters (80 feet)
   - Pterodactyl   1 meter (3.5 feet)
   - Triceratops   8 meters (26 feet)
   - Brachiosaurus   15 meters (50 feet)
   - Velociraptor   2 meters (7 feet)
   - Gigantosaurus   13 meters (43 feet)
   - Oculudentavis   1.27 cm (1/2 inch)

3. The footprint of a T-rex is 3 1/2 feet long. Draw one on the concrete using your sidewalk chalk and predict how many of your footprints (or handprints) would fit inside. Write down your prediction.

4. Once everyone has made their predictions, choose a person's foot (or hand) to trace over and over inside of your footprint and count how many actual footprints (or handprints) you could fit inside.

Fossils

😊 😊 **EXPLORATION: Dinosaur Diorama**

For this activity, you will need:

- Book or video about dinosaurs from the Library List or the YouTube playlist for this unit
- "Dinosaur Diorama" pieces from the Printable Pack. There are three choices: one from the Cretaceous, one from the Jurassic, and one from the Triassic
- Shoe box
- Paint and paintbrushes or markers, crayons, or colored pencils
- Construction paper
- Scissors
- School glue

1. Read a book or watch a video about dinosaurs. Pay special attention to the habitat dinosaurs lived in.
2. Choose a time period for your dinosaur diorama: Cretaceous, Jurassic, or Triassic. Color and cut out the dinosaurs that match your chosen time period from the "Dinosaur Diorama" pieces.
3. Craft a background for your dinosaurs inside the shoe box. Use paints, construction paper, and any other craft supplies you like to make sky, trees, plants, water, and earth or rocks. Once everything is dry, glue your dinosaurs into the diorama box.
4. Present and explain your diorama to an audience, like your family at dinner time.

Step 3: Show What You Know

During this unit, choose one of the assignments below to show what you have learned during the unit. Add this work to your Layers of Learning Notebook. You can also use

Writer's Workshop

Search online for a recent news story about paleontology. Print the article.

As you read the article, use a highlighter pen to mark when the author of the story tells Who, What, When, Where, Why, and How, the five W's & an H of a good news piece. Is it in the first paragraph? The first sentence?

Write your own article about a paleontology discovery (real or imaginary) and include the 5 W's & an H.

For help in writing news articles, check out the *Writer's Workshop: True Stories* unit.

Additional Layer

Just for fun, end this unit by giving your kids "movie tickets" to watch one of these movies together as a family. For extra fun, serve dino nuggets or other fun treats during the show. Please preview any movies before showing them to your family.

- *The Good Dinosaur*
- *Jurassic Park*
- *The Land Before Time*
- *Dinosaur* (Disney)
- *Ice Age, Dawn of the Dinosaurs*
- *Dinotopia*
- *Walking With Dinosaurs*

Earth & Space

Unit Trivia Questions

1. True or false - All fossils show evidence of ancient dinosaurs.

   False. Some fossils are dinosaurs, but lots of other plants and animals have been fossilized too.

2. What is the name of a scientist who specializes in the study of fossils and prehistoric life forms?

   Paleontologist

3. When dissolved minerals in water replace the bone with rock, we call that _____.

   Permineralization

4. Put these time periods in order from earliest to latest: Jurassic, Cretaceous, Triassic.

   Triassic, Jurassic, Cretaceous

5. Fill in the blanks: An _____ is useful for dating and correlating the _____, or layers of rock, in which it is found.

   index fossil, strata

6. Most plant fossils are _____.
   a) Fossil casts
   b) Trace fossils
   c) Carbon film fossils
   d) Amber fossils

7. Dinosaurs have all of these characteristics except:
   a) Lay eggs
   b) Hind limbs beneath the body
   c) Simple hinge ankle joints
   d) Cold-blooded
   e) Live most of their life on land

---

this assignment to show your supervising teacher or your charter school as a sample of what you've been working on in your homeschool, if needed.

There are more ideas for writing assignments in the "Writer's Workshop" sidebars.

Coloring or Narration Page

For this activity, you will need:

- "Fossils" from the Printable Pack
- Writing or drawing utensils

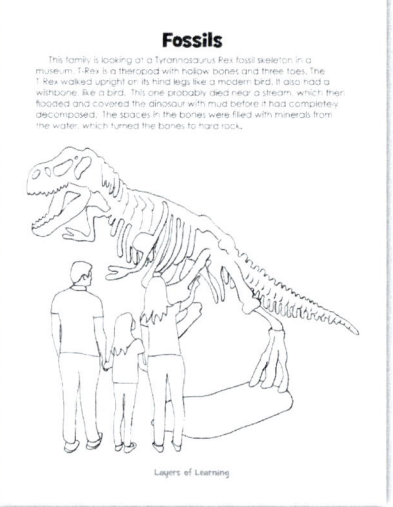

1. Depending on the age and ability of the child, choose either the "Fossils" coloring sheet or the "Fossils" narration page from the Printable Pack.

2. Younger kids can color the coloring sheet as you review some of the things you learned about during this unit. You might talk about fossils, extinction, or dinosaurs. On the bottom of the coloring page, kids can write a sentence about what they learned. Very young children can explain their ideas orally while a parent writes for them.

3. Older kids can write about some of the concepts you learned on the narration page and color the picture as well.

4. Add this to the Science section of your Layers of Learning Notebook.

Writer's Workshop

For this activity, you will need:

- A computer or a piece of paper and a writing utensil

Choose from one of the ideas below or write about something else you learned during this unit. Each of these prompts corresponds with one of the units from the Layers of Learning Writer's Workshop curriculum, so you may choose to coordinate the assignment with the monthly unit you are learning about in Writer's Workshop.

- **Sentences, Paragraphs, & Narrations:** Write a narration about how fossils are formed and what conditions

Fossils

must be met.

- **Descriptions & Instructions:** Choose one specific dinosaur species and write a description that is very detailed but doesn't reveal the name of the species you chose. See if someone can figure out which species it is just based on your description.
- **Fanciful Stories**: Write a story about a kid who found a dinosaur egg in his yard.
- **Poetry:** Write a shape poem about dinosaurs.
- **True Stories:** Look up information about a real paleontologist and tell his or her story.
- **Reports and Essays:** Choose a dinosaur to write a speech about. Present it to an audience.
- **Letters:** Write an essay about what the fossil record reveals and why it is an important branch of science to study.
- **Persuasive Writing:** Write a persuasive essay about why dinosaurs became extinct and the events you believe led up to their extinction.

😊 😊 😊 **Big Book of Knowledge**

For this activity, you will need:

- "Big Book of Knowledge: Fossils" printable from the Printable Pack, printed on card stock
- Writing or drawing utensils
- Big Book of Knowledge

1. Color, draw on, or write on the Big Book of Knowledge page. Record concepts, definitions, and facts you learned during this unit. It's a record of the things you learned and hope to remember. Add the page to your Big Book of Knowledge.

2. Use your Big Book of Knowledge regularly to help you review, quiz, or create games that will help you commit the things you've learned to memory.

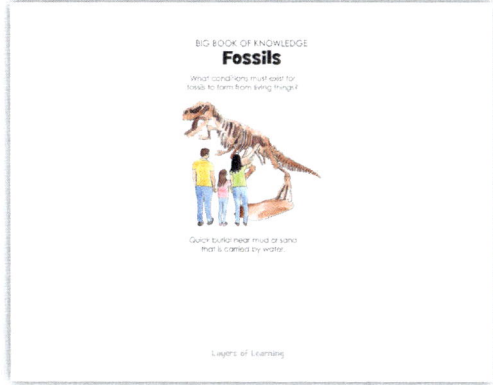

Big Book of Knowledge

The Big Book of Knowledge is a book for you, the mentor, to use as a constant review of all of the things you're learning about. You can use it to quiz your kids or prepare tests or review games. Whenever you learn something in Layers of Learning that you want your kids to remember, add it to your Big Book of Knowledge.

Assemble your Big Book of Knowledge in a binder or with binder rings. Divide it into sections for each subject.

In the Printable Pack for this unit you will find a "Big Book of Knowledge" sheet. You can add this sheet to others you collect or create yourself as you progress through the Layers of Learning curriculum. Customize the Big Book of Knowledge to your family by adding facts and topics that you enjoyed exploring as you were learning.

Visit Layers of Learning online to find more information on how to assemble and use your own Big Book of Knowledge.

You will also find cover and section pages to print along with creative games to play with your Big Book of Knowledge to keep school, even the tests, fun!

Earth & Space

Unit Overview

Key Concepts:
- Earth has seasons because the tilt of the earth changes the amount of sunlight we receive.
- Earth's atmosphere has layers. It is made up of many different gases that are heated by the sun.
- Climates are determined by latitude and elevation as well as proximity to large bodies of water.
- Earth's climate has changed many times over its history and is always changing.
- Humans may be affecting the climate of Earth because of our pollution over the last 300 years.

Vocabulary:
- Seasons
- June solstice
- December solstice
- September equinox
- March equinox
- Atmosphere
- Atmospheric pressure
- Climate
- Weather
- Greenhouse gas
- Ice age
- Carbon cycle

Theories, Laws, & Hypotheses:
- Maunder minimum hypothesis
- Milankovitch cycle theory
- Anthropomorphic climate change hypothesis

SEASONS & CLIMATE

Since the earth is tilted on its axis, we have seasons. When the Northern Hemisphere is tilted toward the sun, it is summer in the north and winter in the south. Six months later, the earth is on the other side of the sun and the north is tilted away from the sun and has winter while the Southern Hemisphere is having summer.

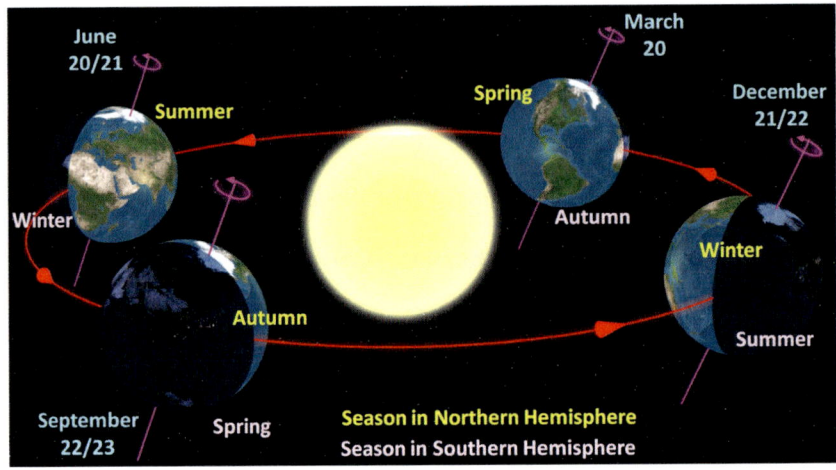

Climates are large areas that have similar weather. In the far north, it is cold and the ground is frozen all year round; we say it has a polar climate. Near the equator, the weather is hot and sunny all year; we say it has a tropical climate. Climate depends on latitude, how far from the equator a place is, and also altitude, how high above sea level a place is.

Tropical rain forest, desert, temperate, and polar climates.

Climates on Earth naturally cycle through warmer and

Seasons & Climate

cooler periods. The whole earth used to be much warmer and dinosaurs lived in the far north and the far south. Earth was also much colder in the past, and huge ice sheets existed as far south as the Great Lakes of North America and covered Germany and Poland in Europe.

Climate is complex and only partially understood today. There are several aspects of the earth that affect climate. The energy the sun puts out is not constant and sometimes the earth receives more heat from the sun than at other times. We also know that the earth's orbit changes shape over time, cycling from nearly a perfect circle to an elongated ellipse. The exact tilt of the earth's axis also changes over time, shifting from 22.1 degrees to 24.5 degrees and back again. The amount of greenhouse gases in the atmosphere can fluctuate over time as well. A small change in one of these factors can affect the others, compounding the effects.

Many scientists also believe that humans can have an effect on climates when we fail to care properly for the planet. If we pollute the air too much, it may increase the temperature of the whole planet. One of the hottest debates in science right now is whether humans are affecting the climate, how much humans are affecting the climate, and what to do about it.

Step 1: Library List

Choose books from your library that go with this topic. Here's a list of some favorites and also a list of search terms so you can utilize what your library offers. Read the books with your kids and/or assign them some to read independently. It is from these books your kids will learn most of the facts they need from this unit.

Search for: seasons, atmosphere, climate, climate change

😊 😊 😊 *Encyclopedia of Science* from DK. Read "Sunshine," "Seasons," "Climates," "Changing Climates," and "Atmosphere" on pages 242-249.

😊 😊 😊 *Kingfisher Science Encyclopedia*. Read "Earth's Atmosphere" on page 10 and "Climate" on page 36.

😊 😊 😊 *The Usborne Science Encyclopedia*. Read "The Atmosphere" on page 184 and "Climate" on page 194.

😊 *Sunshine Makes the Seasons* by Franklyn M. Branley. A picture book that is heavy on science. Excellent author!

😊 *The Reasons For Seasons* by Gail Gibbons. Explains how the earth's orbit and tilt make seasons.

Family School Levels

The colored smilies in this unit help you choose the correct levels of books and activities for your child.

😊 = Ages 6-9
😊 = Ages 10-13
😊 = Ages 14-18

On the Web

For videos, web pages, games, and more to add to this unit, visit the Earth & Space Resources at Layers-of-Learning.com.

You will find a link to video playlists, web links, and more.

Bookworms

If you're looking for a family read-aloud, we'd like to suggest this one.

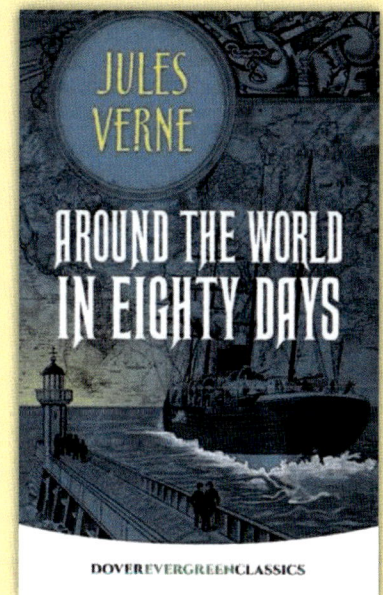

Around the World In 80 Days by Jules Verne is about an inventor, Phineas Fogg, who sets out to travel around the world and into foreign climates at a breakneck speed, while pursued by a policeman who is convinced he is evading the law.

Earth & Space

Teaching Tip

People & Planet: North America has more Explorations and learning activities about climate from a geographical perspective rather than a scientific one.

Fabulous Fact

The sun is highest in the sky during May, June, and July in the Northern Hemisphere and during November, December, and January in the Southern Hemisphere. However, the warmest time of the year begins and ends a month later.

This delay time is called seasonal lag. Seasonal lag happens mostly because of the water on Earth that absorbs and then releases heat later. In polar regions, the lag can be as short as two weeks and in places near the coast it can be as much as ten weeks.

Deep Thoughts

Climate determines how we live our lives. Can you think of some things it affects?

Hint: Think of the different types or constructions of homes people live in because of the climate.

The Year At Maple Hill Farm by Alice Provensen. A picture book that follows farm animals through an entire year as they respond to the seasons.

Climate by Torrey Maloof. A basic look at the difference between weather and climate, how scientists study past climates to make predictions about the future, and also climate zones and climate change.

The Climate Zones by Kristen Rajczak talks about the major climates on Earth and how each one creates a different landscape.

A Giant Shield: A Study of the Atmosphere by Baby Professor. Not too many words on a page, but good, solid science. Talks about the composition and layers of the atmosphere and how it protects the life on Earth.

Bill Nye the Science Guy: Earth's Seasons. Sometimes you can find Bill Nye on YouTube by searching. This video does a great job explaining science concepts simply and with excellent, entertaining visuals. Also look for *Atmosphere* and *Climates*.

Polar Climates by Cath Senker. Discusses where the polar climate is, what conditions are like there, what animals live there, and why the Arctic needs to be protected. Look for other titles by this author including: *Tropical Climates*, *Temperate Climates*, and *Desert Climates*.

18 Miles: the Epic Drama of Our Atmosphere and Its Weather by Christopher Dewdney. Starts with how the atmosphere was formed then goes into the composition of the atmosphere, extreme weather events, weather, and global climate. Can get a bit sensational and emotional but is filled with great storytelling.

Earth System Science: A Very Short Introduction by Tim Lenton. This 144-page book looks at how all of the systems of Earth: the water cycle, the atmosphere, the tides, plate tectonics, and life intertwine to create a single, balanced system that regulates the climate and the resources.

Climate: A Very Short Introduction by Mark Maslin. Written by an actual scientist, this 152-page book explains how the climate on Earth is regulated by oceans, currents, air flow, and the sun. The author explains how climate and weather are different but related.

Cosmology and Astronomy from KhanAcademy.org. To add a lecture for your high schooler, you can add a Khan Academy course. During this unit, study "Earth Geological and Climatic History: Earth's Rotation and Tilt."

Seasons & Climate

Step 2: Explore

Choose a few hands-on explorations from this section to work on as a family. They should be appealing activities that will create mental hooks so your kids remember the information in the unit. Save the rest of the explorations for the next time you do this unit in four years when your kids are older. You can also read the sidebars together and explore some little rabbit trails.

This unit includes printables. See the introduction for instructions on retrieving your Printable Pack.

Seasons

EXPLORATION: Four Seasons Poster

For this activity, you will need:

- "Seasons" from the Printable Pack
- Crayons or colored pencils
- Scissors
- Glue stick
- Protractor (optional, helps get the earth's tilt just right)
- Poster board
- Magazines or the season pictures from the printables

As it orbits, or revolves around the sun, the earth is tilted. That means that sometimes the North Pole is tilted toward the sun and sometimes it is tilted away. The **seasons** change because of the amount of sunlight certain parts of the earth get. If your part of the earth is tilted toward the sun, it is summer where you live.

Deep Thoughts

People who live in temperate climates normally think of four seasons: spring, summer, fall, and winter, but organizing seasons this way is partly cultural. In India, many people recognize six seasons. Some tropical places have only two seasons: the wet and the dry.

Think about the turn of the year where you live. If you could define the seasons, how many would there be and what would mark the change from one to the next? Why?

What would you call your seasons?

Memorization Station

Seasons: each of the four divisions of the year, resulting from the earth's changing position around the sun

Memorize the four seasons: winter, spring, summer, and fall (autumn).

Additional Layer

Make a tree for each of the seasons by drawing four tree trunks and then adding leaves and other details using washable paint and your fingerprints.

Earth & Space

Fabulous Fact

Scientists use models when they can't experiment directly. This is common in earth science since scientists are often working with things like the tectonic plates, the moon, the oceans, or the atmosphere - things that are too big to put in a lab.

Models are purposely simplified aspects of large, complex systems. Many of the experiments in this unit are models. A model will never be as reliable as a controlled experiment, but can still be useful and reveal truths.

Fabulous Fact

In *Earth & Space: Planet Earth* we learned that a giant planet collided with Earth while the solar system was still brand new, forming the moon.

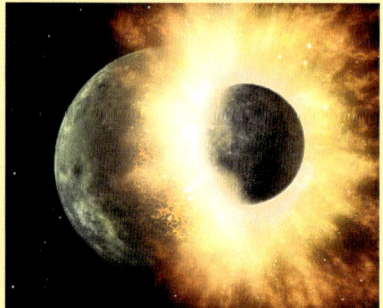

During this collision, the earth was tilted. That is the reason we have seasons. The moon keeps the earth's tilt stable.

Expedition

Go for a season walk. As you walk outside, look for evidence of what season you are in. For example, in the spring you may see eggs, new plants, and rain.

1. Draw the sun in the middle of a sheet of poster board. Around the sun, make a long oval to show earth's orbit.

2. Color the four Earths from the "Seasons" printable. Cut them out. Glue them along Earth's orbit. One should be above the sun, one below, one to the right, and one to the left. Make sure you tilt them all at the same angle. If you want to get it just right, use a protractor to find 23.5 degrees, the amount Earth's axis is tilted.

3. Determine which Earth shows summer where you live. Write "summer" next to that Earth. Cut pictures of summer scenes out of magazines or the printables and paste them next to that Earth. Repeat for each season.

4. Display this poster on your wall throughout this unit.

☺ ☺ EXPLORATION: Seasons Sun & Earth Model

For this activity, you will need:

- A book or video about seasons from the Library List or YouTube playlist
- Globe
- Flashlight
- At least two helpers
- Science Notebook
- Colored pencils or crayons

The earth's rotation around the sun and the tilt of the earth are what cause seasons.

1. Darken a room so the light is dim.

2. Have one person stand in the center of the room and hold the flashlight so it shines straight on the globe.

3. Another person holds the globe, so the base is horizontal to the floor. The poles should be tilted in relation to the "sun." Note how the light is shining on the globe. Where

Seasons & Climate

are the sun's rays most direct? Where is it summer?

4. The person with the globe should slowly walk around the sun, keeping the tilt of the poles in the same direction as you move. The "sun" needs to rotate so the light is shining directly on the globe the entire time. Observe how the direct sunlight on the earth changes position as you move around the "sun."

5. Read a book or watch a video about seasons.

6. Draw a picture of how the earth's tilt causes seasons in your Science Notebook.

😊 😊 **EXPERIMENT: Spreading Out the Light**

For this activity, you will need:

- Flashlight
- Cardboard box or a step stool
- Masking tape
- Graph paper
- Markers
- Flat surface like a clipboard or cutting board
- Protractor
- Science Notebook

When a given amount of light is spread over a larger area, the light is indirect and weaker. It is not the slight increase in distance that the tilt of the earth gives that changes the seasons, but the amount of direct light.

1. Set a flashlight on top of a cardboard box or a small step stool. Tape it in place, if necessary.

2. Tape a piece of graph paper to a flat surface, like a cutting board or clipboard.

3. Turn the flashlight on and place the graph paper in front of the flashlight, straight on. Move the paper back and

Bookworms

This adorable book, *Sing a Song of Seasons* by Frann Preston-Gannon and Fiona Waters, has one nature poem for each day of the year.

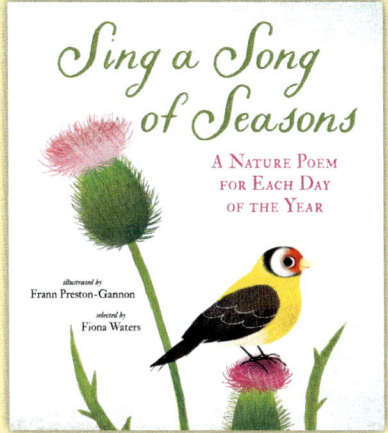

Perfect to read your child at bedtime or for morning meeting.

Additional Layer

The North Pole always points toward Polaris, also known as the North Star.

☆

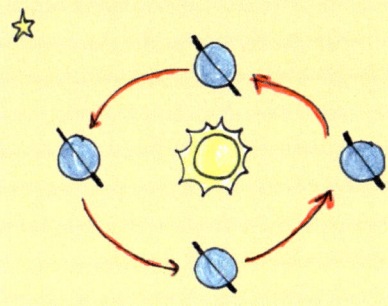

This constancy is why the earth sometimes tilts toward the sun and sometimes tilts away.

Draw a picture of the earth revolving around the sun and show where the North Star is.

The North Star is so far away that even as Earth travels millions of miles across space, it always looks like it is straight overhead.

Earth & Space

Bookworms

For ages nine and up, *I Begin With Spring* is part nature journal, part biography about a famous American philosopher and naturalist, Henry David Thoreau.

Memorization Station

Here's a fun poem to memorize during this unit:

Autumn Fires
by Robert Louis Stevenson

*In the other gardens
And all up the vale,
From the autumn bonfires
See the smoke trail!
Pleasant summer over
And all the summer flowers,
The red fire blazes,
The grey smoke towers.
Sing a song of seasons!
Something bright in all!
Flowers in the summer,
Fires in the fall!*

forth, closer to and further from the flashlight, until you get a nice sharp circle of light on the paper.

4. Draw a sketch of your set up in your Science Notebook. What do you think will happen to the light when you tilt the graph paper backward, away from the light, so the light is indirect? Write a hypothesis.

5. Observe the intensity of the light when the light is straight on. Trace the circle of light with a colored marker.

6. Keeping the base of your graph paper at the same position, tilt the paper backward until it is at 105°. Use a protractor to check the angle. Observe the intensity of the light. Trace the new shape of the light on the graph paper with a different colored marker.

7. Repeat at 120° and 135° using a different colored marker for each test.

8. Now, fill in a chart like this in your Science Notebook. Count the number of squares inside each of the shapes you traced on the graph paper. If you have a partial square, count it as .25 or .50 or .75 of a square.

Degree of Tilt	Number of squares lit up	Observed intensity of light
90°		5
105°		
120°		
135°		

In the "observed intensity of light" column, write a number from 1-5. Assign the 0° of tilt an intensity of 5.

9. Discuss why the brightness of light decreased as the tilt increased. How does this relate to seasons on Earth?

10. Tape your graph paper to your page in your Science Notebook along the top edge so you will be able to lift the paper to see the writing below.

😊 😊 😊 EXPLORATION: What Causes the Seasons?

For this activity, you will need:

- "What Causes the Seasons?" from the Printable Pack, 2 pages
- Scissors
- Glue stick
- Colored pencils or crayons
- Science Notebook
- Book or video about the seasons

Seasons occur as the earth moves around the sun. It takes one year for the earth to travel all the way around the

Seasons & Climate

sun. As it travels, the axis remains tilted the same direction. When the North Pole is tilted directly toward the sun, this is the **June solstice**, the beginning of summer in the Northern Hemisphere. When the North Pole is tilted exactly away from the sun, this is the **December solstice**, the beginning of winter in the Northern Hemisphere. The points exactly halfway between the June and December solstices are called the **September equinox** and **March equinox**. At the equinoxes, the sun appears to be directly over the equator.

1. Read a book or watch a video about the seasons.
2. Color the title "What Causes the Seasons?" and then cut it out and paste it into a page in your Science Notebook. Add the title to your table of contents.
3. Color the little pictures of the earth in the boxes at the bottom of the first page. Then, cut them out. Cut out the large rectangle on the solid lines. Fold on the dashed lines.
4. Glue the back of the shutter-fold book to your Science Notebook. Color each of the flaps. Glue the correct picture on each flap. They should match the description.
5. Inside each flap, finish the sentence that is begun on the

Deep Thoughts

What if the earth weren't tilted? What would it be like if the earth had no seasons?

How would the poles be different? How would the equator be different?

How would the weather be different?

How would plants and animals be different?

After discussing this, you might want to go online and search for "what if earth had no seasons" to see what scientists think.

Memorization Station

Memorize what these mean and also how the sun and earth are aligned.

June solstice: the longest day of the year in the Northern Hemisphere, when the sun appears to reach furthest north

December solstice: the longest day of the year in the Southern Hemisphere, when the sun appears to reach furthest south

September equinox: the point when the sun appears to leave the Northern Hemisphere and move into the Southern Hemisphere

March equinox: the point when the sun appears to leave the Southern Hemisphere and move into the Northern Hemisphere

Earth & Space

Additional Layer

Discuss what the climate is like where you live.

How much rainfall do you get on average? How much did you get in the past year? Was it above, below, or right on the average?

What are the high temperatures in winter and summer where you live? The low temperatures in winter and summer?

Do you have a four season climate or not? What do people call the seasons where you are?

Additional Layer

Discuss micro-climates. Within the large temperate band of North America, there are places that are very different from each other. Glacier National Park in Montana has much colder and earlier winters than land a few hundred miles to the west, in central Washington. Glacier National Park is very high in the Rockies and has an alpine climate.

Places near the ocean are affected greatly by the gulf streams that pass near the shore. Western Washington has a much warmer and wetter climate than the eastern part of Washington State because of the warmth and wetness of the ocean. England, with a much higher latitude, has a milder climate than the Central Plains of North America.

What else affects the climate?

What factors determine the temperature and weather patterns of Earth?

---

front of the flap. Include information you learned from your reading.

6. On the second page of the printable, color each of the spaces for the months in the larger circle. Then color each of the quadrants in the smaller circle.

7. Cut out the small word tags. Glue the season names in the correct space on the smaller circle. Spring comes between March 19-20 and June 20-22 and so on.

8. Then, on the larger circle, glue the correct tags to their spaces. Winter solstice should be in December, spring equinox in March, summer solstice in June, and fall equinox in September.

9. Glue the smaller circle inside the larger circle so that the winter solstice, December 20-22, is lined up with approximately that date on the larger circle.

10. Glue the circles to your Science Notebook.

11. Inside each of the seasons boxes in the long strip, draw a tree for each season. Glue the season strip to your Science Notebook.

🙂🙂🙂 EXPLORATION: Seasons North & Seasons South

For this activity, you will need:

- Foam ball, 6-8 inches (15-20 cm)
- Wooden skewer
- Toothpicks
- Paint & brushes or markers
- Blue spray paint
- Black permanent marker
- Masking tape
- Flashlight
- Globe

The seasons in the Northern and Southern Hemispheres are exactly opposite of one another. Because if the north is tilted toward the sun, then the south must be tilted away.

1. Ahead of time, paint a foam ball blue with spray paint. Let it dry completely.

2. Insert a wooden skewer directly through the center of the foam ball, all of the way through and out the other side. This is the axis of your earth.

3. Next to one end of the axis, write "N" for north and at the other end write "S" for south. Use the marker to draw the Equator halfway between the North and South Poles and all of the way around the ball.

4. Paint or color the land onto the foam ball. Don't worry about it being totally accurate; just do your best. Use a globe to help you.

Seasons & Climate

5. Stick a toothpick in the foam ball at your location on Earth. Stick another toothpick in at the location exactly opposite of you. Label both of these toothpicks with masking tape flags.

6. Use a flashlight to demonstrate how the seasons for you are exactly opposite to the seasons on the other side of the world. If your part of the earth is tilted toward the sun and you are getting direct sunlight, then the people on the other side of the world must be getting indirect, weak sun.

7. Use the globe you made to demonstrate what happens to the sunlight at the poles in the summer and in the winter. Why is it bright all summer at one pole and dim all winter?

8. On your globe, look for the arctic circles. These are the lines that show which portion of the globe has no sunrise in the winter.

9. Next, find the Tropic of Cancer and the Tropic of Capricorn. These lines show the furthest north and furthest south that sun is ever directly overhead. If you live north or south of these lines, then you will never see the sun straight over head, even in the middle of the summer.

10. Draw the arctic circles and the two tropics on your foam globe. Use the flashlight to model how the sun appears to change its position in the sky as the earth revolves around the sun and the seasons change.

Writer's Workshop

Use "Seasonal Art Journaling" from the Printable Pack to create your own creative page, then write a poem about each of the seasons. See *Writer's Workshop: Poetry* for fun ideas.

Bookworms

Moonstick: The Seasons of the Sioux by Eve Bunting is a picture book about a young boy and his father who mark a stick to show each new moon. Through the story, the young boy watches the world change around him as each stick is marked.

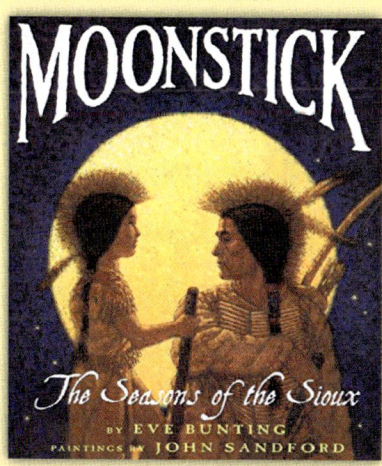

This is a fascinating look at how a different culture perceives and marks seasons as they pass.

Earth & Space

Memorization Station

Memorize the layers of the atmosphere in order.

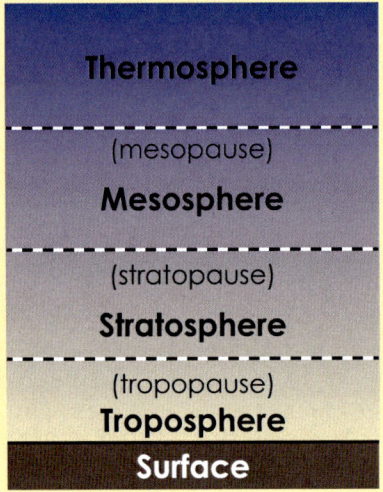

Additional Layer

Aurora borealis (or northern lights) and aurora australis (or southern lights) are caused by solar winds blowing across Earth's magnetosphere, or magnetic shield. Particles in the atmosphere are excited and create the colorful lights we see in the sky.

Learn more about the northern and southern lights and find out:

- How they are the same
- How they are different from each other
- What causes them
- When and where you can see them
- How high in the atmosphere they occur
- What color is most common

Atmosphere

The earth is surrounded by a pocket of gases called the **atmosphere**. All of the planets in our solar system have atmospheres. Earth has an atmosphere made of layers of gases that we rely on to make our planet habitable.

😊😊😊 EXPLORATION: Layers of the Sky

For this activity, you will need:

- White paper - 7 sheets
- Mathematical compass
- Watercolor paints
- Scissors
- Glue
- Black permanent marker

The sky isn't one consistent body trailing off into space; it has layers. The layer nearest the earth's surface is called the troposphere. It is 10 kilometers thick and contains all the weather on Earth. If you see a giant cumulonimbus anvil cloud that trails off in a straight line high up, you are seeing the upper limit of the troposphere.

The next layer is the stratosphere, which contains the ozone layer. The ozone layer is toward the bottom of the stratosphere and, since the ozone layer absorbs radiation from the sun, the stratosphere is colder at the bottom and gets warmer as the altitude increases.

Above the stratosphere is the mesosphere. The temperatures in this layer start out warmer and become colder as altitude increases. The mesosphere contains lots of turbulence which mixes the parts of the mesosphere thoroughly. The upper boundary of this layer is called the mesopause and this is the coldest part of the atmosphere.

The final layer is the thermosphere, which is where the auroras occur and noctilucent clouds form. The thermosphere is also where most meteors burn up as

Seasons & Climate

shooting stars. This layer contains gases separated out by weight, with heavier ones floating below lighter ones. This level also absorbs lots of radiation and is warmer than the mesosphere beneath it. Most artificial satellites, including the International Space Station, orbit inside the thermosphere.

Sometimes the exosphere is included as a layer of the atmosphere as well, but it is mostly outer space with a few escaped molecules of atmosphere from Earth. The density of molecules is so low that they rarely collide with each other. This layer gradually thins out and becomes space.

1. Draw a circle with a radius of 5 cm on a piece of paper. Freehand paint the circle with watercolor paints to look like the earth with green continents and blue oceans.
2. Use watercolor paints to paint 4 other sheets of paper with blue, shading each piece to be a little darker than the one before.
3. Paint your last piece of paper with black watercolor paints.
4. Let the papers dry, then trace circles with increasing diameters starting with 7 cm for the lightest blue, then 9 cm for the next, 11 cm for the third blue, and 15 cm for the final, darkest blue paper. You will only need a half circle of each color, so it's okay if your entire circle doesn't fit on a paper.
5. Cut each circle in half, creating a semicircle. Glue the darkest blue to the black paper so they share a straight line at the bottom of the page. Then, glue each concentric circle on top of the last, ending with the earth.
6. Label each of the layers using a black permanent marker from lowest to highest: troposphere, stratosphere, mesosphere, thermosphere. If you'd like, you can also label the black paper the exosphere.

😊 😊 😊 **EXPLORATION: What is the Atmosphere Made Of?**
For this activity, you will need:

- Book or video about Earth's atmosphere from the Library List or YouTube playlist
- 22 balloons - 15 blue, 4 white, 2 yellow, and 1 red
- Permanent marker
- Science Notebook
- Colored pencils or crayons

The atmosphere is 78% nitrogen, 21% oxygen, 1% argon,

Memorization Station

Atmosphere: the envelope of gases surrounding the earth or another planet

Without our atmosphere, our Earth couldn't support life. It protects us from the sun's radiation, provides enough pressure for water to exist here, gives us oxygen to breathe, and warms our planet.

Additional Layer

Most of Earth's atmosphere is nitrogen. Nitrogen is essential for life, but only a very few living things can get nitrogen directly from the air. Instead, plants get it from the soil, and then animals eat plants.

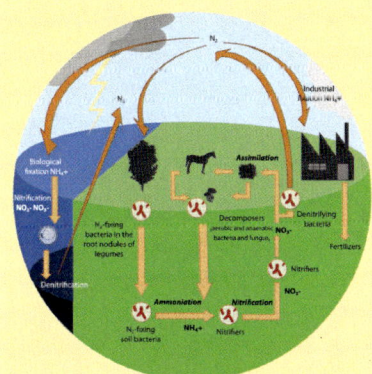

Learn more about the nitrogen cycle as nitrogen moves from the earth, to the air, to the soil, to living things, and then back to the earth.

Earth & Space

Famous Folks

Frenchman Leon Teisserenc de Bort invented weather balloons and sent up over 200 as he studied the sky.

He discovered the first two layers of the atmosphere and named them troposphere and stratosphere.

Bookworms

The Aeronauts by James Glaisher is the original 1862 account, by the scientist, of the first balloonists to ascend into the upper atmosphere for science.

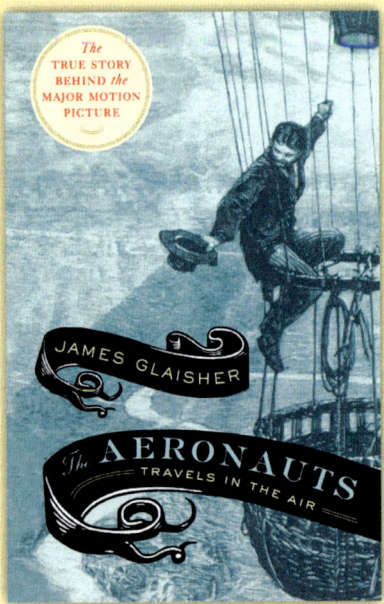

The 2019 movie, *The Aeronauts,* was based on this epic ascent into the heavens.

and a tiny .04% trace gases. The trace gases include carbon dioxide, helium, hydrogen, krypton, methane, and neon.

1. Read a book or watch a video about Earth's atmosphere.
2. Blow up and tie off all of the balloons. Blow the red balloon only half full.
3. Mark each balloon with a chemical symbol for the type of atom that it represents in the atmosphere. Blue balloons should be marked with N_2 for nitrogen, white with O_2 for oxygen, yellow with Ar for argon, and write "trace" on the red balloon.
4. Put all the balloons in one room and have fun bouncing them around, keeping as many up at a time as you can.

   The proportions of the elements in the air are close to the proportions of the balloons bouncing around. And like the balloons, the molecules of gases in the air are always in motion, bouncing around and hitting one another.

5. Draw a picture in your Science Notebook of the molecules. Draw 15 nitrogens, 4 oxygens, 2 argons, and 1 tiny trace molecule. Write a paragraph about the composition of molecules in the atmosphere.

Don't forget to give your page a title and add it to your table of contents.

😊 😊 😊 EXPERIMENT: Sun Heats the Air

WARNING: This activity includes very hot water. Use caution!

For this activity, you will need:

- Shallow dish
- Water, boiling or near boiling
- Erlenmeyer flask or jar with a narrow mouth
- Balloon
- Video about the sun causing climates and weather
- Science Notebook

The weather on Earth is mostly caused by the sun's heat. Heat from the sun affects the temperature and the movement of the air. It also evaporates water, causing rain and snow.

1. Watch a video about how the sun causes the climates and weather.
2. Pour about 5 cm of very hot water into a shallow dish.

Seasons & Climate

3. Pre-blow a balloon to stretch out the rubber a bit, then deflate it again. Stretch the deflated balloon over the mouth of a flask.

4. Place the flask with the balloon in the hot water. Observe the balloon.

   The balloon begins to blow up as the hot air in the jar moves and expands. The air in earth's atmosphere is also heated and moves and expands with the heat.

5. Draw a picture of your experiment in your Science Notebook. Label the picture. Write a sentence or two about how the sun's heat moves and expands the air, causing the weather.

☺ ☺ ☺ **EXPERIMENT: Atmospheric Pressure**

WARNING: This activity includes fire. Use caution!

For this activity, you will need:

- Book or video about atmospheric pressure
- Beaker or large jar
- Shallow dish - like a pie pan
- Water
- Candle
- Matches or lighter
- Science Notebook

Air is made up of molecules of gas, which are being pulled toward the center of the planet by gravity. Their weight presses down on everything on the surface. This is called **atmospheric pressure**.

1. Head a new page in your Science Notebook "Atmospheric Pressure" and add it to your table of contents.

2. Watch a video about atmospheric pressure.

Memorization Station

Atmospheric pressure: the weight of the air pressing down on the earth

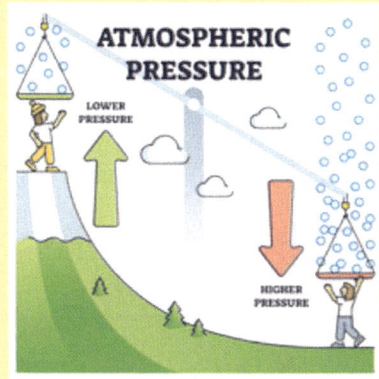

Air pressure is caused by the weight of the air molecules above. Each molecule only weighs a tiny bit, but there are huge numbers of molecules that all add up.

Famous Folks

Japanese geophysicist Syukuro Manabe first developed the models that show how air actually flows and circulates in the atmosphere.

Photo by Bengt Nyman of Vaxholm, Sweden, CC by SA 2.0 Wikimedia

He also developed computer models to simulate the effects of CO_2 on the climate.

Earth & Space

Additional Layer

To demonstrate air pressure simply to little ones, blow up a balloon and then let it go, watching it buzz around on its own air power. Explain that even though we can't see air, it is real and causes things to move. Without air pressure, clouds wouldn't move; airplanes wouldn't fly; and your lungs wouldn't inflate. You wouldn't be able to breathe!

Additional Layer

Sunspots are dark spots on the surface of the sun. They are areas that are cooler than the rest of the sun. The number of sunspots increases and decreases in an 11-year cycle.

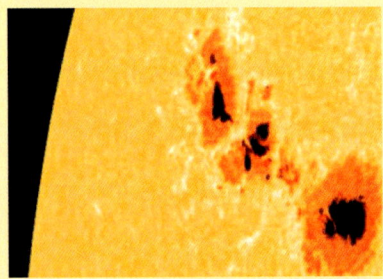

Some scientists think that sunspots may be related to overall weather patterns and climate. Go find out more.

3. Pour water into a shallow pan so it is about half full.

4. Put a candle into the center of the baking dish and light it. Write a hypothesis in your Science Notebook about what you think will happen if you place a jar upside down over the candle.

5. Place a jar upside down over the candle.

6. Observe carefully as the candle burns up the oxygen inside the jar and goes out. What happens to the water level in the jar? Why?

The candle burns up a portion of the air inside the jar, creating a partial vacuum where there is less air pressure. The reduced air pressure causes the water level inside the jar to rise.

This same phenomenon happens in nature when rising warm air leaves an area of reduced pressure, allowing cold air to rush in to fill the space. This is how wind storms and hurricanes begin.

7. Draw and label a picture of your experiment in your Science Notebook. Add a paragraph about what you learned about the weight of the air.

EXPERIMENT: Air Contracts & Expands

WARNING: This activity includes very hot water. Use caution!

For this activity, you will need:

- Transparent bottle with a narrow mouth
- Dish soap
- Water, nearly boiling and cold water

166

Seasons & Climate

- Ice
- 2 containers with high sides, about the size of a shoe box
- 1 small dish
- Science Notebook

When air warms, it expands and rises. When air cools, it contracts and sinks. This is true of the air in the whole atmosphere, which explains a lot about the weather we experience on Earth.

1. Put a few squirts of dish soap into the small container and dilute it with an equal amount of water, gently stirring to mix it.
2. Fill one of your large containers one third full with cold water. Add at least 12 ice cubes to cool it further.
3. Fill the other large container one third full with very hot water, heated almost to boiling on a stove or in a microwave.
4. Carefully dip the open end of the narrow-mouthed bottle in the soap mixture so a thin film of soap stretches across the opening. Place the bottle in the cold water and observe what happens to the film of soap.

This is the bottle in cold water. You can see the soap line way below the mouth of the bottle.

This is the bottle in hot water. The soap has formed a big bubble above the bottle.

5. Draw a picture of your experiment in your Science Notebook. Label it.
6. Hypothesize what will happen when you place the bottle in the hot water. Try it and see!
7. Write a paragraph about what you learned about the behavior of hot and cold air.

Fabulous Fact

If the Earth were just a little bit bigger, gravity would be too great for a proper atmosphere. If it were just a tiny bit smaller, Earth wouldn't have enough of a magnetic field to keep the harmful radiation of the sun from stripping away our atmosphere.

Famous Folks

The first barometer was invented by Evangelista Torricelli in 1644.

Famous Folks

Susan Solomon went to Antarctica to study the then recently discovered hole in the Ozone Layer in 1986.

She hypothesized that the hole was caused by CFCs, chemical propellants used in aerosols and in industry. Her work resulted in the worldwide ban on CFCs in 1989.

Earth & Space

Bookworms

Read about both sides of the climate change argument to compare and decide for yourself. Keeping an open mind means listening, really listening, then using your reason and experience to decide. You have to be willing to find out you were wrong. That requires humility.

It's Getting Hot In Here by Bridget Heos is a pro-global warming book that explains the science behind the argument. It is written for ages 12 and up.

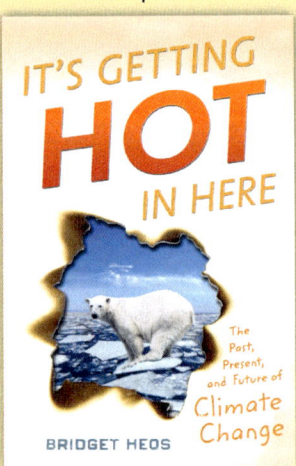

Next, read *The Geology of Climate Change* by Gene D. Robinson. This is written by a geologist who uses the record and data from the rocks to refute the climate change argument.

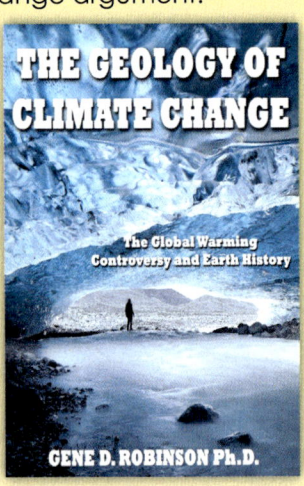

😊😊😊 EXPERIMENT: Ozone Layer

For this activity, you will need:

- 2 sheets of clear plastic, like from food packaging
- Dark colored paper
- Clear tape
- Clipboard
- Science Notebook
- Video about the ozone layer from the YouTube playlist

Near the lower part of the stratosphere is a thin layer of ozone. Ozone is three oxygen molecules bonded together. Ozone is created by radiation from the sun striking normal oxygen gas, O_2, and splitting it into individual atoms. Each uncombined oxygen atom then combines with normal molecules of O_2, making O_3. Each ozone molecule is unstable, but because of the sun's radiation, there is a steady supply in the stratosphere. The thin layer of ozone absorbs much of the harmful radiation from the sun, protecting life on Earth.

1. Watch a video about the ozone layer.

2. Make a model of the way the ozone layer protects life on Earth using sunscreen. First, spread sunscreen on one piece of clear plastic. It should be a thin layer that doesn't block the sunlight by being opaque.

3. Put a sheet of colored paper outside in the sun. Tape the clear plastic piece to the paper.

4. What do you think will happen to the paper exposed to sun versus the paper protected by the sunscreen? Write down your hypothesis in your Science Notebook.

5. Leave the paper out in the sun for three hours or more. When the time is up, check the paper for effects of the

Seasons & Climate

sun. Did the sunscreen protect the paper? How is this like the ozone layer?

6. Draw a picture of your experiment and write your observations and conclusions in your Science Notebook.

Climate

Climate is the overall weather trends and conditions in a particular place over time. Climatologists average the weather over a 30-year period to arrive at a climate classification. It is different from **weather** because weather changes from day to day and hour-to-hour. You can have extremely hot weather in a cold climate and extremely cold weather in a hot climate.

😊 😊 😊 **EXPLORATION: Climate Map**
For this activity, you will need:

- "Climate Map" from the Printable Pack
- Colored pencils
- Book or video about climate from the Library List or YouTube playlist

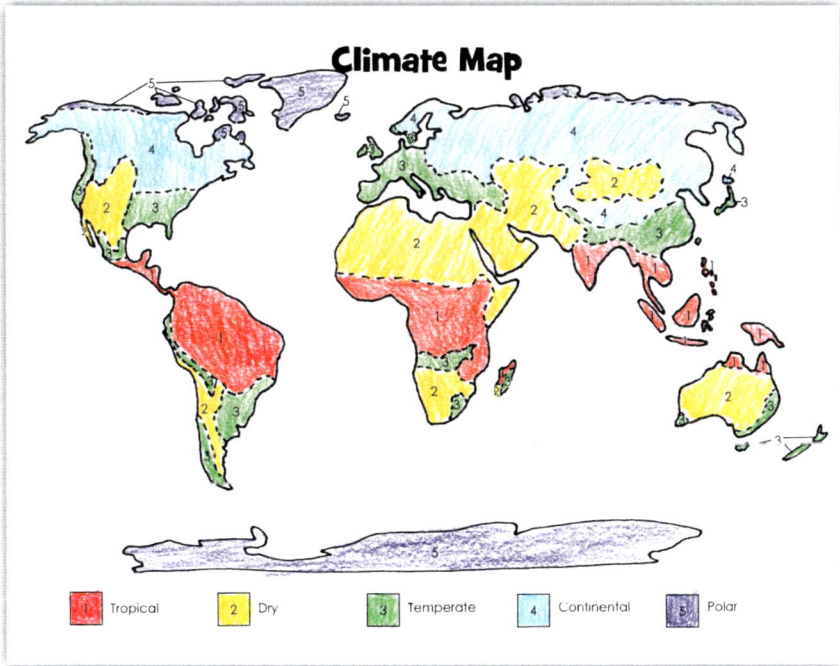

Earth has an overall climate, but there are also climate zones on Earth. Climate is a 30-year average of weather in a particular place, including temperature, humidity, precipitation, and wind. Climate is affected by latitude, elevation, proximity to oceans, and terrain. The Köppen climate classification system recognizes five main types of climate: tropical, dry, temperate, continental, and polar.

Additional Layer

Climate is far more complex than the map on this page shows. This is a generalized map that shows the whole earth. Look up a climate map of your country or region to see more detail. Also, look up micro-climates. A tiny unique climate might exist against a wall in your yard.

Teaching Tip

You'll also find a simplified "Climate Zones On Earth" in the Printable Pack that kids can paint with watercolor paints to learn the basics of climate with fewer details than the "Climate Map." Use the image below to help you paint the map correctly.

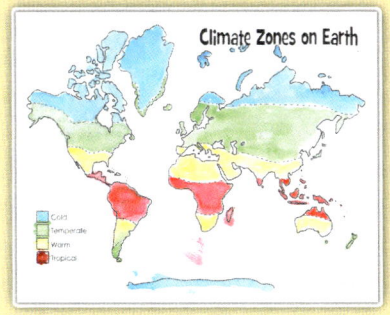

Memorization Station

Learn the definitions of weather and climate.

Climate: the long-term average of weather in a particular place that includes average precipitation, temperature, humidity, wind, and atmospheric pressure

Weather: the condition of the atmosphere in a particular place at a given moment and includes measures of precipitation, wind, temperature, humidity, and atmospheric pressure

Earth & Space

Famous Folks

Astronomer Edward Maunder married his assistant, Annie Russell, and together, they studied sunspot records.

They found that there had been almost no sunspots between 1645 and 1715, during a time known as the "Little Ice Age."

The Maunders concluded that there must be a connection between the lack of sunspots and the climate. Modern scientists are still debating the Maunder Minimum hypothesis.

Memorization Station

Greenhouse gas: a gas that can absorb radiation from the sun and then release it back out, thereby increasing the temperature of the earth

Additional Layer

Look up information on your hometown and make a graph showing temperatures or rainfall for a past period of time, like highest temperatures over the last ten years or the amount of rainfall during each month of the last year.

1. Color the "Climate Map" according to the numbers in the key on the printable.
2. Read a book or watch a video about climate.
3. Add the map to the Science section of your Layers of Learning Notebook.

☺☺☺ **EXPERIMENT: Greenhouse Gases**

For this activity, you will need:

- 2 beakers or jars
- Cold water
- Thermometer
- Plastic bag
- Science Notebook
- Books or videos about greenhouse gases and about the atmosphere
- Timer

Greenhouse gases are the part of the atmosphere that traps the sun's heat at the surface of the earth. Without greenhouse gases, the earth would be intensely cold and frozen. Greenhouse gases include water vapor, carbon dioxide, carbon monoxide, and other minor gases.

The amount of greenhouse gases in the atmosphere has a huge effect on the earth's climate.

1. Fill each jar with 200 ml of cold water.
2. Cover one jar loosely with a plastic bag. Leave both jars in the sun.
3. Head a new page in your Science Notebook "Greenhouse Gases" and add it to your table of contents. Draw a labeled diagram of your experiment. Write a hypothesis of what you think will happen to the temperature in each jar.

Seasons & Climate

4. Check the temperature of the water in each jar every 15 minutes for at least an hour. Record the data in a table.

5. While you are waiting in between temperature checks, watch a video and read books about the atmosphere and greenhouse gases.

6. Draw a graph of the temperature of the water in each jar. Explain what you think happened.

7. 😊 Discuss:

   a. How is this model similar to and different from the real atmosphere?

   b. Do you think this is a good model for learning about the real atmosphere?

   c. How could you make a better model?

😊 😊 😊 **EXPERIMENT: Ice Ages and Ocean Currents**

For this activity, you will need:

- Shallow pan
- Clay or salt dough (1/2 cup warm tap water, 1/4 cup salt, 4 tablespoons cooking oil, 2 cups flour)
- Ice water with blue food coloring
- Hot water with red food coloring
- Globe
- Science Notebook

An **ice age** is an extended period when the earth cools and ice sheets expand from the poles toward the equator. Anytime there is permanent ice at the poles is an ice age. Earth's climate alternates between ice ages and greenhouse periods when the earth is so warm that there are no glaciers or ice sheets. Ice ages last for 100,000 years or so. Currently, Earth is in its fifth ice age.

One of the major factors that causes an ice age is the position of continents. If warm equatorial ocean water is prevented from flowing to the poles, ice begins to build up.

1. Look at a globe of the earth. Can warm ocean water flow easily to the poles today?

2. Build continents out of clay in a shallow pan so that the poles are blocked partially or completely.

3. Fill the pan with ice cold water, but not over the top of the "continents." Let the water settle for a minute.

4. Put several drops of red food coloring into very hot water. Carefully pour the hot water in the central part

---

Famous Folks

American geologist Wallace S. Broecker discovered the global oceanic "conveyor belt" system of deep ocean currents, a major factor in global climate.

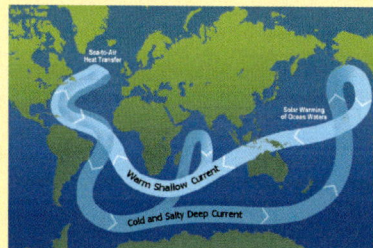

A graphic of the ocean circulation conveyor belt, this is a major discovery by Broecker.

He also helped construct the carbon cycle. Broecker is known as the "grandfather of climate science."

He also worked on carbon sequestration, methods of capturing and storing CO_2 from the atmosphere.

Memorization Station

Ice age: an extended period of cold, earth-wide climate that results in permanent ice caps at the poles

Within an ice age, there are fluctuations. Colder periods are called glacials and warmer periods are called interglacials. During a glacial, the ice advances from the poles. During an interglacial, the ice retreats toward the poles. An interglacial lasts from around 10 to 20 thousand years.

Right now Earth is in the Pleistocene ice age, but we are experiencing an interglacial period, an intermittent warm phase called the Holocene.

Earth & Space

Additional Layer

El Niño is a weather pattern caused by shifting ocean currents that happens in the Pacific Ocean along the equator. During an el Niño year, the western Pacific experiences droughts while the eastern Pacific has floods. The weather across half the globe shifts dramatically just because of these ocean currents.

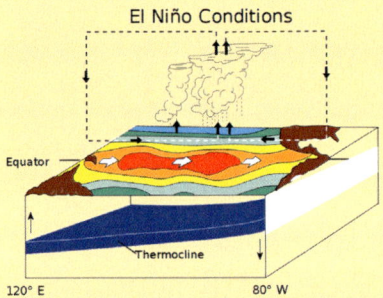

Learn more about El Niño.

Famous Folks

Milutin Milanković was arrested in Austria at the outbreak of WWI for being a Serbian.

He arrived in prison with nothing but his suitcase, which was full of his calculations on the climate, orbits, and precession, and lots of blank paper.

Find out more about how Milanković discovered the cycles that lead to major climate shifts on Earth.

---

of the dish, where the equator would be. How well does the warmer water reach the poles?

5. Head a new page in your Science Notebook "Ice Ages and Ocean Currents" and add it to your table of contents. Draw a labeled diagram of your experiment. Write your observations and conclusions.

6. Repeat the experiment, but position continents so they do not block the poles. Add the new trial to your Science Notebook.

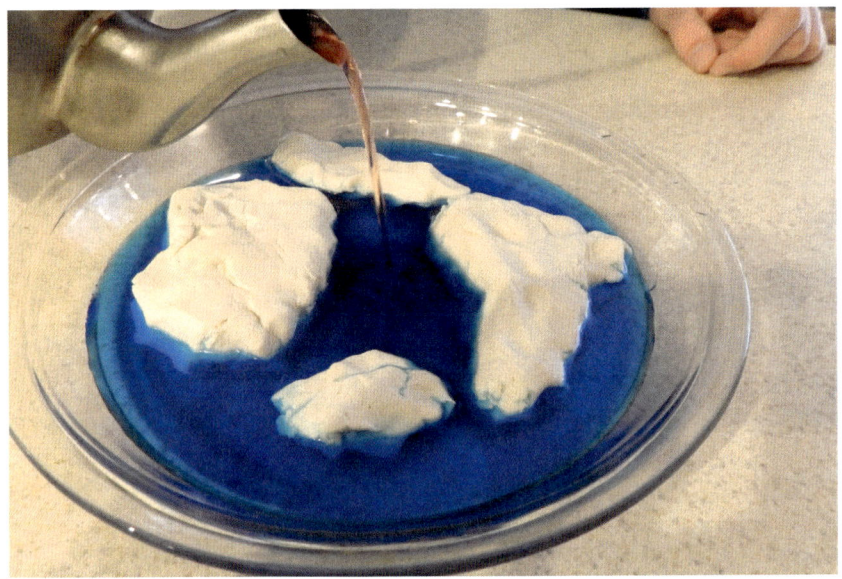

😊 😊 EXPLORATION: Milankovitch Cycles & Ice Cores

For this activity, you will need:

- Tall disposable can, like from Pringles potato chips or tennis balls
- Water
- Blue food coloring
- Ash and carbonated water (optional)
- Freezer
- Metric ruler
- Video about the Milankovitch cycles from the YouTube playlist for this unit

The overall climate of Earth depends on three things related to Earth's position in space:

- Eccentricity: the shape of the Earth's orbit
- The tilt of the axis
- Precession: the wobbling of the pole so that the direction of Earth's axis tilt changes

All these factors together add up to regular, cyclical changes in the overall climate of Earth. The Milankovitch

Seasons & Climate

cycle takes about 100,000 years to go from the start of one ice age to the start of the next.

We know that the math of the Milankovitch cycles coincides with actual ice ages on Earth because of ice cores. In places where the ice never melts, like the Vostok Station in Antarctica, we can drill deep into the ice and take a long sample out. Winter ice is less dense than summer ice because summer ice melts just a little bit. This makes rings, like tree rings. The thickness of the ice layers and the things trapped in the ice, like ash, insects, or bubbles of gas, let us know what the earth was like in past ages. We can tell how long ago ice ages occurred.

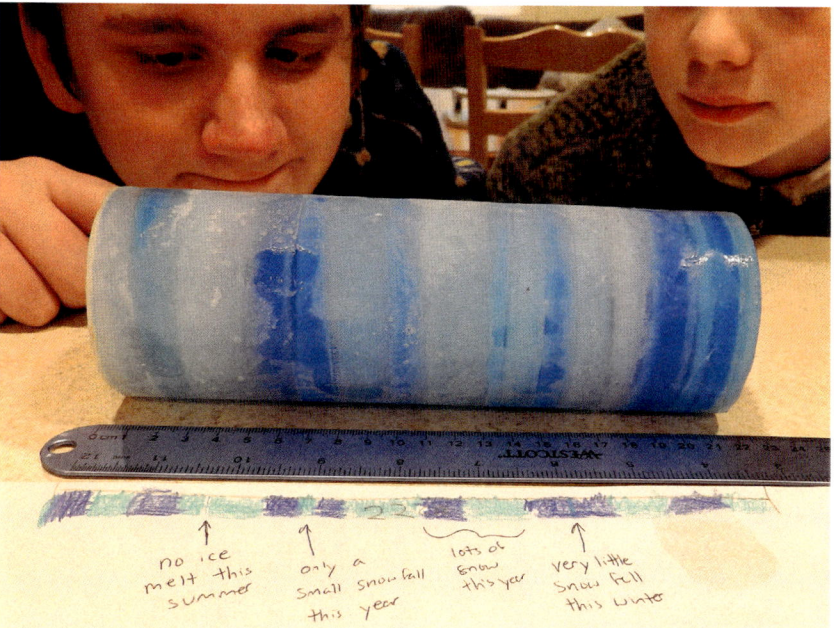

1. Prepare an "ice core" ahead of time. Pour about 2 cm of clear water into the bottom of a tall potato chip or tennis ball can. The clear water represents winter ice. Put it in the freezer and let it freeze completely.

   Add several drops of blue food coloring to a pitcher of water. Pour a thin layer of blue water over the ice in the bottom of the can. The blue is for summer ice. Freeze completely.

   If you'd like, you can add a little bit of ash (to show a volcanic eruption) or some carbonated water (to show trapped gas bubbles) to the layers randomly.

   Repeat freezing layers of water until the can is full. Some layers should be thicker than others. This process may take several days. If you start with already chilled water, it will be a bit quicker.

2. Watch a video about the Milankovitch cycle.

Writer's Workshop

Look up the definitions of climate and weather. Write a paragraph comparing and contrasting climate and weather. How are they related and how are they different?

Fabulous Fact

By looking at ice cores, scientists have found that atmospheric rises in carbon dioxide coincided with warmer periods on Earth. Since 1958, scientists at the Mauna Loa observatory in Hawaii, which has exceptionally clean air but is also near an active volcano, have been directly measuring levels of carbon dioxide in the atmosphere. CO_2 has steadily climbed from less than 320 parts per million to more than 420 parts per million during that time.

Many scientists hypothesize that the increase in carbon dioxide is due to human activities like burning coal and gasoline and clear cutting forests because the carbon dioxide began to climb around the time of the Industrial Revolution.

Fabulous Fact

Global warming or global cooling results in changes in habitats. For example, a 3° C rise in temperature means climate zones shift around 300 or so kilometers closer to the poles.

Animals and plants that thrive 300 km south of where you live (in the Northern Hemisphere) would now do well in your location.

Earth & Space

Famous Folks

Swedish meteorologist Lennart O. Bengtsson has received numerous awards from all over the world, has published over 180 peer-reviewed journals, and is a climate skeptic.

Photo by Vogler, CC by SA 4.0 Wikimedia

Bengtsson is most famous for being forced by political and academic pressure to recant his criticisms of *Environmental Research Letters*, a scientific journal, for refusing to publish his paper for what Bengtsson thought was political reasons, and resign from a climate skeptic organization, the GWPF.

Additional Layer

Climate is always changing on Earth and usually these changes are slow.

However, the Younger Dryas event in Greenland that occurred around 12,000 years ago was very abrupt.

Learn more about this event, what caused it, and what the results were for the animals and plants that lived in Greenland at the time.

Consider what an abrupt climate change in your region would mean for you.

3. Head a new page in your Science Notebook "Ice Cores" and add it to your table of contents.

4. Remove the cardboard can from the ice core.

5. Measure the thickness of each layer and record your measurements in your Science Notebook. Make observations about each "year" in your ice core.

Draw a sketch of your ice core and label with the observations about each year.

Was it a year of high snowfall or low? Was there a volcanic eruption that year? Why are there more bubbles in some layers? **(The bubbles represent carbon dioxide and mean a much warmer climate with more CO_2 in the air.)**

😊 😊 😊 EXPERIMENT: Feedback Loops & Albedo

For this activity, you will need:

- 2 sheets of paper, one black and one white
- Tape
- 2 thermometers (one will work, if that's all you have)
- Heat lamp or a hot, sunny day
- Video on feedback loops from the YouTube playlist for this unit

Feedback is when a system creates a product that amplifies the tendency of the system. For example, snow reflects sunlight and keeps the climate cold so more snow accumulates. The production of snow feeds back into the system, making even more snow.

The climate has many factors that can create feedback loops including albedo, CO_2, volcanoes, land near the poles, and ocean currents.

Albedo is the reflective quality of a surface. A surface with high albedo, like snow and ice, reflects a lot of light. This means less heat on the surface and ice that expands even further.

1. Fold your black sheet of paper in half, hamburger-style and use tape to secure the sides. Do the same with the white sheet of paper.

2. Slip the bulb end of a thermometer into each of the paper rectangles. Set the paper and thermometers under a heat lamp or outside in direct sunlight. Record the temperature every two minutes for 14 minutes.

If you only have one thermometer, you can run this test twice, once with the black paper and once with the

Seasons & Climate

white paper.

3. Head a new page in your Science Notebook "Feedback Loops" and add it to your table of contents. Draw a labeled diagram of your experiment. Write down your hypothesis of what will happen to the two temperatures in the papers.

4. Watch a video about feedback loops. Take notes from the video in your Science Notebook.

5. Discuss how the albedo of the white paper kept the temperature cooler. What does this have to do with ice and the climate? Of course, land that is not covered with snow isn't usually black. What do you think is really happening in the real world?

6. Write down your conclusions from your experiment in your Science Notebook.

😊 😊 😊 EXPERIMENT: CO_2 as a Greenhouse Gas

For this activity, you will need:

- Two identical beakers or glass jars
- Flask or jar with a narrow neck
- Acetic acid (vinegar)
- Sodium bicarbonate (baking soda)
- Black sheet of paper
- Two thermometers
- Electronic balance
- Graduated cylinder
- Clay or play dough
- Rubber tubing
- Large bowl
- Water, room temperature
- Strong lamp that you can direct straight down, a heat lamp is nice

Some of the gases in the atmosphere have molecular bonds that resonate with the heat radiation from the earth's surface and can, therefore, absorb heat and keep it in the atmosphere, making the earth a warmer place than it would otherwise be. These are greenhouse gases. The heat-absorbing gases have to have three or more atoms, so oxygen (O_2) and Nitrogen (N_2), which make up 99% of the

Additional Layer

Make a climate chart that shows the five factors that determine or affect climate:

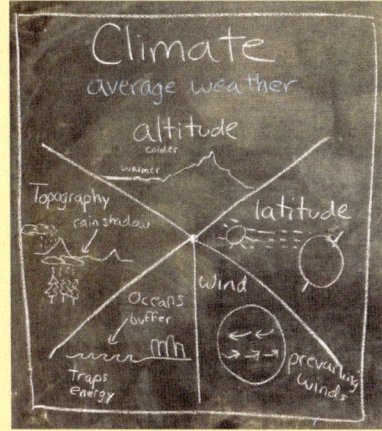

1. Altitude
2. Topography (esp. mountains)
3. Latitude
4. Oceans
5. Prevailing winds

Draw the chart on a piece of paper and put it in your Science Notebook.

Deep Thoughts

Climate is incredibly complex and impossible to predict with any certainty. Scientists have developed complex computer models of the atmosphere, but the models are consistently wrong.

So, it's possible we are heading for man-made climate change that will cool the earth or warm the earth or cause epic storms. The truth is - we just don't know.

However, we do know that polluting the place we live isn't a good idea.

Discuss some of the uncertainties about climate science, the problems of pollution, and some of the solutions that have been floated to solve the problems.

Earth & Space

Fabulous Fact

Volcanoes release about 0.3 billion tons per year. Humans release about 32 billion tons of CO_2 every year. All natural sources release about 750 billion tons per year.

Deep Thoughts

If we assume climate change is happening and is caused by human activity, there are several proposed solutions.

1. Remove more CO_2 from the atmosphere by planting forests, etc.
2. Phase out fossil fuels by using other energy production.
3. Tax people who emit more carbon than the government allows or give people "carbon quotas."
4. Encourage lifestyle changes, such as lowering consumption, eating a vegetarian diet, and living car-free.

Debate which of these solutions you think are most effective and most likely to happen.

What would be the political and economic consequences of each of these?

How would technology and infrastructure (like the way cities are designed) have to change to make some of these happen?

atmosphere, do not act as greenhouse gases.

In order of their heat absorbing capabilities: water vapor, carbon dioxide, methane, and nitrous oxide are the main greenhouse gases. Water vapor is the most important greenhouse gas. Carbon dioxide (CO_2) only makes up about .04% of the atmosphere, but even so, carbon dioxide has an inordinately large effect on the climate. Carbon dioxide stays in the atmosphere for a long time, up to a thousand years or longer. Carbon dioxide is abundant throughout the layers of the atmosphere while most water vapor is closer to the ground. Carbon dioxide also absorbs a different spectrum of radiation than water vapor or methane.

1. First, collect carbon dioxide gas. Fill a large bowl nearly to the top with room temperature water. Put a beaker in the bowl of water and fill it completely so there are no air bubbles inside. Then, turn it upside down.

2. Soften a large chunk of clay by kneading it with your hands. Mold it around the end of a piece of rubber tubing. Make sure the clay with the rubber tubing will completely seal off the end of your flask.

3. Prepare more clay into thick rings. These will be placed on the black paper. You will be putting the two beakers upside down onto the rings of clay to seal them off from the air in the room, so make sure the rings of clay are the right size for the beakers. Put the red bulb ends of two thermometers through the clay and into the center of the rings. They will be measuring the temperature inside of the beakers.

4. Measure 75 ml of acetic acid (vinegar) in a graduated cylinder.

Seasons & Climate

5. Measure 8 g of sodium bicarbonate (baking soda) and put it into the flask.

6. Position the non-clay end of the rubber tubing under the edge of the beaker that is inside the bowl of water. Dump the acetic acid into the flask with the sodium bicarbonate and quickly cover the flask with the clay and rubber tubing. You will need to hold the rubber tubing in place on both ends as gas is quickly formed in the reaction.

7. Keeping the CO_2 beaker upside down, quickly remove it from the water and set it on a clay seal on the sheet of black paper.

8. Place the second beaker, just filled with normal air from the room, upside down next to it on the other clay seal.

9. Turn the lamp on so the light is directed straight at the two beakers. Set a timer for 10 minutes.

10. Head a new page in your Science Notebook "CO_2 as a Greenhouse Gas" Write a hypothesis about what you think will happen to the temperature in each beaker. Draw a labeled diagram of your experiment and write down the steps you had to take.

11. Once the timer goes off, observe the temperature in each beaker. Turn off the light and set the timer for another ten minutes.

12. Record your results and your observations. Finish recording your entire experiment. When the timer goes off again, observe the temperature.

13. Discuss your results. How could you change this experiment to more closely model what happens in the real atmosphere?

Deep Thoughts

Those who oppose heavy government intervention in people's lives over climate change cite these reasons:

1. The climate has been much hotter and much colder than it is today, so we don't need to worry.
2. Warmer climates are good for plants and animals.
3. There is correlation, but no causation between human CO_2 outputs and warming climates.
4. Climate science is so political that it can't be trusted.
5. Efforts to force people to reduce their CO_2 consumption will increase poverty, destroy jobs, and cause hunger.
6. Climate is so complex and so powerful that human intervention can only have minor effects and we can't even know for sure that humans are affecting the climate.

There may be other reasons as well. Think about each of these arguments. Do more research on one or two that interest you. Are they valid and compelling? Why?

Writer's Workshop

Choose one of these climate scientists and write a one-page biography describing his or her education and work.

- Richard S. Lindzen
- Nir J. Shaviv
- John R. Christy
- Tom M.L. Wigley
- Veerabhadran Ramanthan
- Michael E. Mann

Earth & Space

Famous Folks

Dr. Judith A. Curry, geophysicist, was forced to retire early from her long-held position as head of Earth and Atmospheric Sciences at Georgia Tech for stressing uncertainties in climate science and urging caution and open scientific debate among her colleagues.

She has testified before the U.S. Congress multiple times about her concerns over the politicization of climate science. You can find videos of her talking about her concerns on YouTube.

Memorization Station

Carbon cycle: the cycle of carbon atoms moving from the atmosphere to organisms and the earth and then back to the atmosphere

It is nature's way of reusing carbon atoms. Most carbon is stored in rocks and sediments, while the rest is stored in the ocean, atmosphere, and living organisms. It's a continuous cycle that never stops.

😀 😀 😀 **EXPLORATION: Carbon Cycle**

For this activity, you will need:

- Poster board - white
- Markers, crayons, or colored pencils

Carbon moves through the earth's systems from the air to the water, to rocks, to living things, back into the air, and on and on. Carbon atoms are always moving in a cycle called the **carbon cycle**. Plants take carbon out of the air during photosynthesis. Then, animals eat the plants. When plants and animals die, they decompose and the carbon in their bodies goes into the soil. If plants don't decompose quickly, they can turn into coal. In the sea, plankton builds up at the bottom of the ocean and turns into limestone. Coal and limestone can be pulled under the surface and melted in magma. The carbon is then inside of the earth. Volcanoes belch carbon back into the atmosphere.

Over the last 300 years or so, humans have been burning much more of the stored carbon from plants and fossil fuels than ever before. This means it is possible that more carbon is in the atmosphere and oceans than the cycle can naturally absorb back into storage in limestone and coal.

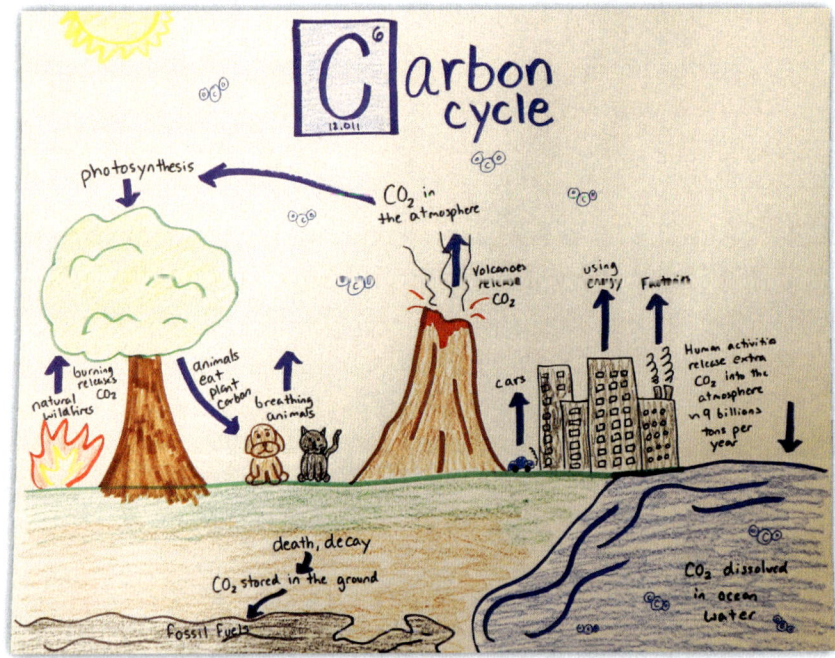

1. Watch a video about the carbon cycle.
2. On a poster board, draw a picture of the carbon cycle.

    Include CO_2 in the atmosphere and ways CO_2 is pulled from the atmosphere into living things and stored in ocean water and rocks.

    Also, include all the ways CO_2 is released back into the

Seasons & Climate

atmosphere. This would be through burning, animals breathing, volcanoes, and human activities.

3. Display your poster on your wall until the end of this unit.
4. Explain the carbon cycle, using the poster, to an audience like a family member or neighbor.

😊 😊 **EXPLORATION: Anthropomorphic Climate Change**
For this activity, you will need:

- Two videos: one arguing for anthropomorphic climate change and one arguing against
- "Anthropomorphic Climate Change Argument" from the Printable Pack

Most people agree that Earth's climate is always changing, but there is a big debate right now about whether humans are affecting climate and how much. The idea that humans are changing the global climate is the anthropomorphic climate change hypothesis.

1. Use the "Anthropomorphic Climate Change Argument" printable to take notes while you watch two videos about climate change. If you want to, watch more than two to get an even better idea of the arguments.
2. After you have taken notes and thought about both sides of the argument, write a persuasive essay explaining why you think one side has a better argument. Give clear examples and line up the evidence to convince someone else.

   Or you can take the position that neither side is completely convincing. If you take this point of view, you must explain what evidence you require in order to be convinced.
3. Put your essay in your Layers of Learning Notebook in the Science section.

Step 3: Show What You Know

During this unit, choose one of the assignments below to show what you have learned during the unit. Add this work to your Layers of Learning Notebook. You can also use this assignment to show your supervising teacher or your charter school as a sample of what you've been working on in your homeschool, if needed.

There are more ideas for writing assignments in the "Writer's Workshop" sidebars.

Bookworms

Ship Breaker by Paolo Bacigalupi takes place in a dystopian future where changing climate has brought about economic destruction for mankind.

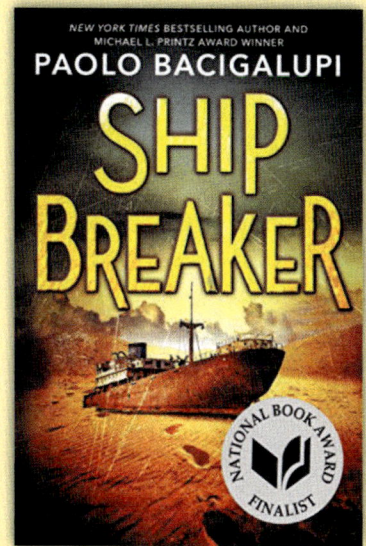

A teen boy, Nailer, works scrapping copper from old tanker ships. He comes across someone he didn't expect. Should he save her in the hope that she can save him?

Memorization Station

Memorize the four steps of the carbon cycle.

- Photosynthesis
- Decomposition
- Respiration
- Combustion

To understand more about this cycle, you can look up some online articles or YouTube videos to see some examples of those four steps in action. Can you identify any of those steps on your Carbon Cycle poster?

Earth & Space

Unit Trivia Questions

1. Which season do you experience when your part of the earth is tilted toward the sun?

   Summer

2. What is the most common gas in our atmosphere?

   a) hydrogen

   b) oxygen

   c) argon

   d) nitrogen

   e) carbon dioxide

3. True or false - The ozone layer harms life on earth.

   False - It protects life by absorbing much of the harmful radiation from the sun.

4. Name the layers of the atmosphere from the ground up.

   Thermosphere, mesosphere, stratosphere, troposphere

5. _____ is the condition of the atmosphere in a particular place at a given moment, while _____ is the long-term average of weather in a particular place.

   Weather, climate

6. True or false - The earth has experienced five ice ages.

   True

7. The earth's climate has always been changing but the debate over whether or not humans are causing the earth's climate to change is heated. What do we call climate change caused by humans?

   Anthropomorphic climate change

😊 😊 Coloring or Narration Page

For this activity, you will need:

- "Seasons & Climate" from the Printable Pack
- Writing or drawing utensils

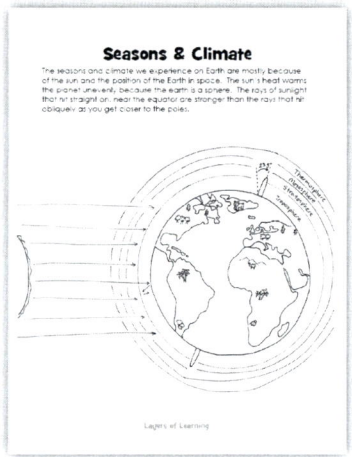

1. Depending on the age and ability of the child, choose either the "Seasons & Climate" coloring sheet or the "Seasons & Climate" narration page from the Printable Pack.

2. Younger kids can color the coloring sheet as you review some of the things you learned about during this unit. On the bottom of the coloring page, kids can write a sentence about what they learned. Very young children can explain their ideas orally while a parent writes for them.

3. Older kids can write about some of the concepts you learned on the narration page and color the picture as well.

4. Add this to the Science section of your Layers of Learning Notebook.

😊 😊 😊 Science Experiment Write-Up

For this activity, you will need:

- The "Experiment" write-up or "Experiment Report Template" from the Printable Pack

1. Choose one of the experiments you completed during this unit and create a careful and complete experiment write-up for it. Make sure you have included every specific detail of each step so your experiment could be repeated by anyone who wanted to try it.

2. Do a careful revision and edit of your write-up, taking it through the writing process, before you turn it in for grading.

😊 😊 😊 Writer's Workshop

For this activity, you will need:

- A computer or a piece of paper and a writing utensil

Choose from one of the ideas below or write about something else you learned during this unit. Each of these prompts corresponds with one of the units from the Layers

Seasons & Climate

of Learning Writer's Workshop curriculum, so you may choose to coordinate the assignment with the monthly unit you are learning about in Writer's Workshop.

- **Sentences, Paragraphs, & Narrations:** Write a narration about the climate in your area and what it is like.
- **Descriptions & Instructions:** Choose your favorite season and write a descriptive paragraph about it.
- **Fanciful Stories**: Write a story about traveling through the layers of the atmosphere.
- **Poetry:** Compose a poem about how the earth's atmosphere protects us.
- **True Stories:** Research a climate scientist and tell the story of his or her career and findings.
- **Reports and Essays:** Write a brief compare and contrast essay about the difference between weather and climate.
- **Letters:** Write a letter to a member of your government about what role you believe the government has in climate change.
- **Persuasive Writing:** Craft a convincing persuasive essay about anthropomorphic climate change.

☺ ☺ ☺ **Big Book of Knowledge**

For this activity, you will need:

- "Big Book of Knowledge: Seasons & Climate" printable from the Printable Pack, printed on card stock
- Writing or drawing utensils
- Big Book of Knowledge

1. Color, draw on, or write on the Big Book of Knowledge page. Record concepts, definitions, and facts you learned during this unit. It's a record of the things you learned and hope to remember. Add the page to your Big Book of Knowledge.

2. Use your Big Book of Knowledge regularly to help you review, quiz, or create games that will help you commit the things you've learned to memory.

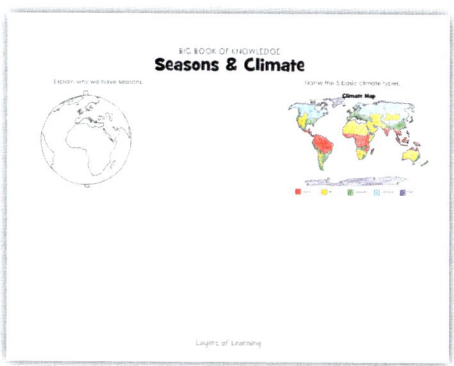

Big Book of Knowledge

The Big Book of Knowledge is a book for you, the mentor, to use as a constant review of all of the things you're learning about. You can use it to quiz your kids or prepare tests or review games. Whenever you learn something in Layers of Learning that you want your kids to remember, add it to your Big Book of Knowledge.

Assemble your Big Book of Knowledge in a binder or with binder rings. Divide it into sections for each subject.

In the Printable Pack for this unit you will find a "Big Book of Knowledge" sheet. You can add this sheet to others you collect or create yourself as you progress through the Layers of Learning curriculum. Customize the Big Book of Knowledge to your family by adding facts and topics that you enjoyed exploring as you were learning.

Visit Layers of Learning online to find more information on how to assemble and use your own Big Book of Knowledge.

You will also find cover and section pages to print along with creative games to play with your Big Book of Knowledge to keep school, even the tests, fun!

Earth & Space

Unit Overview

Key Concepts:
- Weather is the state of the atmosphere at a place and time.
- It is caused by things like air pressure, heating and cooling, the water cycle, and the movement of air.
- Meteorologists use tools to measure, observe, and study the weather.
- There are lots of extreme kinds of weather beyond the day-to-day weather patterns we observe.

Vocabulary:
- Rain gauge
- Precipitation
- Hygrometer
- Humidity
- Wind
- Anemometer
- Barometer
- Prevailing winds
- Thermometer
- Temperature
- Lightning
- Thunder
- Tornado
- Blizzard

WEATHER

Weather is the wind, precipitation, temperature, and humidity at a particular place and time. Weather all happens in the lowest layer of the atmosphere, the troposphere.

Weather is caused by the sun unevenly heating the surface of the earth. Land is heated more effectively than water. Lower latitudes are heated more than upper latitudes. Lower elevations are heated more than higher elevations. Since hot air rises and cooler air sinks, this uneven heating causes the air to move. Moving air creates wind, and wind is constantly carrying moisture or dryness with it to new locations.

The weather on Earth is chaotic. However, it can be predicted in very short terms of a few days and sometimes as much as a week. Predictions are based on past patterns, air pressure, and observation of the wind and clouds. In our modern day, technology like Doppler radar can help meteorologists to track moving weather from space and give people advanced warning of everything from a rain shower to a hurricane.

As you learn about weather during this unit, we encourage you to keep a weather log. You'll find one at the beginning of the Printable Pack for this unit. Each day, you'll record what the weather is like where you live. If you'd like to, you can make predictions about what you think the weather will be, then compare your predictions with your actual results. Even professional meteorologists are just making educated guesses; sometimes they are right and sometimes they are wrong. As you learn more about weather during this unit, you'll learn how they make their

Weather

predictions and what tools they use.

Step 1: Library List

Choose books from your library that go with this topic. Here's a list of some favorites and also a list of search terms so you can utilize what your library offers. Read the books with your kids and/or assign them some to read independently. It is from these books your kids will learn most of the facts they need from this unit.

Search for: weather, clouds, rain, snow, forecasting, storms, hurricanes, tornadoes, cyclones, rainbows, aurora

🙂 🙂 🙂 *The Usborne Science Encyclopedia*. Read "Weather" on pages 192-193.

🙂 🙂 🙂 *Encyclopedia of Science* from DK. Read "Air Pressure," "Temperature," "Humidity," "Fronts," "Winds," "Wind Strength," "Thunder and Lightning," "Hurricanes," "Tornadoes," "Clouds," "Formation of Clouds," "Fog, Mist, and Smog," "Rain," "Snow," "Hail," "Frost, Dew, and Ice," "Special Effects," and "Forecasting" on pages 250-271.

🙂 🙂 🙂 *The Kingfisher Science Encyclopedia*. Read "Rain and Snow," "Clouds and Fog," "Weather Forecasting," and "Winds, Storms, and Floods" on pages 36-45.

🙂 🙂 🙂 *Nature's Fury* from National Geographic. This is a documentary you can stream online or find in DVD form. Great family viewing for all ages, this especially focuses on extreme weather and storms.

🙂 🙂 🙂 *Bill Nye, the Science Guy* has episodes about both *Storms* and *Wind* your family may enjoy. You can find these online.

🙂 *Weather Words and What They Mean* by Gail Gibbons. Simple, clear explanations of terms like air pressure, moisture, precipitation, fog, frost, thunder, and so on. Also look for *Weather Forecasting* by the same author.

🙂 *What Will The Weather Be?* by Lynda DeWitt. Simply explains weather forecasting for the youngest kids. We love this series! It also includes *What Makes A Blizzard?*, *Down Comes the Rain*, *Feel the Wind*, and other specific titles about weather phenomena.

🙂 *Clouds* by Anne Rockwell. Explains the different types of clouds and what they tell you about the weather.

🙂 *Flash, Crash, Rumble, and Roll* by Franklyn M. Branley. Explains the science behind thunderstorms.

Family School Levels

The colored smilies in this unit help you choose the correct levels of books and activities for your child.

🙂 = Ages 6-9
🙂 = Ages 10-13
🙂 = Ages 14-18

On the Web

For videos, web pages, games, and more to add to this unit, visit the Earth & Space Resources at Layers-of-Learning.com.

You will find a link to video playlists, web links, and more.

Bookworms

If you're looking for a family read-aloud, we'd like to suggest this one.

Night of the Twisters by Ivy Ruckman is a fictional account of a real tornado event. It brings this kind of natural disaster home. What would it really mean to be caught in a tornado, from the fright of the event to the massive clean up afterward?

Earth & Space

Teaching Tip

Throughout this unit, you'll be keeping a Weather Log, a record of the weather in your area. Many of the Explorations encourage you to add to your record. Even if you don't complete every one of those Explorations, you can keep a weather log. For example, if you don't make a homemade barometer, you can still look up whether you are experiencing high or low pressure online each day, and record it on your Weather Log.

Additional Layer

A windsock is colorful and useful to see wind direction and get an idea of wind strength.

Make one with fabric, a plastic hoop cut from a coffee or margarine lid, fabric glue, and wide ribbon.

Cut your fabric into a rectangle a bit wider than the circumference of your hoop and .25 meters long.

Glue long ribbons to the bottom of the fabric cylinder to make long tails. Glue your fabric into a cylinder. Then glue the cylinder onto the hoop by wrapping it around the hoop. Then tie strings to the hoop and tie the windsock to your porch roof or a tree limb.

☺ *Rainbow* by Marion Dane Bauer. A very simple book about how rainbows form. Also look for *Clouds, Rain, Wind, Snow,* and *Sun* by the same author.

☺ *The Magic School Bus Inside A Hurricane* by Joanna Cole. Part of the original series, these books are full of real science with kid-friendly delivery.

☺ *You Wouldn't Want to Live Without Extreme Weather* by Roger Canavan. Fun illustrations and an interesting look at the weather.

☺ ☺ *Storms* by Seymour Simon. Full-page color photos of storms around the world with just the right amount of text for upper elementary or middle schoolers. Look for *Hurricanes, Lightning, Tornadoes,* and *Weather* by this author as well.

☺ *Can It Really Rain Frogs?* by Spencer Christian. Written by an actual meteorologist, this book is about weird weather events, like raining frogs.

☺ *The Kids' Book of Weather Forecasting* by Mark Breen. Tons of information and activities about the weather.

☺ *Eyewitness Weather* by DK. Color photos and diagrams, lots of interesting text. This is an excellent everything-in-one book about the weather.

☺ *Khan Academy: Weather & Climate*, an online course. This is directed to middle schoolers and is a traditional online course that will walk you through weather concepts.

☺ ☺ *Extraordinary Weather* by Richard Hamblyn. Gorgeous full-page photos of weather events from dust storms to lighting to clouds with short text explanations of each one. Also look for *Extraordinary Clouds* by the same author.

☺ ☺ *Exploring the Sky By Day* by Terence Dickinson. Covers the atmosphere, clouds, precipitation, storms, humidity, fog, sunsets, the aurora, forecasting, and more.

☺ *The Lost Art of Reading Nature's Signs* by Tristan Gooley. This includes how to read the natural world to forecast the weather but it goes way beyond weather to everything in nature.

☺ *The Cloudspotter's Guide* by Gavin Pretor-Pinney. Takes each cloud type one by one and explains the history, culture, and science behind them and then teaches you how to find them in the sky. Also check out the companion book, *The Cloud Collector's Handbook*.

☺ *The Weather Machine* by Andrew Blum. We take weather forecasts for granted, but we shouldn't. This book explains the history and science behind weather forecasting.

Weather

🙂 *Reading Weather* by Jim Woodmency. A great, basic meteorology book to help you predict the weather, for at least the next few hours.

🙂 *Bozeman Science* online course. For a high school lecture, study "Meteorology" during this unit.

Step 2: Explore

Choose a few hands-on explorations from this section to work on as a family. They should be appealing activities that will create mental hooks so your kids remember the information in the unit. Save the rest of the explorations for the next time you do this unit in four years when your kids are older. You can also read the sidebars together and explore some little rabbit trails.

This unit includes printables. See the introduction for instructions on retrieving your Printable Pack.

Recording & Forecasting

Meteorologists use all kinds of tools to help record and forecast the weather. You may enjoy setting up a weather station at your home during this unit.

🙂🙂🙂 EXPLORATION: Weather Log

For this activity, you will need:

- "Weather Log" from the Printable Pack (Choose between the simple one for younger kids or the more complex one for older kids.)
- Markers
- Scissors
- Glue
- Science Notebook

Throughout this unit, you'll be keeping a weather log each day and observing the weather where you live.

1. Choose the same time of the day each day to record the weather in your area. You may check using measurement tools you make or already own or your own observations. You can also look up the data online.
2. Write or draw in the data on your weather log.
3. Cut the "Weather Log" on the heavy line and glue it into your Science Notebook. You'll continue to use it throughout this unit. Make sure to add it to your table of contents and be prepared to add data to it each day

---

Additional Layer

Before modern forecasting methods, sailors and farmers needed to know what weather was on the way. There are many folklore sayings about the weather, but which ones actually work?

Choose one weather folklore to test. Make careful observations and see if it actually is accurate or not. Here are some to try.

Red sky in the morning, sailor's warning. Red sky at night, sailor's delight.

If crows fly low, wind's going to blow; if crows fly high, winds going to die.

When sea birds fly to land, there truly is a storm at hand.

Yellow streaks in sunset sky, wind and rain day long is nigh.

Rainbow at noon, more rain soon.

Rain before seven, quit by eleven.

Teaching Tip

In this section, you'll be learning about some of the instruments meteorologists use to record and forecast the weather.

Make some note cards with each of the weather instruments and the things they measure written on the cards. Play a matching game where you practice matching each instrument with what it measures. For example, a rain gauge measures the amount of precipitation.

Earth & Space

Famous Folks

Sir Francis Beaufort was an Irish sailor and hydrographer for the Royal Navy.

He developed the Beaufort wind scale early in his career and its use became widespread after he became the head hydrographer for the Navy in the 1830s.

Memorization Station

Rain gauge: an instrument that measures the amount of rainfall

Precipitation: condensed water vapor that falls from clouds to the ground - rain, snow, sleet, or hail

Additional Layer

For more advanced weather vocabulary, fill out "A to Z Weather Words" from the Printable Pack.

as you learn about and record the weather. The log for older kids lasts a month. The log for younger kids only lasts a week. You can print off more if you decide to keep logging after the week is up.

😊 😊 😊 EXPERIMENT: Rain Gauge

For this activity, you will need:

- Book or video about weather from the Library List or YouTube playlist
- "Weather Log" from the Printable Pack
- Jar with straight sides and a flat bottom
- Ruler
- Masking tape
- Permanent marker
- Science Notebook

A **rain gauge** measures the amount of **precipitation** a place receives. These numbers are recorded. Then, the record is used to calculate average rainfall for a certain area over a month, a year, a decade, or a 30-year period.

1. Read a book or watch a video about weather.
2. Stick a strip of masking tape on the side of the jar from bottom to top. Use a ruler and permanent marker to make marks on the masking tape at each centimeter.
3. Set the rain gauge outside in a clear space, not under trees or shaded by buildings.
4. Choose a time of day and check, record, and empty your rain gauge once a day. Older kids can track rainfall until the end of this unit using the "Weather Log."

Weather

😊 😊 😊 **EXPERIMENT: Measuring Snowfall**

For this activity, you will need:

- Book or video about weather from the Library List or YouTube playlist
- "Weather Log" from the Printable Pack
- Board, 2 feet by 2 feet
- White paint
- Metric ruler or meter stick
- Long stake (optional)

If you live in a place with snow and you are studying weather in the winter, you may want to measure snow instead of rain.

1. Read a book or watch a video about weather.
2. Paint your board with white paint on one side and let it dry.
3. Set the board outside on a flat, open space, not covered by trees or too near buildings. It's also important not to set the board in a place where you know snow drifts. You may need to mark the location of your board with a stake so you can find the board after a large snowfall.
4. After a snowfall, measure the amount of snow using a metric ruler. Measure to the nearest half centimeter.
5. Clear all the snow off the board and replace it after you measure.
6. Measure at the same time of day each day. Older kids can record measurements on the "Weather Log."

Additional Layer

A psychrometer is a tool used to measure how the humidity makes the temperature feel. A cold, humid day feels much colder than a dry day at the same temperature.

You can make a psychrometer. Put two thermometers side by side on a table. Cover the bulb of one with a cotton ball soaked in water. Then turn a fan on the two thermometers. Observe the difference in the temperatures.

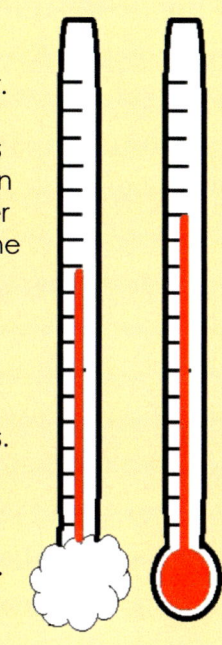

Fabulous Fact

One lesser known weather measuring device is a hail pad. It is a florist's foam pad that is covered by aluminum foil then set out before a storm. The falling hailstones dent the pad and allow someone to measure the size of the hailstones accurately.

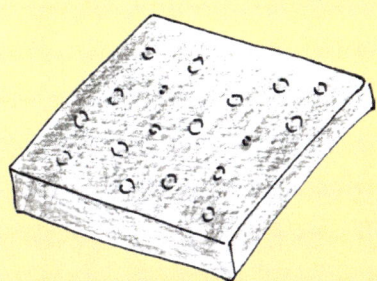

You can make one for yourself if you live in an area that gets hailstorms.

Earth & Space

Additional Layer

When a high and low pressure zone meet, wind shear is created. The air is turbulent and wind direction and speed are unpredictable. A quick downdraft can send an airplane to the ground.

Go read about what happened to Delta Flight 191.

😊 😊 😊 EXPERIMENT: Humidity

For this activity, you will need:

- Book or video about humidity from the Library List or YouTube playlist
- Someone with long hair

A **hygrometer** is used to measure **humidity**, or the amount of water vapor in the air. Human hair is actually used to make some hygrometers. Hair strands tend to relax and get longer when there is more moisture in the air and contract when there's less.

1. Read a book or watch a video about humidity.

2. Examine your own hair or the hair of others nearby. Some hygrometers actually use hair that they measure to see how relaxed or contracted it is. Can you detect anything about humidity based on their hair? Hint: Hair tends to get frizzier when it's humid. Discuss your observations.

Memorization Station

Hygrometer: An instrument that measures humidity

Humidity: the concentration of water vapor in the air

Wind: the massive flow of gases in the atmosphere

Anemometer: an instrument that measures the speed of the wind

Barometer: an instrument that measures air pressure

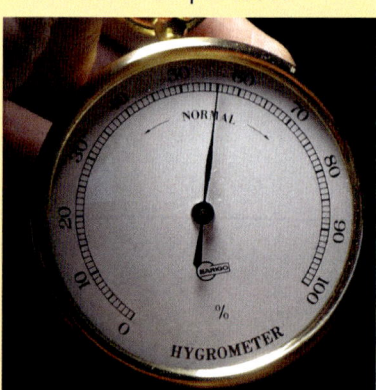

This hygrometer measures humidity.

😊 😊 😊 EXPERIMENT: Wind Detector

For this activity, you will need:

- "Wind Speed" and "Weather Log" from the Printable Pack
- Paper plate
- Scissors
- Glue
- Wide ribbon
- Staples and stapler
- Book or video about weather from the Library List or YouTube playlist

Wind speed can be measured with an **anemometer** or with the naked eye and the Beaufort scale. The Beaufort scale measures wind speed in knots because that is how sailors measured speed. The Beaufort scale is printed on the "Wind Speed" printable.

1. Read a book or watch a video about weather.

2. Cut out the "Wind Speed" along the circle. Glue to the middle of the back side of a paper plate.

3. Cut four ribbons, each 45 cm long. Staple the ribbons, one each, to the four points of the compass on the rim of the plate.

4. Take your wind detector outside. Orient it so that N on the plate faces north from your position. Hold the plate horizontal to the ground. Observe the direction of the wind by watching the way your ribbons blow. Observe the trees and use the Beaufort scale to determine the strength of the wind. Record your findings.

Weather

5. Older kids can track the wind speed and direction on the "Weather Log" until the end of this unit.

😊 😊 😊 EXPERIMENT: Homemade Barometer

For this activity, you will need:

- Wide mouth jar
- Balloon
- Scissors
- Rubber band
- Drinking straw
- Piece of card stock
- School glue
- Pencil
- Straight pin (optional)
- Book or video about weather from the Library List or YouTube playlist
- "Weather Log" from the Printable Pack

A **barometer** is a tool that measures air pressure. When air pressure is high, the air will press down on the balloon. When air pressure is low, the balloon will bulge up a bit. High pressure usually means clear weather. Low pressure means you can expect wind, rain, and clouds.

1. Read a book or watch a video about weather.

2. Cut the neck of the balloon off. Stretch the remaining piece of the balloon over the mouth of the jar. Secure it with a rubber band.

3. Glue one end of a straw to the center of the balloon so it is sticking out parallel to the work surface. You may want to glue a straight pin to the opposite end of the straw, if you want a more accurate pointer.

4. Create a scale on the piece of card stock. First, fold the card stock in half the short way, hamburger-style.

Fabulous Fact

Meteorologists use wind socks to look at wind direction, but they also use anemometers which measure exact wind speed.

Additional Layer

For a simple demonstration of air pressure, poke three holes in the side of an empty milk jug, one near the top, one in the center, and one near the bottom. Fill it with water, Observe the streams as the water flows out. The one near the bottom will shoot out the furthest because there is more pressure on it from the water above. Air pressure works the same. As you go higher, there is less air pressure because there is less air pressing down from above.

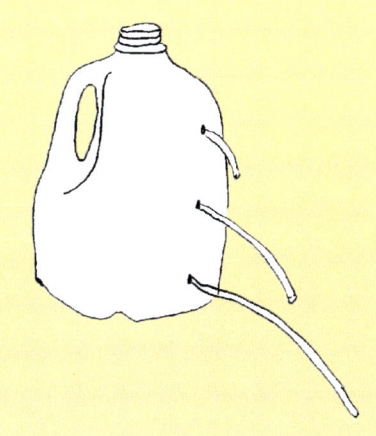

Earth & Space

Expedition

Weather balloons are sent up at least once a day from more than 800 locations worldwide.

Find out how weather balloons work and what they are used for, then go see one near you.

Memorization Station

Prevailing winds: a zone where the wind usually blows the same direction

Deep Thoughts

Early scientists were polymaths. They didn't specialize; they learned about the natural world in many areas, from weather to worms to waves. Today, all scientists specialize.

Why do you think scientists used to learn about broad areas, but not today? What are the advantages and disadvantages to specialization?

Make a mark every centimeter on your scale. Have your numbering start at the bottom and progress all of the way to the top of the paper. If you don't want to be as exact, you can just use the labels "high" and "low." In the center, where the straw rests, make a heavier, longer mark, so you will know if the gauge has risen or fallen from "normal."

5. Place the barometer outside in the shade. Tape the paper to a wall or set it up next to the barometer. The fold will keep the paper upright. Check the barometer once or twice a day to see what the air pressure is doing. Record your observations. What kind of weather do you see when your barometer indicates low pressure? High pressure? Can you accurately predict coming rain? When the air is pressing on the balloon's surface, it forces the balloon down, making the tip of the straw rise higher. Likewise, when the pressure is low and not pushing on the balloon, the straw falls lower.

6. Older kids can record whether you are experiencing high pressure or low pressure on the "Weather Log" in the "Barometer" column.

😊😊😊 EXPLORATION: Pressure Zones

For this activity, you will need:

- "Pressure Zones" from the Printable Pack
- Colored pencils
- Scissors
- Glue stick
- Globe or map of Earth
- Video about prevailing winds from the YouTube playlist

Weather

There are four zones on Earth that maintain a pretty consistent pressure. One of these is the low pressure zone along the equator. Since the equator gets the most direct sunlight and is the hottest part of earth, the air there is rising pretty consistently. This also means you can expect lots of rain along the equator.

The more northerly zones that maintain their pressure are related to the trade winds. The subtropical highs are dry places with little rainfall. The sub-polar lows are places where lots of rain and snow falls. In each of these zones, there are **prevailing winds** that always blow in the same general direction.

1. Watch a video about prevailing winds.

2. Using the printable "Pressure Zones," cut out the tags. Glue them to the correct places on the map.

3. Color the low pressure zones blue because they get lots of rain. Color the high pressure zones yellow because they are dry.

4. Color the prevailing wind zones green.

5. Compare your Pressure Zones map with a globe or world map. Do the sub-tropical highs match up with deserts on Earth? Are there rainforests in the Equatorial low zone? What is happening in climates around 60 degrees north and south? Add your map to the Science section of your Layers of Learning Notebook.

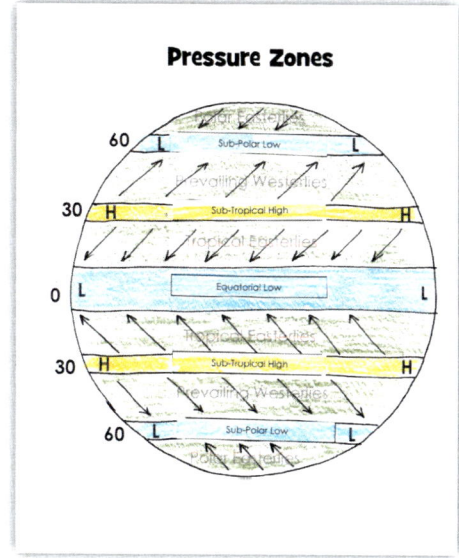

☺ ☺ ☺ EXPERIMENT: Homemade Thermometer

For this activity, you will need:

- A clean, clear, empty water bottle
- A clear drinking straw
- Water
- Isopropyl alcohol
- Red food coloring
- Clay or play dough
- Hair dryer

Additional Layer

Stevenson screens are enclosed little boxes set up on a high pole out in a field away from buildings and trees. They contain minimum and maximum thermometers that automatically record the low and high temperature each day.

Learn more about how these are used to find average temperatures all over the world.

Teaching Tip

The amount of change in the mercury of a thermometer is actually very small. You can compare a real thermometer you have with your homemade thermometer and look at how tiny the tube is that the mercury goes in compared with the straw you used. The liquid rises only a tiny bit, but if we have the right scale on it, we can see the temperature variations.

Earth & Space

Memorization Station
Thermometer: an instrument for measuring temperature

Temperature: a measure of heat in the atmosphere

Teaching Tip
You can learn more about climate and how it relates to weather in Layers of Learning *Earth & Space: Seasons & Climate*.

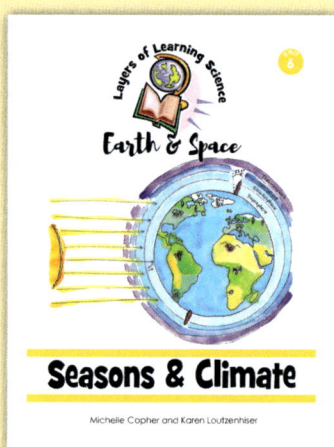

Bookworms

The Man Who Named the Clouds by Julie Hanna and Joan Holub is the true story of Luke Howard, the man who classified the clouds. He started keeping a weather journal when he was ten years old.

Thermometers work because, as liquids heat, they expand. The expanding liquid rises up the tube of the thermometer with the rising **temperature** of the liquid.

1. Start by filling the bottle halfway with water. Fill the remaining half with isopropyl alcohol. Add a few drops of red food coloring to make the liquid bright red. This just makes it visible as your liquid level changes.

2. Use the clay to surround the straw and then press the clay on to the top of the bottle, completely sealing it so it's airtight. Make sure the bottom of the straw is a few centimeters from the bottom of the bottle, allowing the red liquid to rise up it.

3. Now your thermometer is ready. We'll apply heat to the liquid and watch the "mercury" rise (We don't have mercury, of course, just red alcohol water, but it is acting as our mercury in this experiment.) Use a hair dryer on low setting to blow warm air at the bottle for a few minutes. Observe how the liquid rises up the straw as the temperature rises.

4. Discuss together or write about what you observe.

😊 😊 😊 **EXPLORATION: Cloud Diagram**
For this activity, you will need:

- Book or video about clouds from the Library List or YouTube playlist
- "Types of Clouds" and "Weather Log" from the Printable Pack
- Blue and green card stock or construction paper
- Cotton balls
- School glue
- Gray paint - black and white mixed

There are ten major types of clouds. High-level clouds include cirrus, cirrocumulus, and cirrostratus. Mid-level clouds include altocumulus, altostratus, and nimbostratus. Low-level clouds include stratus, cumulus, cumulonimbus, and stratocumulus.

Weather

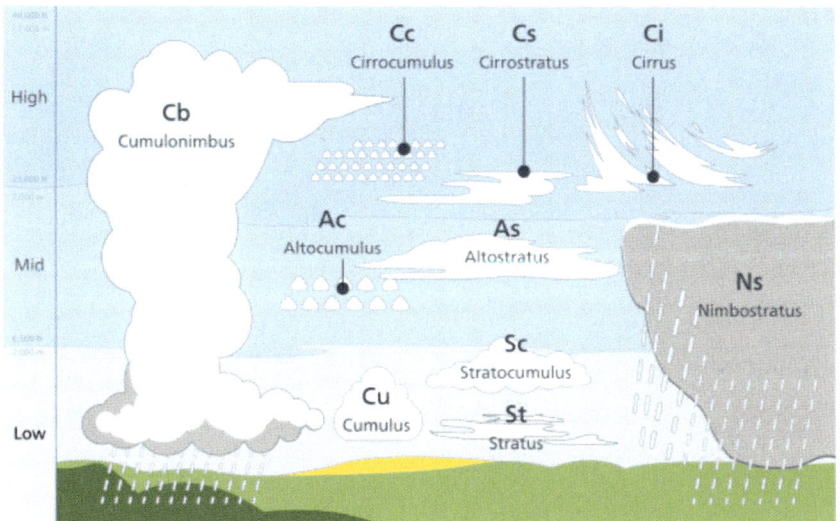

Ten Types of Clouds, Cloud Classification image shared by Valentine de Bruyn under CC 3.0 license

1. Read a book or watch a video about clouds.
2. Read and color the "Types of Clouds" chart from the Printable Pack. Take the chart outside and identify which types of clouds you have right now, if any.
3. Cut a thin strip of green card stock from the long edge of the paper. Glue this to one edge of the blue paper to make the ground beneath a blue sky.
4. Stretch out and manipulate the cotton balls to make them look like each of the ten types of clouds. Glue the clouds to the paper with school glue.
5. Paint some of the cotton balls gray to darken the rain clouds.

Fabulous Fact

Because water turns to gas at 100° C and freezes at 0° C, when water vapor rises in Earth's atmosphere, it cools and turns to liquid and then to a solid. All other gases remain gas until much, much lower temperatures. They escape into space, but water doesn't. It falls back to Earth as rain or snow. If not for this property, water would have been depleted from Earth long ago and life could not survive here. The same water has been cycling around and around since the beginning.

Teaching Tip

As you're learning the types of clouds, recognize the clues within their names.

If you hear "nimbus" anywhere in the name, that means precipitation falls from that kind of cloud.

If you hear "cumulo" anywhere in the name, that mean it is puffy or mounded.

The root "cirro" means curl of hair. These clouds are wispy. They are high altitude clouds made of ice crystals.

"Strato" means layer. These clouds form a low layer and don't let sun through.

"Alto" refers to altitude. These clouds are mid-altitude clouds, not low-lying and not high.

Memorization Station

Memorize the three families of clouds.

- Cirrus
- Stratus
- Cumulus

Earth & Space

Additional Layer

Find out about other temperature scales besides the one most commonly used where you live. Fahrenheit created the first scale, based on the freezing and boiling points of saline water. Later, Anders Celsius created another scale with the freezing point of pure water at zero degrees and the boiling point at 100 degrees. Lord Kelvin created the Kelvin scale even later than that, and also introduced the idea of absolute zero, or the point at which there is no heat present at all.

Additional Layer

Some weather forecasters are also meteorologists, but not all of them are.

A meteorologist is a scientist who studies the air circulation patterns in the troposphere. They have to understand how oceans, heat from the sun, mountains, and different banks of air interact to make the weather on Earth. They have a college degree in meteorology. Some of them forecast the weather on TV, others teach at universities, and some work for agencies like NASA.

6. Once your cloud painting is dry, display it on a wall until the end of this unit.

7. Practice identifying the real clouds in the sky each day while you are doing this unit. You can record the types of clouds you see on your "Weather Log."

EXPEDITION: Cloud Viewer

For this activity, you will need:

- "Cloud Viewer" from the Printable Pack, printed on card stock (and laminated if you'd like it to last)
- Scissors
- Science Notebook
- Drawing and writing utensils

1. Make your cloud viewer by copying the printable on to card stock and cutting out the center window. You can laminate it if you'd like it to last. We keep one in our science supplies.

2. Go outside on any cloudy day with your cloud viewer. Look through the window and use the identification photos to help you identify the kinds of clouds that are in the sky. The ones along the top are higher altitude clouds and as you get lower along the viewer, the clouds are lower altitude clouds.

3. As you identify clouds, take some time to observe them quietly, draw them in your Science Notebook with descriptions of what you observe, and begin to learn the small differences between the various types of clouds.

EXPLORATION: Weather Report Art

For this activity, you will need:

- Thin cardboard, like from a cereal box
- Paint
- Glitter (optional)
- Scissors
- School glue
- Permanent marker

Use these thermometers to report the weather in a fun, colorful way.

1. Cut out three identical thermometer shapes from cardboard.

2. Paint the first one to show the four major types of clouds: cirrus, cumulus, stratus, and cumulonimbus.

194

Weather

3. Paint the second one to show the basic kinds of weather you get in your location. You could show snow, rain, sun, and clouds, for example.
4. Paint the third one to show temperature in degrees C or, if you live in the United States, in degrees F.
5. After the paint dries, use a permanent marker to label each thermometer.
6. Make a cardboard tab that wraps around the thermometer and slides up and down. Cut out a window inside the tab so you can see the weather.
7. Add glitter or other embellishments as desired.
8. Post these on your fridge or wall and change them each day according to the weather.

😊 😊 😊 EXPEDITION: Visit A Forecasting Station

For this activity, you will need:

- A local forecasting station to visit
- Science Notebook

1. Make arrangements to go on a tour of a local weather forecasting station. TV stations, airports, and some science centers have weather forecasting stations. Call ahead and make arrangements to visit one.
2. Go prepared with a few good questions to ask your tour guide about the methods they use to forecast the weather. Bring your Science Notebook along and take notes about what you learn.

Additional Layer

Weather forecasters use certain symbols on maps to show what the weather is doing.

A warm front means warm air is moving in to take the place of colder air. A cold front is cold air moving in to take the place of warmer air. If a warm and cold front collide, there will be a big storm.

An occluded front is when you have both warm and cold air moving the same way and mixing together. A stationary front is a mass of cold air and warm air butting heads but not getting very far.

Learn about other weather symbols and watch the weather report, looking for the symbols.

Fabulous Fact

If you count the number of times a cricket chirps in 25 seconds, divide by 3 and add 4, you will get the temperature in Celsius.

Practice doing the math. What is the temperature if a cricket chirps 48 times?

20 degrees Celsius

Earth & Space

Fabulous Fact

Sandstorms are wind storms in dry places that blow sand, dirt, and grit into the air.

This is the front edge of a sandstorm in Al Asad, Iraq.

Sandstorms can damage buildings, electric networks, and roads. People and animals that are caught out in a sandstorm can become lost in the near zero visibility. Sometimes people die of asphyxiation in a sandstorm.

Entire cities have been buried by sandstorms. The city of Tanis in Egypt was abandoned and then buried under sand.

Writer's Workshop

At the mouth of the Catatumbo River, where it empties into Lake Maracqaibo in Venezuela, there is a lighting storm that rages almost all year long, all the time.

Learn more about this perpetual lighting storm and what causes it. Then, write it into a short adventure story where the lighting plays a role.

😊 😊 **EXPLORATION: Weather Forecaster**

For this activity, you will need:

- Access to view a weather report
- "My Weather Map" from the Printable Pack (or a map of your area if outside of the United States)
- Clear tape
- Magnetic tape
- Scissors
- Cookie sheet or another magnetic metal surface
- Video camera (optional)

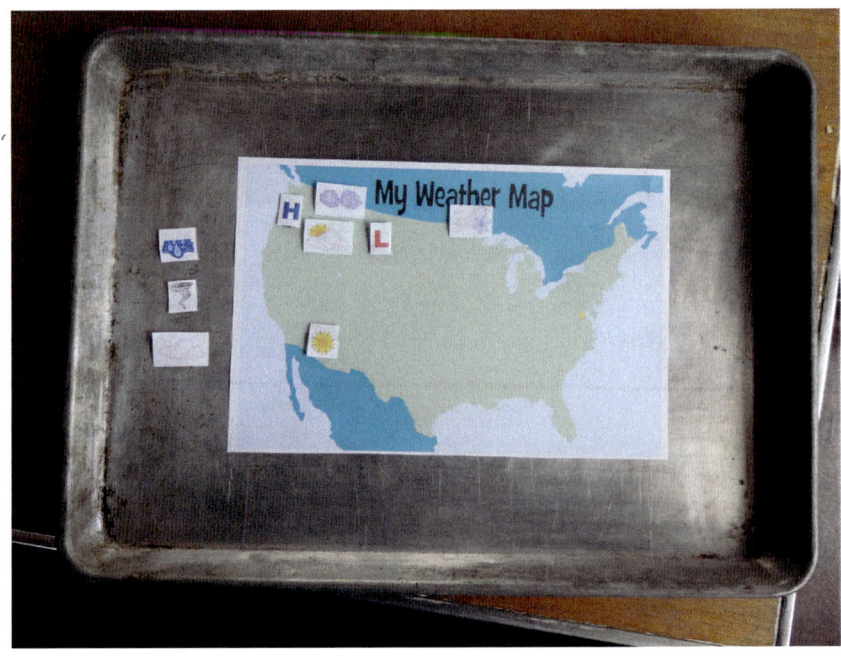

Weather forecasters stand in front of a camera on the

196

Weather

news and explain the weather forecast. They use maps and weather symbols to explain the coming weather to the public. They also broadcast the coming weather over the radio and on internet sites or apps.

1. First, watch one or more weather forecasters. Take note of how they use maps and symbols to show what is happening with the weather.
2. Print the "My Weather Map" on card stock. Cut out the map and the pieces along the bottom edge.
3. Tape the weather map to the metal cookie sheet. Cut the magnetic tape into short pieces. Attach the magnetic tape pieces to the back of the weather symbols.
4. Use the map and the symbols to give a weather forecast to your family. You can do this live or you can even record a video of yourself, just for fun.

Precipitation

😊 😊 😊 **EXPERIMENT: Cloud in a Bottle**

WARNING: This activity uses very hot water. Use caution and keep away from young children.

For this activity, you will need:

- Transparent 2-liter bottle
- Hot water
- Container with a spout, like a teapot
- Ice
- Small dish
- Science Notebook

Clouds form when air, laden with water vapor, rises and cools enough for the water vapor to clump together. The water vapor condenses and forms droplets or ice crystals. As the water droplets continue to condense, they become heavy enough to fall to the ground as rain.

1. Bring water to boil in a teapot or container with a spout. Pour the hot water into a 2-liter bottle until it is about 1/3 full.

Memorization Station

Learn the four basic types of precipitation: rain, snow, sleet, and hail.

Make a diagram in your Science Notebook with an illustration and label for each of the four types.

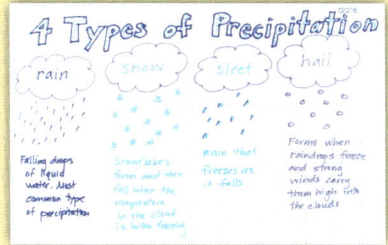

Fabulous Fact

Clouds can hold millions of gallons of water. They are made up of tiny droplets of water that rise with warm air. Learn more about the water cycle and how our world just keeps recycling its water over and over again.

Additional Layer

Because the earth is spinning, currents in the atmosphere and in the ocean are deflected to the right in the Northern Hemisphere and to the left in the Southern Hemisphere. They create the ocean gyres and the turn of cyclones.

Learn more about the Coriolis Effect.

Earth & Space

Fabulous Fact

Wildfires can make their own weather as the fire heats the air and causes updrafts that draw in fresh, cooler air from the surroundings. The cooler air creates wind that fans the flames even more.

Fire whirls, tornadoes made of flame, can also occur.

Bookworms

Snowflake Bentley by Jacqueline Briggs Martin is the amazing, true story of a man named Wilson Bentley who was fascinated by snowflakes and began photographing them.

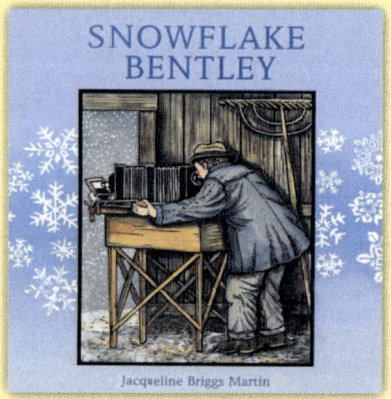

He loved the unique crystals of snowflakes and took pictures of thousands of them.

2. Fill a small container most of the way with ice cubes. Balance the cold container on top of the 2-liter bottle. Observe as a cloud forms within your bottle.

3. In your Science Notebook, draw a labeled diagram of what you observe. Write your conclusions about the way water droplets form in the atmosphere.

😊 😊 😊 EXPERIMENT: Warm and Cold Fronts

WARNING: This activity uses hot water and will make a mess. It should be a demonstration by an adult or older teen. We recommend doing it over a shallow pan.

For this activity, you will need:

- Hot tap water
- Ice water
- Two small transparent jars that are identical
- Index card or piece of thin cardboard
- Red and blue food dye
- Science Notebook

Fronts are moving masses of air. They can be cold air or warm air. If a cold front and a warm front collide, the warm front usually rises over the cold front because warm air is less dense than cold air. Warm air often holds quite a bit of water vapor, but, as the warm air rises, it cools and the water vapor condenses out, forming clouds and sometimes rain.

1. Pour hot tap water into one jar until it is mostly full. Add a few drops of red food coloring to the water. Top off the jar with more hot water until it is full to the brim.

2. Fill the second jar mostly full with cold ice water. Add a few drops of blue food coloring to the jar, then top it off until the jar is full to the brim.

3. Cover the red jar with an index card and hold it tightly while you invert it over the blue jar. Line the two jars up carefully. Pull the index card out all at once.

4. Press the lips of the jars tightly together and gently turn them on their sides. Observe how the hot and cold fronts travel in relation to one another.

Weather

5. Draw a picture of what you did and write down your observations in your Science Notebook. Give your page a title and add it to your table of contents.

🙂 🙂 **EXPLORATION: Paper Snowflakes**
For this activity, you will need:

- White paper
- Scissors
- Iron and ironing board (optional)

Snowflakes are formed high up in the troposphere with tiny bits of vapor. The water vapor clings to a piece of dust or pollen. As the frozen water vapor falls, it attracts more bits of water vapor and the speck turns into a flake with six arms. All snowflakes have six sides, but each snowflake is also unique.

1. Read a book or watch a video about the formation of snowflakes.

2. Make your piece of paper square by folding the paper into a right triangle and trimming off the extra.

3. Fold the paper in half to make a triangle, then in half again to make a smaller triangle.

4. Fold the small triangle into thirds so that the two lower points of the triangle overlap and the sides match up, then crease it.

5. Cut off the pointed ends of the triangle that are sticking out below. Now, cut out bits off the paper triangle here and there, as desired.

Writer's Workshop

It can "rain" frogs or fish or other objects if a tornado forms over water, scoops up frogs or fish, and then moves them to land and lets them go. Write a story about something crazy falling from the sky.

Fabulous Fact

Snow can only form if there's dust or pollen in the air. It starts with a cold water droplet freezing onto a particle of pollen or dust and becoming an ice crystal.

Additional Layer

The exact shape of the crystals that form within snowflakes depends on the path they take through the clouds. They always form symmetrically and with six arms, but no two snowflakes are precisely the same because no two snowflakes take the exact same path. Learn more about why snow crystals have six arms and how they form.

Earth & Space

Bookworms

Magic Treehouse: Twister on Tuesday by Mary Pope Osborne, as well as its companion Fact Tracker, *Twisters and Other Terrible Storms*, are fun read-alouds to add to this unit. Jack and Annie go back in time to the pioneer era within the United States and learn about storm cellars and why they were so important to the people in the states on the Great Plains who faced severe windstorms.

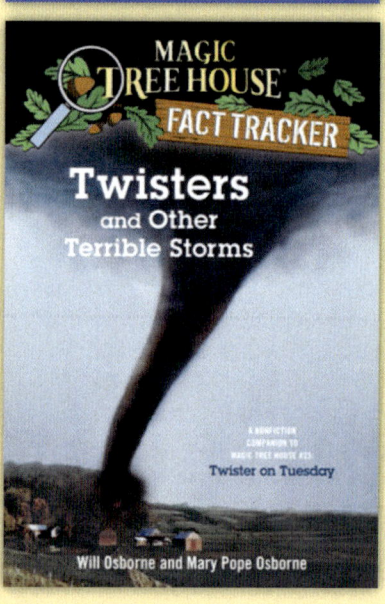

6. Carefully unfold the triangle and smooth it out with your hands. If you want your snowflake to be really flat, iron it on low temperature.

7. Hang your snowflakes on a wall or in a window until the end of this unit.

Storms

🙂🙂🙂 **EXPERIMENT: Storm in a Jar**

For this activity, you will need:

- Tall transparent jar or glass
- Foam shaving cream
- Food coloring
- Spoon
- Glass liquid measuring cup
- Science Notebook

Clouds form in the sky from water that has evaporated in the sun's heat. Once enough water has evaporated, the clouds get too heavy and can no longer hold any more, causing it to rain, snow, or hail.

1. Fill a tall jar half full of water. Spray shaving cream on

Weather

top of the water until the jar is 3/4 full. Use a spoon to carefully level the top of the shaving cream.

2. Add 10 drops of food coloring to a 1/2 cup of water in a liquid measuring cup. Mix the color in with a spoon. Drizzle the colored water slowly on top of the shaving cream until it begins to "storm" inside the jar.

The shaving cream can absorb water just like the atmosphere can, but once it hits saturation, the water begins to fall out the bottom and precipitate down.

3. Draw a picture of your experiment and write your observations in your Science Notebook.

😊 🟢 EXPLORATION: Lightning

For this activity, you will need:

- Book or video about lightning
- Socks - wool works best, but cotton should do
- A room with a rug

Lighting occurs when violent winds, high in the sky, cause ice particles to move rapidly back and forth, rubbing against one another. The movement causes static electricity to build up. Eventually, the charge grows so great that it has to be released into the ground.

1. Read a book or watch a video about lightning and how it is formed.
2. Put on a pair of socks and shuffle your feet over a rug, rubbing the particles in your socks against the particles in the rug.
3. Now, slowly reach your finger toward a metal doorknob. A spark of miniature lightning (static electricity) will jump between your finger and the doorknob as you get close enough. If you do this in a darkened room, you might be able to see the spark.
4. Draw a picture in your Science Notebook of your experiment with miniature lightning. Write a description of how lightning is formed in the atmosphere.

😊 🟢 EXPLORATION: Thunder

For this activity you need:

- Book or video about thunder and lightning
- Paper sack - lunch size is best

Thunder is produced when lighting creates heat, causing the air to expand very quickly. The fast expansion of air

---

Memorization Station

Lightning: natural electrical discharge between a cloud and the ground or between two clouds

Thunder: a loud rumbling or crashing noise heard after a lightning flash, caused by rapidly heated air expanding

Writer's Workshop

An almanac is a long-term forecast of the weather. It tells when to plant your crops for the best harvest, shows the cycles of the moon, and has a calendar with witty sayings.

Write your own almanac for the next year. Put down what you think the weather will be like for each month. Predict when you think major storms will happen or if it will be an especially wet summer, and so on.

Give the date for the most auspicious time to plant your garden. Add quotes, pithy sayings, or your best advice to each page. You can make one page per month.

Fabulous Fact

The longer the time between the flash of lightning and the sound of thunder, the further you are away from the storm. It takes the sound longer to travel to you than the light.

Earth & Space

Additional Layer

Learn more about severe weather. Here are a few kinds of storms that may interest you.

- Tornado
- Hurricane
- Dust storm
- Flood
- Hail storm
- Ice storm
- Tropical cyclone

Choose one to learn about and then make a mobile or poster report about it.

Memorization Station

Tornado: a violently rotating column of air, usually attached to the base of a thunderstorm

Blizzard: a severe snowstorm with high winds and low visibility

Additional Layer

What kind of severe weather would you be most afraid of?

Are there any kinds of severe weather phenomena that particularly afflict the area of the world you live in?

Are there things you can do to prepare for severe weather?

You may want to go over your emergency plan as a family and talk about what to do if a storm strikes.

causes thunder.

1. Read a book or watch a video about thunder and lightning.
2. Open a paper bag completely, then gather the open end in your hand so only a small opening is left. Blow air into the sack, then squeeze the opening shut so the air is trapped.
3. Smack the bottom of the bag hard with your other hand. The air in the bag is quickly forced out and creates a mini thunder clap.

😀😀😀 EXPERIMENT: Tornado Tube

For this activity, you will need:

- Two 2-liter plastic pop bottles
- Plastic vortex bottle connector (search online)
- Water
- Blue food coloring (optional)

A **tornado** is a column of air that is swirling madly in a circle. A hurricane is also a rapidly swirling vortex of air, but on a much larger scale. Both a tornado and a hurricane have an eye in the center, a zone of low pressure surrounded by moist, warm air that is rising rapidly.

1. Read a book or watch a video about cyclones.
2. Fill one of the 2-liter bottles with water. Add a couple of drops of blue food coloring if you want.
3. Secure the two bottles together with the connector.
4. Tip the bottle over so the empty one is on the bottom. Give the bottles a good swirl to get the water moving.

Weather

Watch as the water drains from the top bottle to the bottom one.

5. You will notice a hole in the middle of the swirling water. This is the eye. The water leaves a hole so that air from the bottom bottle can move into the top bottle. This is the low pressure zone that also forms inside a tornado or hurricane.

6. Draw a picture of your tornado tube experiment in your Science Notebook. Write a description of how tornadoes are created in nature next to your picture. Don't forget to title your page and add it in your table of contents.

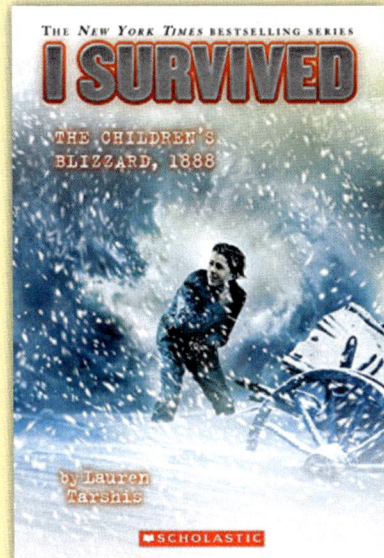

Bookworms

I Survived: The Children's Blizzard, 1888 by Lauren Tarshis is part of the I Survived Series. It's about an 11-year old boy who survived a brutal blizzard in the Midwestern states of the United States that killed hundreds. This is historical fiction - a story set in a real historical time period. It's well-written and fast-paced.

**EXPLORATION: Blizzard in a Jar**

WARNING: This activiy uses a hot glue gun. Be careful!

For this activity, you will need:

- Video about blizzards from the YouTube playlist
- Clear jar with a lid
- Polymer clay - white
- Acrylic paints or permanent markers
- Glycerin (from the health or personal care aisles)
- Glitter - clear or iridescent glitter works best
- Distilled water (automotive aisle)
- Hot glue gun and hot glue

Blizzards are severe snowstorms where the wind is blowing at least 48 km/h or 30 mph for 3 hours or more. They are created when a mass of warm air and a mass of cold air collide really quickly. The meeting of the two fronts causes strong winds and storm clouds. Snow falls from the sky and is whipped around by the wind; snow is also picked up from the ground and swirled into the sky. Blizzards can be so thick with snow that you can't see your hand in front of your face.

1. Watch a video all about blizzards.
2. Use the polymer clay to craft a snowman. Bake the clay according to the directions on the package.

Additional Layer

Which do you think holds more heat - air or water? Fill one glass jar with water and set another empty jar by it. This one is filled with air. Place both glasses in the freezer for ten minutes. Remove them. Which one feels warmer?

The glass with water will feel warmer because water holds more heat than air.

Earth & Space

Memorization Station

Memorize *The Wind* by Robert Louis Stevenson.

I saw you toss the kites on high
And blow the birds about the sky;
And all around I heard you pass,
Like ladies skirts across the grass.

O wind, a blowing all day long,
O wind, that sings so loud a song!

I saw the different things you did,
But always you yourself you hid.
I felt you push, I heard you call,
I could not see yourself at all.

O wind, a blowing all day long,
O wind, that sings so loud a song!

O you that are so strong and cold,
O blower, are you young or old?
Are you a beast of field and tree,
Or just a stronger child than me?

O wind, a blowing all day long,
O wind, that sings so loud a song!

Deep Thoughts

St. Elmo's Fire appears to be a faint light on the pointed edges of things like power lines, church steeples, and airplane wings. It is actually caused by electricity in the atmosphere that creates a faint light.

3. Once the clay is baked and cooled, paint your snowman's face and details with acrylic paints or use permanent markers. Let the paint dry completely.
4. Hot glue the snowman to the inside of the lid of the jar.
5. Fill the jar 3/4 full of distilled water. Add 1 tsp glycerin to the water. Add a generous amount of glitter. Stir it all together. Over a sink, fill the jar to the top with water. Insert your lid with your snowman into the jar and twist to secure. Some water will likely spill out when you do this. Put a ring of hot glue around the lid to seal it tightly.

Special Effects

😊 😊 😊 EXPERIMENT: Make a Rainbow

For this activity, you will need:

- Book or video about how rainbows are formed from the Library List or YouTube playlist
- CD
- Flashlight or lamp
- White paper & pencil
- Tape
- Colored pencils or crayons
- Science Notebook
- Glue stick
- Scissors

Rainbows are formed when light from the sun hits raindrops in the sky. The raindrops bend the light, scattering the white light into its component colors and making a rainbow.

1. Read a book or watch a video about how rainbows are formed.
2. Tape a piece of paper to a wall in a dim room.

Weather

3. Hold the shiny side of a CD horizontally in front of the paper. Shine a light at the CD so it reflects off and onto the paper. Move the CD and the flashlight around so that a rainbow shows up on the paper.
4. Trace the lines of the rainbow and color the paper to match the rainbow you see. You should see red, orange, yellow, green, blue, indigo (dark blue), and violet (purple).
5. Cut out your rainbow and paste it in your Science Notebook. Write a description of how rainbows are formed in the sky.

😊 😊 😊 EXPERIMENT: Rainbow Spinner

For this activity, you will need:

- "Rainbow Spinner" from the Printable Pack
- Thin cardboard, like from a cereal box
- Glue stick
- Scissors
- Tempera paints in rainbow colors
- Pencil
- String

It's hard to believe that the colors of a rainbow come from white light. This experiment shows that combining colors can make white.

1. Paint the two circles from the "Rainbow Spinner" with rainbow colors, one color in each section of the circles: red, orange, yellow, green, blue, indigo, violet. Let it dry completely.
2. Cut out the two "Rainbow Spinner" circles. Glue one

Additional Layer

Mirages are optical illusions caused by atmospheric conditions. Often, they appear to be a sheet of water on a stretch of dry land or roadway. Actually, it is from the refraction of light by heated air.

Writer's Workshop

Use the "Weather in the News" printable and add a 5-day weather forecast along with some articles that feature storms or other newsworthy weather.

Additional Layer

In 2011, astronomers discovered an old, large mass of water in the universe. It's a gigantic twelve billion year old cloud holding 140 trillion times more water than all of Earth's oceans combined. The space cloud surrounds a supermassive black hole that is about 12 billion light years from Earth.

Earth & Space

Fabulous Fact

The Earth's atmosphere has changed a great deal over time. During the Cambrian Period, the carbon dioxide (CO_2) levels in the atmosphere were roughly sixteen times higher than they are now.

Expedition

On a windy day, go out and fly a kite!

Deep Thoughts

Do you trust the weather forecast on TV? On the internet? Do you think it's valuable or a waste of time to report about weather?

circle to a piece of thin cardboard. Cut out the thin cardboard around the circle shape. Glue your second circle to the back side.

3. Poke two holes near each other in the center of the circle. Thread 30 cm of string through the holes and tie the string into a loop.

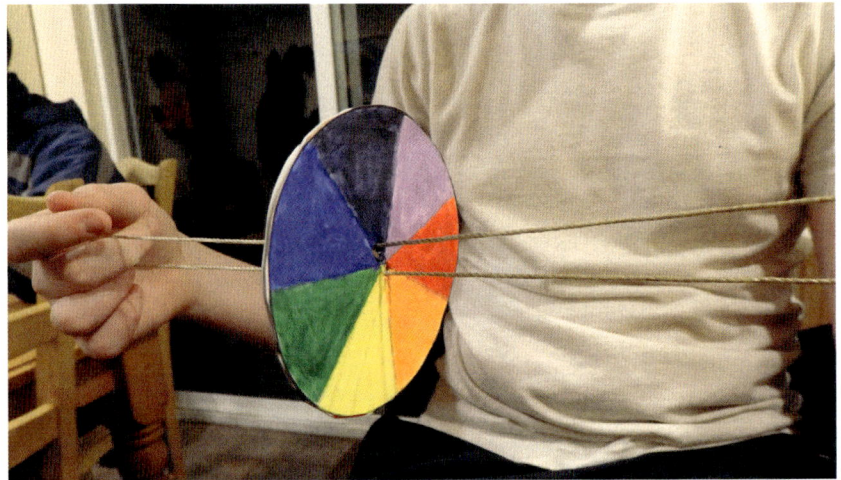

4. Gripping opposite sides of the string, Twirl the circles around and around, so the string gets twisted up. Pull straight out from the disc in the center, making it spin. Pull and release in a rhythm to keep the disc spinning. Observe what happens to the colored disc as it gets spinning faster and faster.

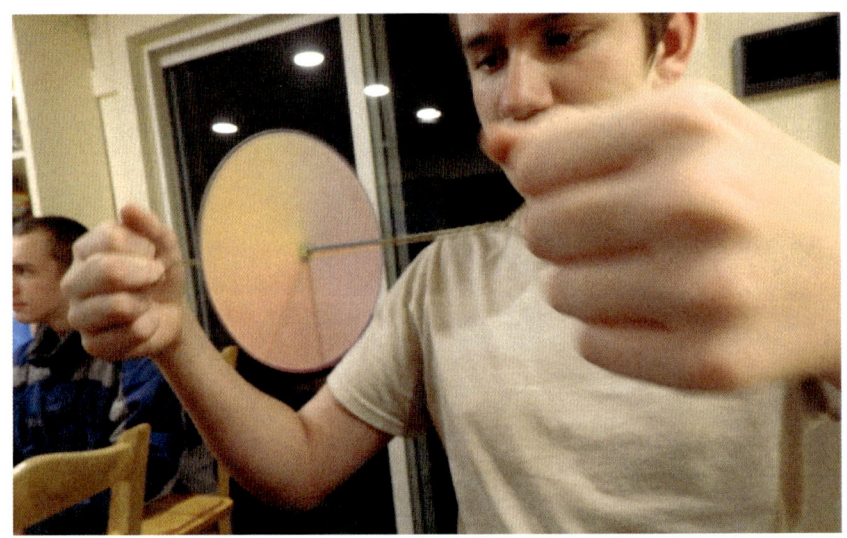

😊 😊 😊 **EXPERIMENT: Noctilucent Clouds**

For this activity, you will need:

- Spray bottle with water
- Dark room
- Flashlight
- Science Notebook

Weather

Noctilucent clouds form very high in the sky, above the troposphere, way up in the mesosphere. You can only see them at twilight, only in the summer, and only in latitudes between 50° and 70° north and south of the equator. They are made of water vapor like other clouds, but are extremely rare because there is normally not much water at all in the mesosphere. They are so thin that you can't see them in bright sunlight, only after the sun has dipped below the horizon but is still shining on the atmosphere.

1. Spray some water from a spray bottle on fine mist setting in a brightly lit room. The spray should be hard to see.

2. Now, go to a darkened room. Turn on a flashlight. Spray the fine mist again. This time the mist should show up very clearly. Light shining off particles in a dark atmosphere makes the particles show up really well.

3. If it is summer and you live in the appropriate latitudes, go outside in the twilight and look for noctilucent clouds.

4. Make a sketch and write about noctilucent clouds in your Science Notebook.

☺☺☺ EXPLORATION: Aurora

For this activity, you will need:

- White sheet of paper - watercolor paper or card stock
- Watercolor paints in lime green, bright blue, navy blue, and black
- Brushes & water
- White tempera paint
- Toothbrush - old, used for crafts
- Black paper
- Pencil
- Scissors
- Glue stick

The Northern and Southern Lights, sometimes called the aurora, are natural light displays in the polar night sky. They are seen only upwards of about 50° latitude. They are caused by solar wind particles getting caught in the Earth's magnetic field, which excites the particles in the atmosphere, making the particles emit light. The magnetic field is strongest close to the poles, which is why you can only see the aurora in those places.

The aurora can have green, blue, yellow, and red lights, with green being the most common.

1. Paint your paper with water to get the paper moist. Work water into bright lime green, blue, and navy paint to prepare it for painting.

Writer's Workshop

Write a paragraph about auroras and how they are formed. Cut it out and glue it to the back of your aurora painting.

Additional Layer

Pine cones can be used to forecast rain. If the weather is warm and dry, pine cones stay open to drop pollen and seeds. As humidity rises, pine cones begin to close up to protect the seeds and pollen inside. They are like Mother Nature's natural hygrometer.

Writer's Workshop

Make an extreme weather mobile. Draw different extreme types of weather on card stock, then cut out the pieces. Write facts about each one on the back of the pictures. Hole punch each one at the top and attach strings. Hang the pieces on a hanger, embroidery hoop, or something similar to create your mobile.

Earth & Space

Famous Folks

Galileo discovered that temperature can be observed through buoyancy. Thermometers like this are named for him. Learn more about Galileo.

Expedition

This is a virtual expedition, but it's worthwhile. You can go on a virtual tour of the National Weather Center in the United States. You'll find the tour by searching online or on this unit's YouTube playlist.

2. Paint 3-4 bright green streaks curved but along a similar path across the page. Paint bright blue streaks around the green. Paint the rest of the page with navy blue. Overlay the navy blue with black paint. Use a dry brush to pull streaks of the blues down into the green paint.

3. While your painting is drying, use the black paper to cut out a silhouette foreground scene. Sketch the outline on the black paper with a pencil and then cut it out.

4. Use white tempera paint and a toothbrush to flick white paint across the watercolor sky to make stars. Let it dry.

5. Glue the foreground silhouette to the bottom of the painting.

6. Show your painting to an audience and explain how auroras are formed. Put your painting in your Layers of Learning Notebook in the Science section.

☺ ☺ ☺ **EXPLORATION: What Makes the Weather?**

For this activity, you will need:

- "What Makes the Weather?" from the Printable Pack
- Science Notebook
- Markers
- Scissors
- Glue stick

1. Write these words in each section of the "What Makes the Weather?" printable:

Weather

- Temperature
- Precipitation
- Humidity
- Wind Direction
- Wind Speed
- Air Pressure

2. Illustrate each section with a picture of the instrument that meteorologists use to measure it.

3. Cut along the solid lines, fold along the dotted lines, and then glue just the center into your Science Notebook.

4. On the back of each flap, write the instrument that is used to measure it.

Step 3: Show What You Know

During this unit, choose one of the assignments below to show what you have learned during the unit. Add this work to your Layers of Learning Notebook. You can also use this assignment to show your supervising teacher or your charter school as a sample of what you've been working on in your homeschool, if needed.

There are more ideas for writing assignments in the "Writer's Workshop" sidebars.

🙂 🙂 Coloring or Narration Page

For this activity, you will need:

- "Weather" from the Printable Pack
- Writing or drawing utensils

1. Depending on the age and ability of the child, choose either the "Weather" coloring sheet or the "Weather" narration page from the Printable Pack.

2. Younger kids can color the coloring sheet as you review some of the things you learned about during this unit. On the bottom of the

Additional Layer

Just for fun, look up some interesting statistics and records about the weather. Find out:

- The highest temperature ever recorded
- The lowest temperature ever recorded
- The most rainfall in 60 seconds
- Most consecutive days with measurable rain
- Most snow in a calendar month
- Fastest wind speed ever recorded
- Largest diameter of hail ever recorded
- Longest lightning bolt
- Highest air pressure ever recorded
- Deadliest tornado on Earth

Famous Folks

Daniel Gabriel Fahrenheit, a German physicist, manufactured the first reliably scaled thermometers. His scale was based on the freezing point of a solution of brine, which temperature he called zero. The Fahrenheit scale is named for him.

Earth & Space

Unit Trivia Questions

1. What kind of precipitation involves small, irregular chunks of ice that fall from the clouds?
   Hail

2. The amount of water vapor in the air is called the _____. It is measured with a _____.
   Humidity, hygrometer

3. Name at least three extreme weather conditions.
   Tornado, hurricane, flood, blizzard, dust storm, etc. (answers will vary)

4. Why does lightning appear faster than the sound of thunder during a storm?
   Because light travels faster than sound.

5. What are the four basic kinds of precipitation?
   Rain, snow, sleet, hail

6. What are the three basic families of clouds?
   Cirrus, stratus, cumulus

7. What measurement scale is used to determine wind speed?
   a) Gusting scale
   b) Beaufort scale
   c) Richter scale
   d) Barometric scale

8. How many sides do snowflakes have?
   Six

9. _____ are moving masses of air that can be hot or cold. When they collide, we often get stormy weather.
   Fronts

coloring page, kids can write a sentence about what they learned. Very young children can explain their ideas orally while a parent writes.

3. Older kids can write about some of the concepts you learned on the narration page and color the picture.

4. Add this to the Science section of your Layers of Learning Notebook.

🙂🙂🙂 **Weather Log**

For this activity, you will need:

- The "Weather Log" you've been keeping in your Science Notebook
- "Weather Graphs" from the Printable Pack
- Markers, crayons, or colored pencils
- Scissors
- Glue

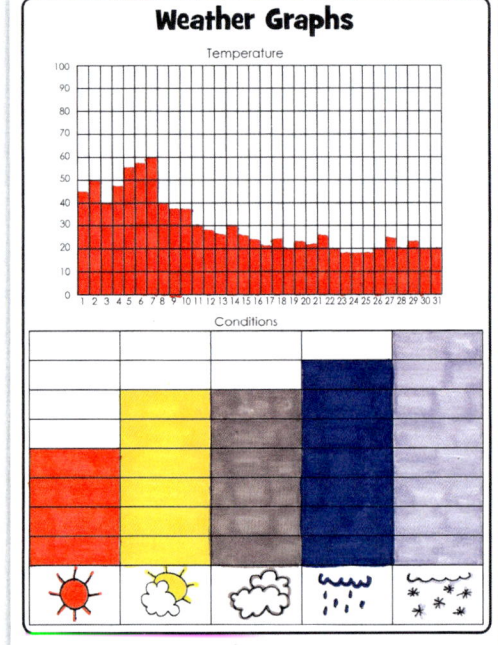

1. Finish the weather log you've been keeping throughout this unit. Make sure it's neat, colorful, and complete.

2. Use the data on your weather log to complete your "Weather Graphs" page. In the top section, create a graph of the daily high temperature. Within the bottom section, create a bar graph of the kinds of weather you experienced each day. Analyze which kinds of weather you've experienced the most and which you've experienced the least. Do the results match what you would expect for your season and location? Did you have any types of weather that weren't listed on your chart? Did you experience any extreme weather?

3. Present your Weather Log, Weather Graphs, and observations to an audience.

4. Add your Weather Graphs to either your Science Notebook or to the Science section of your Layers of Learning Notebook.

Weather

😊 😊 😊 Science Experiment Write-Up
For this activity, you will need:

- The "Experiment" write-up or "Experiment Report Template" from the Printable Pack

1. Choose one of the experiments you completed during this unit and create a careful and complete experiment write-up for it. Make sure you have included every specific detail of each step so your experiment could be repeated by anyone who wanted to try it.

2. Do a careful revision and edit of your write-up, taking it through the writing process, before you turn it in for grading.

😊 😊 😊 Weather Quiz
For this activity, you will need:

- "Weather Quiz" and "Weather Quiz Answers" from the Printable Pack

1. Give everyone the "Weather Quiz" to see what they remember from this unit.

2. You can add short answer questions about things you learned for older kids as well.

😊 😊 😊 Big Book of Knowledge
For this activity, you will need:

- "Big Book of Knowledge: Weather" printable from the Printable Pack, printed on card stock
- Writing or drawing utensils
- Big Book of Knowledge

1. Color, draw on, or write on the Big Book of Knowledge page. Record concepts, definitions, and facts you learned during this unit. It's a record of the things you learned and hope to remember. Add the page to your Big Book of Knowledge.

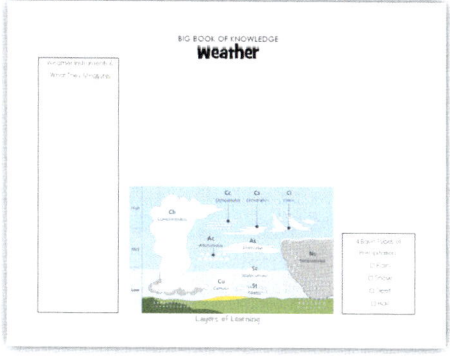

2. Use your Big Book of Knowledge regularly to help you review, quiz, or create games that will help you commit the things you've learned to memory.

Big Book of Knowledge

The Big Book of Knowledge is a book for you, the mentor, to use as a constant review of all of the things you're learning about. You can use it to quiz your kids or prepare tests or review games. Whenever you learn something in Layers of Learning that you want your kids to remember, add it to your Big Book of Knowledge.

Assemble your Big Book of Knowledge in a binder or with binder rings. Divide it into sections for each subject.

In the Printable Pack for this unit you will find a "Big Book of Knowledge" sheet. You can add this sheet to others you collect or create yourself as you progress through the Layers of Learning curriculum. Customize the Big Book of Knowledge to your family by adding facts and topics that you enjoyed exploring as you were learning.

Visit Layers of Learning online to find more information on how to assemble and use your own Big Book of Knowledge.

You will also find cover and section pages to print along with creative games to play with your Big Book of Knowledge to keep school, even the tests, fun!

Earth & Space

Unit Overview

Key Concepts:
- The universe is unimaginably big and it is getting bigger as it expands.
- Stars are burning balls of gas that can be classified, identified, and mapped in the night sky.
- The universe is full of objects like quasars, black holes, galaxies, stars, nebulae, and planets. Mankind is only beginning to learn about everything that is out there.

Vocabulary:
- Universe
- Stars
- Red giant
- White dwarf
- Red dwarf
- Neutron
- Supergiant
- Main sequence
- Constellation
- Galaxy
- Nebula
- Black hole
- Open cluster
- Globular cluster
- Quasar
- Exoplanet

Important Scientists:
- Georges Lemaître
- Edwin Hubble

Theories, Laws, & Hypotheses:
- Dark matter hypothesis
- Big Bang Theory
- Hubble's Law

UNIVERSE

The universe is all of the matter, space, energy, and time in existence. Outer space isn't as empty as it seems. It is full of stars clustered into galaxies, planets, dust, gas clouds, and atoms. Connecting all these parts are filaments made of hydrogen gas interspersed with voids. It turns out that most of the universe is made of something we can't see, something called dark matter. It is dark and invisible because it does not reflect or emit light. It does have gravity though, so we can tell it is there.

This is artist Pablo Carlos Budassi's concept of the universe, as seen from Earth. The solar system is on the left, distant galaxies in the center, and the most distant objects, including quasars and galaxies, on the far right. As you move left to right the scale jumps logarithmically, so Earth appears very large. CC by SA 4.0.

Besides matter, the universe is also full of energy. There is chemical energy from stars and gravitational energy of things falling or being pulled together. The most important source of energy is something astrophysicists are just beginning to understand. It is called dark energy. It is the energy that is causing the universe to expand, grow, and change. As space expands, the amount of dark energy also expands.

No one knows how big the universe is exactly, and it is expanding so fast that we probably can never know. It's possible the universe is infinite and has no edge. The observable universe, the part we can see while standing on Earth, is about 93 billion light years across. We can't see further because light has a speed limit and we can't see without light. We do know there are around 100 billion stars in our galaxy and there are hundreds of billions of galaxies. The universe is so big, it's beyond our minds to comprehend.

Astronomers use light to estimate the age of the

Universe

universe at about 13.7 billion years old. By walking that time backward, scientists visualize the universe contracting until it is a tiny, incomprehensibly dense and hot single speck. No one knows how or why, but the theory is that the tiny speck exploded, released light, created matter, and began to expand in an event nicknamed the "Big Bang." The process of creation and expansion are still underway.

Step 1: Library List

Choose books from your library that go with this topic. Here's a list of some favorites and also a list of search terms so you can utilize what your library offers. Read the books with your kids and/or assign them some to read independently. It is from these books your kids will learn most of the facts they need from this unit.

WARNING: You will encounter both the Big Bang Theory and the Creation within the Library List, YouTube playlist, and unit.

Search for: stars, universe, Big Bang, Hubble, astronomy

☺ ☺ ☺ *Encyclopedia of Science* from DK. Read "Universe," "Origin of the Universe," "Galaxies," "Stars," "Life cycle of Stars," and "Constellations" on pages 274-282.

☺ ☺ ☺ *The Kingfisher Science Encyclopedia*. During this unit, read "The Universe," "The Universe: Origins and Future," "Galaxies," and "Stars" on pages 386-393. Also read "Studying the Universe" and "Astronomical Telescopes" on pages 414-417.

☺ ☺ ☺ *The Usborne Science Encyclopedia*. Read "The Universe," "Galaxies," and "Stars" on pages 154-161.

☺ ☺ ☺ *Find the Constellations* by H.A. Rey. This is, by far, the best beginner constellation book. Using this book, you will be able to identify and find constellations in the night sky.

☺ ☺ ☺ *Seeing In the Dark* from PBS. A video documentary about telescopes and the wonders of outer space.

☺ ☺ ☺ *50 Things to See With a Telescope* by John Reed. Helps you make the most of your telescope by pointing you at nebulae, planets, stars, galaxies, and more.

☺ ☺ ☺ *Night Sky* by Carole Stott. Lots of captioned illustrations about all things space.

☺ *Older Than the Stars* by Karen C. Fox. Talks about the formation of the universe, the Big Bang, the formation of the elements, and the beginning of stars and galaxies.

Family School Levels

The colored smilies in this unit help you choose the correct levels of books and activities for your child.

☺ = Ages 6-9
☺ = Ages 10-13
☺ = Ages 14-18

On the Web

For videos, web pages, games, and more to add to this unit, visit the Earth & Space Resources at Layers-of-Learning.com.

You will find a link to video playlists, web links, and more.

Bookworms

If you're looking for a family read-aloud, we'd like to suggest this one.

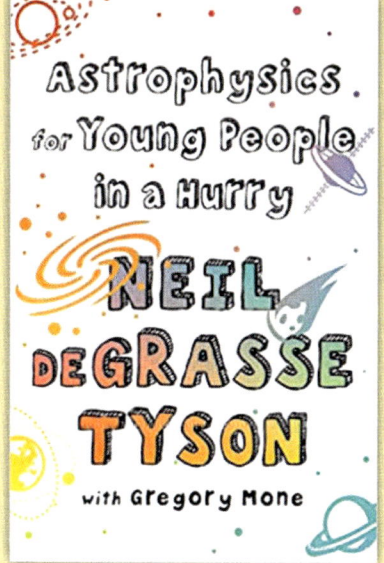

Astrophysics for Young People In a Hurry by Neil deGrasse Tyson breaks down the universe, light, matter, and how it all formed into simple language and interesting tidbits. For example, do you know how to talk to an alien?

Earth & Space

Fabulous Fact

An astronomer studies stars, planets, comets, galaxies and so on.

Cosmology is a branch of astronomy that studies the origin and evolution of the universe.

Astrophysics is another branch of astronomy that seeks to know what things in the universe are made of.

Teaching Tip

You don't need a telescope to study the stars. You can see gas giants, star clusters, nebulae, galaxies, planets, comets, and meteors with nothing but your eyes and a dark night.

We recommend that you don't buy a telescope until and unless you get into star gazing and have already learned many constellations, bright stars, and other visible objects in the sky.

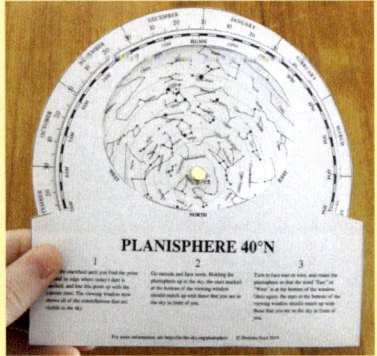

This is a planisphere that we printed from an online site.

What you do need is a guide to help you find the stars. You can get a guidebook, like H. A. Rey's *Find the Constellations*, get a planisphere, or download a phone app that helps you find the constellations and other space objects.

☺ *Stargazers* by Gail Gibbons. Easy introduction to astronomers, stars, galaxies, and telescopes.

☺ *Caroline's Comets* by Emily Arnold McCully. The true story of Caroline Herschel, the first woman to become a paid, professional scientist and astronomer.

☺ *Your Place in the Universe* by Jason Chin. A visual comparison of the size of things that goes clear up to the vastness of the universe. A winner of many awards for both content and illustrations, your kids will love this one.

☺ *Galaxies, Galaxies!* by Gail Gibbons. A journey into galaxies beyond the Milky Way.

☺ ☺ *The Mysteries of the Universe* by Will Gater. Illustrations and photographs pair with paragraphs and captions to explore the solar system and deep space. At 224 pages, this book is perfect for hours and hours of browsing.

☺ *Stars* by Seymour Simon. Lots of information and gorgeous full-color, full-page photos of the universe.

☺ *Space, Stars, and the Beginning of Time* by Elaine Scott. Explains the mission of the Hubble telescope, shows many photos captured by Hubble, and then explains what we have learned from this amazing tool.

☺ ☺ *The Astronomy Book* by DK. Discusses planets, stars, black holes, and more. It also gives a brief overview of the most important discoveries in astronomy since earliest times.

☺ ☺ *Bang! The Complete History of the Universe* by Brian May, et al. An excellent and short overview of everything in the universe from the Big Bang to size to stars and on.

☺ *Astronomy: A Self-Teaching Guide* by Dinah L. Moche. If you want your high schooler to have a text book approach with self quizzes and all, this is the book for you. Use it during this unit and the next, *Solar System*.

☺ *Big Bang: The Origin of the Universe* by Simon Singh. This is a popular level science book about the Big Bang theory of the formation of the universe.

☺ *The God of the Big Bang* by Leslie Wickman, PhD. A former astronaut and research scientists explains how modern science and belief in God and creation dovetail instead of conflict. For people of faith who need help melding their faith in science with their faith in God.

☺ *A Brief History of Time* by Stephen Hawking. Hawking explains his ideas to a general audience. It covers the universe, light, time, and space. It can get deep in some places, but it's okay to skim through the equations.

Universe

😊 *The Universe in Your Hand* by Christophe Galfard. Big Bang Theory, string theory, black holes, dark matter, stars, and more, entertainingly and clearly explained. This book is aimed at teens, but is written by a physicist who really knows his stuff.

😊 *Cosmology and Astronomy* from KhanAcademy.org. Add a lecture course for your high schooler with this Khan Academy course. During this unit, study "Scale of the Universe" and "Stars, Black Holes, and Galaxies."

Step 2: Explore

Choose a few hands-on explorations from this section to work on as a family. They should be appealing activities that will create mental hooks so your kids remember the information in the unit. Save the rest of the explorations for the next time you do this unit in four years when your kids are older. You can also read the sidebars together and explore some little rabbit trails.

This unit includes printables. See the introduction for instructions on retrieving your Printable Pack.

Outer Space

😊😊😊 **EXPERIMENT: Parts of a Telescope**
For this activity, you will need:

- "Parts of a Telescope" from the Printable Pack
- Telescope (optional)
- Book or video about telescopes

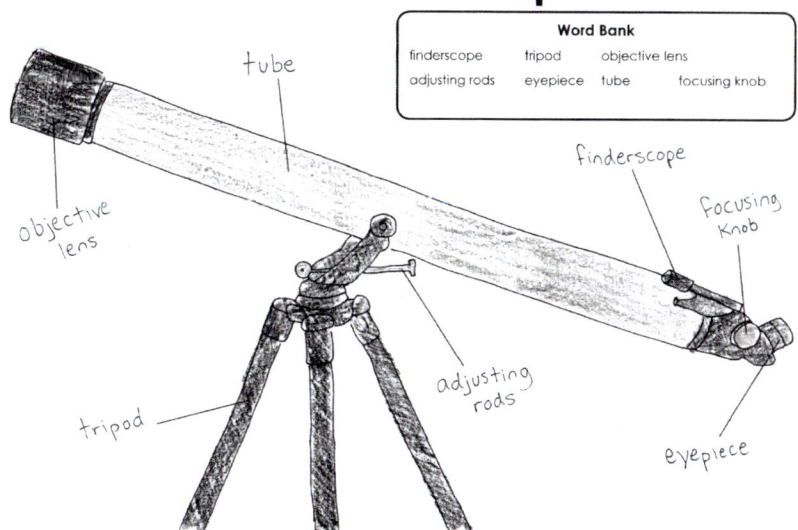

Famous Folks

Carl Sagan was an American astronomer who believed strongly in the possibility of extra terrestrial life. He pioneered the Search for Extra Terrestrial Intelligence (SETI) program.

Additional Layer

The Printable Pack includes a basic timeline of the "History of Stargazing" for you to complete. Cut out the timeline tags, read the descriptions, and then glue the squares into the proper places on the timeline.

Fabulous Fact

Scientists can be divided into two philosophical camps: materialists and creationists.

Materialists believe that nothing exists beyond the physical universe.

Creationists believe that a creator god or being caused the universe to exist.

Courageous scientists search for the truth even if the truth contradicts or seems to contradict their philosophy.

Earth & Space

Recent discoveries about outer space have almost all been made with the aid of telescopes. They magnify light and allow us to see much further than we could see with our eyes alone.

1. Use the "Parts of a Telescope" printable and label it. Use the image as an answer key.
2. If you have a real telescope, find those parts on your telescope. Play with the focusing knobs and adjusting knobs to understand how they work.
3. Read a book or watch a video about telescopes.

😊 💜 **EXPLORATION: Light-Years & Parallax**

For this activity, you will need:

- "Measuring With Parallax" from the Printable Pack
- A large, empty field
- Objects to mark your position, like wooden boards
- Meter stick
- Small table or stool
- Heavy duty rubber band
- Large rock or brick
- Metric measuring tape

Distances in outer space are so vast that using kilometers would be absurd. Instead, we measure distance in light-years. A light-year is the distance light can travel in one year. Light travels at 300,000 kilometers per second, which works out to 9.46 trillion kilometers in a year. The star nearest to Earth, apart from the Sun, is Proxima Centauri, which is 4.22 light-years away.

Fabulous Fact

A parsec is another unit used for measuring distance in space. A parsec is figured out using parallax and trigonometry. It works out to about 31 trillion kilometers, or about 3.26 light-years. Parsecs are used more often in scientific astronomy literature, but popular books use the more familiar light-year.

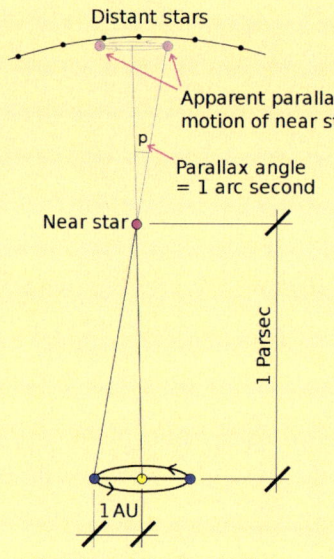

This image shows how a parsec is calculated. One parsec is the distance between the earth and an object that has a parallax angle of 1/60th of 1°.

Parsecs are an SI unit for astronomy, along with kiloparsecs (a thousand parsecs), megaparsecs (a million parsecs), and gigaparsecs (a billion parsecs).

Writer's Workshop

Craft a five sentence paragraph with a topic sentence, three points, and a conclusion sentence, about the difference between parsecs and light-years.

Universe

Astronomers measure distances in outer space using a technique called parallax.

1. In a large open field, find an object that represents a distant star. It should be something easily visible, but some distance away. A tree works well.

2. As far away as you can get from your target object, place your boards on the ground one meter apart from each other, one to your left and one to your right as you face your target object.

3. Place the small table two meters in front of your two boards and directly between them. Place a large rock or brick on the table and use a rubber band to wrap around the rock and around a meter stick. The goal is to get the meter stick horizontal just above the table top. The rock or brick holds the meter stick in place.

4. The center point between your boards, the center of the meter stick, and the target object need to all line up straight.

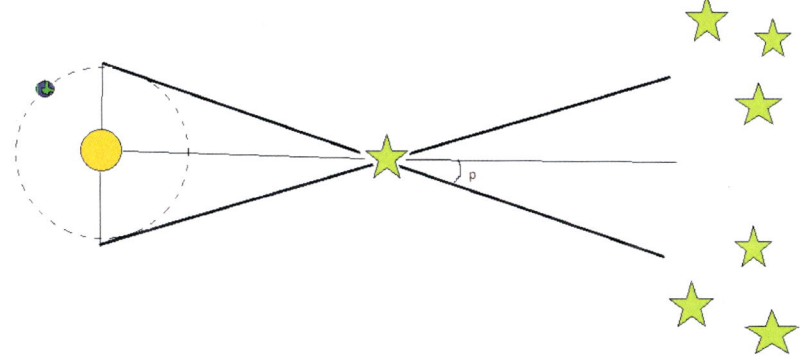

5. Stand on the left board and look at the target object. Note which cm mark on the meter stick the distant object appears to line up with. Record this on the "Measuring With Parallax" data sheet. Then, stand on the right board and repeat.

6. Move the table with the meter stick and the rock forward, toward the distant object, another two meters. Repeat standing on the left then the right board and noting which cm mark the distant object appears to line up with.

7. Repeat this process at 6 meters, 8 meters, 10 meters, and 12 meters.

8. Calculate the values in the fourth column of "Measuring With Parallax" by subtracting the value in the second column from the value in the third column for each row.

9. Make a line graph of the data on the "Measuring With

Bookworms

Ada and the Galaxies by Alan Lightman is an adorable picture book about a New York City girl who goes to Maine to visit her grandparents and see the stars.

The illustrations are overlaid on gorgeous photographs from the Hubble Space Telescope.

Additional Layer

Light pollution is artificial light at night. It helps people see, work at night, and cuts down on crime, but it also has harmful effects. It affects animals, disrupts the sleep patterns and health of humans, and makes it so you can't see the stars.

Find out more about light pollution, why it is a problem, and what can be done about it.

Deep Thoughts

We know the observable universe (the part we can see) is ~93 billion light-years in diameter.

But how big is the whole universe? Is it infinite?

What do you think?

Earth & Space

Fabulous Fact

Dark matter is still mostly in the hypothesis stage of scientific inquiry. There is quite a bit of evidence that dark matter exists based on the way objects in space react gravitationally with something we can't see, but no one knows for sure what dark matter is made of or how it behaves, except that it has gravity.

Astrophysicists are hard at work learning more about dark matter.

Bookworms

See You In The Cosmos by Jack Cheng is about Alex and his dog, Carl Sagan.

Alex is obsessed with outer space and records life on Earth on his iPod in the hopes he can send it out into the cosmos. Along the way, he learns the truth about his father's death and meets some long-lost family members. This is an emotional and optimistic middle grades novel for ages 10 and up.

Parallax" sheet. The horizontal x axis is the distance from the meter stick table. The vertical y axis is the distance the object appeared to move.

10. Think about the data. How are the distances measured related to the real distance of the target object?

Parallax is the way a distant object appears to shift positions when viewed from different perspectives. When viewing stars, astronomers view a star from Earth compared to its position with other stars. Then they wait six months for Earth to orbit to the other side of the Sun and measure the same stars, comparing the nearer stars to the more distant ones. The amount the nearer stars appear to move compared to the more distant stars tells astronomers how far away the stars are.

In the experiment above, the two different positions of Earth's orbit are like the two boards placed on the ground. The meter stick on the table is like the nearer stars, and the distant target object is like the further stars.

😊 😊 😊 EXPLORATION: Dark Matter & Gravitational Lensing

For this activity, you will need:

- Sheet of white card stock paper
- Watercolor paints, brushes, and a water cup
- White poster paint
- Stiff brush, like a toothbrush
- Curved piece of glass, like a drinking glass

Gravity is a powerful force in the universe. One of the things it can do is bend light so the light no longer travels in a straight path, or rather, mass can bend space so the light travels along the curve of space. The more massive something is, the more it bends space. Astronomers have observed light bending in space where it shouldn't, unless something we can't see is out there making it bend with the power of its gravity. This bending of light is called gravitational lensing.

1. Work water into bright pink, purple, and black watercolor paints so the paint is vibrant.

2. Paint a streak of bright pink across the middle of your paper. Surround the pink with purple and cover the whole sheet. Then, go across the sheet with black paint, covering most of the purple. This represents a nebula in the darkness of space.

3. Use white poster paints and a stiff brush to sprinkle white paint across the whole paper. These are stars in the night sky. Let the paint dry completely.

4. Set the curved glass on the paper and move it across the page observing how the stars appear to shift and move. The curved glass is a lens that bends light, distorting the position of the stars, just as mass bends light in outer space in gravitational lensing.

🙂🙂🙂 **EXPLORATION: Big Bang Theory**

For this activity, you will need:

- Book or video on the Big Bang Theory from this unit's Library List or YouTube playlist
- Balloon
- Glitter glue, paint pen, or marker
- Clip
- Science Notebook

For most of history, people have believed that the **universe** was static and unchanging. In the early 1900s, astronomers observed that nearby galaxies seemed to be moving further away from us here on Earth. Georges Lemaître, a Belgian Catholic priest and physics professor at Catholic University of Louvain, proposed that the universe is actually not static, but constantly expanding, which also meant that at one time it had been an infinitesimally small point containing all the matter and energy of the universe. Lemaître called it the "hypothesis of the primeval atom" and the "beginning of the world." His critics, including astronomer Fred Hoyle, disparagingly called it the Big Bang. Evidence has mounted that Lemaître was right all along and, today, most astronomers and physicists accept the Big Bang Theory.

Memorization Station

Universe: all of space and all of the matter and energy that space contains

Famous Folks

This is Georges Lemaître, the scientist who first proposed the hypothesis that the universe was expanding.

His ideas were based on Einstein's theory of relativity and observations of light by astronomers. Einstein initially rejected Lemaître's hypothesis even though he knew the math was sound. He just couldn't accept that the universe began as a single point of matter and energy. To his credit, Einstein did admit he had been wrong once the evidence convinced him.

Deep Thoughts

You may believe in the Creation. You may believe in the Big Bang Theory. You may even believe in both.

Whatever you believe in, discuss the various theories and beliefs to understand and evaluate them and have intelligent conversations about both viewpoints.

Earth & Space

Additional Layer

Hubble's Law states that:

Galaxies are moving away from Earth at speeds proportional to the distance from Earth.

This observation is the main reason astronomers believe the universe is expanding.

Astronomers are mathematicians. There is a lot of fancy math involved in calculating how fast the universe is expanding. If you have a mathematician in your house, go look up the math as well.

Famous Folks

Edwin Hubble first observed redshift in distant objects in the universe. In 1929, he proposed that the universe is expanding, shocking the world.

He also discovered Hubble's Law, that galaxies move faster and faster away the further they are from Earth. This law suggests that the universe is expanding.

The Hubble Space Telescope was named in his honor.

1. Read a book or watch a video about the Big Bang theory.

2. Blow up a balloon until it is about the size of your fist. Clip the mouth closed so no air can escape. Then, draw dots all over the balloon with glitter glue, a paint pen, or markers. Each dot represents a galaxy.

3. Remove the clip and blow the balloon up more. Watch what happens to the dots as the balloon expands.

   Notice that the galaxies move away from each other and the galaxies themselves also expand and grow larger. The galaxy dots represent the normal matter and energy in the universe. The balloon, itself, represents the dark matter and dark energy in the universe.

4. Draw a picture of your balloon universe expansion in your Science Notebook. Give the page a title and add it to your table of contents.

5. At the bottom of your page, write "Big Bang Theory" and explain what the Big Bang Theory is and why it is important.

☺ ☺ **EXPERIMENT: Expanding Universe & Redshift**

For this activity, you will need:

- 2 long cardboard tubes, like from gift wrap
- Scissors
- Tape
- 10 or more marbles
- Stopwatch or timer

Light is made up of the colors of the rainbow, from red to violet. When something moves away from Earth, the light

Universe

it gives off is shifted toward the red end of the spectrum as its wavelength gets longer. If it moves towards Earth, the light is shifted toward the blue end of the spectrum as its wavelength gets shorter.

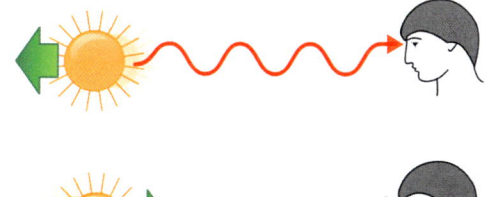

When a star moves away, the wavelength appears longer, shifting toward red. When an object moves closer, the wavelength appears shorter, shifting toward blue. Image by Aleš Tošovský, CC by SA 3.0, Wikimedia.

It's the same effect that happens to the sound of a police siren as it passes you on the road. While its zooming toward you, the sound is high pitched, but after it passes, the pitch drops lower. This is called the Doppler effect, and it happens to light as well as sound.

Because light moves so fast, this shift in light is only observable at the massive distances and speeds of space. When standing on Earth, nearly all of the galaxies we observe are shifted toward the red end of the spectrum. That means the galaxies are all, on every side of us, moving away from us. The further a galaxy is from Earth, the larger the redshift. In other words, the more distant the galaxy is, the faster it is moving away from us. This only makes sense if the entire universe is expanding outward in all directions at an accelerating rate.

If the universe is expanding faster and faster, then there must be some energy source making it do so. The energy doesn't come from light or gravity or magnetism. It comes from something we can't see, touch, or manipulate. Astronomers have called this mysterious energy in outer space "dark energy."

1. Cut the long cardboard tubes in half the long way so you have four long troughs. Tape the

Bookworms

The Boy Whose Head Was Filled With Stars by Isabelle Marinov is a picture book biography of the great astronomer, Edwin Hubble.

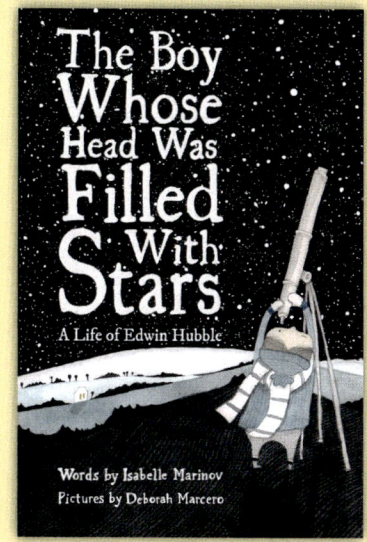

He overcame great difficulties to one day discover that ours is not the only galaxy and that our universe grows bigger every moment.

Teaching Tip

If you have a budding astronomer in your house, consider subscribing to an astronomy magazine to feed the passion.

On the Web

EarthSky is an online site and email subscription that keeps you up to date on things to look for in the night sky as well as the latest news in the world of astronomy, weather, and space travel.

Go there to read up-to-date articles and subscribe to get news of current objects or events in the cosmos.

Earth & Space

Memorization Station

Stars: huge balls of gas in space that produce light and heat

Famous Folks

In the early 1900s, American astronomer Annie Jump Canon developed the system to classify stars based on their temperature.

She was able to do this because she worked for decades cataloging stars at the Harvard Observatory. The men worked the telescopes and took observations while Annie and other women examined the data, did astronomical calculations and cataloged the photographs captured from the telescopes.

She also discovered 300 variable stars, five novas, and a binary star system.

Memorization Station

Memorize the star classification letters in order, from brightest to dimmest.

O B A F G K M

You can use the mnemonic:

Oh, be a fine girl, kiss me

to help you remember.

---

troughs together, end to end.

2. Set the trough up on a slight slope so the marbles will roll down it. Release the marbles, one every second using a stopwatch to time the release. Observe the distance between the marbles. This distance is like wavelength, the pulses between particles of light coming from a star. The hand releasing the marbles is the "star," or source of the light particles.

3. Repeat the experiment, but this time, slowly move backward, up the slope of the trough as you release the marbles, still at one second intervals. Observe the distance between the marbles. This is like a star moving away. Even though the light particles are released at the same intervals, they appear to be further apart than they ought to be.

4. Try the experiment again, but move the hand releasing the marbles slowly down the trough as the marbles are released at one second intervals. What happens this time? This is like blue shift where the star is moving toward the observer.

Stars

😊 😊 😊 EXPLORATION: Star Classification

For this activity, you will need:

- Candle
- Matches or lighter
- Colored pencils
- Paper
- "Star Classification" from the Printable Pack
- Star guide book, planisphere, or phone app that helps you locate constellations and stars
- "Stars to Find" from the Printable Pack (Choose the applicable printable based on the month.)

Stars are grouped into seven categories based on their temperatures. Each type of star is given a letter: O, B, A, F, G, K, and M, with O being the hottest and M the coolest stars. We can tell the temperature of stars because different temperatures give off different colors of light.

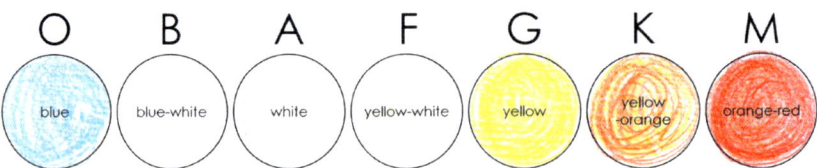

Universe

1. Light a candle and observe the flame very closely. Draw a detailed picture of the candle flame, using different colored pencils to depict what you see. Which part of the candle flame is the hottest? What color was it? Have you noticed the colors of flame in other situations (campfire, a rocket taking off, a gas stove). Blue flame is hotter than yellow flame, which is hotter than orange or red flame. These color differences exist in stars as well.

2. Color the stars on the "Star Classification" sheet. Read the descriptions of each type of star. Also, memorize the different types of stars - **red giants, white dwarves, red dwarves, neutrons, supergiants,** and **main sequence stars**.

3. Go outside on a dark night and locate one of each type of star in the sky. Use the "Stars to Find" from the Printable Pack for names of the stars, general locations, and some facts about each one. The chart works in the Northern or Southern Hemispheres. Choose the one with the months that work for you. You will need a star guidebook or phone app to pinpoint each star. Note that most stars look white or blue to the naked eye. If you have a telescope, look at each star through the telescope to see if you can distinguish some color.

☺ ☺ ☺ **EXPLORATION: Life Cycle of a Star**
For this activity, you will need:

- Book or YouTube video about the life cycle of stars
- "Life Cycle of a Star" and "Life Cycle of a Massive Star" from the Printable Pack
- Colored pencils
- Scissors
- Glue stick

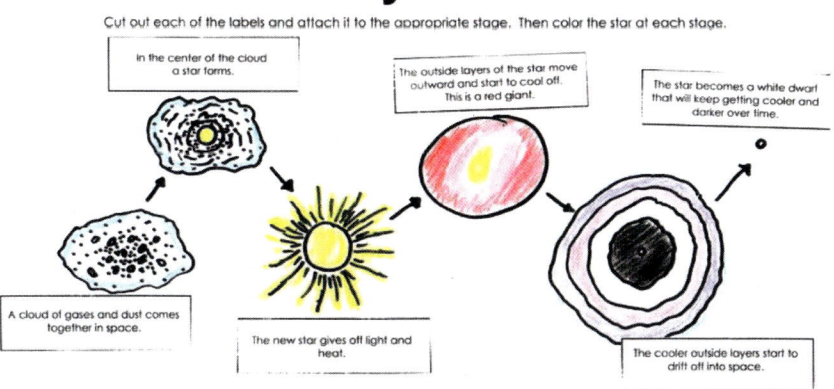

Stars form from a cloud of gases called a nebula. A protostar, or new star, forms in the center of the nebula.

Memorization Station

Memorize the a few of the different types of stars.

Red giant: an old star that has used up most of its fuel, but grows up to 100 times its original size

White dwarf: a star that has completely used up all of its hydrogen fuel and collapses into its own gravity, still glows white-hot, but will slowly cool down

Red dwarf: a low-mass star that burns cooler, but much longer than an average star

Neutron: a star with a high enough mass to end its life in a supernova explosion and is composed completely of neutrons because its intense gravity crushes protons and electrons together to make neutrons

Supergiant: the most massive stars in the universe, many times larger than our Sun, that consumes their fuel rapidly, detonating as supernovae in the end

Main sequence: stars in the prime of life, burning hydrogen gas in their cores, converting it into helium and releasing enormous amounts of energy in the process (Most of the stars in the universe are main sequence.)

Fabulous Fact

Stars are hot balls of burning matter, held together by their own gravity. They are mostly made of hydrogen and helium with a tiny bit of heavier elements like iron and chromium.

Earth & Space

The new star gives off light and heat. Over time, the outside layers of the star move outward from the center. As they do, they begin to cool. The cooler layers on the outside start to drift off into space. Eventually, the star continues to get darker and cooler over time.

1. Read a book or watch a video about star life cycles.

2. Complete the "Life Cycle of a Star" sheet by cutting the word strips off the bottom of the sheet and cutting them apart. Color the sheet. Then glue the word strips to the sheet next to the image that shows each stage. Use the image above as an answer key. There's also a life cycle of a massive star coloring sheet.

3. Add your printables to the Science section of your Layers of Learning Notebook.

😊 🟢 EXPLORATION: Constellation Viewer

For this activity, you will need:

- Aluminum soda pop can - empty and rinsed out
- Graph paper
- Constellation guide book or the internet
- Tape
- Small nail and hammer
- Dark blue, black, or purple colored paper
- Crayons

Constellations are groups of stars in the sky that form a pattern. People have looked up and thought they could see a plow or a swan or a goat in the patterns the stars made. Constellations are useful to learn because once you can identify several of them, the night sky begins to become familiar and organized in your mind.

Additional Layer

People have been navigating for thousands of years using the stars as their guides.

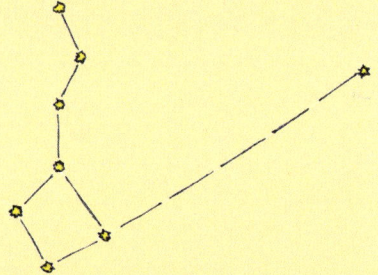

In the Northern Hemisphere, you have to find Polaris, the pole star, by following the line from the Big Dipper.

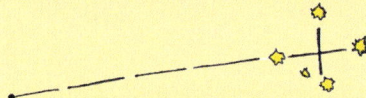

If you live in the Southern Hemisphere, finding your direction is a bit trickier since there is no southern pole star to sight from. You have to start by finding the southern pole in the sky. Find the southern cross. Then draw an imaginary line between the two stars at the head and the foot of the cross. Continue that line for four more lengths. That spot in the sky is the south celestial pole.

Memorization Station

Constellation: a group of stars that form a picture or pattern

On the Web

Search for images from NASA's James Webb telescope. It is capturing images that teach us new things about the universe.

Universe

1. Cut out a small, round piece of graph paper to match the bottom of your pop can. Draw the stars of a constellation on your graph paper using a constellation guide book to help you.

2. Once you have the stars plotted, flip the paper over and mark the stars from the reverse side. It is the reverse side you want facing out, so that when you look at your constellation from the inside of your can, it will be facing the right way.

3. Tape the graph paper to the bottom of the can and drive small nails through the paper and through the can at each "star" point. Look through the opening of your can at your constellation.

4. Cover the outside of the can with construction paper, decorated with the stars and name of your constellation.

5. Now you can go outside at night and find your constellation in the sky. (Be sure the constellation you choose is visible at the time of year you do this Exploration.)

😊 😊 😊 **EXPERIMENT: Astrolabe and Star Map**

For this activity, you will need:

- Card stock
- "Astrolabe" from the Printable Pack
- Scissors
- Drinking straw
- Tape
- String
- Weight, like a washer or a paper clip
- "Star Chart" from the Printable Pack

Writer's Workshop

From ancient times, people have made up stories about the constellations in the sky. The constellation Orion, for example, is named after a mythological Greek hunter.

Look up at the night sky. Take some time finding a pattern or a picture of your own in the stars. Go back out and find it night after night so you will always know it.

Name your constellation and then invent a story about it. Write the story in your Writer's Notebook along with a sketch of the pattern the stars make in the sky.

Additional Layer

A nebula is a cloud of gas and dust where stars are born. The Orion Nebula is very bright and can be seen with the naked eye.

Learn more about nebulae, the Orion Nebula in particular, and then go and find the Orion Nebula. It is the middle "star" in Orion's sword. If it is a very dark night and you have good eye sight, you can tell the "star" is fuzzy and not quite like a star at all.

If you have a telescope, train it at the Orion nebula and see what you can see.

Earth & Space

Bookworms

The Last Stargazers by Emily Levesque is a memoir and history of recent astronomy as told by the astronomer author. Entertaining and well-written.

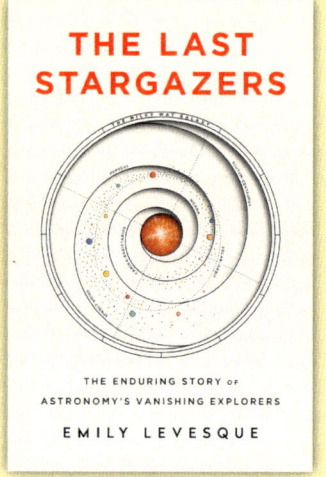

Famous Folks

In 1924, scientists believed that the composition of the earth, Moon, Sun, and other planets and stars were approximately the same.

Then, in 1925, Cecilia Payne hypothesized that the Sun was actually mostly made of just two elements: hydrogen and helium.

The idea that different astronomical objects have different compositions was groundbreaking and laid the foundation for astrophysics.

An astrolabe (pronounced astro-lay-b) is a tool used to find the altitude of stars above the horizon. It is used in making star charts. It can also be used to find latitude on the surface of the earth.

1. Print "Astrolabe" onto card stock. Cut the astrolabe out.

2. Attach a straw along the top edge of the astrolabe using tape. You want the astrolabe suspended from the straw, not taped directly to the straw.

3. Poke a hole through the astrolabe in the corner where the dot is. Tie a string through this hole. Tie a washer onto the other end of the string.

4. To use the astrolabe, look through the straw at a star. Have another person read the degrees that the string is hanging on the astrolabe. That is the number of degrees above the horizon the star is located at.

5. To find your latitude on Earth, measure the angle from the horizon to the pole star if you are in the Northern Hemisphere or to the celestial pole in the Southern Hemisphere. Your latitude is equal to the angle between the horizon and the pole star or point.

226

Universe

6. Use your astrolabe to find the altitudes of some of the brighter stars, perhaps stars you have become familiar with already, and make a star chart. Use the printable "Star Chart" from the end of this unit. Measure the location of the star from the northern (or southern) horizon. Then measure again from the western (or eastern) horizon. Plot your star on the chart. Label it with the degrees from the horizons and the name of the star.

7. Add your Star Chart to the Science section of your Layers of Learning Notebook.

😊 😊 😊 **EXPEDITION: Stargazing**

For this activity, you will need:

- Constellation guidebook, planisphere, or phone app for finding constellations
- Flashlight with a red filter (Put red cellophane over a normal flashlight to preserve your night vision.)
- Blankets, chairs, cushions, snacks, etc. for comfort
- Dark location outside of a city (You can still see stars from inside a city or in the suburbs, but not nearly as many because the lights from the city will wash out the sky. Also, consult a moon chart to get a moonless night and the weather to get a mostly cloudless night.)
- "Constellations" from the Printable Pack
- Scissors
- Glue
- Science Notebook

The more time you spend looking up at the night sky, the more familiar it will become to you. Objects in the night sky are categorized by their brightness as viewed from Earth. The lower the number, the brighter the object is. The brightest stars are magnitude 1. The second brightest are magnitude 2. The next level is magnitude 3. Dim stars are magnitude 4. Very dim stars are magnitude 5. On star maps, brighter stars have larger dots than dimmer stars. The smallest stars on a star map are usually about a magnitude 5. If the night is dark enough, you may be able to see even dimmer stars. Many people report being able to see 6.5 magnitude stars or higher.

1. Find a dark location away from a city where you can see the stars without tall trees, mountains, or buildings blocking your view. You will want to bring snacks, comfy chairs, blankets and anything else that will make your evening pleasant. Don't forget your constellation guidebooks and red flashlights. Red flashlights preserve your night vision so your pupils remain dilated to bring in the most light possible.

Fabulous Fact

You can see the Andromeda galaxy with your eyes alone if you are in a dark location, away from a city. It is located in the Andromeda constellation. Use a planisphere and look for M31, the other name for the Andromeda galaxy.

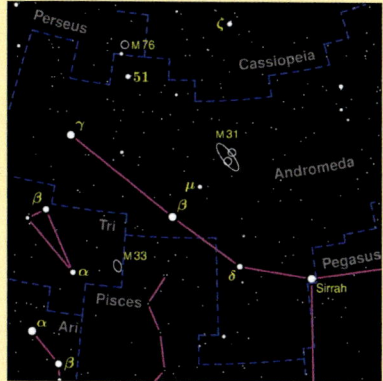

This is a map of the constellation Andromeda. You can see M31, the Andromeda Galaxy, near the center of the image.

It is easiest to see in October in the evening. To the naked eye, it appears as a dim, hazy patch. With a telescope, you should be able to pick out some details.

Additional Layer

The ancient Greeks gave us the names of most of our stars and constellations in the Northern Hemisphere.

They searched the skies for meaning and found their myths written in the stars to remind humans of the consequences of angering the gods. Along the way, they became scientists, calculating the size of the earth and predicting events in the night sky.

Find out more about the Greeks and their astronomical achievements.

Earth & Space

Additional Layer

Remote mountain tops in places with little humidity are the best possible places on Earth to observe the night sky from, and this is where many observatories are placed.

Antarctica is an ideal location for astronomy because it is so dark, cold, dry, and has a thinner atmosphere.

There is, in fact, a South Pole Telescope at Amundsen-Scott Station in Antarctica.

Find out more about astronomy and other science that happens in Antarctica.

Writer's Workshop

Brainstorm a list of everything you know about the Sun. Put the list in your Writing Journal. You can use it later as inspiration for writing a report, a poem, or anything else.

Fabulous Fact

The Sun goes through an 11-year cycle of increased sunspots and solar activity. At the end of each 11-year period, the Sun's magnetic field flips.

No one knows why or how the Sun does this.

We do know it affects the weather on Earth, but we don't know to what extent. So many questions.

2. Spend an hour or more observing the night sky. Search for constellations first. Once you become familiar with some of these, you can find the brightest stars (which have names like Regulus, Sirius, Arcturus, and Vega) and planets on a second outing.

3. Finally, you can find nebulae, galaxies, and clusters of stars on later outings.

4. Cut out the cards and the pocket from the "Constellation" printable and follow the instructions to add them to a page in your Science Notebook.

☺ ☺ EXPLORATION: Sun Catcher

WARNNG: This activity uses sharp tools and a hot iron. These steps should be done by an adult or older teen.

For this activity, you will need:

- Book or video about the Sun from the Library List or YouTube playlist
- Paper plates
- Crayons
- Waxed paper
- Scissors
- School glue
- Stapler
- Ribbon or string
- An iron
- Newspapers
- Hand grater, pencil sharpener, or sharp knife

The Sun is a star. It is our nearest star and is at the center of our solar system. It gives Earth all of the light and energy we need for plants and animals to thrive. The Sun is made of hydrogen and helium gases, heated to incandescence by nuclear fusion reactions in its core which turn matter into energy. It is a G-type star, also known as a yellow dwarf. The Sun is one star on one arm of the Milky Way Galaxy.

Universe

1. Read a book or watch a video about the Sun.
2. Grate yellow, orange, and red crayons with a hand grater, pencil sharpener, or sharp knife.
3. Use a paper plate to trace two circles onto waxed paper. Cut out two paper plate-sized circles from the waxed paper.
4. Turn an iron to a low setting without steam to preheat.
5. Layer these items on your work surface: newspaper, a waxed paper circle, then a sprinkling of wax from the crayons, a second waxed paper circle, then a second layer of newspaper.
6. Slowly iron over the newspapers and wax to melt the crayon wax. Turn off the iron and let it cool to the side when you are finished melting the wax.
7. Cut out the center of two paper plates to create a frame. Sandwich your waxed paper circles with the melted crayons between the two paper plates, using glue to secure.
8. Use a permanent marker to draw the Sun on the waxed paper with the melted wax.
9. Hang the Sun catcher in a window with a piece of ribbon or string and leave it until the end of this unit.

Star Clusters & Galaxies

😀 😊 🙂 **EXPLORATION: Galaxy Shapes Mobile**
For this activity, you will need:

- "Galaxy Mobile" from the Printable Pack, 2 pages
- Card Stock
- Scissors
- Colored pencils
- Internet access (optional)
- School glue
- Paintbrush
- Glitter
- Cardboard - heavy corrugated
- Black paint (spray paint works well)
- String

A **galaxy** is stars, planets, **nebulae**, dark matter, and other objects, all held together with gravity and orbiting a central massive region. Galaxies come in four basic shapes: elliptical, spiral, lenticular, or irregular.

Elliptical galaxies are smooth and featureless, just discs of light. Spiral galaxies are flat, rotating discs of stars with a central bulge. Some spiral galaxies have a bar shape in the middle of them. Lenticular galaxies are disc-shaped, with a

Deep Thoughts

In 1920, astronomers held what is known as The Great Debate to determine whether the Milky Way was the entire universe or not.

Astronomer Harlow Shapley argued that the nebulae that could be seen in the sky were relatively close and inside the Milky Way. Heber Curtis said, no, the nebulae were much further away and were, in fact, galaxies outside our own. Both astronomers had valid reasons and many of their conclusions were correct, but Curtis was proved right when Edwin Hubble collected further data that proved there are, in fact, at least 200 billion galaxies in the universe.

Part of discovery is a willingness to be wrong and change your mind. Have you ever changed your mind about something you once believed?

This is what is meant by having an open mind. Discuss the benefits of being open to change.

Memorization Station

Galaxy: a system of stars, dust, and dark matter bound together by gravity

Nebula: an enormous cloud of gas and dust that forms a birth place for new stars (plural = nebulae)

Additional Layer

Create some artwork to display about space, stars, constellations, or galaxies. Hang it up throughout this unit for everyone to enjoy.

Earth & Space

central bulge of light but no arms radiating from the center. Irregular galaxies have no obvious shape or form, they are like nebulous clouds of stars. Usually, irregular galaxies are smaller than elliptical or spiral galaxies.

Fabulous Fact

Some clusters and galaxies have names, like "Andromeda," but most are just given numbers. There are two numbering systems.

The Messier catalog was compiled by French astronomer Charles Messier in the late 1700s and includes 110 nebulae, galaxies, and star clusters. Objects from this catalog will have numbers that begin with an M, like M31.

This is a Hubble photograph of the Antenna Galaxies, two galaxies colliding. They are called NGC 4038 and NGC 4039. Image by ESA/Hubble & NASA, CC by SA 4.0, Wikimedia

The New General Catalogue was compiled in 1888 by John Louis Emil Dreyer. Objects in this catalog begin with the letters NGC, like NGC 3982.

There are other catalogs of stars as well, and no one authoritative source.

Memorization Station

Black hole: a region where gravity is so strong that nothing, not even light, can escape from it

1. Print the two "Galaxy Mobile" pages onto card stock

2. Color both sides of each galaxy with colored pencils. Use blues, purples, and yellows. Each galaxy is labeled with its name. Some galaxies have normal names, like Pinwheel Galaxy, but most are just assigned numbers. You can look each galaxy up online to see actual photos of the galaxies.

3. Paint a thin layer of glue on to each galaxy, then sprinkle glitter on, as desired.

4. Cut out the galaxies. Also, cut a cardboard circle with a diameter of about 30 cm. You can use a dinner plate as a circle to trace. Paint the cardboard circle black. Add glue and glitter to the cardboard circle as well.

5. Cut eight pieces of string between 15 and 30 cm long. Use glue to glue one string to each galaxy and the other end of each string to the cardboard circle.

   Can you sort the galaxies into their types?

Universe

😊 😀 EXPLORATION: Milky Way

For this activity, you will need:

- Book or video about the Milky Way from the Library List or YouTube playlist
- "Map of the Milky Way" from the Printable Pack
- Oil pastels, crayons, paints, or any art supplies you prefer
- Glitter and glue or glitter glue

The Milky Way is our galaxy, the one Earth lives in. If you look up on a cloudless night, you can see a hazy band of light going clear across the sky. This is the view of the Milky Way we can see from Earth. That hazy band of light is really more than 100 billion stars, too many to pick out individually with the naked eye.

The Milky Way is a flat spinning disc with curved arms radiating out from a center bar shape. This type of galaxy is called a spiral galaxy. Earth is positioned on the inner edge of the Orion spur. As you near the center of the Milky Way, the concentration of stars becomes higher and higher until, in the center, there are so many stars that they form a light-filled, bar-shaped bulge. At the very center of that bulge is thought to be a **black hole** four million times as massive as our Sun. The entire galaxy is rotating around this center.

1. Read a book or watch a video about the Milky Way.
2. Color or paint the "Map of the Milky Way" any way you like. Let the paint dry, then add glitter or glitter glue to make the stars sparkle.
3. Take note of the location of the Sun in the Milky Way.

😊 😀 😃 EXPERIMENT: Star Clusters

For this activity, you will need:

- "Star Cluster Sorting" from the Printable Pack (2 pages)
- Card stock
- Scissors
- Internet search engine

Most stars are "born" in huge clouds of gas and dust, called nebulae, that give rise to dozens, hundreds, or even

Fabulous Fact

The Milky Way is just one galaxy in the cluster of galaxies known as the Local Group. The Milky Way and the Andromeda Galaxy each have smaller galaxies clustered round them, and these groups rotate around each other, making a dumbbell-shaped group of galaxies.

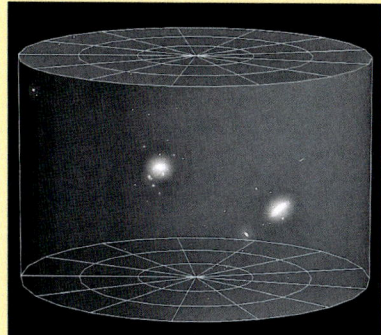

This is a drawing of the Local Group. The two large galaxies are the Milky Way and Andromeda. Each of these is surrounded by smaller galaxies. Image by Andrew Z. Colvin, CC by SA 3.0, Wikimedia.

Famous Folks

Neil deGrasse Tyson is an American astrophysicist who has spent his career studying star formation and galactic bulges and educating the public about the universe.

Photo by Bruce F Press, CC by SA 3.0 Wikimedia

Earth & Space

Memorization Station

Open cluster: a group of a few thousand stars or fewer that are all about the same age and formed from the same dust cloud

Globular cluster: a spherical group of stars that orbits a point in space

Quasar: a massive and bright celestial object that emits large amounts of energy

Exoplanet: a planet outside of our solar system

Famous Folks

Stephen Hawking was a British astrophysicist who predicted that black holes emit radiation.

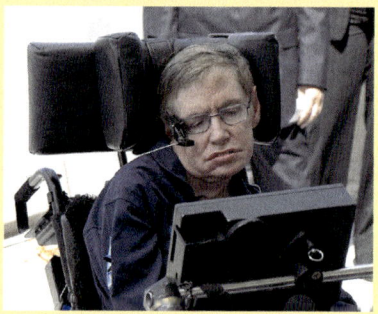

He also worked on the "Theory of Everything," which seeks to unite quantum mechanics with general relativity to explain how the universe works.

Deep Thoughts

Big telescopes, skilled astronomers, computer data processing software, and space telescopes cost lots of money.

Discuss the cost of pursuing knowledge about the universe. What are the benefits? Is it worth it to mankind? Why or why not?

---

many thousands of stars. These stars stay near one another, forming clusters. All of the stars in a cluster are about the same age as the others in the cluster. If there are fewer stars, between a dozen and a few thousand, they are loosely bound together in **open clusters**. Open clusters tend to be young, made up of mostly blue stars, and form in the arms of a spiral galaxy.

If there are more stars, like hundreds of thousands of stars, they are grouped in a heavy gravity field that forms a **globular cluster**. These massive globular clusters form spherical shapes because their overall gravity is so great. Globular clusters orbit near the center of a galaxy and are very old, with many red stars.

Stars like our Sun either were born alone or they broke out of a cluster through evaporation. Evaporation is when a star is flung out of a cluster when the other stars tug on its orbit with gravity. Eventually, all clusters are broken apart this way.

1. Print the two pages of the "Star Cluster Sorting" sheets
2. Cut the cards apart on the heavy lines.
3. Sort the cards into two groups: open clusters and globular clusters.

   Open clusters: M45, NGC 2547, NGC 346, NGC 2367, NGC 3572, and M7.

   Globular clusters: M80, M22, M4, M54, and M92.

4. Observe the two groups closely. What are differences you see? What are similarities? Write down any questions that occur to you. Use a search engine to see if you can find the answers to your questions.

Universe

🙂 😊 **EXPLORATION: Quasars & Galaxy Formation**

For this activity, you will need:

- "Facts About Galaxies" from the Printable Pack
- Scissors
- Blank sheet(s) of paper and pen or pencil
- Internet search engine

A **quasar** is a super massive black hole that is surrounded by an especially large and bright cloud. As the mass surrounding the black hole falls toward the center, it releases heat and light from gamma waves to visible light to radio waves. Sometimes quasars have a super bright jet of light erupting from the center. Even with powerful telescopes, they look like stars, because they are so far away. However, we can tell they aren't stars because of the light and radio waves they give off.

Quasars were first discovered in the 1950s as astronomers picked up their radio waves from outer space. There are no quasars anywhere close to Earth, which might mean that quasars are extinct since the light from distant quasars has traveled for many billions of years to reach us. There is speculation that quasars are an early part of the life cycle of galaxies from the early period of the formation of the universe.

1. Use the "Facts About Galaxies" sheet and an internet search engine to assemble as many facts about galaxies as you can.

2. Cut apart the cards on the "Facts about Galaxies" sheet so you can rearrange the cards any way you like. There are two blank cards that you can write your own facts on. You can use more paper to make more cards as needed.

3. Think about the facts you have and come up with a hypothesis about how you think galaxies form. What information is missing that you think would help prove your theory? Write down your hypothesis and your missing information.

🙂 😊 😊 **EXPERIMENT: Exoplanets**

For this activity, you will need:

- Large poster board (at least 26 cm wide)
- Scissors
- Pencil
- Meter stick
- Mathematical compass
- Poster paints: black, blue, yellow, plus other colors as desired
- Paintbrushes
- Cups or plates for mixing paint

Additional Layer

No quasars can be seen without a telescope, but if you have a decent amateur telescope, you can probably see 3C 273, which is in the constellation Virgo.

This is quasar 3C 273. It is surrounded by a galaxy, but the quasar in the center is so bright the galaxy is not visible. Image by ESA/Hubble & NASA.

It is the most distant and therefore oldest object you can see with an amateur telescope. Look for it.

Fabulous Fact

Sometimes exoplanets can be seen directly. Fomalhaut b is a planet orbiting the star Fomalhaut, which the Hubble Space Telescope was able to photograph. In 2015, Fomalhaut b was given the official name Dagon, after a Semitic deity that was half man, half fish.

On the Web

NASA scientists took the data from telescope observations and turned it into music. The light wavelengths match the sound wavelengths.

You can listen to it at the Chandra X-ray Observatory website.

Earth & Space

Bookworms

The Astronomer Who Questioned Everything by Laura Alary is a picture book biography about Maria Mitchell, an American astronomer of the 1800s.

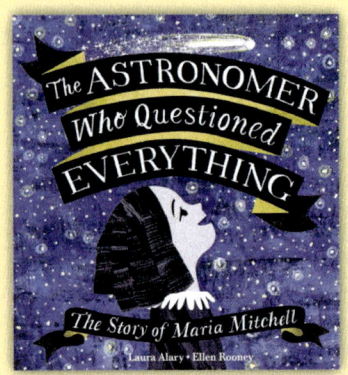

This is a positive book about having the courage to follow your dreams.

Deep Thoughts

We tend to think of art and science as polar opposites.

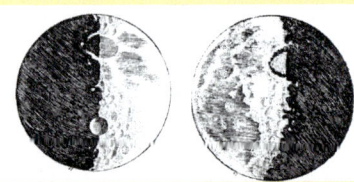

But from Galileo's use of the new techniques of perspective and chiaroscuro in depicting the surface of the Moon to the images from the Hubble Telescope that saved it from the scrap heap, art is actually integral to science.

Discuss how art and science need each other.

- String
- Paper clip
- Air dry clay
- White paint pen or white marker
- Craft glue

An **exoplanet** is a planet outside of our solar system, a planet orbiting another star. They are discovered by one of three methods. Exoplanets can be imaged, photographed directly with a powerful telescope. They can be detected with radial-velocity, by watching tiny wobbles in a star which indicates that some mass is pulling the star slightly off balance. Or planets can be detected with the transit method, observing a dip in the brightness of a star as the planet passes in front of the star.

Five exoplanets orbiting the star Kepler 186 were discovered with the transit method in 2014. One of these planets, Kepler 186 f, is in the habitable zone. That means the planet orbits in an area of space where it could have liquid water for at least part of the year, so it is possible that life could exist there.

1. Cut your poster board into a square. Measure the short side of the poster board. Then, trim off the long side so it matches the length of the short side.

2. Find the center of the poster board by aligning a meter stick from one corner to the other and making a light pencil mark line near the center. Then, move the meter stick so it goes across the poster board in the other direction. Make another short line. The point at which the two lines cross is the middle of your poster.

3. Use a mathematical compass to draw a circle with a radius of 1.3 cm from the center of the poster. This is the radius of the star Kepler 186. Make a second circle with a 12.8 cm radius.

Universe

4. Next, you will make a third circle with a radius of 26 cm. This is too large for a math compass, so instead, you will use a piece of string, tied to a paper clip. Put a pencil through the paper clip and set the pencil tip at the 26 cm mark along the meter stick. Grip the string exactly at the 0 cm point. Hold the string at the center of the poster and circle the other end around this point to make a large circle on the poster.

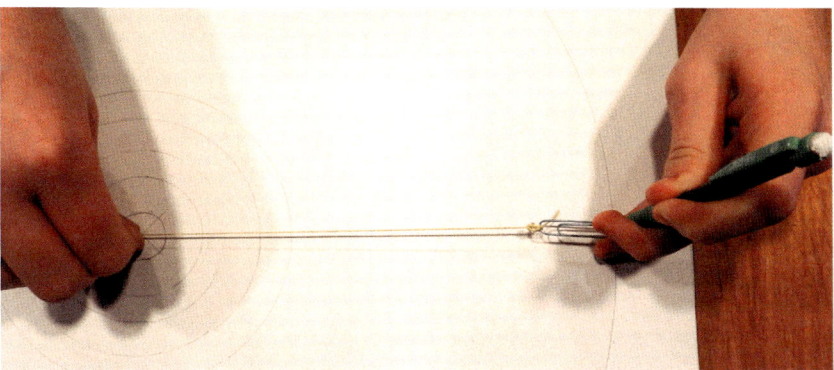

5. Mix a bit of water with black paint to make the paint thinner and easier to spread. Paint it around the outside of the largest circle. Then paint between the smallest circle and the second circle with black.

6. Water down some blue paint and paint between the second and third circles. The blue area is the habitable zone around the star.

7. Paint inside the star area with yellow paint.

8. Use air dry clay to make a round star with a diameter of about 1.3 cm. It should pretty much fill up the circle in the center. Paint this star yellow.

9. Use the air dry clay to make 5 more small balls, each with a diameter of about 1 cm. These are the five planets circling Kepler 186. Paint them with yellow, brown, blue, orange, or any colors you like. No one knows what these planets are made of or how they look in real life, so be creative.

10. Once all the paint is dry, use the compass to make circles on the poster board at radii of 3.2 cm, 4.8 cm, 6.4 cm, 8 cm, and 23 cm. These are the orbits of the five planets. Trace over the orbits with a white paint pen. Glue each planet to an orbit.

11. Label the poster board with a white paint pen. The star should be labeled "Kepler 186." The blue zone should be labeled "Habitable Zone." Each planet should be labeled in order from the star outward "b," "c," "d," "e," and "f."

Famous Folks

Jocelyn Bell Burnell, an astrophysicist from Northern Ireland, was the first to discover pulsars in 1967 when she was a post graduate student at Cambridge.

Photo by Roger W Haworth, CC by SA 2.0, Wikimedia

Pulsars are rotating neutron stars that emit electromagnetic radiation from their poles. The radiation can only be detected from Earth when the star's pole is pointed toward the earth, so they pulse, like a lighthouse beam, as they rotate.

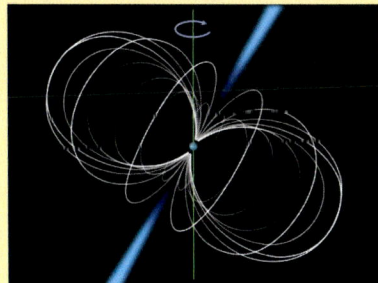

Image by Mysid, CC by SA 3.0, Wikimedia

This image above is a schematic drawing of a pulsar. The strong magnetic fields (white lines) direct the electromagnetic radiation out the poles of the star. Then, the star rotates at a set speed.

Earth & Space

Fabulous Fact

Just as the earth revolves around the Sun, so the Sun revolves around the center of our Milky Way Galaxy.

It takes about 240 million years for the Sun to orbit completely around its center.

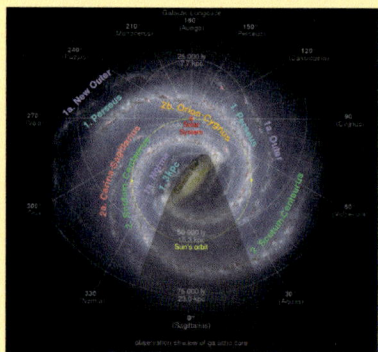

In this image, above, the red dot is our solar system and the yellow circle is its orbital path. The entire Milky Way rotates together.

A habitable zone is an area where water can exist in liquid form. We don't know whether life actually does exist on Kepler 186 f or not. What else would be necessary for life to exist on an exoplanet?

😊😊🌐 **EXPEDITION: Visit an Observatory**

For this activity, you will need:

- An observatory near you

Observatories are places people view the universe. They usually contain powerful telescopes. The best locations for observatories are away from cities with their bright lights that obscure the sky. High elevations are nice too because it gets the telescope above the thickest parts of the atmosphere.

1. Find out if there is an observatory within traveling distance and if you are allowed to visit.

2. Take a tour and be ready with a good question or two.

Step 3: Show What You Know

During this unit, choose one of the assignments below to show what you have learned during the unit. Add this work to your Layers of Learning Notebook. You can also use this assignment to show your supervising teacher or your charter school as a sample of what you've been working on in your homeschool, if needed.

Additional Layer

Many, many poems have been written about the stars. Go read some. Here is a short list.

- "Twinkle, Twinkle, Little Star"
- "Evening Star" by Edgar Allan Poe
- "When I Heard the Learned Astronomer" by Walt Whitman
- "Starlight" by William Meredith
- "To the North Star" by William B. Tappan
- "The Stars Are Mansions Built by Nature's Hand" by William Wordsworth
- "But Outer Space" by Robert Frost
- "The Light of Stars" by Longfellow
- "Ah Moon - and Star" by Emily Dickinson

😊😊 **Coloring or Narration Page**

For this activity, you will need:

- "Universe" from the Printable Pack
- Writing or drawing utensils

1. Depending on the age and ability of the child, choose either the "Universe" coloring sheet or the "Universe" narration page from the Printable Pack.

2. Younger kids can color the coloring sheet as you review some of the things you learned about during this unit.

236

Universe

On the bottom of the coloring page, kids can write a sentence about what they learned. Very young children can explain their ideas orally while a parent writes for them.

3. Older kids can write about some of the concepts you learned on the narration page and color the picture as well.

4. Add this to the Science section of your Layers of Learning Notebook.

😊 😊 😊 Science Experiment Write-Up
For this activity, you will need:

- The "Experiment" write-up or "Experiment Report Template" from the Printable Pack

1. Choose one of the experiments you completed during this unit and create a careful and complete experiment write-up for it. Make sure you have included every specific detail of each step so your experiment could be repeated by anyone who wanted to try it.

2. Do a careful revision and edit of your write-up, taking it through the writing process, before you turn it in for grading.

😊 😊 😊 Constellation Challenge
For this activity, you will need:

- "Astrolabe" and "Star Chart" from the Printable Pack
- Chairs, snack and other comforts for stargazing
- A dark clear night location
- Star guidebook or phone app (optional)

1. Go outside with all your stargazing comforts like chairs, binoculars, telescopes, blankets, and snacks.

2. Have each child work independently, identifying as many constellations and stars as they can, from memory, without the use of a guidebook. Older kids can map the stars and constellations on the "Star Chart" using an "Astrolabe." Younger kids can just point them out in the night sky to an adult. Give a time limit of an hour or whatever time period you like.

3. Grade the completed star chart, giving a point for each plotted star or constellation. Determine how may objects you expect identified based on your previous stargazing experiences. If you know your kids can identify ten constellations, then make the total available

Deep Thoughts
We can't be sure that our universe is the only one. Some astronomers believe in a multiverse, or infinite universes.

But can we ever know? Is the multiverse hypothesis falsifiable?

Remember that being falsifiable is a necessary condition for science.

Bookworms
Discoverers of the Universe: William and Caroline Herschel by Michael Hoskin is about the brother-sister team who discovered Uranus and revealed the universe to be dynamic and changing instead of the mechanical static thing previous generations had believed in.

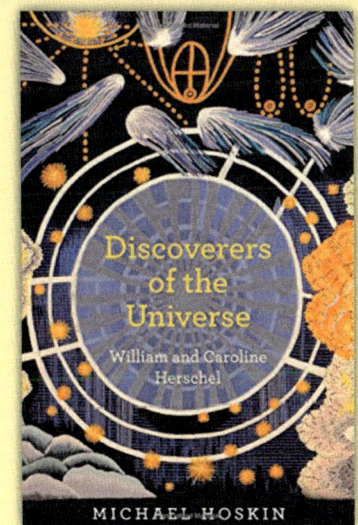

For 14 and up.

Writer's Workshop
Make a poster advertisement for an observatory. Are you selling tours, trying to get public donations for science, or doing community outreach?

Earth & Space

Unit Trivia Questions

1. Light-years measure:
   a) Speed
   b) Distance
   c) Time

2. The Big Bang Theory explains that the universe:
   a) Began as a tiny speck containing everything
   b) Is expanding and constantly changing.
   c) Both a and b

3. Name the star classifications in order, starting with the hottest stars.
   O B A F G K M

4. New stars form from a cloud of gases called a _____.
   nebula

5. True or false - Constellations are groups of stars in the sky that form a pattern. Every culture names the same groups and they are absolute.
   False. The constellations are arbitrary and depend on the culture that names them.

6. What is the name of the star closest to Earth?
   The Sun

7. The Milky Way is a _____ shaped galaxy.
   spiral

8. True or false - There are many planets orbiting other stars besides our sun.
   True. Planets orbiting other stars, or exoplanets, have been observed directly and inferred from data about gravitation and star brightness.

points ten. If they get extra objects, give them bonus points. The adult may want to have a guidebook or star finder app on hand to check the work.

😊 😊 😊 Writer's Workshop

For this activity, you will need:

- A computer or a piece of paper and a writing utensil

Choose from one of the ideas below or write about something else you learned during this unit. Each of these prompts corresponds with one of the units from the Layers of Learning Writer's Workshop curriculum, so you may choose to coordinate the assignment with the monthly unit you are learning about in Writer's Workshop.

- **Sentences, Paragraphs, & Narrations:** Use the "Silly Sentence Dice" printable to write sentences with outer space themes.
- **Descriptions & Instructions:** Write a paragraph about stars. Then go back and look for passive verbs like is, were, and was, and replace them with active verbs.
- **Fanciful Stories**: Learn about a real exoplanet and what scientists think it is like. Then, use it as a setting in a short story or scene.
- **Poetry:** Write a rhyming poem about your favorite astronomer.
- **True Stories:** Search the news for a recent astronomy story. Print the story. Circle the who, what, where, when, and why. Do they appear in the first paragraph? Rewrite the article in your own words.
- **Reports and Essays:** Pick an astronomy topic from this unit. Use your research skills to find a reliable book, magazine, and online source about the topic. Write a

Universe

bibliography of your three sources.
- **Letters:** Pretend you want a job at an observatory. Write a resume for the job. Find out what qualifications are needed and put them on your imaginary resume.
- **Persuasive Writing:** Write a convincing hook (first line) of an essay to persuade people that funding a new space telescope would be a good use of tax payer money.

😊 😊 😊 Big Book of Knowledge

For this activity, you will need:

- "Big Book of Knowledge: Universe" printable from the Printable Pack, printed on card stock
- Writing or drawing utensils
- Big Book of Knowledge

1. Color, draw on, or write on the Big Book of Knowledge page. Record concepts, definitions, and facts you learned during this unit. It's a record of the things you learned and hope to remember. Add the page to your Big Book of Knowledge.

2. Use your Big Book of Knowledge regularly to help you review, quiz, or create games that will help you commit the things you've learned to memory.

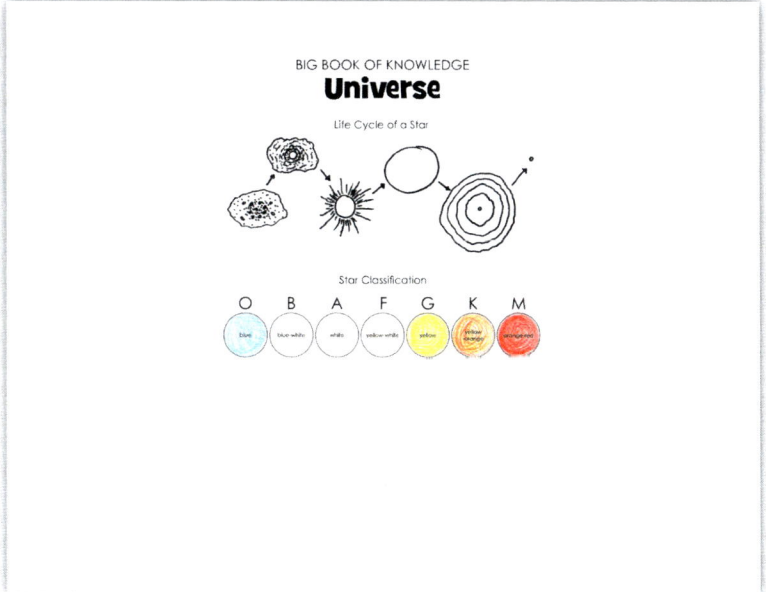

Big Book of Knowledge

The Big Book of Knowledge is a book for you, the mentor, to use as a constant review of all of the things you're learning about. You can use it to quiz your kids or prepare tests or review games. Whenever you learn something in Layers of Learning that you want your kids to remember, add it to your Big Book of Knowledge.

Assemble your Big Book of Knowledge in a binder or with binder rings. Divide it into sections for each subject.

In the Printable Pack for this unit you will find a "Big Book of Knowledge" sheet. You can add this sheet to others you collect or create yourself as you progress through the Layers of Learning curriculum. Customize the Big Book of Knowledge to your family by adding facts and topics that you enjoyed exploring as you were learning.

Visit Layers of Learning online to find more information on how to assemble and use your own Big Book of Knowledge.

You will also find cover and section pages to print along with creative games to play with your Big Book of Knowledge to keep school, even the tests, fun!

Earth & Space

Unit Overview

Key Concepts:
- There are eight major planets in our solar system. They each orbit around the Sun.
- Comets, asteroids, and meteoroids are space rocks that did not fully form into planets but are still drifting in space.
- Modernly, many people have traveled to space. We have launched rockets, put satellites into orbit, walked on the Moon, and even built a space station where astronauts live and conduct experiments.

Vocabulary:
- Solar system
- Planet
- Dwarf planet
- Moon
- Asteroid
- Orbit
- Rotation
- Comet
- Craters
- Meteoroids
- Meteors
- Meteorites
- Satellite
- Astronaut

Theories, Laws, & Hypotheses:
- Heliocentric theory of the solar system
- Kepler's three laws of planetary motion

SOLAR SYSTEM

The solar system is made up of planets, asteroids, comets, and other objects orbiting the Sun, all held together by gravity. From the Sun, first, you meet Mercury, then Venus, Earth and its Moon, Mars and its moons, then the asteroid belt and dwarf planets. Next, you'll see Jupiter and its moons and asteroids, Saturn and its moons, Uranus and its moons, and Neptune and its moons. Finally, beyond the eight planets is the Kuiper Belt with its asteroids and dwarf planets.

People have been exploring the solar system and the planets with their eyes since ancient times, but in the 20th century, people began to visit the solar system in person and with machines. There are plans to put people on the Moon again, to go to Mars, and to establish space stations and bases all over the solar system. We also have satellites, telescopes, and other technology that helps us photograph, communicate, and learn more about space.

Step 1: Library List

Choose books from your library that go with this topic. Here's a list of some favorites and also a list of search terms so you can utilize what your library offers. Read the books with your kids and/or assign them some to read independently. It is from these books your kids will learn most of the facts they need from this unit.

Search for: solar system, planets, astronauts

☺☺☺*Encyclopedia of Science* from DK. Read "Solar System" through "Space Stations" on pages 283-304.

☺☺☺*Kingfisher Science Encyclopedia*. Read "The Solar System" through "Artificial Satellites" on pages 398-425.

☺☺☺*The Usborne Science Encyclopedia*. Read "The Sun" through "Space Exploration" on pages 162-177.

Solar System

🙂🙂🙂 *50 Things To See on the Moon* by John A. Read. A guide to viewing the craters, lunar seas, and mountains on the Moon through a telescope or binoculars.

🙂🙂🙂 *Bill Nye the Science Guy: Space Exploration*. An excellent video to use as an introduction to this unit. Also look for these related episodes: *The Planets, The Sun, The Moon, Comets & Meteors,* and *Outer Space*.

🙂 *Me and My Place in Space* by Joan Sweeney. Takes little kids on a tour of the solar system.

🙂 *The Magic School Bus Lost in the Solar System* by Joanna Cole. If you buy one book on the solar system for younger kids, this is the one. Kids take a field trip in their magic bus to visit each of the planets and learn facts about them.

🙂 *Astronaut Handbook* by Meghan McCarthy. Humorous book that "trains" kids to be astronauts.

🙂 *Mae Among the Stars* by Roda Ahmed. A picture book biography of Mae Jemison, an American astronaut. This book is also about following your dreams.

🙂 *Solar System* by Gregory Vogt. Simple text about each of the planets in our solar system.

🙂 *Rockets and Space Ships* by Karen Wallace. A simple, leveled reader for little ones.

🙂 *Spacebusters: Race to the Moon* by Philip Wilkinson. Teaches about the first moon landing.

🙂 *The Moon Book* by Gail Gibbons. Explains the Moon simply but well, including the phases, eclipses, and more. Also look for *The Planets* by the same author.

🙂 *The Skies Above My Eyes* by Charlotte Guillain. This book takes you up through the atmosphere and out into space, examining all of the things that are in the sky.

🙂🙂 *Our Solar System* by Seymour Simon. Wonderful full-color, full-page photos are accompanied by paragraphs of text with just the right amount information for upper elementary and middle grades students.

🙂🙂 *13 Planets: The Latest View of the Solar System* by David A. Aguilar. From National Geographic, it talks about the eight main planets, their moons, and the dwarf planets including Pluto, Eris, Makemake, Haumea, and Ceres.

🙂🙂 *Neil Armstrong: Young Flyer* by Montrew Dunham. This chapter book biography focuses on the childhood of Armstrong and seeks to make him a role model for kids.

Family School Levels

The colored smilies in this unit help you choose the correct levels of books and activities for your child.

🙂 = Ages 6-9
🙂 = Ages 10-13
🙂 = Ages 14-18

On the Web

For videos, web pages, games, and more to add to this unit, visit the Earth & Space Resources at Layers-of-Learning.com.

You will find a link to video playlists, web links, and more.

Bookworms

If you're looking for a family read-aloud, we'd like to suggest this one.

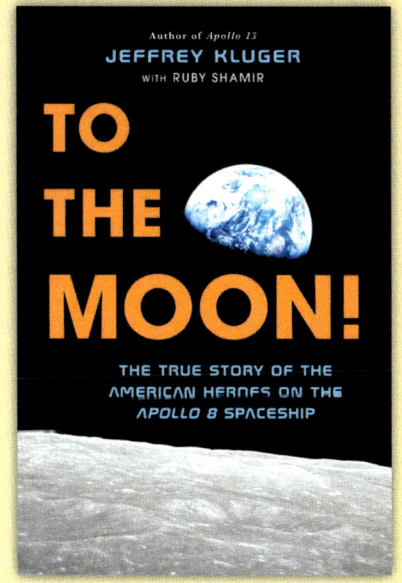

To the Moon by Jeffrey Kluger and Ruby Shamir is the true story of the Apollo 8 spaceship, the first to break Earth's orbit and travel to the Moon. Aimed at a young audience, this 288-page book is a perfect read aloud about space and astronauts.

Earth & Space

Memorization Station

Solar system: everything that orbits a star

Planet: a large spherical body that orbits a star and clears other objects of a similar size out of its path

Dwarf planet: a body that directly orbits the Sun, has a spherical shape, but has not cleared other objects from its orbital path

Moon: a large body that orbits a planet or a dwarf planet

Asteroid: a rocky body that orbits the Sun, is larger than 1 meter across, and is not large enough to be spherical

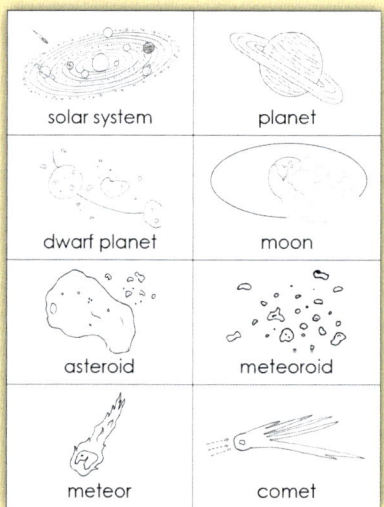

The Printable Pack for this unit includes some vocabulary cards for some of the most important vocabulary words in this unit. Write definitions on the back.

Memorization Station

Memorize the planets with this mnemonic: **M**y **V**ery **E**ager **M**other **J**ust **S**erved **U**s **N**oodles.

Mercury, **V**enus, **E**arth, **M**ars, **J**upiter, **S**aturn, **U**ranus, **N**eptune.

☺ ☺ *You Wouldn't Want to Be on Apollo 13!* by Ian Graham. This book puts the reader into the story. Find out what it was like to be aboard the disastrous Apollo 13 space mission.

☺ *Science Comics: Solar System* by Rosemary Mosco. Graphic novel-format, this is great for reluctant readers. It's packed with information about the solar system while telling the story of two girls who design a spaceship.

☺ ☺ *Ask an Astronaut: My Guide To Life in Space* by Tim Peake. Written by an astronaut, this is a question and answer book. People ask Tim questions like, "What was your scariest moment in space?" He answers them.

☺ ☺ *The Planets: The Definitive Visual Guide to Our Solar System* by Robert Dinwiddie, et al. This is a big coffee table-style book from DK that has amazing illustrations of things like the structure of Venus and how a solar eclipse works. Use this as a reference and browsing book.

☺ ☺ *Endurance (Young Readers Edition)* by Scott Kelly. This is the story of an astronaut who spent an entire year on the International Space Station. It begins with his troubled childhood (alcohol and abuse alert!) and then talks about what it's really like to be on the space station.

☺ *Vacation Guide to the Solar System: Science For the Savvy Space Traveler* by Olivia Koski and Jana Grcevich. Tells you how to prepare, what to pack, and how to get around the solar system.

☺ *How I Killed Pluto and Why It Had It Coming* by Mike Brown. Mike Brown is the astronomer who discovered thousands of ice balls orbiting the Sun in the deep reaches of our solar system. His discovery led to Pluto being demoted as a planet.

☺ *A Man on the Moon* by Andrew Chaikin. A 700-page tome about the Apollo Space Program.

☺ *Dialogue Concerning the Two Chief World Systems* by Galileo Galilei. Written in 1633 and presented as a debate between three philosophers about which solar system is the correct one - a geocentric or a heliocentric. Galileo doesn't just argue for the earth revolving around the Sun, he also argues against merely relying on Aristotle and others as authorities and instead using observation and mathematics to discover truth in the natural world. This book set off the Scientific Revolution. Look for the Stillman Drake translation. This is a Great Book of the world.

☺ *Cosmology and Astronomy* from KhanAcademy.org. To add a high school lecture, you can add a Khan Academy

Solar System

course. During this unit, study "Earth Geological and Climatic History: Moon Phases and Eclipses."

> ## Step 2: Explore
>
> Choose a few hands-on explorations from this section to work on as a family. They should be appealing activities that will create mental hooks so your kids remember the information in the unit. Save the rest of the explorations for the next time you do this unit in four years when your kids are older. You can also read the sidebars together and explore some little rabbit trails.
>
> This unit includes printables. See the introduction for instructions on retrieving your Printable Pack.

Planets

EXPLORATION: Map of the Solar System
For this activity, you will need:

- Two pages of "Map of the Solar System" from the Printable Pack
- Scissors
- Glue stick
- Black ink pen
- Colored Pencils

The **solar system** contains eight major **planets**, **dwarf planets**, **moons**, and four regions of **asteroids**. It's a good idea to have the basic order of these places in your mind. The "Map of the Solar System" from the Printable Pack is a schematic map. Nothing is to scale or shows actual locations; instead, it just shows the relative position of things. You can tell that Mars is closer to the Sun than the asteroid belt, but not exactly how far from the Sun or each other they are.

1. Trim the edge off the second sheet of the "Map of the Solar System." Glue the two halves of the map together, lining up the edges and rings of Saturn.

2. Label each of the planets, dwarf planets, asteroid belts,

Famous Folks

The Italian astronomer Galileo used an early telescope that he designed himself to study the night sky.

He discovered the moons of Jupiter and noticed that Venus moves between Earth and the Sun and is also sometimes on the other side of the Sun. Both discoveries upset the widely-held beliefs of the time that everything in the heavens orbited Earth.

Galileo was put on trial for heresy and convicted in 1633. He was forced to recant his opinion that the earth moves around the Sun and spent the last nine years of his life under house arrest.

The book that got Galileo into trouble is called *Dialogue Concerning the Two Chief World Systems*. In it, philosophers argue about whether a heliocentric solar system or a geocentric solar system makes the most sense.

Galileo was forced to present the book as though there were valid arguments on both sides, but he couldn't quite manage it and the questioners during his Inquisition saw through it.

Earth & Space

Famous Folks

Ptolemy of ancient Greece believed the earth was at the center of the universe and the stars were fixed to a celestial sphere, all at an equal distance from Earth.

Aristarchus of Samos put the Sun in the center and said the stars were like our Sun, only further away.

Aristotle accepted and promoted Ptolemy's idea over Aristarchus. Aristotle was so highly respected that everyone else accepted a geocentric model for centuries.

Nicolaus Copernicus was the first of the modern era to come up with a model of the solar system that put the Sun at the center.

He was so afraid of what people would think about his ideas that he didn't allow them to be published until he was on his death bed.

Galileo read and agreed with Copernicus. He maintained that Aristotle was wrong.

Science is a process.

and moons. Here is a key, starting with the Sun. Moons and minor planets are in parenthesis following their planet or asteroid belt and from bottom to top.

- Sun
- Mercury
- Venus
- Earth (Moon)
- Mars (Phobos, Deimos)
- Asteroid Belt (Pallas, Ceres, Juno, Vesta)
- Trojan Asteroids
- Greek Asteroids
- Jupiter (Io, Europa, Ganymede, Callisto)
- Saturn (Mimos, Enceladus, Tethys, Dione, Rhea, Titan, Hyperion, Iapetus)
- Uranus (Miranda, Ariel, Umbriel, Titania, Oberon)
- Neptune (Triton)
- Kuiper Belt (Haumea, Pluto {Charon}, Makemake, Eris)

3. Color the map with colored pencils and hang it up to display during this unit.

😊 😊 EXPLORATION: Solar System Model

For this activity, you will need:

- Foam balls : 1- 18 cm (7"), 1 - 12 cm (4.5"), 1 - 10 cm (4"), 2 - 6 cm (2.5"), and 4 - 4 cm (2") (In other words, you need a huge ball, two big balls, two medium balls, and four small balls - exact sizes don't matter.)
- Poster paint and paintbrushes
- Paper rings cut out with scissors
- String to hang the planets (optional)
- Internet (optional)

1. Paint each of the foam balls to resemble a part of the solar system. The largest ball is the Sun. The next largest is Jupiter. The third largest is Saturn. The next two are Earth and Neptune, and the four smallest are Mercury, Venus, Mars, and Uranus. If you aren't sure what colors to use, look up pictures of each of the planets online.

Solar System

2. Once the paint is dry, add a paper ring to Saturn. Make the ring just large enough to fit around the planet. It should stay put without glue.

3. Hang the planets from the ceiling or set them along a shelf in order from the Sun to Neptune.

🙂 🙂 🙂 **EXPERIMENT: The Solar System to Scale**

For this activity, you will need:

- Construction Paper
- Scissors
- Large craft sticks
- Tape
- Long outdoor measuring tape
- Large park or open field
- Science Notebook

The solar system is so big, with such huge distances that you can never see it properly on a piece of paper or an indoor model.

1. Start by making a paper Sun and paper planets with construction paper. Include Pluto so you can see the distance of some of the furthest objects. Tape each one to a large craft stick.

2. Place the Sun at one end of a field. Stick the craft stick into the ground so the Sun stands up.

3. Run the tape measure out as far as it will reach with 0 at the Sun. Stick each planet into the ground at the following distances from your Sun.

   Mercury - 40 cm (1 ft 4 inches)
   Venus - 78 cm (2 feet 7 inches)

Additional Layer

Mars has a regressive orbit. This means that Mars will be moving along the night sky, but then it will appear to move backward night after night. Suddenly, it rights itself and starts moving like the other planets again. Get two toy cars and a block. Move the cars along in the same direction, one slower than the other with the block in the background as a point of reference.

From the point of view of the faster car, it looks like the slower car is moving backward, but it isn't, it's just slower. Mars orbits slower than Earth so it looks like it is going backward for part of its orbit.

Writer's Workshop

Make a poster featuring the planet of your choice. Include its location in the solar system, its atmosphere, the structure, its size, three or four interesting facts, and the story of its discovery. Use lots of hand-drawn illustrations along with captions and short paragraphs.

Earth & Space

Memorization Station

For ages 14 and up:

Kepler's first law of planetary motion says that planets orbit in an ellipse with the Sun at one focus.

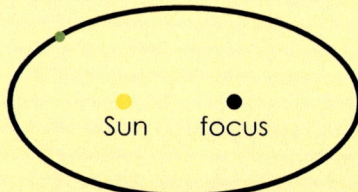

Kepler's second law is that a radius vector extending from the Sun to the orbiting body sweeps out an equal amount of area in an equal amount of time. In other words, as planets get nearer to the focus, they move faster.

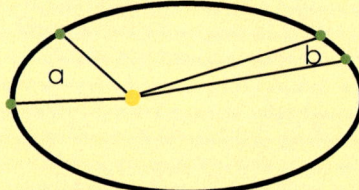

Kepler's third law states that the square of the time it takes for a body to complete one orbit (its period) is proportional to the semi-major axis cubed.

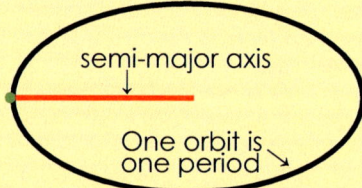

If you use Earth years and astronomical units (the distance from the earth to the Sun is 1 AU), then the equation is this:

$$P^2 = a^3$$

Period^2 = axis^3

Planets closer to the Sun move faster than planets further from the Sun.

Earth - 1 meter (3 feet 6 inches)
Mars - 1.6 meters (5 feet 4 inches)
Jupiter - 5.6 meters (18 feet 4 inches)
Saturn - 10 meters (33 feet 8 inches)
Uranus - 20.6 meters (67 feet 8 inches)
Neptune - 32 meters (106 feet)
Pluto - 42.5 meters (139 feet 5 inches)

4. Observe the distances, then draw a small diagram of the large model you just made in your Science Notebook. Make sure to title your page and add it to the table of contents.

🙂 EXPLORATION: Coloring Book of the Planets

For this activity, you will need:

- Video about the solar system
- "The Planets In Our Solar System" from the Printable Pack (including the cover page through "Neptune")
- Crayons or colored pencils
- Stapler

1. Turn on a video about the solar system and let kids color the pages while they watch. Each page has the name of the planet to trace, a few facts, and coloring instructions.

2. Staple the edges of the pages together to make a book.

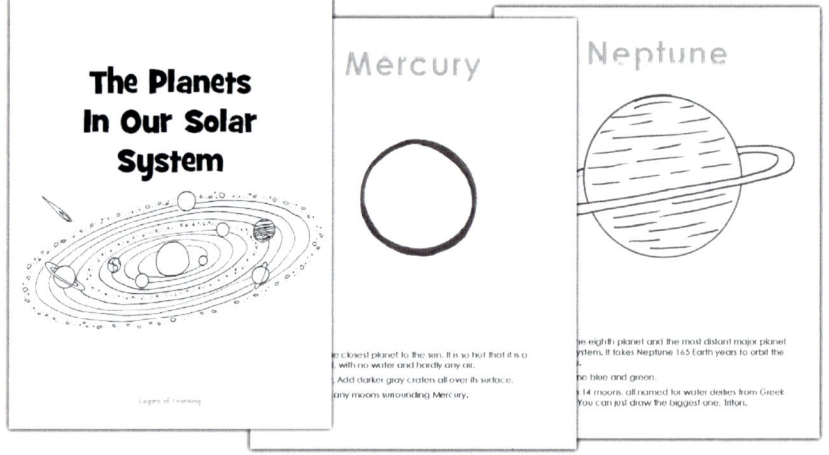

🙂 🙂 🙂 EXPLORATION: Planet Fact Fans

For this activity, you will need:

- "Planet Fact Fan" from the Printable Pack, 4 pages, printed on white card stock
- Watercolor paints, paintbrushes, and a water cup

Solar System

- Markers
- Scissors
- Hole punch
- Brad
- Internet or books about the planets

1. Use watercolor paints and markers to color each of the planet fact fan pieces.
2. Cut each one out, punch a hole at the circle, and attach your fan in order using a brad.
3. Fill in the information and facts about each planet by researching each one online or in a book.

🙂 **EXPLORATION: Earth, Moon, and Stars Mobile**
For this activity, you will need:

- "Earth, Moon, and Stars Mobile" from the Printable Pack
- White card stock
- Crayons or markers
- Scissors
- Hole punch or needle
- Craft wire
- String

1. Print the mobile onto white card stock. Color the mobile pieces. Cut them out.
2. Bend a piece of craft wire into a spiral. Hang the mobile pieces from the wire with string.

Fabulous Fact

1 AU (astronomical unit) is the distance from the Sun to the earth, or about 150 million kilometers. It isn't an official SI unit, but it is often used in scientific literature when discussing distances in the solar system or other star systems in the universe.

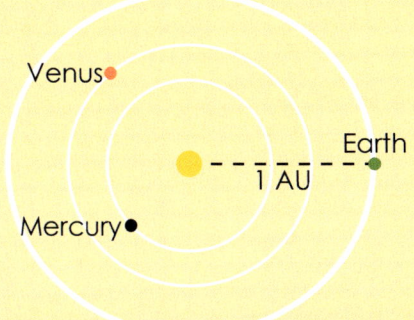

An AU is too small to be useful over larger distances like the distance between stars or galaxies.

Famous Folks

German astronomer Johannes Kepler is best known for his laws on planetary motion, which you can learn on the opposite sidebar.

Isaac Newton's ideas about motion were based on Kepler's.

Earth & Space

Additional Layer

Use books or the internet to find some basic facts about each planet. Record your information on "Planet Survey" from the Printable Pack.

Deep Thoughts

How unique is our solar system? Are there other living planets out there?

This may be the biggest question in astronomy and no one knows the answer.

Discuss your belief and the reasons for it.

Additional Layer

Create an Oreo cookie Moon phases chart, and then enjoy a treat together.

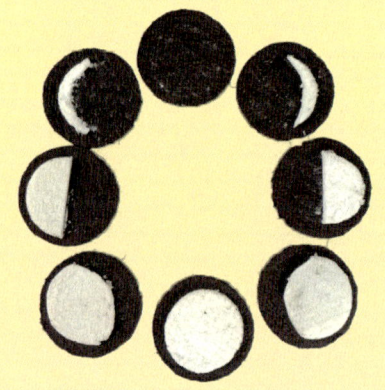

😊😊🙂 EXPLORATION: Moon Phases

For this activity, you will need:

- "Moon Portrait" from the Printable Pack
- Ball - about 5 cm diameter or larger, white or light colors work best
- Lamp without a shade

Throughout each month, the Moon disappears, then grows larger until it is full, then gradually gets smaller until it disappears again. The Moon isn't really changing in size. We can only see the Moon when the light from the Sun shines on it. As the Moon orbits the earth, sometimes the Moon is only partially lit up or not lit up at all.

1. Observe the Moon each night for at least two weeks (a full month is best) either right before or after this activity. Have kids make a sketch of the Moon each night using the "Moon Portrait" printable.

2. Stand a lit lamp without a shade in the middle of a darkened room. Hold the ball out in front of you on your palm. The lamp is the Sun and the ball is the Moon. You are Earth.

3. Stand facing the light and holding the Moon between you and the Sun. You can only see the parts of the Moon that are lit up by the Sun.

4. Now, turn an eighth turn counterclockwise. How much of the Moon is lit up now? Keep turning an eighth turn at a time and observing how much of the Moon is lit up each time.

5. Add your chart to the Science section of your Layers of Learning Notebook.

Solar System

😊 😊 **EXPERIMENT: Temperature Based on Place in Space**

For this activity, you will need:

- Lamp with an incandescent bulb
- Two or more thermometers
- Science Notebook

The location of a planet in relation to the Sun generally determines how hot or cold that planet is. Mercury is very close to the Sun so it is warmer than Earth, which is much warmer than Neptune.

1. Set a lamp on a smooth surface, like a countertop. Place one thermometer near the lamp and in the beam of the light. Place a second thermometer further from the lamp but still within the beam of light. If you have more thermometers, you can place them further and further.
2. Check the temperatures of the thermometers at the beginning, then once every two minutes for ten minutes.
3. Record your findings in your Science Notebook and apply your experiment to space.

😊 😊 **EXPERIMENT: The Evening and Morning Star**

For this activity, you will need:

- Two balls, one very small and the other larger
- A lamp with the shade removed

Venus is easy to spot in the sky. It is far brighter than any other "star," but you can only see it in the evening or in

Fabulous Fact

Distance from a heat source matters. Mercury's daytime temperatures make it too hot for humans to survive. Planets further from the Sun never get enough heat to make life possible. However, the distance from the Sun doesn't always line up perfectly with the planets' temperatures. Because of its atmosphere, Venus is hotter than Mercury even though it's further away from the Sun.

Famous Folks

Neil Armstrong and Buzz Aldrin were the first of twelve people to walk on the Moon. Learn more about them and the Apollo missions.

Bookworms

Space Case by Stuart Gibbs is a middle grades murder mystery set on the Moon.

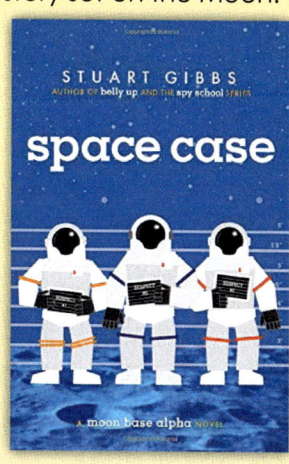

Earth & Space

Writer's Workshop

Read some myths about the Moon. Native Americans see a rabbit in the Moon. Europeans often see a man in the Moon. There are stories about men transforming into werewolves under a full Moon. Chang'e is the Chinese goddess of the Moon.

This is a scene from a Jules Verne book about people who went to the Moon.

Many stories have been told about the Moon. Make up your own magical story about the Moon.

Deep Thoughts

One of the reasons people talk about colonizing the Moon or Mars is so we can move industry and mining to these worlds, keeping Earth cleaner.

But what about these environments? Should we be worried about polluting other places in the solar system and beyond?

the early morning. That is why it is called the evening and morning star.

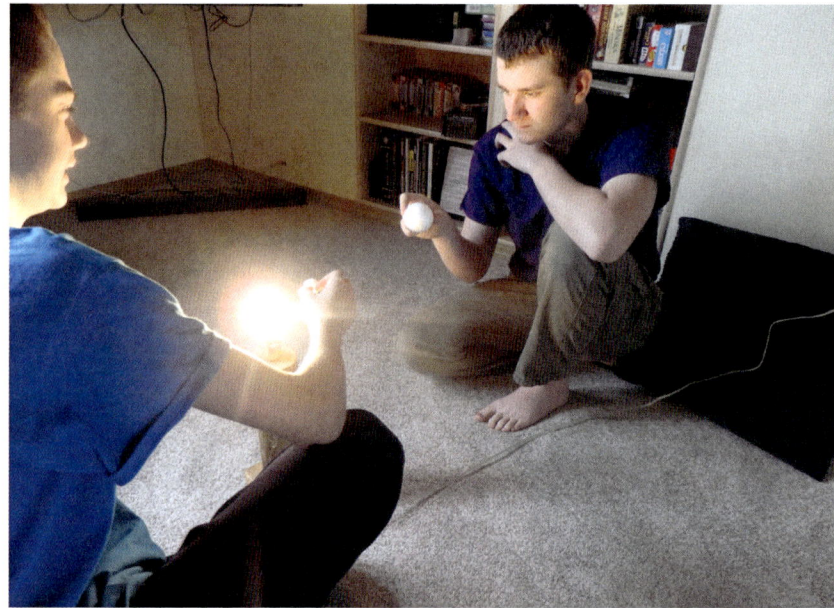

1. Place a lit lamp without a shade in the center of a room. Darken the other lights in the room. Have another person hold a small ball near the lamp and orbit the lamp. The lamp represents the Sun and the small ball represents Venus.

2. Have a second person hold the larger ball, stand further from the lamp, and also orbit the lamp.

3. Every now and then, call, "Freeze!" Both of the planets stop orbiting. Determine if Venus could be seen from Earth in that position. Venus cannot be seen from Earth if it is on the other side of the Sun or if it is directly between the Sun and Earth. Where would Venus be in the sky? In the middle of the day the Sun is too bright and obscures the light from Venus. Could you see Venus if you were on the dark side of Earth? When can you see Venus?

😊 😊 EXPERIMENT: Elliptical Orbits

For this activity, you will need:

- String
- Scissors
- Large sheet of paper or poster board
- Pencil
- Markers or crayons
- Ruler
- Science Notebook

The **orbits** of the planets around the Sun aren't circular; they're elliptical. An ellipse is an oval or elongated circle. Neptune, for example, is 4.46 billion kilometers from the Sun at its closest point and 4.54 billion kilometers from the Sun at its furthest point. The point when a planet is at the closest

Solar System

point is called the perihelion and when it is at the furthest point is called the aphelion.

1. Cut the string so it is 40 cm long. Tie the string into a loop.
2. Near the center of the large sheet of paper, draw two dots, 2.5 cm apart. Draw a Sun around one of the dots.

   The Sun is one of the foci, or centers of gravity, in the orbit of each object in the solar system. The other focus (your other dot) is a spot in space a little distance from the center of the Sun. This is because the Sun and Neptune (or Earth or Mars, etc) are actually orbiting each other. The second focus is at the center of gravity for the two objects. Since the Sun is much more massive than any planet, the second focus for each of the planets in our solar system is actually still inside the Sun.

3. Place two fingers on the dots on the paper and inside the string loop. Put a pencil inside the string loop and pull it taut against your fingers. Trace an oval around the foci with the taut string as your guide.
4. The path you traced looks circular, but measure the diameter at different points on the circle to see if it really is a circle or if it is actually an ellipse. Try drawing different ellipses with your fingers spaced differently or with different lengths of string.
5. Draw a planet on each of your elliptical orbits. Where are the foci? Where are the aphelion and the perihelion? Label each of them on your picture.
6. Write an entry about elliptical orbits in your Science Notebook.

Bookworms

Zero G by Dan Wells is about a boy who embarks on a space voyage with his family.

Everyone is put into stasis sleep, but Zero is awakened early while the ship is still in the solar system, only to find that space pirates are trying to hijack the whole thing.

For ages 8 and up. This is the first in a series.

Additional Layer

Add an illustration and an entry in your Science Notebook that shows the difference between orbit and rotation.

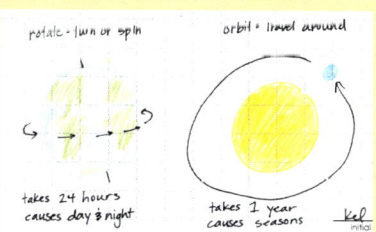

Memorization Station

Orbit: the curved path of a celestial object around a star, planet, or moon

Earth & Space

Memorization Station

Rotation: the circular action of an object around its center

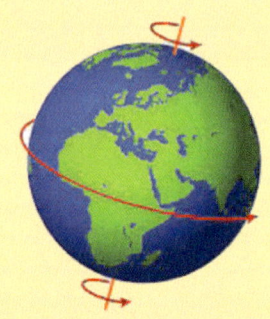

Comet: space object made of frozen gases and rock that is orbiting a star

Famous Folks

English astronomer Edmond Halley predicted that the comet he observed in 1682 would appear again in 1758.

Halley holding a picture of his hypothesis that the earth is hollow. You can't always be right.

People waited breathlessly to see if he would be right. He was, and they named the comet after him.

🙂 🙂 🙂 **EXPERIMENT: Planetary Rotation**

For this activity, you will need:

- Paper plate
- String - about 60 cm long
- Tape
- Paper clips
- Markers, colored pencils, or crayons

All planets, moons, and other bodies are also in **rotation** as they orbit. Each planet and moon in our solar system rotates at a different rate. Earth rotates once in 24 hours. Venus rotates much slower, only once every 243 Earth days. It also spins backwards as compared to the earth and the other planets in the solar system. Uranus rotates on its side. They all rotate though. The reason everything rotates is because of gravity. As objects get pulled toward a center they spin around that center, like water going down a drain.

Spinning is very important to keep everything in balance. If the planets weren't spinning, they would be randomly drifting, first one way and then the other, creating forces that would throw the orbits off and turn our solar system into cosmic bumper cars instead of nice dependable orbits.

1. Color the top surface of a paper plate to look like a planet, real or imaginary.

2. Place four paper clips around the rim of a paper plate, one at each quarter and equidistant from one another.

3. Attach a string directly to the center of the plate with tape.

4. Holding onto the end of the string furthest from the plate, swing the plate in front of you from left to right like

Solar System

a pendulum. What do you notice about the motion of the plate?

5. Now get the plate spinning before you begin to swing it. What changes about the motion of the plate? The spinning should stabilize the plate so it doesn't wobble back and forth.

Comets, Asteroids, Meteors

😊 😊 😊 **EXPLORATION: Comets**

Please wear goggles and use gloves. Dry ice can be dangerous.

For this activity, you will need:

- "Halley's Comet" from the Printable Pack
- Book or video about comets from the Library List or YouTube playlist
- Safety goggles and gloves
- A disposable bowl
- A wooden spoon
- 1 liter of water
- 2 cups of dirt
- 1 Tbsp. syrup
- 1 Tbsp. vinegar
- 5 pounds dry ice, pre-crushed into bits with a hammer

A **comet** is made of frozen gases and rock. We'll make our own.

Additional Layer

Comets move from deep space, in the outer edges of the solar system, to near the Sun and then back out in an elongated elliptical orbit. When a comet nears the Sun, the Sun's heat begins to melt the comet a little and some of the ice melts into gas. This gives the comet an atmosphere of gas and dust called a coma. The coma can drift off the comet in two long tails. One tail is made of gas and the other is made of dust. The tails always point away from the Sun, no matter which direction the comet is moving.

Fabulous Fact

There are comets in the sky almost every year, but most of them are dim and difficult to see.

Great comets are especially bright as viewed from Earth, but they only appear about once in a decade.

Earth & Space

Fabulous Fact

Centaurs are bodies that cross the orbits of the gas giants in the outer solar system. This pulls their orbits out of whack as the gravity from these planets destabilizes them.

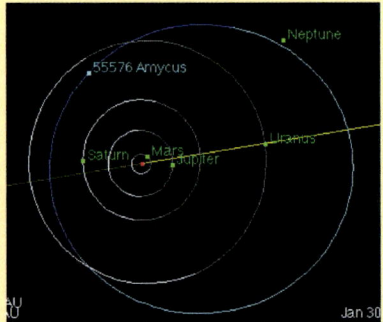

The orbit of Amycus, a centaur, can be seen as the blue line. It's orbit crosses those of Uranus and Neptune.

They look like asteroids, but they orbit like comets. That's why they are called centaurs, mythological creatures that are part horse and part human.

Bookworms

There are a lot of fun interactive adventure books centered around space. Look for *Apollo 11 Moon Landing*, *International Space Station*, *Mars Exploration Rovers*, and *Space Race*.

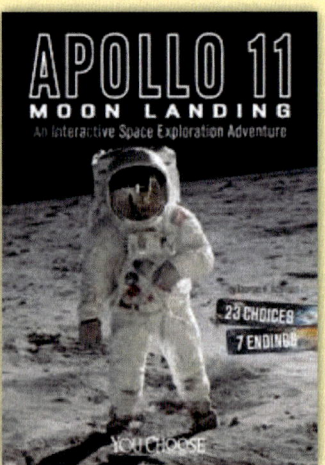

1. Begin by pouring 1 liter of water into a disposable bowl. Comets contain lots of water. Stir in 2 cups of dirt. This represents the minerals and dust that comets have.

2. Next, add in 1 Tbsp. of syrup (represents organic material within comets), 1 Tbsp. vinegar (represents the amino acids in comets), and 1 Tbsp. rubbing alcohol (represents the methanol in comets). Stir everything.

3. Making sure you're wearing gloves, add in 5 pounds of dry ice to your bowl. Use the gloves to help you combine the dirt mixture with the dry ice. Those are the ingredients of a comet. You just made your own!

4. Watch a video or read a book about comets.

5. Color "Halley's Comet" sheet from the Printable Pack. Discuss the parts of a comet and the orbit of a comet. This worksheet shows the orbit of Halley's Comet, which comes from the Kuiper Belt, passes near the Sun, and returns to the Kuiper Belt every 75 years. Notice how the tail of the comet always points away from the Sun because of the solar wind. Find the aphelion (furthest point from the Sun in an orbit) and the perihelion (closest point to the Sun in an orbit) for Halley's Comet.

☺ ☺ EXPERIMENT: Asteroid Belt

For this activity, you will need:

- Book or video about asteroids from the Library List or YouTube playlist
- Salt dough (1/2 cup warm tap water, 1/4 cup salt, 4 tablespoons cooking oil, 2 cups flour)
- Acrylic paints, paintbrushes, and a water cup
- Poster board
- Markers and crayons

Solar System

1. Read a book or watch a video about asteroids.
2. Make salt dough. Use the salt dough to mold dozens of asteroids in any shape and size you like. Keep them all smaller than a golf ball though. If you'd like, you can craft your asteroids to look like, real, named asteroids.
3. Paint the asteroids with gray, black, purple, dark blue, and sparkly paint. You can leave white streaks too. Keep the paint thin.
4. While the paint dries, color a poster board with the Sun in the middle of the sheet. Draw orbits for Mercury, Venus, Earth, Mars, and Jupiter around the Sun. Draw each of these planets on their orbital path.
5. Place your asteroids in an orbital path between Mars and Jupiter. This is the asteroid belt.
6. Place a few in two groups on Jupiter's path as well. These are the Trojan asteroids.
7. Show your asteroid poster to an audience and explain what asteroids are and where they are found in the solar system.

😊 😊 😊 **EXPERIMENT: Asteroid Impact**

For this activity, you will need:

- Long roll of paper (Freezer paper works great.)
- Washable paints
- Water balloons
- Sink with water to fill balloons
- Metric ruler
- Paper and pencil

Asteroids are rocks that orbit the Sun. They are leftover bits from the formation of our solar system. They didn't clump together well enough or grow large enough to form a rounded shape and become planets or moons. Some asteroids are as big as Texas while others are as small as a go-cart. Most of them orbit in the asteroid belt between Mars and Jupiter or in Jupiter's orbital path, but asteroids can be found all over the solar system. Sometimes they crash into each other, planets, moons, or the Sun. The **craters** you can see on the Moon were caused by asteroid impacts.

1. Get a long roll of paper and take it outside to a flat surface like a driveway or patio. Stretch out a few meters of paper and cut it off from the roll.
2. Squirt a bit of washable paint into a water balloon. Fill the water balloon the rest of the way with water.

Fabulous Fact

There are millions and millions of asteroids in our solar system alone. One of the reasons so many of them are in the asteroid belt is that Jupiter is so massive that its gravity is holding them near it.

Memorization Station

Craters: large, bowl-shaped cavities in the ground or on the surface of a planet or the Moon

Writer's Workshop

Write an acrostic for a comet, meteor, or asteroid.

Considered a bad omen
Orbits the Sun
Miniature compared to planets
Etymology: hair of the head
Tail trailing behind

Earth & Space

Memorization Station

Meteoroids: small rocks floating in space

Meteors: burning rocks that have entered Earth's atmosphere

They are also called shooting stars. Usually you can only see meteors at night, but sometimes they can be bright enough to see in the day time.

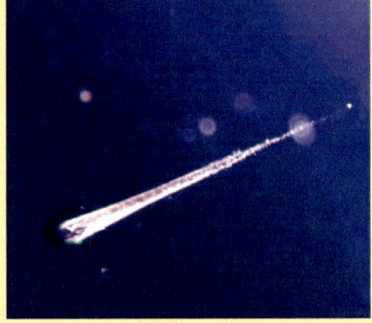

Meteorites: rocks from space that have survived the atmosphere to land on Earth

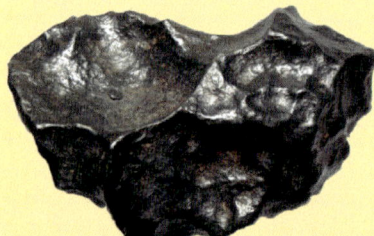

Meteorites like this one often look partially melted because they were. Falling through the atmosphere generates friction which makes the rocks burn. Photo by H. Raab, CC by SA 3.0, Wikimedia.

Squish it around a bit to mix the paint and water. The water balloon represents an asteroid while the paper represents a planet or moon surface.

3. Measure the balloon width and record it on a sheet of paper.

4. Drop the balloon with some force onto the paper so that the balloon explodes. Like an asteroid, the balloon explosion leaves little of itself behind, but it does make an impact.

5. Measure the width of the impact splash. Compare that to the original size of the asteroid. A relatively small asteroid can make a huge impact. Most asteroid impacts are 10 to 20 times the size of the asteroid. How does that compare to your balloon impacts?

6. Repeat with more balloons as many times as desired, recording your data as you go.

☺ ☺ ☺ **EXPEDITION: Meteor Shower**

For this activity, you will need:

- Internet
- Blankets, chairs, snacks, and whatever else you need to be comfy for an hour or so outside

Meteoroids are like asteroids except smaller. They range from one meter diameter down to a grain of sand. Meteoroids are mostly debris from impacts by larger bodies. You can see them in the sky at night if they enter our atmosphere and get hot and bright from the friction. Once they do enter our atmosphere they are known as **meteors** or shooting stars. If those meteors make it all of the way to the surface of the earth, we call them **meteorites**.

Solar System

There are meteors every night, but at certain times they are especially easy to see because Earth passes through a cloud of space debris. These clouds are usually left behind by passing comets. During mid-July to early August, we pass through the orbit of the Swift-Tuttle meteor and can view the Perseid meteor shower. In the second week of December, you can see the Geminids meteor shower.

1. Search online for "meteor showers" to find a date to plan to go out and watch for meteors.
2. Go outside on a dark and cloudless night and watch for meteoroids entering our atmosphere as meteors.

😊 😊 😊 EXPLORATION: Impact Craters

For this activity, you will need:

- Flour
- Ruler
- Clay
- Shallow dish, like a cake pan
- Science Notebook

Often meteors burn up when they hit the atmosphere, but some meteorites make it through to impact. If a meteor hits the earth, it makes a crater. If it is a tiny meteor, it makes a tiny crater. If it is a big meteor, it makes a big crater.

1. Fill a shallow dish three quarters full of flour and smooth the surface so it is flat.
2. Roll clay into balls of three different sizes, beginning with a tiny ball.
3. Head a page in your Science Notebook "Impact Craters" and put it in your table of contents. Draw a picture of your pan of flour and your three balls.

Fabulous Fact

In 1967, the Outer Space Treaty was signed by the United States and Russia. The treaty says that the Moon belongs to all mankind and can only be used for peaceful purposes.

Famous Folks

William and Caroline Herschel were a brother and sister duo of astronomers who worked together to catalog the night sky including nebulae, star clusters, and other objects.

William discovered the planet Uranus and Caroline discovered several comets, including the Herschel-Rigollet comet which is named after her. She was also the first woman to be paid for doing scientific work.

Teaching Tip

While you're outside watching for meteors, review constellations and stars you have learned and keep an eye out for man-made satellites.

Earth & Space

Famous Folks

Yuri Gagarin was the first human in space and was also the first man to orbit the earth in space. He is the most famous cosmonaut in the world. He was from Russia and died at the young age of 34.

Learn more about him.

Additional Layer

Humans have been in space but so have a number of animals. Do some research and learn more about some of the animals who have traveled to space.

Bookworms

American Moonshot (Young Readers Edition) by Douglas Brinkley is a riveting history of the space race and how America landed astronauts on the Moon.

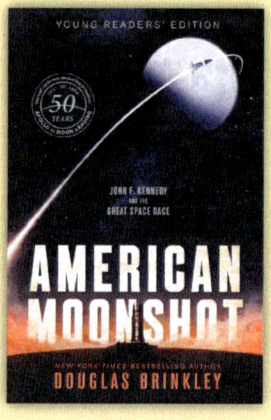

4. Measure the three diameters of the three balls. Record the diameters in your Science Notebook. Predict how large the crater will be when you drop each ball into the flour.

5. Drop each ball into the flour, one at a time, all from the same height. Measure each crater's diameter and record it. Smooth the flour between each trial. How close was your prediction?

6. Do the same thing, dropping all three balls, but from a greater height this time. Does the crater size change?

7. Finally, do a third trial, this time throwing the balls with some force at the pan of flour. Does the crater size change?

8. Discuss what you think might happen to Earth if a large meteor hit the surface with the speed of the planets orbiting through space.

Humans in Space

😊 😊 😊 EXPLORATION: Space Base

For this activity, you will need:

- Saved objects like cardboard boxes, food packaging, paper cups, toilet paper rolls, straws, and so on
- Construction paper
- Scissors
- Spray paint
- School glue (or hot glue with supervision, if desired)

Solar System

- A piece of cardboard to be the base

People at space agencies are making plans to not only visit the Moon, Mars, and other planets but to make permanent space stations in these places. To live on the Moon or Mars, you would have to overcome the things that make life impossible in those places. You would need temperature control, water, oxygen, and a way to get food and dispose of waste. You might also need to create artificial gravity and places to play or relax. What else would you want in a space station?

1. Make a list of everything you would want in a space station if you had to live there for six months, a year, or the rest of your life.

2. Use your saved objects to design a space station with all of the parts you would need.

3. Explain your space station to an audience.

😊 😊 😊 EXPLORATION: Artificial Satellites
For this activity, you will need:

- "Parts of a Satellite" from the Printable Pack
- "Newspaper Article On Satellites" from the Printable Pack

A **satellite** is any body that orbits another body, so the Moon is a satellite of Earth. An artificial satellite is put into space intentionally by people. Artificial satellites can be space stations used to do scientific research, telescopes to observe outer space, communication tools for internet,

Deep Thoughts
Leaving the planet and going into outer space is a huge step scientifically but also socially, economically, and for the development of humanity.

The "Blue Marble" photo, below, was taken by the Apollo 17 crew in 1972.

This photo hit home to many people that while the earth may seem huge and "everything" to us, really it is tiny and fragile. As humans, our common experience outweighs our differences.

Discuss the ways you think space exploration has changed things for us Earthlings.

Memorization Station
Satellite: an artificial body placed in orbit around the earth or moon or another planet

Earth & Space

Deep Thoughts

Space exploration, whether with ever more powerful telescopes or with space ships, is extravagantly expensive.

SpaceX, a private company, can launch a rocket for $57 million, the lowest sticker price in the industry. The Mars Curiosity Rover cost about $2 billion.

What are the benefits of space exploration? Is it worth it?

Where else could we be spending our money, time, and effort that might be a better investment?

Can we explore outer space and meet other goals or do we have to choose?

Additional Layer

Sputnik, a small spherical satellite, the first object to be launched into orbit, was built by the Soviet Union in 1957.

Learn more about it and the things that motivated people to attempt leaving the planet.

---

radio, television, or GPS, weather satellites to track cloud systems, observation for things like Google maps, and other purposes.

Since satellites have so many different purposes, they look different and have different parts. However, there are some basic shared parts. They all have a bus, which is the main body of the satellite, solar panels to power the satellite, rocket thrusters to keep the satellite on course, and a communication device to send data to people on Earth.

This was taken from the International Space Station, the biggest satellite in orbit. It was built over many years, beginning in 1998.

1. Color the "Parts of a Satellite" sheet from the Printable Pack. Put the matching letters in each of the boxes. Here are the answers: **A rocket thrusters, B solar panels, C bus, D communication device.**

2. Look at the picture of the International Space Station and imagine many satellites like this orbiting the earth.

3. Read the newspaper article from CNN about satellite pollution and discuss it. Do you think unregulated satellites are a potential threat, a potential benefit, or both?

🙂 🙂 EXPERIMENT: Spacesuit Design

For this activity, you will need:

- Website about spacesuits
- Drawing utensils - pencils, pens, or colored pencils
- Science Notebook

A spacesuit has to protect a person from the cold, heat, and other dangers of space. It has to provide oxygen and

Solar System

pressure. NASA has described a spacesuit as a one-person spacecraft.

1. Search online for information about spacesuits. NASA's website provides interesting information.

2. After reading up on it, design your own spacesuit in your Science Notebook. Begin by brainstorming all the things a spacesuit would need to keep a person alive in space. Sketch the items and label them on your design.

3. Explain to an audience all of the parts of your suit and how they protect you in space.

🙂 😀 **EXPLORATION: Timeline of Space Exploration Turntable**

For this activity, you will need:

- "Big Dates In Space Exploration" from the Printable Pack, plus the two pages that follow
- Card stock
- Colored pencils
- Glue stick
- Scissors
- Brads

During the 1900s, humans began to not only learn about the stars and planets by looking at them, but to learn to actually leave our planet and visit other worlds. Since that time, lots of **astronauts** have visited space. This was an important development. Learn the most important dates associated with space exploration.

1. Print the three pages starting with "Big Dates In Space Exploration" on card stock.

2. Color each of the ten circles with images and dates. One of the cards has the names of the various space agencies around the world and the date each was established. There are dozens more space agencies not mentioned on this card. The rest of the cards are landmark events in space exploration. Look them up, one by one, to find out what happened and why the event was significant.

Bookworms

Hidden Figures by Margot Lee Shetterly and Laura Freeman is a picture book about four black women who were the mathematicians behind the space program in the 1960s.

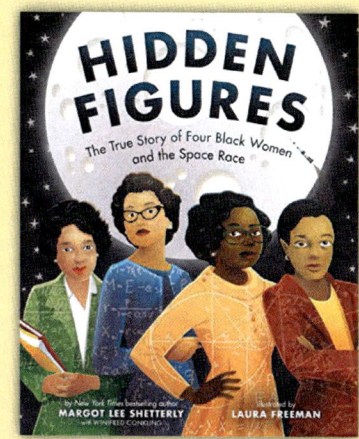

Hidden Figures Young Reader's Edition by Margot Lee Shetterly is a biography for ages 9 and up about the same women and their contributions to space exploration.

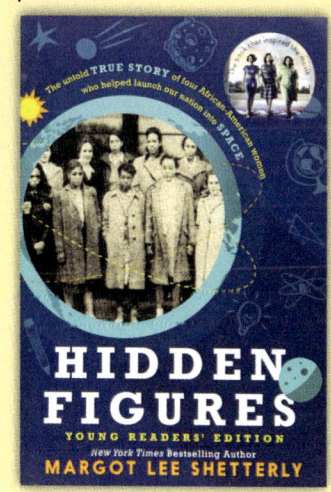

Memorization Station

Astronaut: a person who is trained to travel in a spacecraft

It comes from Greek words that mean "space sailor."

Earth & Space

Bookworms

The Astronaut Who Painted the Moon by Dean Robbins is a picture book about Alan Bean, the fourth man to step on the moon and a trained artist, who came home and painted what he saw.

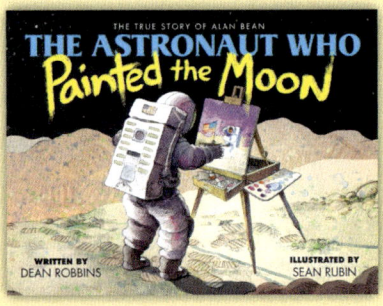

Additional Layer

You can purchase a kit to launch your own rocket. It won't make it all of the way to space, but it's a fun chance to see how rockets are propelled upward.

3. Cut out the large circle with the solid line. Poke a hole through the circle at the center mark and a hole through the circle with the dashed line on the main "Big Dates In Space Travel" page. Attach these two circles together with a brad through the center so that the cut out circle sits on top of the full sheet.

4. Fold back the flaps on each of the date circles and glue them to the circle on the dashed rectangle spaces. The circle can spin as you read the dates and the date circles can fold down to sit flat inside a notebook.

😊😊😊 EXPLORATION: Rocket Launch

For this activity, you will need:

- Video of a real space rocket launch from the YouTube playlist
- String
- Drinking straw
- Balloons
- "Rocket" from the Printable Pack, printed on card stock
- Scotch tape
- Markers or crayons
- Scissors

1. Watch a video of a real rocket launch.

2. Go back to a frame where you can see the rocket just ready to launch and pause on that scene. Discuss and write down your ideas:

   a. What can you identify and name in this image of the rocket launch?

   b. What do you wonder about this scene?

3. Use the internet individually or as a group to look up things you did not know, such as the names of structures, the sequence of launching, the type of vehicle in the launch, where the astronauts sit, and so on.

Solar System

4. Tie one end of a string to a stationary object. Stretch the string across the space as far as you can and then cut it.

5. Use the "Rocket" printable to create your own space craft, decorated however you'd like. Color and cut out your rocket. There are two per sheet, so you can share. Tape your rocket to the straw, then thread it on to the open end of the string.

6. Blow up a balloon and hold the opening closed, but do not tie it off. Tape the balloon to the rocket that is on the string so that the balloon stem is pointing at the tail of the rocket.

7. Let the balloon go. It will release air and make your rocket zoom across the string. Did it make it all the way? Does adding different amounts of air change the speed and distance your rocket balloon can fly? Does adjusting the angle or tightness of the string have an effect?

😊😊😊 EXPLORATION: Science in Space

For this activity, you will need:

- Video about the International Space Station from the YouTube playlist

One of the major roles of the space program today is doing science experiments in space. How do things change when they are in micro-gravity? Learning these answers helps us understand things on Earth better.

1. Watch videos about the International Space Station.

2. Have a discussion.

Deep Thoughts

Astronomer Carl Sagan once said, "If there is life on Mars, I believe we should do nothing with Mars. Mars then belongs to the Martians, even if the Martians are only microbes."

Discuss this idea. What do you think?

Deep Thoughts

Today there are tens of thousands of artificial satellites and bits of space junk orbiting Earth including launch stages, communication satellites, random bits of metal, abandoned spaceship parts, and so on.

Space debris is dangerous for space craft. Even a screw or a paint fleck can cause great damage because they are orbiting at high speeds.

The Space Shuttle Endeavour was hit with a piece of space junk that put a hole in part of the ship.

Sometimes this space debris comes back down to Earth and could potentially endanger life and property.

People also worry that, as time goes on, the space junk could accumulate enough to impact astronomy and our view of the sky.

Do a little reading then discuss the problem and possible prevention and clean up solutions.

Earth & Space

Bookworms

Sally Ride: A Photobiography of America's Pioneering Woman in Space by Tam O'Shaughnessy is a fascinating look at the first American woman to go to space.

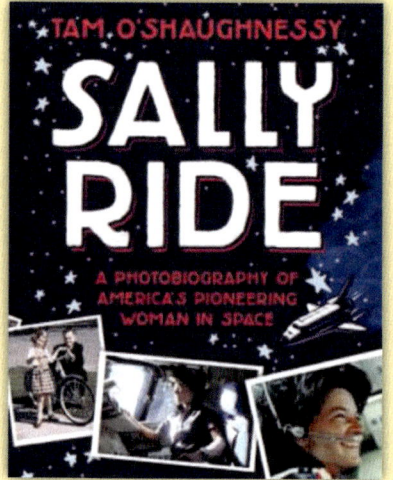

On the Web

You can visit the ISS National Laboratory website to see what experiments they are doing right now. Some of those experiments were designed by students.

Additional Layer

Learn all about Starlink and how this network of satellites is changing both the world and our view of space. This was one of the launches that delivered 60 Starlink satellites to orbit from Cape Canaveral, Florida, USA.

a. What do astronauts do while they are on the ISS?

b. How is life different for them? Are there any ways that life is the same?

c. Why do astronauts do experiments in space?

d. Are these experiments useful? Could they be important for further exploration into space?

e. Would you want to travel to the International Space Station? Would you be willing to leave Earth and live there for an entire year?

f. Are there any scientific discoveries or breakthroughs you would hope to achieve?

😊 😊 😊 EXPLORATION: Docking in Space

For this activity, you will need:

- Video of a space shuttle docking with the ISS from the YouTube playlist
- Model rocket (built from a kit, paper, toilet paper tubes, Legos, clay, or any other materials you like)
- Paper cup
- String

1. Watch a video of a shuttle docking with the International Space Station. As you watch them dock, remember that both ships are in orbit and traveling at millions of km per hour. Not only do they have to carefully and accurately ease into position, but the rocket has to aim at the spot where the International Space Station will be when the rocket travels there.

2. Build a rocket model either from a kit or out of paper and toilet paper rolls, Legos, clay, or any other materials.

3. Tie a string to the tail of your rocket so it can hang nose down.

Solar System

4. Tie another string around the wrists of two people, one on each end of the string. Tie your rocket string to the middle of this longer string.

5. Try to "dock" the rocket in the paper cup perfectly, without knocking the cup over.

Step 3: Show What You Know

During this unit, choose one of the assignments below to show what you have learned during the unit. Add this work to your Layers of Learning Notebook. You can also use this assignment to show your supervising teacher or your charter school as a sample of what you've been working on in your homeschool, if needed.

😊 😊 Coloring or Narration Page

For this activity, you will need:

- "Solar System" from the Printable Pack
- Writing or drawing utensils

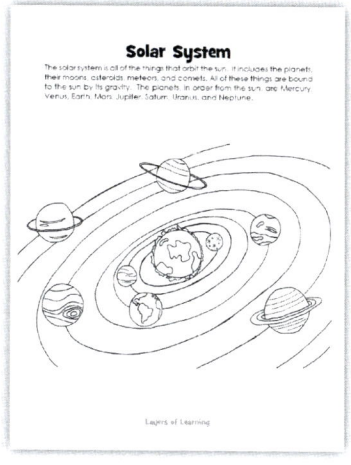

1. Depending on the age and ability of the child, choose either the "Solar System" coloring sheet or the "Solar System" narration page from the Printable Pack.

2. Younger kids can color the coloring sheet as you review some of the things you learned about during this unit. On the bottom of the coloring page, kids can write a sentence about what they learned. Very young children can explain their ideas orally while a parent writes for them.

3. Older kids can write about some of the concepts you learned on the narration page and color the picture as well.

4. Add this to the Science section of your Layers of Learning Notebook.

😊 😊 😊 Science Experiment Write-Up

For this activity, you will need:

- The "Experiment" write-up or "Experiment Report Template" from the Printable Pack

1. Choose one of the experiments you completed during

Expedition

Go visit a planetarium. Beyond the displays, they usually offer educational shows or presentations. Go prepared to ask questions and get involved!

A planetarium is a specially designed theater with a domed ceiling onto which images of the night sky can be projected while an astronomer or educator teaches the audience about stars, planets, and other space objects. Often colleges and universities have a planetarium or sometimes they are associated with a museum. They usually charge an entrance fee.

On the Web

Search for images from the James Webb telescope. NASA has an amazing collection of images from space captured by the James Webb. You can also learn more about this telescope and what NASA is hoping to accomplish with it.

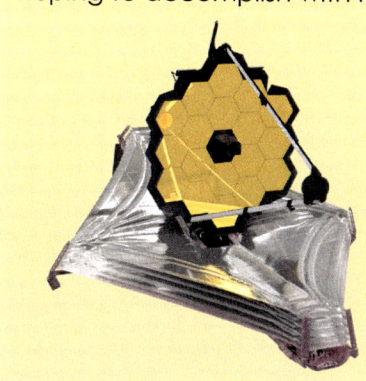

Earth & Space

Unit Trivia Questions

1. Name the eight planets in our solar system.

   Mercury, Venus, Earth, Mars, Jupiter, Saturn, Uranus, Neptune

2. Which planet rotates on its side?

   Uranus

3. How many moons does Earth have?

   One

4. Which moon phase has no visible Moon?

   A. Full moon

   B. New moon

   C. Waxing crescent

   D. Waning gibbous

5. Who was the first man in space?

   Yuri Gagarin

6. True or false: The asteroid belt is found between Jupiter and Saturn.

   False - Mars and Jupiter

7. What is the largest star in our solar system?

   The Sun

8. How many planets in our solar system are known as the gas giants?

   Four

9. What is also known as a one-person spacecraft?

   A spacesuit

10. What do we call space rocks that have survived the atmosphere and hit the earth's surface?

    A. Meteorites

    B. Meteors

    C. Satellites

    D. Meteoroids

---

this unit and create a careful and complete experiment write-up for it. Make sure you have included every specific detail of each step so your experiment could be repeated by anyone who wanted to try it.

2. Do a careful revision and edit of your write-up, taking it through the writing process, before you turn it in for grading.

😀😀😀 Planets Quiz Game

For this activity, you will need:

- Buzzers, bells, or another noisemaker (optional)
- White board or sheet of paper to keep score
- Prizes (optional)

1. Gather everyone together and call out questions about the planets. Whoever knows the answer can be the first to buzz in and guess the answer.

2. Give a point for each correct answer and declare a winner at the end. Optionally, you can give a prize to the winner. Here are a few questions to get you started, but don't limit yourself to these:

   a. What is the biggest planet in the solar system? **Jupiter**

   b. Which planet rotates on its side? **Uranus**

   c. Which planet has the most life forms? **Earth**

   d. Which planet is nearest the Sun? **Mercury**

   e. Which planet has such low density, it could float on water? **Saturn**

   f. Which planet is called the red planet? **Mars**

😀😀😀 Writer's Workshop

For this activity, you will need:

- A computer or a piece of paper and a writing utensil

Choose from one of the ideas below or write about something else you learned during this unit. Each of these prompts corresponds with one of the units from the Layers of Learning Writer's Workshop curriculum, so you may choose to coordinate the assignment with the monthly unit you are learning about in Writer's Workshop.

- **Sentences, Paragraphs, & Narrations:** In a few sentences, tell what name you would give a comet if you discovered one, and why.
- **Descriptions & Instructions:** Write a descriptive paragraph

Solar System

about what it would be like to fly through the asteroid belt.
- **Fanciful Stories**: Imagine you were the first person ever to travel to space. Write about what it's like up there all by yourself.
- **Poetry:** Create a solar system haiku.
- **True Stories:** Choose one space mission or rocket launch and tell the story of what happened.
- **Reports and Essays:** Research and then compose an essay comparing and contrasting the differences between the rocky planets and the gas giants.
- **Letters:** Compose a letter from one planet to another, telling what it loves and admires about the other.
- **Persuasive Writing:** Convince me that Pluto should still be classified as a planet.

🙂 🙂 🙂 **Big Book of Knowledge**

For this activity, you will need:

- "Big Book of Knowledge: Solar System" printable from the Printable Pack, printed on card stock
- Writing or drawing utensils
- Big Book of Knowledge

1. Color, draw on, or write on the Big Book of Knowledge page. Record concepts, definitions, and facts you learned during this unit. It's a record of the things you learned and hope to remember. Add the page to your Big Book of Knowledge.

2. Use your Big Book of Knowledge regularly to help you review, quiz, or create games that will help you commit the things you've learned to memory.

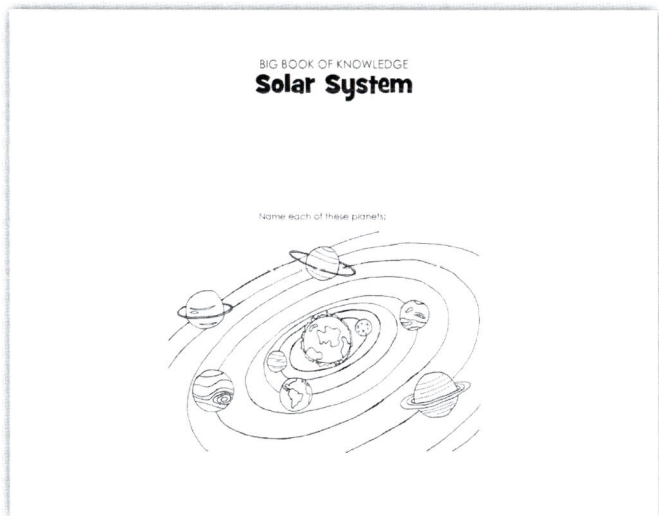

Big Book of Knowledge

The Big Book of Knowledge is a book for you, the mentor, to use as a constant review of all of the things you're learning about. You can use it to quiz your kids or prepare tests or review games. Whenever you learn something in Layers of Learning that you want your kids to remember, add it to your Big Book of Knowledge.

Assemble your Big Book of Knowledge in a binder or with binder rings. Divide it into sections for each subject.

In the Printable Pack for this unit you will find a "Big Book of Knowledge" sheet. You can add this sheet to others you collect or create yourself as you progress through the Layers of Learning curriculum. Customize the Big Book of Knowledge to your family by adding facts and topics that you enjoyed exploring as you were learning.

Visit Layers of Learning online to find more information on how to assemble and use your own Big Book of Knowledge.

You will also find cover and section pages to print along with creative games to play with your Big Book of Knowledge to keep school, even the tests, fun!

Glossary

Amber: a small organism is trapped in sap, which fossilizes into rock   131

Anemometer: an instrument that measures the speed of the wind   188

Asteroid: a rocky body that orbits the Sun, is larger than 1 meter across, and is not large enough to be spherical   242

Astronaut: a person who is trained to travel in a spacecraft   261

Atmosphere: the envelope of gases surrounding the earth or another planet   163

Atmospheric pressure: the weight of the air pressing down on the earth   165

Barometer: an instrument that measures air pressure   188

Biology: study of life   21

Black hole: a region where gravity is so strong that nothing, not even light, can escape from it   230

Blizzard: a severe snowstorm with high winds and low visibility   202

Block mountains: caused by faults in the crust where blocks of rock move past each other   85

Brackish water: water that has more salt than freshwater, but less than saltwater, usually occurs where fresh ground water mixes with water from the ocean   52

BYA: billion years ago   44

Carbon cycle: the cycle of carbon atoms moving from the atmosphere to organisms and the earth and then back to the atmosphere   178

Carbon film: the organism is compressed between layers of sedimentary rock, leaving only an outline or impression   131

Carnivore: an animal that feeds on flesh, or other animals   147

Chemistry: study of materials and how they combine   21

Climate: the long-term average of weather in a particular place that includes average precipitation, temperature, humidity, wind, and atmospheric pressure   169

Comet: space object made of frozen gases and rock that is orbiting a star   252

Constellation: a group of stars that form a picture or pattern   224

Contact metamorphism: occurs deep in the earth where pressure builds up and are able to create a chemical change in rocks   113

Continental crust: the relatively thick part of the earth's crust that forms landmasses   42

Control group: a group in which all variable factors are kept constant   26

Convergent boundary: place where plates are moving toward one another and colliding   68

Craters: large, bowl-shaped cavities in the ground or on the surface of a planet or the Moon   255

Crust: the thin outermost layer that wraps around the earth   38

Crystals: a homogeneous substance that has a regular geometric shape   99

Current: a steady flow of fluid   55

December solstice: the longest day of the year in the Southern Hemisphere, when the sun appears to reach furthest south   159

Dependent variable: the variable being tested, it will change depending on the independent variable   26

Deposition: when sediment is dropped or deposited in a new location   117

Dinosaur: extinct, warm-blooded reptiles that lay eggs, have hind limbs extending directly beneath the body, have a simple hinge ankle joint, have a hole between the eye socket and nostril, and live most of life on land   143

Divergent boundary: place where plates are moving apart from one another   68

Double blind: When neither the scientist nor his test subjects know which sample is which   28

Dwarf planet: a body that directly orbits

the Sun, has a spherical shape, but has not cleared other objects from its orbital path   242

Earthquake: shaking of the earth caused by moving plates   80

Earth & Space: study of Earth and the universe   21

Effusive eruption: lava steadily and slowly flows from a fissure   73

Epicenter: the spot on the surface directly above the focus of an earthquake   80

Erosion: the movement of sediment from one location to another by means of ice, wind, or water   117

Exoplanet: a planet outside of our solar system   232

Experimental group: a group in which one variable is changed to test its effects   26

Explosive eruption: a violent volcanic eruption where gas, ash, and magma are forcibly ejected from a fissure   73

Extinct: when a species dies out completely and there are no more left on Earth   126

Faulting: the crust fractures and mass displacement of rock layers occurs   88

Felsic: rocks that are lighter in color and less dense   104

Focus: the spot in the crust at the center of the earthquake, also called a hypocenter   80

Folding: layers of rock are bent or curved in a permanent deformation.   88

Fold mountains: occur where two plates collide, pushing the continental material up   85

Foliation: the parallel arrangement of mineral grains that give rocks a striped appearance   113

Fossil: a remnant or trace of a deceased ancient organism   126

Fossil cast: a complete impression of soft tissues is left on the rock   129

Freshwater: water that is not salty, like the water within lakes, streams, and rivers   52

Galaxy: a system of stars, dust, and dark matter bound together by gravity   229

Globular cluster: a spherical group of stars that orbits a point in space   232

Greenhouse gas: a gas that can absorb radiation from the sun and then release it back out, thereby increasing the temperature of the earth   170

Herbivore: an animal that feeds on plants   147

Humidity: the concentration of water vapor in the air   188

Hygrometer: An instrument that measures humidity   188

Hypothesis: Prediction of what will happen in an experiment   23

Ice age: an extended period of cold, earth-wide climate that results in permanent ice caps at the poles   171

Igneous intrusion: magma pushes upward beneath the surface, cooling and solidifying underground   88

Igneous: rocks that solidify from magma   103

Independent variable: the variable that is changed in a scientific experiment   26

Index fossils: fossils that are useful for dating and correlating the strata in which it is found   139

Inner core: the solid material in the center of the earth that is at an extremely high temperature and pressure   38

June solstice: the longest day of the year in the Northern Hemisphere, when the sun appears to reach furthest north   159

Lava: hot molten rock on the surface of the crust   73, 106

Law: a description of what happens in a natural process, often expressed with mathematics   25

Lightning: natural electrical discharge between a cloud and the ground or between two clouds   201

Mafic: rocks that are dense and dark in color   104

Magma: hot molten rock found under the surface of the crust   73, 106

Main sequence: stars in the prime of life, burning hydrogen gas in their cores, converting it into helium and releasing enormous amounts of energy in the process (Most of the stars in the universe are main sequence.) 223

Mantle: the layer of the earth between the crust and the core that is made of silicate rock   38

March equinox: the point when the sun appears to leave the Southern Hemisphere and move into the Northern Hemisphere   159

Metamorphic: rocks that are transformed by heat or pressure (or both) deep in the crust   103

Metamorphism: heat and pressure deep in the crust deform rocks and pushes them into ridges and folds   88

Meteorites: rocks from space that have survived the atmosphere to land on Earth   256

Meteoroids: small rocks floating in space   256

Meteors: burning rocks that have entered Earth's atmosphere   256

Minerals: made of specific elements and often forming regular crystals, minerals are the building blocks of rocks   99

Moon: a large body that orbits a planet or a dwarf planet   242

MYA: million years ago   44

Nebula: an enormous cloud of gas and dust that forms a birth place for new stars (plural = nebulae)   229

Neutron: a star with a high enough mass to end its life in a supernova explosion and is composed completely of neutrons because its intense gravity crushes protons and electrons together to make neutrons   223

Oceanic crust: the relatively thin part of the earth's crust which is found under the oceans   42

Omnivore: an animal that eats both plants and flesh, or other animals   147

Open cluster: a group of a few thousand stars or fewer that are all about the same age and formed from the same dust cloud   232

Orbit: the curved path of a celestial object around a star, planet, or moon   251

Outer core: a fluid layer of the earth composed mostly of iron and nickel   38

Paleontologist: a scientist who specializes in the study of fossils and prehistoric life forms   143

Paleontology: the study of fossilized animals and plants from the past   126

Pangaea: a supercontinent that formed about 335 million years ago and has since broken apart due to plate tectonics   68

Permineralization: dissolved minerals in water replace the bone with rock   129

Physics: study of motion, forces, and energy on a large and atomic scale   21

Planet: a large spherical body that orbits a star and clears other objects of a similar size out of its path   242

Plate: a large piece of Earth's crust that reacts and moves as a unit   66

Precipitation: condensed water vapor that falls from clouds to the ground - rain, snow, sleet, or hail   186

Prevailing winds: a zone where the wind usually blows the same direction   190

P waves: or primary waves, travel through the ground like a water wave   83

Pyroclastic flow: a fast moving "river" of hot ash and rock that flows out of a volcano and along the ground   73

Qualitative observations: data that is focused on characteristics or qualities   10

Quantitative observations: data that can quantified, or expressed using numbers and values (They must be measured as accurately as possible.)   10

Quasar: a massive and bright celestial object that emits large amounts of energy   232

Rain gauge: an instrument that measures the amount of rainfall   186

Red dwarf: a low-mass star that burns cooler, but much longer than an average star   223

Red giant: an old star that has used up most of its fuel, but grows up to 100 times its original size   223

Regional metamorphism: occurs when rocks are heated by nearby magma   113

Rotation: the circular action of an object around its center   252

Salinity: the amount of salt in water   55

Saltwater: contains high concentrations of dissolved salts and minerals   52

Satellite: an artificial body placed in orbit around the earth or moon or another planet   259

Science: the study of nature and the way things in nature behave   8

Scientific method: A method of research in which a problem is identified, relevant data are gathered, a hypothesis is formulated from these data, and the hypothesis is empirically tested   23

Seasons: each of the four divisions of the year, resulting from the earth's changing position around the sun   155

Sedimentary: rocks that form from sediment deposited by water or wind   103

Sediment: solid material that is moved and deposited in a new location   109

Seismic waves: waves of energy that travel through the earth   83

Seismometer: an instrument that detects and records earthquakes   81

September equinox: the point when the sun appears to leave the Northern Hemisphere and move into the Southern Hemisphere   159

Soil horizon: the layers of the soil that are revealed as you dig down from the surface   119

Soil profile: the pattern of soil horizons in a particular location   119

Solar system: everything that orbits a star   242

Specific heat: the energy required to raise 1 gram, 1 degree   58

Stars: huge balls of gas in space that produce light and heat   222

Strata: layers of rock   134

Supercontinent: when all of Earth's land masses assemble into one big continent   68

Supergiant: the most massive stars in the universe, many times larger than our Sun, that consumes their fuel rapidly, detonating as supernovae in the end   223

S waves: or secondary waves, shake the ground up and down, perpendicular to the direction the P wave is moving   83

Temperature: a measure of heat in the atmosphere   192

Theory: explains the mechanism of a natural process   25

Thermometer: an instrument for measuring temperature   192

Thunder: a loud rumbling or crashing noise heard after a lightning flash, caused by rapidly heated air expanding   201

Tornado: a violently rotating column of air, usually attached to the base of a thunderstorm   202

Trace fossils: a fossil of a footprint, trail, burrow, or other trace of an animal rather than of the animal itself   131

Transform boundary: place where plates are sliding past one another longitudinally   68

Unifying theory: an overall idea that explains how everything else within a scientific discipline works   71

Universe: all of space and all of the matter and energy that space contains   219

Volcanic activity: a rupture in the earth's crust allows hot material from the magma chamber to rise and spill out onto the surface   88

Volcanic mountains: occur along the margins of plates where oceanic crust is pushed underneath continental crust, causing melting of crust material   85

Volcano: a place where the earth's crust is ruptured and lava, gas, and ash escape from inside the earth to the surface   73

Water cycle: the continuous recycling of the earth's water that causes it to circulate within the earth and the atmosphere   58

Weathering: the breaking down of rocks and minerals   117

Weather: the condition of the atmosphere in a particular place at a given moment and includes measures of precipitation, wind, temperature, humidity, and atmospheric pressure   169

White dwarf: a star that has completely used up all of its hydrogen fuel and collapses into its own gravity, still glows white-hot, but will slowly cool down   223

Wind: the massive flow of gases in the atmosphere   188

People

A

Aldrin, Buzz 249

Alvarez, Luis 138

Alvarez, Walter 138

Anning, Mary 127

Aristarchus of Samos 244

Aristotle 244

Armstrong, Neil 249

Aryabhata 16

B

Bacon, Roger 23

Baltz, Vera 121

Bascom, Florence 101

Beaufort, Francis 186

Bengtsson, Lennart O. 174

Benioff, Hugo 68

Bentley, Wilson 198

Berners-Lee, Tim 22

Birch, Francis 39

Bird, Peter 89

Boltwood, Bertram 136

Broecker, Wallace S. 171

Burnell, Jocelyn Bell 235

C

Canon, Annie Jump 222

Carver, George Washington 22

Christy, John R. 177

Cope, Edward 137

Copernicus, Nicolaus 244

Curie, Marie 22

Curry, Judith A. 178

Curtis, Heber 229

Cuvier, Georges 128

D

Daly, Marie Maynard 31

Darwin, Charles 22

da Vinci, Leonardo 21

de Bort, Leon Teisserenc 164

Dokuchaev, Vasily 120

Dong Zhiming 144

Dreyer, John Louis Emil 230

E

Edison, Thomas 21, 22

Einstein, Albert 22, 31, 219

Ewing, Maurice 66

F

Fahrenheit, Daniel Gabriel 209

Flamel, Nicolas 19

Franklin, Benjamin 21

G

Gagarin, Yuri 258

Galileo 208, 234, 243, 244

Glaisher, James 164

Goodall, Jane 22

Griffith, Frederick 29

Gutenberg, Beno 81

H

Halley, Edmond 252

Hawking, Stephen 232

Herschel, Caroline 237, 257

Herschel, William 237, 257

Howard, Luke 192

Hubble, Edwin 22, 220, 229

Hutton, James 98

I

Irving, Ted 69

J

Jason 54

Johnson, Tim 106

K

Kepler, Johannes 246, 247

Kidinnu 17

Krafft, Katia 77

Krafft, Maurice 77

L

Lal, Rattan 118

Lehmann, Inge 37

Lemaître, Georges 219

Lindzen, Richard S. 177

Li Yumin 147

Lyell, Charles 87

M

Manabe, Syukuro 165

Mann, Michael E. 177

Marsh, Othniel 137

Maunder, Edward 170

Messier, Charles 230

Milanković, Milutin 172

Mitchell, Maria 234

Mohs, Friedrich 121

Munk, Walter 53

P

Payne, Cecilia 226

Planck, Max 18

Ptolemy 244

R

Ramanthan, Veerabhadran 177

Richter, Charles 81

Ride, Sally 264

Russell, Annie 170

S

Sagan, Carl 215, 263

Shapley, Harlow 229

Shaviv, Nir J. 177

Shen Kuo 27

Smith, William 100, 108

Solomon, Susan 167

T

Tesla, Nikola 21

Thales of Miletus 21

Tharp, Maria 57

Thoreau, Henry David 158

Torricelli, Evangelista 167

Trouvelot, Étienne Léopold 9

Tyson, Neil deGrasse 231

V

Vulcan 79

W

Wadati, Kiyoo 68

Walcott, Charles Doolittle 130

Wegener, Alfred 70

Wiffen, Joan 141

Wigley, Tom M.L. 177

Wilson, John Tuzo 67

About the Authors

Michelle and Karen are sisters from Idaho, USA. They grew up playing in the woods and on the lakes of the northern Rockies. Karen is married with four children, two boys and two girls. Michelle is married with six kids, all boys.

Michelle has a BS in biology and Karen has a BA in education. Since the early 2000s, they have been homeschooling their kids and taking them to the lake as often as possible.

In 2008, at a family reunion (at the lake, of course), they were opining about all the things they wished they could have in a homeschool curriculum. Their mom suggested they write their own curriculum. They looked at each other in doubt, then thought, "Why not?" And Layers of Learning was born. Thanks, Mom.

Visit **Layers-of-Learning.com** for more family-style curriculum, planners, and resources to add to every unit.

Made in United States
Orlando, FL
24 September 2023